FROMMER'S

COMPREHENSIVE TRAVEL GUIDE

SAN FRANCISCO '95

by Dan Levine

MACMILLAN • USA

About the Author:

Dan Levine has a degree in history from New York University. An inveterate traveler and demanding gourmand, he is the author of Frommer guides to California, Los Angeles, Miami, and Prague and of *Frommer's London on $45 a Day*. He is also co-author of two walking tour books—to London and England's Favorite Cities—and contributes to *Frommer's Europe on $50 a Day*. When he is not on the road, Dan lives and writes in Santa Barbara.

Macmillan Travel
A Prentice Hall Macmillan Company
15 Columbus Circle
New York, NY 10023

ISBN 0-671-88381-X
ISSN 0899-3254

Design by Robert Bull Design
Maps by Geografix Inc. and Ortelius Design

Special Sales

Bulk purchases (10+ copies) of Frommer's Travel Guides are available to corporations at special discounts. The Special Sales Department can produce custom editions to be used as premiums and/or for sales promotions to suit individual needs. Existing editions can be produced with custom cover imprints, such as corporate logos. For more information write to: Special Sales, Prentice Hall, 15 Columbus Circle, New York, NY 10023.

Manufactured in the United States of America

CONTENTS

LIST OF MAPS

WHAT THE SYMBOLS MEAN

 FROMMER'S FAVORITES — hotels, restaurants, attractions, and entertainments you should not miss

 SUPER-SPECIAL VALUES — really exceptional values

 FROMMER'S SMART TRAVELER TIPS — hints on how to secure the best value for your money

IN HOTEL AND OTHER LISTINGS

The following symbols refer to the standard amenities available in all rooms:

A/C air conditioning   TEL telephone   TV television
MINIBAR refrigerator stocked with beverages and snacks

The following abbreviations are used for credit cards:

AE American Express   DC Diners Club   MC MasterCard
CB Carte Blanche   DISC Discover   V Visa

TRIP PLANNING WITH THIS GUIDE

Use the following features:

What Things Cost In . . . to help you plan your daily budget
Calendar of Events . . . to plan for or avoid
Suggested Itineraries . . . for seeing the city and environs
What's Special About Checklist . . . a summary of the city's highlights—which lets you check off those that appeal most to you
Easy-to-Read Maps . . . walking tours, city sights, hotel and restaurant locations—all referring to or keyed to the text
Fast Facts . . . all the essentials at a glance: emergencies, safety, taxes, tipping, and more

OTHER SPECIAL FROMMER FEATURES

Cool for Kids — attractions
Did You Know . . . ? — offbeat, fun facts
Famous People — the city's greats
Impressions — what others have said

INVITATION TO THE READERS

In researching this book, I have come across many wonderful establishments, the best of which I have included here. I'm sure that many of you will also come across appealing hotels, inns, restaurants, guesthouses, shops, and attractions. Please don't keep them to yourself. Share your experiences, especially if you want to comment on places covered in this edition that have changed for the worse. You can address your letters to me:

Dan Levine
Frommer's San Francisco '95
c/o Macmillan Travel
15 Columbus Circle
New York, NY 10023

A DISCLAIMER

Readers are advised that prices fluctuate in the course of time and travel information changes under the impact of the varied and volatile factors that affect the travel industry. The author and publisher cannot be held responsible for the experiences of readers while traveling. Readers are invited to write to the publisher with ideas, comments, and suggestions for future editions.

SAFETY ADVISORY

Whenever you're traveling in an unfamiliar city or country, stay alert. Be aware of your immediate surroundings. Wear a moneybelt and keep a close eye on your possessions. Be particularly careful with cameras, purses, and wallets, all favorite targets of thieves and pickpockets.

CHAPTER 1

INTRODUCING SAN FRANCISCO

San Francisco's enchanting beauty is its primary charm. Built across dozens of hills, the city is shaped like a compressed accordion; its gingerbread houses cling to steep hillsides like displaced alpine cottages. Both first-time visitors and long-time locals are stirred by the sights and sounds of San Francisco: the glitter of sunshine on the golden pagoda roofs of Chinatown, unexpected glimpses of ocean when you stop climbing and look back over your shoulder, and the bell-clanking onrush of toylike cable cars that seem to have escaped from an amusement park.

Few of the world's cities project as positive an image as America's "City by the Bay." In a national survey, the vast majority of those questioned named San Francisco as the city in which they'd most like to live. The funny thing is that many respondents had never even been to San Francisco! Indeed, San Francisco is a living legend, a national treasure, and a harbinger of the future. It is the cultural and financial center of northern California and one of this country's greatest wonders. Yet San Francisco is more than just the sum of its parts. The gold rush that led to its development is long gone, but the city still glitters with the same alluring promise that drew thousands of prospectors to the West Coast a century and a half ago.

1. CULTURE, HISTORY & BACKGROUND

GEOGRAPHY & PEOPLE

San Francisco occupies the tip of a 32-mile-long peninsula between San Francisco Bay and the Pacific Ocean. Its land area measures about 46 square miles—comparable in size to Manhattan, but minute by the standards of, say, Chicago or Los Angeles. Don't be misled by this. The city's downtown section is wonderfully compact (especially North Beach and Chinatown), but the rest of the city meanders over 43 hills, many of which become positively mountainous when you're in the process of climbing them. Twin Peaks, in the geographic center of the city, is over 900 feet high.

WHAT'S SPECIAL ABOUT SAN FRANCISCO

The Arts

☐ ACT and other city theater companies, well known for excellent, innovative staging.

☐ The world-renowned San Francisco Opera and Ballet.

☐ World-class galleries, many of which highlight works by local artists.

Public Transportation

☐ The city's trademark cable cars—fun, historic, and utilitarian.

☐ BART, fast and futuristic, one of the world's best high-speed commuter railways.

Geographical Features

☐ Golden Gate Park: It's easy to get lost among the ponds, trees, and museums of one of the world's greatest urban parks.

☐ The Presidio of San Francisco: The city's largest and newest park is in an exciting stage of transformation.

☐ San Francisco's hills: Each highpoint offers its own unique perspective of the city.

☐ The Bay: It remains San Francisco's most important asset.

Bridges

☐ The Golden Gate Bridge, one of the world's most elegant spans, connecting a beautiful city with the bucolic countryside.

☐ The San Francisco–Oakland Bay Bridge, the city's busiest bridge and a spectacular engineering feat.

Neighborhoods

☐ North Beach, the city's Italian and bohemian quarter, known for its restaurants and nightlife.

☐ Haight-Ashbury, the famed hippie district, still a great place to shop for the latest street fashions.

☐ The Castro, a unique neighborhood that's synonymous with the city's gay culture.

☐ Chinatown, one of the Occidental world's largest Asian communities and one of the best places in San Francisco for strolling, shopping, and eating.

San Francisco's hills count among the city's chief charms. They offer sudden, breathless views of moving ships and creeping fog banks on the harbor below or of rolling stretches of open countryside at what seems arm's-length. It has been said that when you get tired of walking around San Francisco, you can always lean against it.

At the turn of the 20th century, just less than half of California's population lived in San Francisco. Today the city is home to about 724,000 people, less than 5% of the state's total. The nine Bay Area counties that surround the city hold an additional 6 million. Despite its small size, the city itself is highly diversified culturally. One out of every three San Franciscans comes

IMPRESSIONS

San Francisco is the most civilized city in America, full of delightful people.
—W. SOMERSET MAUGHAM

Cities are like gentlemen. They are born, not made. Size has nothing to do with it. I bet San Francisco was a city from the very first time it had a dozen settlers.
—WILL ROGERS

---

from a home where a language other than English is spoken. The city is 13% Chinese, 9% Irish, 8% German, and 6% Italian. Filipinos, Mexicans, Russians, French, and Japanese are also significantly represented.

Despite its unusually broad ethnicity, San Francisco is best known as a spawning ground and haven for alternative lifestyles. Indeed, this was the town that sheltered the hippie counterculture and the "beat generation" before it. Most of all, however, the Bay Area is internationally known as a liberal oasis for gays and lesbians. The Castro district remains the center of the city's gay community, while the lesbian stronghold is in Oakland, across the bay.

HISTORY & POLITICS

HISTORY   This city by the bay began life, under the name Yerba Buena ("good herb"), as a mission post founded by Spanish monks in 1776. Annexed by Mexico in 1821, after that country gained independence from Spain, Yerba Buena remained a sleepy little village of 30 or so families, grouped around an adobe customshouse and guarded by a "company" of nine cavalrymen, who were rarely paid.

In June 1846, English-speaking Californians launched the so-called Bear Flag Rebellion against Mexican rule, fighting under a grizzly bear emblem that the Mexicans mocked as a hog. The Anglos won hands down and promptly founded what was possibly the shortest-lived republic on record. It lasted just 26 days before it was absorbed by the United States. A year later the town was renamed San Francisco

There's no telling how long the place would have remained a drowsy village if it hadn't been for the cry of "*Gold!*" in 1848. Within a year the peninsula's population soared from about 800 to 25,000. Few prospectors, however, found any gold worth shouting about, and disappointed diggers were soon committing suicide at the rate of

DATELINE

- **1542**   Juan Cabrillo sails up the California coast.
- **1579**   Sir Francis Drake lands in the Bay Area, missing the entrance to the Golden Gate.
- **1769**   Members of the Spanish expedition led by Gaspar de Portola become the first foreigners to see San Francisco Bay.
- **1775**   The first European ship, *San Carlos*, sails into San Francisco Bay.
- **1776**   Captain Juan Bautista de Anza establishes a presidio (military fort); San Francisco
  (continues)

DATELINE

de Asis Mission opens.

- **1821** Mexico wins independence from Spain and annexes California.
- **1835** The town of Yerba Buena develops around the port: the United States tries unsuccessfully to purchase San Francisco Bay from Mexico.
- **1846** Mexican-American War.
- **1847** Americans annex Yerba Buena and rename it San Francisco.
- **1848** Gold is discovered near what is now Sacramento.
- **1849** In the year of the gold rush, San Francisco's population swells from about 800 to 25,000.
- **1851** Lawlessness becomes particularly acute before attempts are made to curb it.
- **1869** The transcontinental railroad reaches San Francisco.
- **1873** Andrew S. Hallidie invents the cable car.
- **1906** The Great Earthquake strikes, and the resulting fire levels the city.
- **1915** The Panama Pacific

(continues)

1,000 a year. Still, the gold rush attracted settlers and single-handedly transformed the town into a roaring, boisterous boom metropolis. It has been said that anything went here, provided you could pay for it.

The small city of San Francisco was a relatively dangerous place, swarming with assorted gangs who called themselves "Hounds" or "Sydney Ducks." Supplying unwilling sailors to windjammers bound for the Far East was 19th-century San Francisco's most infamous form of thuggery. This was usually accomplished by slipping would-be seamen drugged whisky in some waterfront tavern, then rowing them unconscious out to a ship. Because the most frequent destination was Shanghai, China, this game was dubbed "shanghaiing." King of the profession was Calico Jim, who at one time shanghaied six policemen sent to arrest him on a murder charge. San Francisco's lawlessness was so acute that successive groups of irate citizens formed vigilance committees in attempts to rid the city of some of the worst cutthroats. Often little more than rapid-order lynch mobs, these committees hanged as many innocents as hoodlums. Almost invariably they degenerated into thuggery themselves, whereupon a new batch of vigilantes had to be roused to get rid of the previous lot.

Prostitution also flourished, earning some of its most prolific practitioners enough money to build mansions that left easterners pop-eyed with wonder. Unfortunately, many of the women were Chinese slaves, kept virtually imprisoned in Chinatown cribs to earn fortunes for their owners. Despite many attempts to clean up the city, gangs became empowered, opium dens flourished, and gambling parlors operated unabated. But everything changed on the morning of April 18, 1906.

San Francisco has never experienced an earthquake as destructive as the one that hit at 5:13am. All but a handful of its 400,000 inhabitants lay fast asleep when the ground beneath the city went into a series of convulsions. As one eyewitness put it, "The earth wasn't shaking—it was undulating, rolling like an ocean breaker." The quake ruptured every water main in the city—and simultaneously started a chain of fires that rapidly fused into one gigantic conflagration. The fire brigades were helpless, and for three days San Francisco burned. Militia troops finally stopped the flames from advancing by dynamiting entire city blocks, but not before more than 28,000 buildings lay in ruins and some 500 people lay buried beneath them. As Jack London wrote in a heartrending newspaper dispatch: "The city of San Francisco . . . is no more."

Happily, he was right—the city that London knew was no more. The earthquake and subsequent fire so decisively changed the city that post-1906 San Francisco bears little resemblance to the town before the quake. Out of the ashes rose a bigger, healthier, and more beautiful town. The natural disaster had accomplished what the reformers had failed to do, and the old, infamous Barbary Coast and opium-reeking Chinatown became mere memories, whispered legends. The new San Francisco expanded into a reasonably law-abiding and cultured, though still somewhat rakish, metropolis.

The city has shed the viciousness of its lurid past but has retained some intriguing aspects of it. It's still a very internationally minded port, more at ease with foreigners than almost any other place in the world; it was chosen as the birthplace of the United Nations in 1945. San Francisco still looks with tolerant amusement at certain human tastes that would mobilize vice squads elsewhere, a quality that has made it the cradle and focal point for every individualist who ever felt out of step with Main Street, U.S.A.—the bohemians of the 1930s, the beatniks of the 1950s, the hippies of the 1960s, and the gays of the 1970s. And although the movements have changed, the easygoing atmosphere in which they thrived lingers on. All of us who love this town hope that it will keep right on lingering.

POLITICS On the city level, San Francisco politics are particularly exciting because of the many divergent cultural and special-interest groups. Gay rights are the highest-profile—and most contentious—issue in the city. Gays and lesbians are among San Francisco's most powerful voting blocs and, along with other sympathetic voters, have created one of the most tolerant official climates in the world. Today, resolution of the issue of gay rights has been successful to the point that whether one is gay or straight would seem to be irrelevant. Gays have for the most part

DATELINE

International Exposition celebrates San Francisco's restoration and the completion of the Panama Canal.

- **1936** The Bay Bridge is built.
- **1937** The Golden Gate Bridge is completed.
- **1945** The United Nations Charter is drafted and adopted by the representatives of 50 countries meeting in San Francisco.
- **1950** The "beat generation" moves into the bars and cafes of North Beach.
- **1967** A free concert in Golden Gate Park attracts 20,000 people, ushering in the "Summer of Love" and the hippie era.
- **1974** BART's high-speed transit system opens the tunnel linking San Francisco with the East Bay.
- **1978** Harvey Milk, a San Francisco city supervisor and America's first openly gay politician, is assassinated, along with Mayor George Moscone, by political rival Dan White.
- **1989** An earthquake registering 7.1 on the Richter scale hits San Francisco during a World Series baseball game, as

(continues)

DATELINE

100 million watch on TV; the city quickly rebuilds.

- **1991** Fire rages through the Berkeley/ Oakland hills, destroying 2,800 homes.

simply flowed into the mainstream—in and around the urban professional Castro district, the industrial and trendy-nightlife South of Market (SoMa) district, and Folsom Street, as well as the unabashedly proper-business-attire set of Pacific Heights and Nob Hill. In achieving many of their goals, gays seemingly have become part of the establishment.

The homeless problem, coupled with a rise in panhandling, has risen to alarming and epidemic proportions in San Francisco. Although this city is no better equipped than any other to resolve national social problems, government officials have considered various propositions to clean up Union Square and the adjacent Tenderloin district. Proposals include the establishment of city-licensed brothels that would rent rooms to prostitutes, check their health, and collect taxes on their earnings.

FAMOUS SAN FRANCISCANS

Francis Ford Coppola (b. 1939) One of America's most successful contemporary filmmakers, Coppola is best known for *Apocalypse Now* and *The Godfather*. His movie *The Conversation* was filmed in San Francisco. Coppola still lives here and works from Columbus Tower, in North Beach.

Joe DiMaggio (b. 1914) In addition to marrying Marilyn Monroe in the 1950s, DiMaggio was one of the greatest baseball players of all time. He began his career with the San Francisco Seals, before becoming the New York Yankees' star centerfielder.

Dianne Feinstein (b. 1933) Born in San Francisco and educated at nearby Stanford, this former city mayor and current U.S. senator is a true San Franciscan. A political "centrist," Feinstein is supportive of alternative lifestyles and reproductive rights.

Lawrence Ferlinghetti (b. 1920) A prominent figure of the "beat movement" of the 1950s, Ferlinghetti is a poet extraordinaire with close links to major cultural figures. In 1953, he founded, and still owns, City Lights Book Store, the first paperback bookshop in America.

Jerry Garcia (b. 1942) Lead guitarist and vocalist of the psychedelic rock band the Grateful Dead, Jerry and the band still live in the Bay Area.

Dashiell Hammet (1894–1961) Drawing on his experience with the Pinkerton Detective Agency, Hammett penned hard-boiled detective novels, including *The Maltese Falcon* and *The Thin Man*. He was imprisoned for refusing to testify during the House Un-American Activities Committee "witch-hunts" in the 1950s.

William Randolph Hearst (1863–1951) Famous for his opulent lifestyle and grand castle at San Simeon, Hearst was a publishing magnate, who as a young man worked on the *San Francisco Examiner*. He later acquired a string of successful radio stations, motion-picture companies, and daily newspapers.

Janis Joplin (1943–70) One of the 1960s' most charismatic rock-and-roll voices, Joplin moved from Texas at the age of 18 and began her career in San Francisco with Big Brother and the Holding Company. She died from an overdose of heroin in 1970.

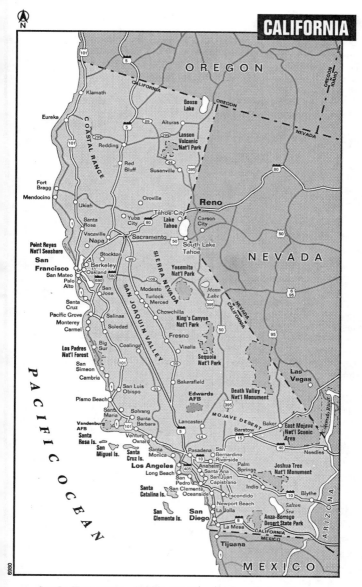

CALIFORNIA

OREGON

Klamath

Eureka

Fort Bragg
Mendocino

COASTAL RANGE

Goose Lake

Alturas

Lassen Volcanic Nat'l Park

Reno

NEVADA

OREGON TRAIL

Redding

Red Bluff

Susanville

Oroville

Ukiah

Santa Rosa

Vacaville

Napa

Yuba City

Tahoe City
Lake Tahoe

Carson City

Point Reyes Nat'l Seashore

San Francisco

Sacramento

South Lake Tahoe

NEVADA

Stockton

Berkeley
Oakland

San Mateo
Palo Alto

San Jose

SIERRA NEVADA

Yosemite Nat'l Park

Santa Cruz

Pacific Grove
Monterey
Carmel

Salinas

Soledad

SAN JOAQUIN VALLEY

Modesto
Turlock
Merced

Chowchilla

King's Canyon Nat'l Park

Mono Lake

Big Sur

Coalinga

Fresno

Visalia

Las Vegas

Los Padres Nat'l Forest

San Simeon

Cambria

San Luis Obispo

Bakersfield

Sequoia Nat'l Park

Pismo Beach

Santa Maria

Solvang

Santa Barbara

Vandenberg AFB

Santa Rosa Is.

Ventura

Oxnard

Edwards AFB

Lancaster

Death Valley Nat'l Monument

Baker

MOJAVE DESERT

Barstow

East Mojave Nat'l Scenic Area

Needles

San Miguel Is.

Santa Cruz Is.

Santa Monica

Pasadena

Los Angeles

Long Beach

San Pedro

San Bernardino
Riverside

Anaheim
Santa Ana
San Juan Capistrano

Palm Springs

Joshua Tree Nat'l Monument

ARIZONA

Santa Catalina Is.

San Clemente Is.

San Clemente
Oceanside

Escondido

Newport Beach

La Jolla

San Diego

Indio

Salton Sea

Anza-Borrego Desert State Park

Blythe

La Mesa

CALIFORNIA
MEXICO

Tijuana

PACIFIC OCEAN

MEXICO

Jack Kerouac (1922–69) The leader of the "beat generation," born in Lowell, Massachusetts, came to San Francisco in the
1950s to write the beats' bible, *On the Road*.

Jack London (1876–1916) Influenced by the ideas of Dar-
win, Nietzsche, and Marx, London is most famous for his
Klondike stories, tales of survival under harsh conditions. The author of such novels as *Call of the Wild* and *White Fang* grew up
along Oakland's waterfront.

Hunter S. Thompson (b. 1939) A long-time political columnist for the *San Francisco Examiner,* Thompson is also the National Affairs Editor at *Rolling Stone,* and author of several bestselling books including *Fear and Loathing in Las Vegas* and *Fear and Loathing on the Campaign Trail.* A self-styled "gonzo" journalist, Thompson claims membership in such diverse organizations as the Sheriff's Advisory Committee of Pitkin County Colorado, the National Organization for the Reform of Marijuana Laws, and the Kona Coast Marlin Fishermen's Association.

ART & ARCHITECTURE

ART Although there may be no distinctive "San Francisco style," the city's art scene is very much at the forefront of American design. In addition to hosting controversial performance-art shows, the city boasts dozens of fine art galleries, most of which are primarily concerned with contemporary collections in all media. A good selection of galleries is listed in Chapter 9, "Shopping from A to Z."

> ✪ **San Francisco's art scene is very much at the forefront of American design.**

The late Beniamino Bufano was one of the world's great contemporary sculptors, and one of this city's most prolific artists. His works are easy to miss because so many of them are placed quite casually outside museums or inside children's playgrounds. But chances are that if you happen to spot a particularly whimsical rabbit, contented cat, or luxuriating seal, it'll be his. Don't miss his wonderfully serene and human statue of St. Francis, which offers outstretched arms to birds and passersby at the edge of a parking lot at the corner of Taylor and Beach.

Some of the city's best public-art pieces are the colorful murals inside the base of Coit Tower, atop Telegraph Hill. Commissioned in 1934 by the federal Public Works of Art Project, the frescoed paintings, recently restored, are a curious mélange of art and politics, a social realist's vision of America during the Great Depression.

ARCHITECTURE The most obvious and stunning architecture in San Francisco is seen in the many Victorian houses that comprise the bulk of the city's residences. There are more than 14,000 "gingerbread" structures, dating from the second half of the 19th century, spread throughout the city. Many have been beautifully restored and ornately painted by residents who are proud of their city's heritage. The Alamo Square Historic District has one of the greatest concentrations of these "Painted Ladies." Many structures from the Victorian age, such as the Haas-Lillienthal House and the Sheraton Palace Hotel's Garden Court, are open to the public. See

> ✪ **The city's more than 14,000 Victorian houses, known as "Painted Ladies," are a prominent feature of the architectural landscape.**

"Architectural Highlights" in Section 2, "More Attractions," of Chapter 7, for complete information.

Dedicated on August 2, 1791, Mission Dolores is the oldest extant structure in the city. Built at the behest of Franciscan Father Junípero Serra, the mission was the sixth in the chain of missions that dot the California coast. The adobe structure is surrounded by a four-foot-thick wall; its small, simple chapel is a curious mixture of Native American construction methods and Spanish-colonial style.

Among contemporary buildings, the Transamerica Pyramid at 600 Montgomery St., in the Financial District, is the most imposing. Standing 853 feet high, it is the tallest structure in the city's futuristic skyline. The building's unique white wedge is capped by a 212-foot spire and has been called by its detractors "San Francisco's dunce cap." The Pyramid was completed in 1972.

The San Francisco Museum of Modern Art, in brand-new headquarters, is worth a visit for its architectural exhibits alone, both permanent and special. Special exhibits are mounted often, so that your visit is likely to coincide with one.

2. RECOMMENDED BOOKS, FILMS & RECORDINGS

From the beginning, artists, musicians, actors, novelists, and poets were an essential part of the mélange that makes up San Francisco. Although their personal stays were often in the nature of passing through, their works have left lasting records of an ever-changing city.

BOOKS General Mark Twain and Bret Harte were in San Francisco in the gold-rush heydays, writing it all down. *Mark Twain's San Francisco* (Greenwood, 1987) is a collection of articles that Twain wrote about what he called "the liveliest, heartiest community on our continent." His book *Roughing It* (Penguin, 1981) includes a moment-by-moment description of the 1906 earthquake. Harte's collection of stories *The Luck of Roaring Camp and Other Sketches* (Star Rover, 1983) reveals the tough lives of gold rush miners.

Joan Didion's *Slouching Toward Bethlehem* (Washington Square Press, 1983) and Hunter S. Thompson's columns for the *San Francisco Examiner* both used a "new journalistic" approach in their studies of San Francisco in the 1960s. Thompson's essays have been brought together in the collection *Generation of Swine* (Summit Books, 1988). Tom Wolfe's *The Electric Kool-Aid Acid Test* (Farrar, Straus & Giroux, 1987) follows the Hell's Angels, the Grateful Dead, and Ken Kesey's Merry Pranksters as they ride through the hallucinogenic 1960s.

Fiction and Biography Frank Norris's *McTeague: A Story of San Francisco* (Penguin, 1982) is a violent tale of love and revenge set in turn-of-the-century San Francisco. Dashiell Hammett's classic *The Maltese Falcon* (Avon, 1974) is a steamy detective novel that captures the seedier side of 1920s San Francisco. *Martin Eden* (Bantam, 1986) is Jack London's semi-autobiographical account of his boyhood on the Oakland shores.

In the 1950s, Jack Kerouac came to the city to write *On the Road* (Penguin, 1976), the bible of the "beat generation." Its bopping prose chronicles a series of cross-country adventures, including high jinx in San Francisco. In *The Crying of Lot 49*

(Harper & Row, 1986), Thomas Pynchon chronicles the adventures of 1960s potheads.

More recently, Amy Tan's gentle, engrossing novels *The Joy Luck Club* (Ivy Books, 1990) and *The Kitchen God's Wife* (G. P. Putnam, 1991) evoke the lives of several generations of women in San Francisco's Chinatown.

FILMS   San Francisco's varied venues, beautiful sites, and close proximity to Hollywood continue to make the city a natural for directors searching for an engrossing, relatively inexpensive film location. Hundreds of movies have been shot here. Some of the most famous include *The Frisco Kid* (1935), a riffraff tale of a shanghaied sailor (James Cagney) who rises to power in the rough-and-tumble 1860s Barbary Coast, and *The Maltese Falcon* (1941), John Huston's film about San Francisco private eye Sam Spade (Humphrey Bogart), perhaps one of the best detective films ever made.

Bird Man of Alcatraz (1962) is about real-life convicted killer Robert Stroud (Burt Lancaster), who studied birds while doing time in the high-security prison. Alfred Hitchcock's thriller *The Birds* (1963) is set on the rugged coast just north of the city.

Bullit (1968) is a cop thriller starring Steve McQueen. It contains what is still the quintessential San Francisco car chase. *Harold and Maude* (1971) is a very funny black comedy about a death-obsessed teenager and his 80-year-old friend. It's a cult classic. *Dirty Harry* (1971), *Magnum Force* (1973), and *The Enforcer* (1976), three thrillers about a neofascist San Francisco cop, affirmed Clint Eastwood's place in the American psyche.

What's Up Doc? (1972), a screwball comedy starring Barbra Streisand and Ryan O'Neal, offers plenty of shots of San Francisco. *The Conversation* (1974), by San Francisco director Francis Ford Coppola, stars Gene Hackman at his finest and is set in and around Union Square.

Foul Play (1978) was one of Goldie Hawn's biggest movies. Dudley Moore and Chevy Chase costar. *Chan Is Missing* (1982) was director Wayne Wang's low-budget sleeper about the Chinese-American experience in San Francisco's Chinatown. *48 Hours* (1982) offers great shots of the city, in which Eddie Murphy prances around with Nick Nolte while trying to wrap up a homicide case.

RECORDINGS   Dave Brubeck, the Oakland-born pianist and jazz composer, brought, international status to West Coast jazz, and Isaac Stern, the noted violinist, spent his formative years in San Francisco. But, with few exceptions, San Francisco is best known for its place in 1960s musical America.

IMPRESSIONS

The extreme geniality of San Francisco's economic, intellectual and political climate makes it the most varied and challenging city in the United States.
—JAMES MICHENER, AUTHOR

I firmly believe that if the U.N. had remained here it would work much better. San Francisco has shown the world that people of diverse races and cultures can live together in peace.
—ADLAI STEVENSON, DURING THE 1952 PRESIDENTIAL CAMPAIGN

San Francisco's rock bands were a key element of the counter-culture scene that blossomed in the city in the mid-sixties; their free-form improvisation was one of the primary expressions of the hippies' "do your own thing" principle. If you attend a concert by the Grateful Dead, the quintessential psychedelic rock band, you'll still find, amid all the tie-dye shirts and blissful smiles, a set of musical values that dates back to the days of Ken Kesey and his Merry Pranksters: a no-holds-barred reliance on spontaneous improvisation, even at the expense of clarity.

The history and style of the Dead is inseparable from that of the hippie movement. Jerry Garcia, the band's leader, played in a number of Bay Area bands before founding the Dead in 1965; they were soon headlining at counterculture strongholds like Bill Graham's Fillmore Theater in San Francisco. From June 1966 through the end of 1967, the Dead lived communally at 710 Ashbury St. in the Haight and played numerous free concerts there. As 1967's "Summer of Love" brought the flower children into full bloom, they were one of the headliners at the legendary Monterey Pop Festival.

The Grateful Dead have been playing together now for nearly 30 years. Over that span, they have released numerous LPs; *American Beauty, Workingman's Dead,* and *Europe '72,* all on Warner Brothers, are some of their better records. But the band's members themselves downplay the importance of their recordings: The only way to get the flavor of this band—and perhaps a glimpse of Haight-Ashbury in 1967—is to mingle with the converted at one of their concerts.

Santana, a local band known for its innovative blending of Latin rhythms and low-key jazz vocals, made its debut at the Fillmore West. Soon after, the group landed a deal with Columbia Records. Other 1960s-era bands to emerge in San Francisco include Jefferson Airplane and the political country band Country Joe and the Fish.

More contemporary Bay Area rockers include Huey Lewis and the News, and Chris Isaak, whose sultry voice, and sultrier videos, represent one of San Francisco's latest contributions to the rock music scene.

In popular music, San Francisco, like other major cities, has inspired its share of songs. Perhaps no song, however, is more closely identified with the Bay City than the ballad made famous by Tony Bennett more than 25 years ago, "I Left My Heart in San Francisco." It quickly replaced as the city's traditional theme song, another popular tune, "San Francisco," introduced by Jeanette MacDonald in the 1936 movie of that name.

IMPRESSIONS

Of all cities in the United States I have seen, San Francisco is the most beautiful.
—Nikita S. Khrushchev

[San Francisco] is remarkable not only for its beauty. It is also, of all the cities in the United States, the one whose name, the world over, conjures up the most visions and more than any other incites one to dream.
—Georges Pompidou, former president of France

CHAPTER 2

PLANNING A TRIP TO SAN FRANCISCO

Although it is possible to arrive in San Francisco without an itinerary or reservations, your trip will be much more rewarding with a little bit of advance planning.

1. INFORMATION & MONEY

In addition to the data and sources listed below, foreign visitors should also see Chapter 3, "For Foreign Visitors," for entry requirements and other pertinent information.

INFORMATION The **San Francisco Convention and Visitors Bureau,** P.O. Box 429097, San Francisco, CA 94142-9097 (tel. 415/391-2000), is the best source for any kind of specialized information about the city. Even if you don't have a specific question, you may want to send them $2 for their 100-page magazine *The San Francisco Book,* which includes a three-month calendar of events, a lodging guide, and several good, clear maps.

Once in the city, visit the **San Francisco Visitor Information Center,** on the lower level of Hallidie Plaza, 900 Market St., at Powell Street (tel. 415/391-2000), for information, brochures, and advice on restaurants, sights, and events in the city. The office is open Monday through Friday from 9am to 5:30pm, on Saturday from 9am to 3pm, and on Sunday from 10am to 2pm. It's closed on Thanksgiving Day, Christmas, and New Year's Day.

For specialized information on Chinatown's shops and services, and on the city's Chinese community in general, contact the **Chinese Chamber of Commerce,** 730 Sacramento St., San Francisco, CA 94108 (tel. 415/982-3000), open Monday through Friday from 9am to 5pm.

The **Visitors Information Center of the Redwood Empire Association,** 785 Market St., 15th Floor, San Francisco, CA 94103 (tel. 415/543-8334), supplies information on areas north of the city. Their informative, annual *Redwood Empire Visitors' Guide* is available for $3 by mail—free if you pick it up in person.

MONEY   In addition to paying close attention to the details below, foreign visitors should also see Chapter 3, "For Foreign Visitors," for monetary descriptions and currency-exchange information.

U.S. dollar traveler's checks are the safest, most negotiable way to carry currency. They are accepted by most restaurants, hotels, and shops, and can be exchanged for cash at banks and check-issuing offices. American Express offices are open Monday through Friday from 9am to 5pm and on Saturday from 9am until noon. See "Fast Facts: San Francisco" in Chapter 4 for office locations.

Most banks offer Automated Teller Machines (ATMs), which accept cards connected to a particular network. **Bank of America,** 485 California St., at Montgomery Street (tel. 415/622-3456), accepts Plus, Star, and Interlink cards. **First Interstate Bank,** 465 California St. (tel. 415/765-4511), is on-line with the Cirrus system. The two banks have over a dozen other branches each around the city. For additional bank locations, dial toll free 800/424-7787 for the Cirrus network, 800/843-7587 for the Plus system.

WHAT THINGS COST IN SAN FRANCISCO   U.S.$

Taxi from airport to city center	30.00
Bus fare to any destination within the city	1.00
Double room at the Four Seasons Clift Hotel (deluxe)	205.00
Double room at Hotel Beresford (moderate)	85.00
Double room at Edward II Inn & Carriage House (budget)	67.00
Lunch for one at Little City (moderate)	15.00
Lunch for one at Amerasian Café (budget)	7.00
Dinner for one, without wine, at Fleur de Lys (deluxe)	75.00
Dinner for one, without wine, at Cha Cha Cha (moderate)	17.00
Dinner for one, without wine, at Hamburger Mary's (budget)	10.00
Glass of beer	2.75
Coca-Cola	1.25
Cup of coffee	.80
Admission to the top of Coit Tower	3.00
Movie ticket	7.50
Theater ticket	10.00–40.00

Credit cards are widely accepted in San Francisco. MasterCard and Visa are the most commonly accepted, followed by American Express, Carte Blanche, Diners Club, and Discover. ATMs at both the above-listed banks will make cash advances against MasterCard and Visa cards. American Express cardholders can write a personal check, guaranteed against their card, for up to $1,000 in cash at an American Express office. See "Fast Facts: San Francisco" in Chapter 4 for office addresses.

2. WHEN TO GO— CLIMATE & EVENTS

Summer is San Francisco's main tourist season, but not necessarily the best time to go. California's beach paradise image was not created here, where summers are often characterized by overcast days and cold nights. Terrific weather has never been the city's main appeal, but skies are usually bluest in late spring and early autumn. The city is a particular delight during winter, when the opera and ballet seasons are in full swing, there is less crowding in restaurants and stores, and some hotel prices are lower than at other times of the year.

CLIMATE

The Bay City's temperate marine climate means relatively mild weather year-round. In summer, temperatures rarely top 70°F, and the city's famous fog rolls in most mornings and evenings. In winter, the mercury seldom falls below freezing, and snow is almost unheard of.

Because of San Francisco's famous fog, the city seldom gets more than a couple of hottish days in a row. Northern California's summer fog bank is produced by a rare combination of waters, winds, and topography. It lies off the coast and is pulled in by rising air currents when the land heats up. Held back by coastal mountains along a 600-mile front, the low clouds probe for any passage they can find. And the access most readily available is the slot where the Pacific Ocean penetrates the continental wall—the Golden Gate.

San Francisco's Average Temperatures & Rainfall

	Jan	Feb	Mar	Apr	May	June	July	Aug	Sept	Oct	Nov	Dec
Avg. High (°F)	56	59	60	61	63	64	64	65	69	68	63	57
Avg. Low (°F)	46	48	49	49	51	53	53	54	56	55	52	47
Rain (in.)	4.5	2.8	2.6	1.5	0.4	0.2	0.1	0.1	0.2	1.1	2.5	3.5

SAN FRANCISCO CALENDAR OF EVENTS

JANUARY

☐ **San Francisco International Boat Show,** Moscone Center. Draws thousands of boat enthusiasts over a nine-day period. Call 415/469-6065 for details. Early January.

FEBRUARY

⭐ *CHINESE NEW YEAR* *In 1995, the year of the Boar, public celebrations will again spill onto every street in Chinatown. Festivities climax during the "Miss Chinatown U.S.A." pageant parade, an incredible mixture of marching bands, rolling floats, barrages of fireworks, and a wonderful block-long dragon writhing in and out of the crowds. Not to be missed.*

Where: Chinatown. When: January or early February, depending on the lunar calendar. How: Arrive early for a good viewing spot on Grant Avenue. For information, call 415/982-3000.

MARCH

☐ **St. Patrick's Day Parade.** Starts at 12:30pm at Market and Second streets and continues past City Hall. The city's large Irish community is in evidence. Call 415/391-2000 for details. The Sunday before March 17.

⭐ *SAN FRANCISCO INTERNATIONAL FILM FESTIVAL* *This is one of America's oldest film festivals. Tickets are relatively inexpensive, and screenings are very accessible to the general public. Entries include new films by beginning and established directors.*

Where: The AMC Kabuki 8 Cinemas, at Fillmore and Post streets. When: During two weeks early in the month. How: You can charge tickets by phone through BASS Ticketmaster (tel. 415/835-3849). For a schedule or information, call 415/931-FILM.

APRIL

☐ **Cherry Blossom Festival,** Japantown and at Golden Gate Park's Japanese Tea Garden. Traditional drumming, flower arranging, origami, and Kabuki theater celebrate the blooming of the cherry trees' pretty pink petals. Around the middle of April.

☐ **Yachting Season Opening Day.** Fills the bay with boats—it seems as though every craft in the Bay Area takes part in this aquatic salute to sailing. Good views can be had from the Golden Gate Bridge, Fisherman's Wharf, and the Marin Headlands. On a Saturday or Sunday at the end of April.

MAY

☐ **Bay to Breakers Foot Race,** Golden Gate Park. One of the city's most popular annual events, it's really more fun than run. Thousands of entrants show up dressed in their best Halloween-style costumes for the approximately seven-mile run across the park. The event is sponsored by the *San Francisco Examiner* (tel. 415/777-7770). Third Sunday of May.

☐ **Black and White Ball,** Civic Center. A fund-raiser for the San Francisco Symphony held on alternate years. Held last in 1993. At $150 each, tickets aren't cheap, but this is no ordinary black-tie event. Festivities take place in several Civic Center buildings, and the streets between them are cordoned off for the party. Food and drink are donated by local restaurants and wineries, and the thousands of revelers dress—appropriately enough—in black and white. For information, call 415/431-5400. Late May.

⭐ *CARNIVAL   The San Francisco Mission District's largest annual event, Carnival, is a week-long series of festivities that culminates with a parade on Mission Street over Memorial Day weekend. More than a half-million spectators line the route, and the samba musicians and dancers continue to play on 14th Street, near Harrison, at the end of the march.*
  Where: Mission Street, between 14th and 24th streets. When: Memorial Day Weekend, late May. How: Just show up. Phone the Mission Economic Cultural Association (tel. 415/826-1401) for more information.

JUNE

☐ **Union Street Spring Festival,** along Union Street. This is the first of a series of city street fairs. From Fillmore Street to Gough Street, stalls sell arts and crafts, as well as food and drink. Music and entertainment are usually provided on a number of stages. Call 415/346-4446 for more information. First weekend of June.

☐ **Haight Street Fair.** Features alternative crafts, ethnic foods, rock bands, and a healthy number of hippies. For details, call 415/661-8025. A Saturday in the middle of June.

☐ **Lesbian and Gay Freedom Day Parade,** Market Street. A prideful event drawing up to half a million participants. The parade ends at Civic Center Plaza, where hundreds of food, art, and information booths are set up around several sound stages. Call 415/864-3733 for information. Last weekend of June.

☐ **Stern Grove Midsummer Music Festival,** in the natural amphitheater at 19th Avenue and Sloat Boulevard. Free jazz, classical, and pop concerts are held every Sunday at 2pm. Call 415/252-6252 for listings. Mid-June through August.

JULY

☐ **Independence Day.** July 4th is celebrated all over town, but the largest festivities are on the waterfront, at Crissy Field. In addition to a 50-cannon salute, there are music concerts, comedy acts, food stands, and fireworks in front of the Golden Gate Bridge at 9pm.

☐ **San Francisco Marathon.** One of the largest marathons in the world. For entry information, contact the Pamakid Runners Club (tel. 415/391-2123). Mid-July.

☐ **Comedy Celebration Day,** at the Polo Field in Golden Gate Park. A free comedy marathon featuring dozens of famous and not-so-famous funny people. For information, call 415/777-7120. Late July.

SEPTEMBER

⭐ *SAN FRANCISCO FAIR* *There are no tractor pulls or monster trucks at San Francisco's rendition of an annual county fair. This sophisticated urban party is attended by thousands and includes restaurant and winery booths, street artists, fine artists, and high-quality local entertainment.*
   Where: *Fort Mason Center.* ***When:*** *Early September.*
How: *For information, call 415/391-2000.*

☐ **San Francisco Blues Festival,** on the grounds of Fort Mason. The largest outdoor blues music event on the West Coast. Local and national musicians perform back-to-back during two marathon days. You can charge tickets by phone through BASS Ticketmaster (tel. 415/835-3849). For schedule information, call 415/826-6837. Usually in mid-September.

☐ **Castro Street Fair.** Celebrates life in the city's most famous gay neighborhood. Late September.

⭐ *SAUSALITO ART FESTIVAL* *A juried exhibit of more than 160 artists is accompanied by music by Bay Area jazz, rock, and blues performers while international cuisine is washed down with wines from some 50 different Napa and Sonoma producers. Parking is impossible; take the Red & White Fleet (tel. 415/546-2628) ferry from Fisherman's Wharf to the festival site.*
   Where: *Sausalito.* ***When:*** *Labor Day weekend, early September.* ***How:*** *For more information, call 415/332-3555.*

OCTOBER

☐ **Columbus Day Festivities.** The 1995 party will celebrate the 503rd anniversary of Christopher Columbus's landing in America. The city's Italian community leads the festivities around Fisherman's Wharf, which include street food fairs, fireworks, the usual curbside entertainment, and a reenactment of the explorer's landing, at Aquatic Park. On Columbus Day itself, a parade marches up Columbus Avenue. Phone 415/434-1492 for information. Second Monday in October.

DECEMBER

☐ **The Nutcracker,** War Memorial Opera House. Performed annually by the San Francisco Ballet (tel. 415/776-1999). Tickets to this Tchaikovsky tradition should be purchased well in advance.

3. INSURANCE & SAFETY

Health and safety are serious issues. Take a little time before your trip to make sure that these concerns don't ruin it. Foreign travelers should see Chapter 3, "For Foreign Visitors," for entry information, safety precautions, and other related matters.

INSURANCE Most travel agents sell low-cost health, loss, and trip-cancellation insurance to their vacationing clients. Compare these rates and services with those offered by local banks as well as by your personal insurance carrier.

Most American travelers are covered by their hometown **health insurance** policies in the event of an accident or sudden illness while away on vacation. Make sure that your health maintenance organization (HMO) or insurance carrier can provide services for you in San Francisco. If there is any doubt, a health-insurance policy that specifically covers your trip is advisable. Foreign travelers should check to see if they are covered by their home insurance companies and refer to Chapter 3, "For Foreign Visitors," for more information.

You can also protect your travel investment with **travel-related insurance** by insuring against lost or damaged baggage and against trip cancellation or interruption costs. These coverages are often combined into a single comprehensive plan and sold through travel agents, credit-card companies, and automobile and other clubs.

SAFETY Innocent tourists are rarely the victims of violent crime. Still, there are precautions you can take to protect yourself and your possessions.

When sightseeing, it's best to plan your route in advance; consult maps indoors before leaving your hotel room. Ask directions from service providers—hotel desk staff, telephone- or power-company employees, or police officers. Avoid asking strangers for directions, and don't discuss your plans with them. If you get lost, find an open business and ask for directions there. Always be aware of your surroundings and leave an area if it appears unsafe. Remember, alcohol consumption diminishes awareness.

Use traveler's checks or credit cards whenever possible. Carry only as much cash as you will need and never display it openly. Carry your wallet in the front pocket of your pants or inside your jacket. Carry pocketbooks and other bags under your arm, not by the handle. While sitting, keep your handbag in your lap. In a restaurant, never sling your purse over the back of a chair. Keep your bag next to you in a public restroom instead of using door hooks. Consider using a "fanny-pack" or a concealable money belt to carry cash and credit cards. Carry some of your cash and credit cards separately, in a second pocket or wallet, and carry new purchases in old bags. Stay especially alert in crowded situations, such as in department stores, at bus stops, and on public transportation.

Don't let your car advertise that you are a visitor. Place maps, travel brochures, this guidebook, and your valuables out of sight—

in the glove compartment or trunk. Never leave wallets, credit cards, checkbooks, or purses anywhere in the vehicle. Always lock your vehicle and take the keys. Park in well-lighted, busy areas. Check the interior of your vehicle before getting in, and, when parking for the night, ask yourself if you've left anything in your car that could be of any value whatsoever—then remove it.

Keep an eye on your luggage when checking in and out of your hotel. Make sure no one hears your name and room number while at the front desk. Phone the front desk to verify the identity of room service and other hotel employees—especially if you did not call for them. Know what the hotel identification badge looks like. Deposit your valuables in the hotel safe and keep an inventory of what was deposited; never leave cash or other valuables in your room. Lock your luggage when it is left in the room, know how to double lock your room door, and use the door viewer to identify anyone trying to gain entry to your room. Never leave your room key at an unattended front desk.

San Francisco's homeless problem is one of the worst in America—panhandlers are especially prevalent around Union Square. Most homeless people are harmless; however, some street people are chronic law violators who may infringe upon the rights of others. We suggest a combination of respect and caution around panhandlers and other strangers.

See "Fast Facts: San Francisco" in Chapter 4 for city-specific safety tips. For additional crime-prevention information, phone San Francisco SAFE (tel. 415/553-1984).

4. WHAT TO PACK

San Francisco's weather can be freezing cold in summer and pleasantly balmy in winter. It can also be both these things on almost any given day, summer or winter, making packing for your trip particularly difficult.

The weather here is usually cooler than you might expect, especially during summer, when you should pack at least one warm sweater and a light jacket. Any time of the year, an all-weather coat is a good idea. The sun is so unpredictable here that it's best to dress in layers. When you get too hot from climbing up the big hills, you can take off a layer; when the wind whips up on the other side, you can put it back on. Good walking shoes are also a must if you want to explore the city's many wonderful neighborhoods.

If you are currently taking medication, pack the prescriptions in case your pills get lost. If you wear eyeglasses, carry the prescription for them, too. If you are visiting in winter, you may want to bring an umbrella. Even if you forget one, however don't worry; virtually everything can be purchased in San Francisco, so keep the "lug" out of your luggage by eliminating items that you may have decided to take along "just in case."

5. TIPS FOR THE DISABLED, SENIORS, FAMILIES & STUDENTS

FOR PEOPLE WITH DISABILITIES Most of San Francisco's major museums and tourist attractions are fitted with wheelchair ramps to accommodate physically challenged visitors. In addition, many hotels offer special accommodations and services for wheelchair-bound and other visitors with disabilities. These include large bathrooms, ramps, and telecommunication devices for deaf people. The San Francisco Convention and Visitor Bureau (see Section 1, "Information and Money," above) has the most up-to-date information.

The **Easter Seal Society of the Bay Area, San Francisco Center,** 6221 Geary Blvd., San Francisco, CA 94121 (tel. 415/752-4888), offers specialized information for disabled people. Travelers in wheelchairs should also obtain a free copy of the "Accessible Route Guide," published by the **San Francisco Municipal Railway,** 949 Presidio Ave., San Francisco, CA 94115. For special public-transportation information by phone, call 415/673-6864 Monday through Friday from 9am to 5pm, or 415/673-MUNI daily, 24 hours.

FOR SENIORS In San Francisco, the term "seniors" usually refers to men and women age 65 and older. Seniors regularly receive discounts at museums and attractions; such discounts, when available, are listed in this guide, under their appropriate headings. Ask for discounts everywhere—at hotels, movie theaters, museums, restaurants, and attractions. You may be surprised how often you'll be offered reduced rates. When making airline reservations, ask about a senior discount—but find out if there is a cheaper promotional fare before committing yourself.

Older travelers are particularly encouraged to purchase travel insurance (see Section 3, "Insurance and Safety," above).

In addition to organizing tours, the **American Association of Retired Persons (AARP) Travel Service,** P.O. Box 7625, Norcross, GA 30091-7625 (tel. toll free 800/927-0111) provides a list of travel suppliers who offer discounts to members.

FOR FAMILIES Children add joys and a different level of experience to travel. They help you see things in a different way and sometimes will draw local people like a magnet—the very same people who, if you were traveling alone, would probably be suspicious and reticent. Taking kids to San Francisco also obviously means more thorough planning. On airplanes, special-order children's meals as far in advance as possible. Most airlines don't carry baby food but will be glad to heat up any you've brought with you. Pack first-aid supplies, such as a thermometer, Band-Aids, cough drops, and children's aspirin; and always carry snacks.

San Francisco is full of sightseeing opportunities and special activities geared toward children. See Section 3, "Cool for Kids," in Chapter 7, "What to See and Do in San Francisco," for information and ideas for visiting families. *Frommer's San Francisco with*

Kids, by Carey Simon and Charlene Marmer Solomon, is a comprehensive guide geared specifically to families; it is available at bookstores or directly from Macmillan General Reference.

FOR STUDENTS Students will find that their valid high school or college ID means discounts on travel, theater and museum tickets, and at some nightspots. Many student specials are listed throughout this book under their appropriate headings.

6. GETTING THERE

San Francisco is easy to get to, but not all transportation options are created equal. Shopping around will ensure that you get there the right way at the best price.

BY PLANE

THE AIRLINES More than a dozen scheduled airlines service San Francisco International Airport. Following are the major U.S. carriers offering regular flights to San Francisco. The airlines share a walk-in reservations office located downtown at 433 California St.: **American Airlines** (tel. 415/398-4434, or toll free 800/433-7300); **Delta Airlines** (tel. 415/552-5700, or toll free 800/221-1212); **Northwest Airlines** (tel. 415/392-2163, or toll free 800/225-2525); **TWA** (tel. 415/864-5731, or toll free 800/221-2000); **United Airlines** (tel. 415/397-2100, or toll free 800/241-6522); and **USAir** (tel. toll free 800/428-4322).

REGULAR AIRFARES Often an inexpensive ticket to San Francisco is not worth enough to travel agents to make them really dig. Therefore, to get the lowest price, I usually do the legwork and make the reservation myself, and then visit my travel agent for ticketing. Similarly, you should check the newspapers for advertisements and call a few of the major carriers before committing yourself.

The lowest **economy-class** fare usually comes with serious restrictions and steep penalties for altering dates and itineraries. When purchasing these tickets, don't use terms like "APEX" and "excursion" or other airline jargon; just ask for the lowest fare. If you're flexible with dates and times, say so. Ask if you can get a fare cheaper by staying an extra day or by flying during the middle of the week. Many airlines won't volunteer this information. At the time of this writing, the lowest round-trip fare from New York was $398; from Chicago, $298; and from Los Angeles, $198. You may find it even lower.

Seats in **business class** can easily cost twice what coach seats do. When buying a full-fare ticket, expect to pay about $1,600 from New York and $1,100 from Chicago. Note, however, that competition is stiff for luxury-class passengers, so that prices are

IMPRESSIONS

The coldest winter I ever spent was a summer in San Francisco.
—MARK TWAIN

sometimes more elastic in this category than they are for economy seats. Again, call several airlines and compare prices before committing yourself.

Many short hops to San Francisco don't even carry a **first-class** section. When they do, they're predictably expensive. Expect to pay about $2,500 from New York and $2,000 from Chicago.

OTHER GOOD VALUE CHOICES   Alternatives to the traditional travel-agent ticket have their advantages (usually in lower prices) and their drawbacks (usually in lack of freedom). Don't overlook a **consolidator,** or "bucket shop," when hunting for domestic fares. By negotiating directly with the airlines, the "buckets" can sell tickets at prices below official rates. On the minus side, consolidators usually don't offer travel counseling and don't book hotels or rental cars. Like the most heavily restricted tickets, these often carry heavy penalties for changing or canceling.

The lowest-priced bucket shops are usually local operations with low profiles and overheads. Look for their advertisements in the travel section or the classifieds of your local newspapers(s). Nationally advertised businesses are usually not as competitive as the smaller, boiler-room operations, but they have toll-free telephone numbers and are easily accessible. Two of the best known are **Travac,** 989 Sixth Ave., New York, NY 10018 (tel. 212/563-3303, or toll free 800/TRAV-800), and **Unitravel,** 1177 N. Warson Rd., (P.O. Box 12485), St. Louis, MO 63132 (tel. 314/569-0900, or toll free 800/325-2222).

Competition among the bucket shops, not to mention fierce competition among the commercial airlines themselves, has pared the number of **charters** somewhat, but there are still plenty to choose from. Most charter operators advertise and sell their seats through travel agents, thus making these local professionals your best source of information for available flights. Before deciding to take a charter flight, check the restrictions on the ticket: You may be asked to purchase a tour package, to pay your fare in advance of the flight, to be amenable if the day of departure or the destination is changed, to pay a service charge, to fly on an airline you're not familiar with (this usually is not the case), and to pay harsh penalties if you cancel but to be understanding if the charter doesn't fill up and is canceled up to ten days before departure. Summer charters fill up more quickly than others and are almost sure to fly, but if you decide on a charter flight, seriously consider cancellation and baggage insurance (see Section 3, "Insurance and Safety," above).

Courier flights are primarily long-haul jobs and are usually not available for short domestic hops. But if you are crossing the country or an ocean, becoming a mule might be the bargain for you. Companies that hire couriers use your luggage allowance for their business baggage; in return, you get a deeply discounted ticket. Flights are often offered at the last minute, and you may have to arrange a pretrip interview to make sure you're right for the job. **Now Voyager, Inc.** (tel. 212/431-1616 Monday through Friday from 10am to 5pm, and Saturday from 10am to 4:30pm), flies from New York and sometimes has flights to San Francisco for as little as $199 round-trip.

BY TRAIN

Traveling by train takes a long time and usually costs as much as, or more than, flying. But if you're afraid of airplanes, or if you

FROMMER'S SMART TRAVELER: AIRFARES

1. Shop all the airlines that fly to your destination.
2. Always ask for the lowest fare, not "discount," "APEX," or "excursion."
3. Keep calling the airline—availability of cheap seats changes daily.
4. Seek out budget alternatives. Phone "bucket shops," charter companies, and discount travel agents.
5. Plan to travel midweek, when rates are usually lower.

want to take a leisurely ride through America's countryside, rail may be a good option.

San Francisco–bound **Amtrak** (tel. toll free 800/USA-RAIL) trains leave daily from New York and cross the country through Chicago and Denver. The journey takes about 3½ days, and seats fill up quickly. As of this writing, the lowest round-trip fare was $287 from New York and $248 from Chicago. These heavily restricted tickets are good for 45 days and allow up to three stops along the way.

Round-trip tickets can often be had from Los Angeles for as little as $115. Trains actually arrive in Oakland and connect with regularly scheduled buses to San Francisco's Transbay Terminal.

CalTrain (tel. 415/495-4546, or toll free 800/660-4287) operates train services between San Francisco and the towns of the peninsula. The city depot is at 700 Fourth St., at Townsend Street.

BY BUS

Bus travel is an inexpensive and often flexible option. **Greyhound/Trailways** (tel. toll free 800/231-2222) can get you here from anywhere, and offers several money-saving multiday bus passes. Round-trip fares vary, depending on your point of origin, but few, if any, ever exceed $200. The main San Francisco bus station is the Transbay Terminal, at First and Mission streets. Greyhound/Trailways no longer operates a single nationwide telephone number, so consult your local directory for the office nearest you.

BY CAR

San Francisco is well connected to the rest of the United States by several major highways, including Interstate 5, which comes in from the north, and U.S. 101, which follows the western seaboard through the heart of San Francisco. Interstate 10, which originates in Jacksonville, Florida, terminates in Los Angeles, 487 miles to the south.

A car is a great way to go if you want to become intimate with the countryside, but after figuring in food, lodging, and automobile expenses, it may not be your cheapest option. Still, driving down the California coast is one of the world's ultimate journeys. Always drive within the speed limits and keep an eye out for "speed traps," where the limit suddenly drops. For tips on getting around San Francisco by car, see Chapter 4, "Getting to Know San Francisco."

Before taking a long car trip, you should seriously consider joining a major automobile association. Not only do they offer travel insurance and helpful information, but they can also perform vacation-saving roadside services, including towing. The **American Automobile Association (AAA),** 1000 AAA Dr., Heathrow, FL 32746-5063 (tel. 407/444-7000, or toll free 800/763-6600), is the nation's largest auto club, with over 850 offices. Membership ranges from about $40 to $60, depending on where you join.

Amoco Motor Club, P.O. Box 9049, Des Moines, IA 50368 (tel. toll free 800/334-3300) is another recommendable choice.

PACKAGES & TOURS

Tours and packages are put together by airlines, charter companies, hotels, and tour operators, and are sold either directly to travelers or through travel agents. A **tour** usually refers to an escorted group and often includes transportation, sightseeing, meals, and accommodations. The entire group travels together, and all share the same preplanned activities. A **package,** on the other hand, can include any or all of the above components, but travelers are usually unescorted and free to make their own itinerary. Many travelers purchase airfare, hotel, and airport transfers from a travel agent, without even knowing that they're buying a tour operator's package. This is perfectly fine—packages can be a very good value. Since packages buy in bulk, they can sometimes sell their services at a discount.

To find out what tours and packages are available to you, check the ads in the travel section of your newspaper or visit your travel agent. Before signing up, however, read the fine print carefully and do some homework:

- **How reputable is the tour operator?** Ask for references of people who have participated in tours run by the same company. Call travel agents and the local Better Business Bureau, and check with the consumer department of the U.S. Tour Operators Association, 211 E. 51st St., Suite 12B, New York, NY 10022 (tel. 212/750-7371). Be leery of any outfit that doesn't give you details of the itinerary before demanding payment.
- **What is the size of the tour?** Decide whether you can handle an experience shared by 40 other people, or if your limit is 20. A smaller tour is generally a better-quality tour.
- **What kinds of hotels will be used and where are they located?** Get the names of the hotels and then look them up in guidebooks or in your travel agent's hotel guide. If you sense that the hotels provide only minimal essentials, so might the entire tour. If the hotel is not conveniently located, it will be less expensive, but you may feel isolated or unsafe, and you'll spend extra money and time getting to and from attractions and nightspots.
- **If meals are included, how elaborate are they?** Is breakfast continental, English, or buffet? Is the menu for the group limited to a few items?
- **How extensive is the sightseeing?** You may have the chance to get on and off the bus many times to explore a number of

attractions, or you may see them only from the bus window. If you like to explore, pick an attraction you're interested in and ask the operator precisely how much time you can expect to spend there. Find out if all admissions are included in the price of the tour.

- **Are the optional activities offered at an additional price?** This is usually the case, so make sure the activities that particularly interest you are included in the tour price.
- **What is the refund policy should you cancel?** Check this carefully; some tour operators are more lenient than others regarding trip cancellations.
- **How is the package price paid?** If a charter flight is involved, make sure that you can pay into an escrow account (ask for the name of the bank) to ensure proper use of the funds or their return in case the operator cancels the trip.

Most of the airlines listed above offer both escorted tours and on-your-own packages. Dozens of other companies also compete for this lucrative business. Discuss your options with a travel agent and compare tour prices with those in this guide.

CHAPTER 3

FOR FOREIGN VISITORS

The pervasiveness of American culture around the world may make you feel that you know the United States well. Still, leaving your own country requires an additional degree of planning, as well as some special advance knowledge of what to expect from a major American city. This chapter will help you become fully prepared.

1. PREPARING FOR YOUR TRIP

NECESSARY DOCUMENTS Canadian citizens may enter the United States without visas; they need only proof of residence. Citizens of the United Kingdom, New Zealand, Japan, and most Western European countries traveling with valid passports may not need a visa for fewer than 90 days of holiday or business travel to the United States, providing that they hold a round-trip or return ticket and enter the United States on an airline or cruise line participating in the visa-waiver program.

(Note that citizens of these visa-exempt countries who first enter the United States may then visit Mexico, Canada, Bermuda, and/or the Caribbean islands and then reenter the United States, by any mode of transportation, without needing a visa. Further information is available from any U.S embassy or consulate.)

Citizens of countries other than those stipulated above, including citizens of Australia, must have two documents: a valid passport, with an expiration date at least six months later than the scheduled end of the visit to the United States; and a tourist visa, available without charge from the nearest United States consulate.

To obtain a visa, the traveler must submit a completed application form (either in person or by mail) with a 1½-inch-square photo and demonstrate binding ties to a residence abroad. Usually you can obtain a visa at once or within 24 hours, but it may take longer during the summer rush from June to August. If you cannot go in person, contact the nearest U.S. embassy or consulate for directions on applying by mail. Your travel agent or airline office may also be able to provide you with visa applications and instructions. The U.S. consulate or embassy that issues your visa will determine whether you will be issued a multiple- or single-entry visa and any restrictions regarding the length of your stay.

MEDICAL REQUIREMENTS   Unless you are arriving from an area known to be suffering from an epidemic, no inoculations or vaccinations are required to enter the United States. Foreign visitors should be sure to hold a doctor's prescription for any controlled substances you are carrying.

TRAVEL INSURANCE   Although it is not required of travelers, health insurance is highly recommended. Unlike many European countries, the United States does not usually offer free or low-cost medical care to its citizens or visitors. Doctors and hospitals are expensive, and in most cases will require advance payment or proof of coverage before they render their services. Policies can cover everything from the loss or theft of your baggage and trip cancellation to the guarantee of bail in case you are arrested. Good policies will also cover costs of an accident, repatriation, or death. Such packages are sold by automobile clubs, as well as by insurance companies and travel agents. See Section 3, "Insurance and Safety," in Chapter 2 for more information.

Insurance for British Travelers   Most big travel agents offer their own insurance, and will probably try to sell you their package when you book a holiday. Think before you sign. Britain's Consumers' Association recommends that you insist on seeing the policy and reading the fine print before buying travel insurance. You might also shop around for better deals. Try **Columbus Travel Insurance Ltd.** (tel. 071/375-0011) or, for students, **Campus Travel** (tel. 071/730-3402). If you're unsure about who can give you the best deal, contact the **Association of British Insurers,** 51 Gresham St., London EC2V 7HQ (tel. 071/600-333).

SAFETY   General   While tourist areas are generally safe, crime is on the increase everywhere, and U.S. urban areas tend to be less safe than those in Europe or Japan. Visitors should always stay alert. This is particularly true of large U.S. cities. It is wise to ask the city or area's tourist office if you're in doubt about which neighborhoods are safe. Avoid deserted areas, especially at night. Don't go into any city park at night unless there is an occasion that attracts crowds. Generally speaking, you can feel safe in areas where there are many people and many open establishments (see "Fast Facts: San Francisco" in Chapter 4 for city-specific safety tips).

Avoid carrying valuables with you on the street, and don't display expensive cameras or electronic equipment. Hold on to your pocketbook, and place your billfold in an inside pocket. In restaurants, theaters, and other public places, keep your possessions in sight.

Remember also that hotels are open to the public, and in a large hotel, security may not be able to screen everyone entering. Always lock your room door; don't assume that once inside your hotel you are automatically safe and need no longer be aware of your surroundings.

Driving   Safety while driving is particularly important. Question your rental agency about personal safety, or ask for a traveler-safety-tips brochure when you pick up your car. Obtain written directions, or a map with the route marked in red, from the agency showing how to get to your destination. And, if possible, arrive and depart during daylight hours.

Recently more and more crime has involved cars and drivers. If you drive off a highway into a doubtful neighborhood, leave the area as quickly as possible. If you have an accident, even on the highway, stay in your car with the doors locked until you assess the situation, or until the police arrive. If you are bumped from behind on the street or are involved in a minor accident with no injuries and the situation appears to be suspicious, motion to the other driver to follow you. *Never* get out of your car in such situations. You can also keep a pre-made sign in your car that reads: PLEASE FOLLOW THIS VEHICLE TO REPORT THE ACCIDENT. Show the sign to the other driver and go directly to the nearest police precinct, well-lighted service station, or 24-hour store.

If you see someone on the road who indicates a need for help, do not stop. Take note of the location, drive on to a well-lighted area, and telephone the police by dialing 911.

Park in well-lighted, well-traveled areas if possible. Always keep your car doors locked, whether attended or unattended. Look around you before you get out of your car, and never leave any packages or valuables in sight. If someone attempts to rob you or steal your car—do not try to resist the thief/carjacker—report the incident to the police department immediately. You may wish to contact the local tourist information bureau at your destination before you arrive. They may be able to provide you with a safety brochure.

2. GETTING TO & AROUND THE U.S.

GETTING TO THE U.S. In addition to the domestic American airlines listed in Section 6, "Getting There," in Chapter 2, several international carriers, including Air Canada (tel. toll free 800/422-6232), British Airways (tel. toll free 800/247-9297), Japan Airlines (tel. toll free 800/525-3663), SAS (tel. toll free 800/221-2350), and Quantas (tel. toll free 800/622-0850), also serve San Francisco International Airport. For the best rates, compare fares and be flexible with the dates and times of travel. See also "Getting There" in Chapter 2 for information on alternative low-cost fares.

GETTING AROUND THE U.S. Some large airlines (for example, Northwest and Delta) offer travelers on their transatlantic or transpacific flights special discount tickets under the name **Visit USA,** allowing travel between any U.S. destinations at minimum rates. They are not on sale in the United States and must be purchased abroad in conjunction with your international ticket. See your travel agent or airline ticket office for full details, including terms and conditions.

International visitors can also buy a **USA Railpass,** good for 15 or 30 days of unlimited travel on Amtrak. The pass is available through many foreign travel agents. Prices in 1994 for a 15-day pass were $208 off-peak, $308 peak; a 30-day pass cost $309 off-peak, $389 peak. (With a foreign passport, you can also buy passes at various Amtrak offices in the United States, including locations in San Francisco, Los Angeles, Chicago, New York, Miami, Boston, and Washington, D.C.) Reservations are generally required and should be made for each part of your trip as early as possible. Visitors should also be aware of the limitations of long-distance rail travel in the United States. With notable exceptions (for instance, the Northeast Corridor line between Boston and Washington, D.C.), service is rarely up to European standards: Delays are common, routes are limited and often infrequently served, and fares are rarely significantly lower than discount airfares. Although the U.S. may see an improved high-speed rail system in the future, for the time being cross-country train travel should be approached with caution.

The cheapest way to travel through the United States is by **bus.** Greyhound/Trailways, the nation's nationwide bus line, offers an **Ameripass** for unlimited travel for 7 days (for $250), 15 days (for $350), and 30 days (for $450). Bus travel in the United States can be both slow and uncomfortable, so this option is not for everyone.

FAST *FOR THE FOREIGN TRAVELER*

Accommodations Some of the major hotels listed in this book maintain overseas reservation networks and can be booked either directly or through travel agents. Some hotels are also included in tour operators' package tours. Since tour companies buy rooms in bulk, they can often offer them at a discount. Discuss this option with your travel agent and compare tour prices with those in this guide. For accommodations in San Francisco, see Chapter 5, "San Francisco Accommodations."

Auto Organizations If you plan on renting a car in the United States, you will probably not need the services of an additional auto organization. If you are planning to buy or borrow a car, automobile association membership is recommended. The **American Automobile Association (AAA),** 1000 AAA Dr., Heathrow, FL 32746-5063 (tel. 800/336-4357), is the country's largest auto club, supplying members with maps, insurance, and, most important, emergency road service. The cost of joining runs $40 to $60, but if you're a member of a foreign auto club with reciprocal arrangements, you can enjoy free AAA service in America. See Section 6, "Getting There," in Chapter 2 for more information.

Automobile Rentals To rent a car you need a major credit card. A valid driver's license is required, and you usually need to be at least 25. Some companies do rent to younger people but add a daily surcharge. Be sure to return your car with the same amount of gas you started out with; rental companies charge excessive prices for gasoline.

Business Hours See "Fast Facts: San Francisco" in Chapter 4.

Climate See "When to Go—Climate & Events," in Chapter 2.

Currency and Exchange The U.S. monetary system has a decimal base: 1 **dollar** ($1) = 100 **cents** (100¢).

The most common **bills** (all green) are the $1 (colloquially, a "buck"), $5, $10, and $20 denominations. There are also $2 bills (seldom encountered), $50, and $100 bills (the last two are not welcome when paying for small purchases.

There are six denominations of **coins:** 1¢ (1 cent, or a penny), 5¢ (5 cents, or a nickel); 10¢ (10 cents, or a dime), 25¢ (25 cents, or a quarter), 50¢ (50 cents, or a half dollar); and—prized by collectors—the rare $1 piece (the older, large silver dollar and the newer, small Susan B. Anthony coin).

Foreign-exchange bureaus are rare in the United States, and most banks are not equipped to handle currency exchange. San Francisco's money-changing offices include: **Bank of America,** 345 Montgomery St. (tel. 415/622-2451), open Monday through Thursday from 9am to 4pm and Friday from 9am to 6pm, and Saturday 9am to 1pm; and **Thomas Cook,** 75 Geary St. (tel. 415/362-3452), open Monday through Friday from 9am to 5pm.

Though **traveler's checks** are widely accepted, make sure that they are denominated in U.S. dollars, as foreign-currency checks are difficult to exchange.

Customs and Immigration Every visitor over 21 years of age may bring in, free of duty, the following: (1) 1 liter of wine or hard liquor; (2) 200 cigarettes, 100 cigars (but *not* from Cuba), or 3 pounds of smoking tobacco; and (3) $400 worth of gifts. These exemptions are offered to travelers who spend at least 72 hours in the United States and who have not claimed them within the preceding 6 months. It is altogether forbidden to bring into the country foodstuffs (particularly cheese, fruit, cooked meats, and canned goods) and plants (vegetables, seeds, tropical plants, and the like). Foreign tourists may bring in or take out up to $10,000 in U.S. or foreign currency with no formalities; larger sums must be declared to Customs on entering or leaving.

Drinking Laws The legal age for purchase and consumption of alcoholic beverages is 21; proof of age is required. In San Francisco, liquor is sold in supermarkets and grocery stores, daily from 6am to 2am. When licensed, restaurants are permitted to sell alcohol during the same hours. Note that many eateries are licensed only for beer and wine.

Electricity U.S. wall outlets give power at 110–115 volts, 60 cycles, compared with 220 volts, 50 cycles, in most of Europe. In addition to a 100-volt transformer, small foreign appliances, such as hairdryers and shavers, will require a plug adapter, with two flat, parallel pins.

Embassies and Consulates All embassies are located in the national capital, Washington, D.C. In addition, several of the major English-speaking countries also have consulates in San Francisco or in Los Angeles. The embassy of **Australia** is at 1601 Massachusetts Ave. NW, Washington, DC 20036 (tel. 202/797-3000); a consulate-general is at 1 Bush St., San Francisco, CA 94104 (tel. 415/362-6160). The embassy of **Canada** is at 501 Pennsylvania Ave. NW, Washington, DC 20001 (tel. 202/682-1740). The embassy of the **Republic of Ireland** is at 2234 Massachusetts Ave. NW, Washington, DC 20008 (tel. 202/462-3939); a consulate is at 655 Montgomery St., Suite 930, San Francisco, CA 94111 (tel. 415/392-4214). The embassy of **New Zealand** is at 37 Observatory Circle NW, Washington, DC 20008 (tel. 202/328-4800); the nearest consulate is in the Tishman Building, 10960 Wilshire Blvd.,

Suite 1530, Los Angeles, CA 90024 (tel. 310/477-8241). The embassy of the **United Kingdom** is at 3100 Massachusetts Ave. NW, Washington, DC 20008 (tel. 202/462-1340); the nearest consulate is at 11766 Wilshire Blvd., Suite 400, Los Angeles, CA 90025 (tel. 310/477-3322). If you are from **another country,** you can get the telephone number of your embassy by calling "Information" (directory assistance) in Washington, D.C.: 202/555-1212.

Emergencies   You can call the police, an ambulance, or the fire department through the single emergency telephone number **911.** Another useful way of reporting an emergency is to call the telephone company operator by dialing **0** (zero, not the letter "O").

Gasoline   Prices vary, but expect to pay anywhere between $1.15 and $1.45 for 1 U.S. gallon (about 3.8 liters) of "regular" unleaded gasoline (petrol). Higher-octane fuels are also available at most gas stations for slightly higher prices. Taxes are already included in the printed price.

Holidays   On the following legal national holidays, banks, government offices, post offices, and many stores, restaurants, and museums are closed: New Year's Day (January 1), Martin Luther King, Jr., Day (third Monday in January), Presidents Day (third Monday in February), Memorial Day (last Monday in May), Independence Day (July 4), Labor Day (first Monday in September), Columbus Day (second Monday in October), Veterans Day (November 11), Thanksgiving Day (last Thursday in November), Christmas Day (December 25). Election Day, for national elections, falls on the Tuesday following the first Monday in November. It is a legal national holiday during a presidential election, which occurs every fourth year.

Information   See Section 1, "Information and Money," in Chapter 2.

Legal Aid   Happily, foreign tourists rarely come into contact with the American legal system. If you are stopped for a minor driving infraction (speeding, for example), *never* attempt to pay the fine directly to a police officer; fines should be paid to the Clerk of the Court, and a receipt should be obtained. If you are accused of a more serious offense, it is wise to say and do nothing before consulting a lawyer. Under U.S. law, an arrested person is allowed one telephone call to a party of his or her choice. You may wish to contact your country's embassy or consulate (see above).

Mail   If you want to receive mail, but aren't exactly sure where you'll be, have it sent to you, in your name, **℅ General Delivery** (Poste Restante) at the main post office of the city or region you're visiting. The addressee must pick it up in person and produce proof of identity (driver's license, credit card, passport). Most post offices will hold your mail up to one month.

Generally found at street intersections, **mailboxes** are blue and carry the inscription U.S. MAIL. If your mail is addressed to a U.S. destination, don't forget to add the five-figure ZIP Code, after the two-letter abbreviation of the state to which the mail is addressed (CA for California).

For domestic and international postage rates, see "Mail" in "Fast Facts: San Francisco" in Chapter 4.

Medical Emergencies   To call an **ambulance,** dial **911** from any phone. No coins are needed. For a list of hospitals and other emergency information, see "Fast Facts: San Francisco" in Chapter 4.

Newspapers and Magazines   Many of San Francisco's newsstands offer a selection of foreign periodicals and newspapers, such as *The Economist, Le Monde,* and *Der Spiegel*. For information on local literature and specific newsstand locations, see "Fast Facts: San Francisco" in Chapter 4.

Post   See "Mail," above.

Radio/Television   Audiovisual media, with four coast-to-coast networks—ABC, CBS, NBC, and Fox—joined in recent years by the Public Broadcasting System (PBS) and the Cable News Network CNN, play a major part in American life. In big cities, televiewers have a choice of about a dozen channels (including the UHF channels), most of them transmitting 24 hours a day, without counting the cable and pay-TV channels showing recent movies or sports events. All options are usually indicated on your hotel TV set. You'll also find a wide choice of local radio stations, each broadcasting particular kinds of talk shows and/or music—classical, country, jazz, pop, gospel—punctuated by news broadcasts and frequent commercials.

Taxes   In the United States there is no VAT (value-added tax) or other indirect tax at a national level. Every state, as well as every city, is allowed to levy its own local **sales tax** on all purchases, including hotel and restaurant checks and airline tickets. Taxes are already included in the price of certain services, such as public transportation, cab fares, phone calls, and gasoline. The amount of sales tax varies from 4% to 10%, depending on the state and city, so when you are making major purchases, such as photographic equipment, clothing, or high-fidelity components, it can be a significant part of the cost.

In addition, many cities charge a separate "bed" or room tax on accommodations, above and beyond any sales tax.

For information on sales and room taxes in and around San Francisco, see "Fast Facts: San Francisco" in Chapter 4.

Telephone, Telegraph, Telex, and Fax   Pay phones can be found almost everywhere—at street corners, in bars and restaurants, and in hotels. Outside the metropolitan area, however, public telephones are more difficult to find; stores and gas stations are your best bet.

Phones do not accept pennies, and few will take anything larger than a quarter. Some public phones, especially those in airports and large hotels, accept credit cards, such as MasterCard, Visa, and American Express. Credit cards are especially handy for international calls; instructions are printed on the phone.

In San Francisco, **local calls** cost 20¢. For domestic **long-distance calls** or **international calls,** stock up with a supply of quarters; a recorded voice will instruct you when and in what quantity you should put them into the slot. For direct overseas calls, dial 011 first, then the country code (Australia, 61; Republic of Ireland, 353; New Zealand, 64; United Kingdom, 44) followed by the city code, and then the number you wish to call. To place a call to Canada or the Caribbean, just dial 1, the area code, and the number you wish to call.

Before calling from a hotel room, always ask the hotel phone operator if there are any telephone surcharges. These can sometimes be reduced by calling collect or by using a telephone charge card. Hotel charges, which can be exorbitant, may be avoided altogether by using a public phone.

For **collect (reversed-charge) calls** and for **person-to-person calls**, dial 0 (zero, not the letter "O") followed by the area code and the number you want; an operator will then come on the line, and you should specify that you are calling collect or person-to-person, or both. If your operator-assisted call is international, just dial 0 and wait for the operator.

For local **"information" (directory inquiries)**, dial 411; for long-distance information in Canada or the United States, dial 1, then the appropriate area code and 555-1212.

Like the telephone system, **telegraph and telex services** are provided by private corporations, such as ITT, MCI, and above all, Western Union. You can bring your telegram to a Western Union office or dictate it over the phone (tel. toll free, 800/325-6000). You can also telegraph money, or have it telegraphed to you, very quickly. In San Francisco, a Western Union office, located near the Civic Center, is at 61 Gough Street, at Market Street (tel. 415/621-2031). There are several other locations around town, too.

Most copy shops also offer **fax services.**

Time The United States is divided into four time zones (six, if Alaska and Hawaii are included). From east to west, these are eastern standard time (EST), central standard time (CST), mountain standard time (MST), and Pacific standard time (PST). There are also Alaska standard time (AST) and Hawaii standard time (HST). San Francisco is on Pacific standard time, which is eight hours behind Greenwich mean time. Noon in New York City (EST) is 11am in Chicago (CST), 10am in Denver (MST), 9am in San Francisco (PST), 8am in Anchorage (AST), and 7am in Honolulu (HST).

Daylight saving time is in effect from the first Sunday in April until 2am on the last Sunday in October, except in Arizona, Hawaii, part of Indiana, and Puerto Rico. Daylight saving time moves the clock one hour ahead of standard time.

Tipping Service in America is some of the best in the world, and tipping is the reason why. The amount you tip should depend on the service you have received. Good service warrants the following tips: bartenders, 15%; bellhops, $2 to $4; cab drivers, 15%; cafeterias and fast-food restaurants, no tip; chambermaids, $1 per per person per day; cinemas, no tip; checkroom attendants, 50¢ to $1 (unless there is a charge, then no tip); gas-station attendants, no tip; hairdressers, 15% to 20%; parking valets, $1; redcaps (in airports and railroad stations), $2 to $4; restaurants and nightclubs, 15%.

Toilets Public toilets can be hard to find. There are none on the streets, and few small stores will allow you access to their facilities. You can almost always find a toilet in restaurants and bars, but if you are not buying from them, you should ask first. Large hotels and fast-food restaurants are probably the best bet for good, clean facilities. Museums, department stores, shopping malls, and, in a pinch, gas stations all have public toilets.

Yellow Pages The *Yellow Pages* telephone directory lists all local services, businesses, and industries by category; it also has an index for quick reference. Categories range from automobile repairs (listed by make of car) and drugstores, or pharmacies, to places of worship and restaurants (listed according to cuisine and geographical location). The *Yellow Pages* directory is also a good source for information of particular interest to the traveler; among other things, it has maps of the city, showing sights and transportation routes. Such information can be found in the "Community Interest Pages" of San Francisco's directory, at the beginning of volume 1.

THE AMERICAN SYSTEM OF MEASUREMENTS

LENGTH

1 inch (in.)	=	2.54cm				
1 foot (ft.)	=	12 in.	=	30.48cm	=	.305m
1 yard	=	3 ft.	=	.915m		
1 mile	=	5,280 ft.	=	1.609km		

To convert miles to kilometers, multiply the number of miles by 1.61 (example: 50 mi. × 1.61 = 80.5km). Also use to convert speeds from miles per hour (m.p.h.) to kilometers per hour (kmph).

To convert kilometers to miles, multiply the number of kilometers by .62 (example: 25km × .62 = 15.5 mi.). Also use to convert kmph to m.p.h.

CAPACITY

1 fluid ounce (fl. oz.)	= 16 fl. oz.	= .03 liter	
1 pint	= 2 pints	= .47 liter	
1 quart	= 4 quarts	= .94 liter	
1 gallon (gal.)	= .83 Imperial gal.	= 3.79 liters	

To convert U.S. gallons to liters, multiply the number of gallons by 3.79 (example: 12 gal. × 3.79 = 45.58 liters.)

To convert liters to U.S. gallons, multiply the number of liters by .26 (example: 50 liters × .26 = 13 U.S. gal.).

To convert U.S. gallons to Imperial gallons, multiply the number of U.S. gallons by .83 (example: 12 U.S. gal. × .83 = 9.95 Imperial gal.).

To convert Imperial gallons to U.S. gallons, multiply the number of Imperial gallons by 1.2 (example: 8 Imperial gal. × 1.2 = 9.6 U.S. gal.).

WEIGHT

1 ounce (oz.)		= 28.35g		
1 pound (lb.)	= 16 oz.	= 453.6g	= .45kg	
1 ton		= 2,000 lb.	= 907kg	

To convert pounds to kilograms, multiply the number of pounds by .45 (example: 90 lb. × .45 = 40.5kg).

To convert kilograms to pounds, multiply the number of kilos by 2.2 (example, 75kg × 2.2 = 165 lb.).

AREA

1 acre		= .41ha	
1 square mile (sq. mi.)	= 640 acres	= 259ha	= 2.6km^2

To convert acres to hectares, multiply the number of acres by .41 (example: 40 acres × .41 = 16.4ha).

To convert hectares to acres, multiply the number of hectares by 2.47 (example: 20ha × 2.47 = 49.4 acres).

To convert square miles to square kilometers, multiply the number of square miles by 2.6 (example: 80 sq. mi. × 2.6 = 208km²).

To convert square kilometers to square miles, multiply the number of square kilometers by .39 (example: 150km² × .39 = 58.5 square miles).

TEMPERATURE

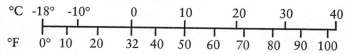

To convert degrees Fahrenheit to degrees Celsius, subtract 32 from °F, multiply by 5, then divide by 9 (example: 85°F − 32 × 5÷9 = 29.4°C).

To convert degrees Celsius to degrees Fahrenheit, multiply °C by 9, divide by 5, and add 32 (example: 20°C × 9÷5 + 32 = 68°F).

CHAPTER 4

GETTING TO KNOW SAN FRANCISCO

etting to San Francisco has come a long way since stagecoach days. Today, in addition to driving, your transportation options include flying, training, and busing. Once here, you will find that negotiating your way around the city is relatively straightforward, but, like all unfamiliar territories, this metropolis will un take a little time to master. This chapter will help familiarize you with the major parts of the city.

1. ORIENTATION

ARRIVING

BY PLANE Two major airports serve the Bay Area: San Francisco International and Oakland International.

San Francisco International Airport Served by almost four dozen major scheduled carriers, San Francisco International Airport (tel. 415/761-0800)—currently completing a $2.4 billion improvement—is one of the busiest in the world. It's located 14 miles south of downtown San Francisco, directly on U.S. 101. Travel time to the downtown area during commuter rush hours is about 40 minutes; at other times it's about 25 minutes. There are several ways of making your way from the airport to your hotel.

First, **taxis** are plentiful and line up in front of a dispatcher's desk outside the airport's arrival terminals. Cabs are metered and cost $25 to $30, plus tip, to a downtown location.

The **SFO Airporter** bus (tel. 415/495-8404) departs from the lower-level luggage-claims area and travels nonstop to downtown San Francisco. Buses leave every 20 minutes from 5am to 11pm and stop at several Union Square–area hotels, including the Grand Hyatt, San Francisco Hilton, San Francisco Marriott, Westin St. Francis, and Parc Fifty Five. No reservations are needed. The cost is $8 one way, $14 round-trip; children two to 12 (accompanied by an adult) pay $4 each way, and children under two ride for free.

Two other private shuttle companies offer door-to-door airport service, in which you share a van with other passengers. **Super-Shuttle** (tel. 415/558-8500) and **Yellow Airport Shuttle** (tel. 415/282-7433) both charge about $11 per person. Each stops every 20 minutes or so and picks up passengers from the marked areas outside the terminals' upper level. Reservations are required for the return trip to the airport only and should be made one day prior to departure

The San Mateo County Transit system, **SamTrans** (tel. 415/ 508-6200, or toll free 800/660-4287 within Northern California) runs two buses between the airport and the Transbay Terminal at First and Missions streets. The 7B bus costs 85¢ and makes the trip in about 55 minutes. The 7F bus costs $1.50 and takes only 35 minutes, but permits only one carry-on bag. Both buses run daily, every half-hour from about 6am to 7pm, then hourly until about midnight.

Oakland International Airport   Located about five miles south of downtown Oakland, at the Hegenberger Road exit of Calif. 17 (U.S. 880), Oakland International Airport (tel. 510/577-4000) is used primarily by passengers with East Bay destinations. Some San Franciscans, however, prefer this uncrowded, accessible airport when flying during busy periods.

Again, **taxis** from the airport to downtown San Francisco are expensive, costing approximately $55, plus tip.

If you make advance reservations, the **AM/PM Airporter,** P.O. Box 2902, Oakland, CA 94609 (tel. 510/547-2155), will take you from the Oakland airport to your hotel any time of the day or night. The price varies, depending on the number of passengers sharing the van, but is usually $35 or less per person; get a quote when you call.

The **AirBART shuttle bus** (tel. 510/832-1464) connects Oakland International Airport with Bay Area Rapid Transit (BART) trains. Buses run about every 15 minutes and stop in front of Terminals 1 and 2 near the GROUND TRANSPORTATION signs. The shuttle ride to BART's Coliseum Station costs $2. BART fares vary, depending on your destination; the trip to downtown San Francisco costs $1.90 and takes 45 minutes. AirBART operates Monday through Saturday from 6am to midnight and on Sunday from 8am to midnight.

BY TRAIN   Passengers traveling to San Francisco by train (see Section 6, "Getting There," in Chapter 2) actually disembark at Amtrak's 16th Street Depot in Oakland (tel. toll free 800/872-7245). Free shuttles connect the Oakland depot with San Francisco's Transbay Terminal at First and Mission streets. The ride takes about 40 minutes. Unfortunately, none of the major car-rental companies has an office at the train station; you'll have to pick up your car from a downtown Oakland or San Francisco location. Hertz (tel. toll free 800/654-3131) will reimburse your cab fare from the train station to its Oakland office at 1001 Broadway, two miles away.

BY BUS   Greyhound/Trailways (tel. 415/558-6789) buses arrive and depart from the Transbay Terminal at First and Mission streets. See Section 6, "Getting There," in Chapter 2 for complete information on traveling by bus.

BY CAR   There are several approaches into San Francisco:
From the North   U.S. 101 crosses the Golden Gate Bridge at the northernmost tip of the peninsula and feeds into city streets.

IMPRESSIONS

When I was a child growing up in Salinas we called San Francisco "The City." Of course it was the only city we knew but I still think of it as The City as does everyone else who has ever associated with it.
—JOHN STEINBECK

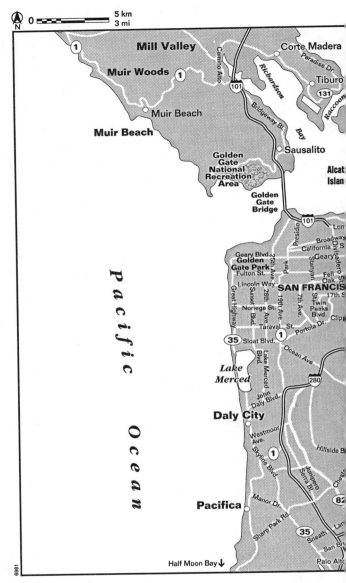

From the East   Interstate 80 crosses the San Francisco–Oakland Bay Bridge and terminates in the city's South of Market district.

From the South   Both Interstate 280 and U.S. 101 come up the peninsula and drop into the city via several downtown off-ramps.

From all three directions, off-ramps are well marked, pointing to Union Square, the Financial District, and Waterfront destinations.

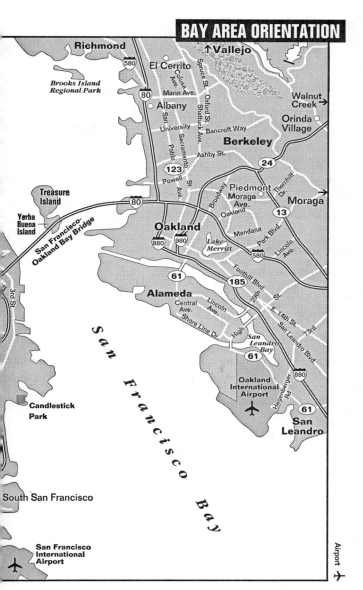

BAY AREA ORIENTATION

Once you're on city streets, you'll see ubiquitous directional signs pointing the way to Chinatown, Fisherman's Wharf, and North Beach.

TOURIST INFORMATION

If you have any questions about what to do and where to go in San Francisco, the people with answers are the cheerful experts at the **San Francisco Visitor Information Center,** on the lower level of Hallidie Plaza, 900 Market St., at Powell Street (tel. 415/391-2000). They can render answers in German, Japanese, French, Italian, and Spanish, as well as English. They're open Monday through Friday from 9am to 5:30pm, on Saturday from 9am to 3pm, and on Sunday from 10am to 2pm. To find the office, descend the escalator at the cable-car turnaround.

When in town, dial 391-2001 any time of day or night for a recorded message about current cultural, theater, music, sports, and other special events. This information is also available in German (tel. 391-2004), French (tel. 391-2003), Japanese (tel. 391-2101), and Spanish (tel. 391-2122).

The **Visitors Information Center of the Redwood Empire Association,** 785 Market St., 15th Floor, San Francisco, CA 94103 (tel. 415/543-8334), offers informative brochures and a very knowledgeable desk staff who are able to plan tours both in San Francisco and north of the city. Their annual *Redwood Empire Visitors' Guide* ($3 by mail, free in person) is crammed with detailed information on everything from San Francisco walking tours and museums to visits to Marin County and the timetable of the Super Skunk train through Mendocino County. The office is open Monday through Friday from 9am to 5pm.

CITY LAYOUT

San Francisco may seem confusing at first, but it quickly becomes easy to negotiate. The city's downtown streets are arranged in a simple grid pattern, with the exception of Market Street and Columbus Avenue, which cut across the grid at right angles to each other. Hills appear to distort this pattern, however, and can seem disorienting. But as you learn your way around, these same hills will become your landmarks and reference points.

MAIN ARTERIES & STREETS **Market Street** is San Francisco's main thoroughfare. Most of the city's buses ply this strip on their way to the Financial District from the bedroom communities to the west and south. The tall office buildings that create the city's stalagmite skyline are clustered at the northeast end of Market; one block beyond lie the Embarcadero and the bay.

The Embarcadero curves north along San Francisco Bay, around the perimeter of the city. It terminates at Fisherman's Wharf, the famous tourist-oriented pier, which is full of restaurants and T-shirt stands. Aquatic Park and the Fort Mason complex are just ahead, occupying the northernmost point of the peninsula.

From here, **Van Ness Avenue** runs due south, back to Market Street. The area I have just described forms a rough triangle, with Market Street as its eastern, the waterfront as its northern, and Van Ness Avenue as its western boundary. Within this triangle lie most of the city's main tourist sights.

FINDING AN ADDRESS Since most of the city's streets are laid out in a grid pattern, finding an address is easy when you know the nearest cross street. All the listings in this book include cross-street information. In addition, the city of San Francisco encompasses more than a dozen distinct neighborhoods. When asking for directions, find out the nearest cross street and the neighborhood in which your destination is located.

NEIGHBORHOODS IN BRIEF

Distinct city neighborhoods like North Beach, Haight-Ashbury, and the Castro have made San Francisco a city of villages. Each is unique and fun to explore.

Union Square Although it's not in the geographic center of the city, Union Square is the true heart of San Francisco. Surrounded by the city's swankiest and seediest shops, the square is also home to large department stores, busy hotels, and tourist-oriented restaurants. It is likely that your hotel will be near here. But even if you're not bedding down within walking distance of Union Square, you will probably pass by sometime during your visit. The grassy square itself was named for a series of violent pro-Union mass demonstrations staged there on the eve of the Civil War. Today the well-manicured little park, which sits atop a huge underground garage, is planted with palms, yews, boxwood, and flowers—centered around a towering memorial to Admiral George Dewey's 1898 victory at Manila Bay. Lunching office workers and assorted homeless people occupy the park's benches, while traffic perpetually jams the surrounding streets.

Financial District Northeast of Union Square, toward San Francisco Bay, is the city's suit-and-tie district. This conservative quarter, centered around Kearny and Sansome streets, swarms with smartly dressed workers on weekdays and is almost deserted on weekends and at night. The Transamerica Pyramid, at Montgomery and Clay streets, is one of the district's most conspicuous architectural features. To its east stands the sprawling Embarcadero Center, an 8½-acre complex housing offices, shops, and restaurants. Farther east still is the World Trade Center, standing adjacent to the old Ferry Building, the city's pre-bridge transportation hub. Ferries to Sausalito and Larkspur still leave from this point.

Chinatown Just blocks north of Union Square and the Financial District, this 24-block labyrinth of restaurants, markets, temples, and shops is one of the largest in North America. For tourists, it is one of the most marvelous walking, shopping, and eating areas in San Francisco.

North Beach At Columbus Avenue, Chinatown blends with North Beach, the city's famous Italian quarter. Although you'll find no beach here, you will discover some of the city's best restaurants, cafes, theaters, and galleries. Telegraph Hill looms over the east side of North Beach, topped by Coit Tower, one of San Francisco's best vantage points.

Nob Hill In San Francisco, height brings prestige, and this high hill in the center of the city is quite a swanky spot. Crossed by cable cars and topped by ritzy apartments and hotels, Nob Hill is also home to Grace Cathedral, one of the finest examples of Gothic architecture in the United States.

Civic Center Although millions of dollars have been expended on brick sidewalks, ornate lampposts, and elaborate street plantings, the southwestern section of Market Street remains downright dilapidated. The Civic Center, at the "bottom" of Market Street, is an exception. This large complex of buildings includes the domed City Hall, the Opera House, Davies Symphony Hall, and the city's main library. The landscaped plaza connecting the buildings is the staging area for San Francisco's frequent demonstrations for or against just about everything.

Cow Hollow Located west of Van Ness Avenue, between Russian Hill and the Presidio, this flat, grazable area was once the city's dairy land. Today, Cow Hollow is largely residential. Its two primary commercial thoroughfares are Lombard Street, known for its plethora of relatively inexpensive motels; and Union Street, a flourishing shopping sector crammed with restaurants, pubs, cafes, and shops. Many of the buildings on Union Street are handsomely painted Victorians transformed into shopping compounds.

SoMa The area south of Market Street, dubbed "SoMa" by young trendies, is in an exciting state of transition. Working warehouses and industrial spaces are rapidly being transformed into nightclubs, galleries, and restaurants. Collectively, they are turning this formerly desolate area into one of the city's most vibrant new neighborhoods.

Haight-Ashbury The Haight, as it is called, was the 1960s stomping ground of America's hippies and the center of the counterculture movement. Today the neighborhood straddling upper Haight Street, on the eastern border of Golden Gate Park, is largely gentrified, but the street life is still colorful, and shops along the strip still include a good number of alternative boutiques.

The Castro Synonymous with San Francisco's gay community, the Castro is a pretty, residential neighborhood centered around bustling Castro Street. Located at the very end of Market Street, at the corner of 17th Street, Castro Street supports dozens of shops, restaurants, and bars, and has one of the best movie houses in America.

STREET MAPS Because San Francisco is relatively compact, and the streets generally follow a rigid grid pattern, the maps included in this guide may be all you need in order to find your way around. The maps printed in the free tourist weeklies *Bay City Guide* and *Key* are also very good for visitors who don't intend on leaving the main tourist areas. These small magazines can be found at most large hotels, around major tourist sites, and in the San Francisco Visitor Information Center (see "Tourist Information," above). More serious explorers should buy one of the accordion-style foldout maps of the city that are sold in hotels, bookshops, and tourist-oriented stores all over town.

2. GETTING AROUND

BY PUBLIC TRANSPORTATION

The **San Francisco Municipal Railway**, better known as **Muni** (tel. 415/673-6864), operates the city's cable cars, buses, and Metro streetcars. Together, these three public-transportation services crisscross the entire city, rendering San Francisco fully accessible to otherwise vehicleless visitors. Buses and Metro streetcars cost $1 for adults, 35¢ for ages five to 17, and 35¢ for seniors over 65. Cable cars cost a whopping $2 and $1 for seniors from 9pm to midnight, and from 6 to 7am. Needless to say, they're packed primarily with tourists. Exact change is required on all vehicles except cable cars. Fares quoted here are subject to change.

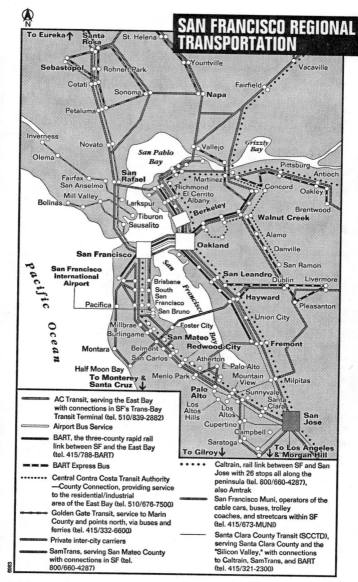

SAN FRANCISCO REGIONAL TRANSPORTATION

Map labels:

To Eureka↑ Santa Rosa, St. Helena, Sebastopol, Rohnert Park, Yountville, Vacaville, Cotati, Sonoma, Fairfield, Petaluma, Napa, Inverness, Novato, Vallejo, *Grizzly Bay*, Olema, *San Pablo Bay*, Pittsburg, Antioch, Fairfax, San Anselmo, San Rafael, Martinez, Richmond, El Cerrito, Albany, Concord, Oakley, Mill Valley, Larkspur, Berkeley, Brentwood, Bolinas, Tiburon, Sausalito, Walnut Creek, Alamo, Oakland, Danville, San Ramon, San Francisco, San Leandro, Dublin, Livermore, San Francisco International Airport, Brisbane, South San Francisco, San Bruno, Hayward, Pleasanton, Pacifica, Union City, Millbrae, Foster City, Burlingame, San Mateo, Redwood City, Fremont, Montara, Belmont, San Carlos, Atherton, Half Moon Bay, E. Palo Alto, To Monterey & Santa Cruz, Menlo Park, Mountain View, Milpitas, Palo Alto, Sunnyvale, Santa Clara, Los Altos Hills, Los Altos, San Jose, Cupertino, Campbell, To Gilroy↓, Saratoga, To Los Angeles & Morgan Hill, *Pacific Ocean*, *San Francisco Bay*

Legend:

━━━ AC Transit, serving the East Bay with connections in SF's Trans-Bay Transit Terminal (tel. 510/839-2882)

━━━ Airport Bus Service

━━━ BART, the three-county rapid rail link between SF and the East Bay (tel. 415/788-BART)

▬▬ BART Express Bus

········ Central Contra Costa Transit Authority —County Connection, providing service to the residential/industrial area of the East Bay (tel. 510/676-7500)

↔↔↔ Golden Gate Transit, service to Marin County and points north, via buses and ferries (tel. 415/332-6600)

░░░ Private inter-city carriers

━━━ SamTrans, serving San Mateo County with connections in SF (tel. 800/660-4287)

•••••• Caltrain, rail link between SF and San Jose with 26 stops all along the peninsula (tel. 800/660-4287), also Amtrak

━━━ San Francisco Muni, operators of the cable cars, buses, trolley coaches, and streetcars within SF (tel. 415/673-MUNI)

━━━ Santa Clara County Transit (SCCTD), serving Santa Clara County and the "Silicon Valley," with connections to Caltrain, SamTrans, and BART (tel. 415/321-2300)

For detailed route information, phone Muni or consult the bus map at the front of the *Yellow Pages*. If you plan on making extensive use of public transportation, you may want to invest in a comprehensive route map ($1.50), sold at the San Francisco Visitor Information Center (see "Tourist Information" in Section 1, "Orientation," above) and in many downtown retail outlets.

Muni discount passes, called "Passports," entitle holders to unlimited rides on buses, Metro streetcars, and cable cars. A Passport costs $6 for one day, and $10 or $15 for three or seven consecutive days. As a bonus, your passport also entitles you to

IMPRESSIONS

What I like best about San Francisco is San Francisco.
—FRANK LLOYD WRIGHT

---

admission discounts at 24 of the city's major attractions, including: the M. H. De Young Memorial Museum, the Asian Art Museum, the California Academy of Sciences, and the Japanese Tea Garden (all in Golden Gate Park); the Museum of Modern Art; Coit Tower; the Exploratorium; the Zoo; and the National Maritime Museum and Historic Ships (where you may visit the U.S.S. *Pampanito* and the S.S. *Jeremiah O'Brien*). Among the places where you can purchase a Passport are the San Francisco Visitors Information Center, the Holiday Inn Civic Center, and the TIX Bay Area booth at Union Square.

BY CABLE CAR San Francisco's cable cars may not be the most practical means of transport, but these rolling symbols of the city are the best loved. They are also official historic landmarks, designated as such by the National Parks Service in 1964. There are three lines in all. The most scenic—and exciting—is the **Powell-Hyde line,** which follows a zigzag route from the corner of Powell and Market streets, over both Nob Hill and Russian Hill, to a turntable at gaslit Victorian Square in front of Aquatic Park. The **Powell-Mason line** starts at the same intersection and climbs over Nob Hill before descending to Bay Street, just three blocks from Fisherman's Wharf. The **California Street line** begins at the foot of Market Street and runs a straight course through Chinatown and over Nob Hill to Van Ness Avenue. All riders must exit at the last stop and wait in line for the return trip. The cable-car system operates from approximately 6:30am to 12:30am.

BY BUS Buses reach almost every corner of San Francisco, and beyond—they travel over the bridges to Marin County and Oakland. Some buses are powered by overhead electric cables; others use conventional gas engines. All are numbered and display their destinations on the front. Stops are designated by signs, curb markings, and yellow bands on adjacent utility poles. Most buses travel along Market Street or pass near Union Square. They run from about 6am to midnight, after which there is infrequent all-night "Owl" service.

Popular tourist routes are traveled by bus nos. 5, 7, and 71, all of which run to Golden Gate Park; by bus nos. 41 and 45, which ply the length of Union Street; and by bus no. 30, which runs between Union Square and Ghirardelli Square.

BY METRO STREETCAR Muni's five Metro streetcar lines, designated J, K, L, M, and N, run underground downtown and on the street in the outer neighborhoods. The sleek railcars make the same stops as BART (see below) along Market Street, including Embarcadero Station (in the Financial District), Montgomery and Powell streets (both near Union Square), and the Civic Center (near City Hall). Past the Civic Center, the routes branch off in different directions: The J line will take you to Mission Dolores; the K, L, and M lines to Castro Street; and the N line parallels Golden Gate Park. Metros run about every 15 minutes—more frequently during rush hours. Service is offered Monday through Friday from 5am to 12:30am, on Saturday from 6am to 12:20am, and on Sunday from 8am to 12:20am.

BY BART BART, an acronym for Bay Area Rapid Transit (tel. 788-BART), is a futuristic-looking, high-speed rail network that connects San Francisco with the East Bay—Oakland, Richmond, Concord, and Fremont. Four stations are located along Market Street (see "By Metro Streetcar" above). Fares range from 80¢ to $3, depending on how far you go. Tickets are dispensed from machines in the stations and are magnetically encoded with a dollar amount. Computerized exits automatically deduct the correct fare. Children 4 and under ride free. Trains run every 15 to 20 minutes, Monday through Friday from 4am to midnight, on Saturday from 6am to midnight, and on Sunday from 8am to midnight.

A $2.5 billion 33-mile BART extension, currently under construction, includes a southern line that is planned to extend all the way to San Francisco International Airport.

BY TAXI

Taxis ply major thoroughfares and can be hailed on the street. When a cab is available for hire, the sign on its roof will be lighted. Like police when you need them, taxis can become suddenly scarce during rain or rush hour. If you can, it's best to phone in advance and request a cab to pick you up at a designated location. The following licensed private companies compete for customers: **Veteran's Cab** (tel. 552-1300), **Desoto Cab Co.** (tel. 673-1414), **Luxor Cabs** (tel. 282-4141), **Yellow Cab** (tel. 262-2345), **City** (tel. 468-7200), and **Pacific** (tel. 986-7220). Rates are approximately $2 for each mile.

BY CAR

You certainly don't need a car to explore San Francisco proper. In fact, in some areas, such as Chinatown and the Financial District, a car is a positive handicap. If, however, you plan on extensive exploration of outlying neighborhoods, or want to tour the Bay Area in general, a car will prove extremely handy. Before venturing very far outside the city, you might want to call about California **road conditions** (tel. 557-3755).

RENTALS Scores of car-rental firms are located in San Francisco, and rates are competitive. The major national companies offer their cheapest economy vehicles for about $30 per day and $100 per week with unlimited mileage.

Most rental firms pad their profits by selling an additional Loss/ Damage Waiver (LDW), which usually costs an extra $9 per day. Before agreeing to this, however, check with your insurance carrier and credit-card company. Many people don't realize that they are already covered by either one or both. If you're not, the LDW is a wise investment.

A minimum-age requirement—ranging from 19 to 25—is set by most rental agencies. Some also have a maximum-age limit. If you're concerned that these limits may affect you, ask about rental requirements at the time of booking to avoid problems later.

Some of the national car-rental companies operating in San Francisco include: **Alamo** (tel. toll free 800/327-9633), **Avis** (tel. toll free 800/331-1212), **Budget** (tel. toll free 800/527-0700), **Dollar** (tel. toll free 800/800-4000), **General** (tel. toll free 800/327-7607), **Hertz** (tel. toll free 800/654-3131, **National** (tel. toll free 800/227-7368), and **Thrifty** (tel. toll free 800/367-2277).

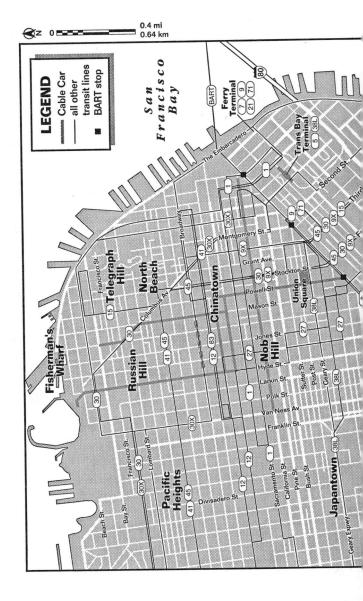

In addition to the big chains, there are dozens of regional rental places in San Francisco, many of which offer lower rates. These include **A-One Rent-A-Car,** 434 O'Farrell St. (tel. 415/771-3977); and **Bay Area Rentals,** 440 O'Farrell St. (tel. 415/441-4779).

PARKING Street parking in San Francisco is extremely limited—and the local cops are the quickest tow I've ever seen. Parking is particularly tough in Chinatown, around Nob Hill, by Fisherman's Wharf, in North Beach, and on Telegraph Hill. Where street parking is not metered, signs will tell you when you can park and for how long. Curb colors also indicate parking regulations—and mean

it! *Red* means no stopping or parking; *blue* is reserved for disabled drivers with a California-issued disabled plate or a placard; *white* means there's a five-minute limit; *green* indicates a 10-minute limit; and *yellow* and *yellow-black* curbs are for commercial vehicles only. Also, don't park at a bus stop or in front of a fire hydrant; watch out, too, for street-cleaning signs. If you violate the law, you may be "booted" (immobilized) or towed away, and that can cost you as much as $100. To get your car back, you must obtain a release from the nearest district police department, then go to the towing company to pick up the vehicle.

When parking on a hill, apply the hand brake, put the car in gear, and *curb your wheels*—toward the curb when facing downhill, away from the curb when facing uphill. Curbing your wheels will not only prevent a possible "runaway" but will also keep you from getting a ticket—an expensive fine that is aggressively enforced.

Parking lots abound, but are usually quite expensive. Parking often costs about $4 to $5 per hour. It's cheaper by the day. In Chinatown the best (and cheapest) place to park is the Portsmouth Square Garage at 733 Kearny St. (enter between Clay and Washington Streets). Between 10:30am and 2:30pm you may have to wait in line to enter. The price is 75¢ for the first hour, $2 for two hours, $4 for three hours, $6.50 for four hours—up to a maximum of $16 for 7 to 24 hours. At the Civic Center, try for the Civic Center Plaza Garage between Polk and Larkin Streets, and downtown, head for the Sutter-Stockton Garage at 330 Sutter St. At Fisherman's Wharf/Ghirardelli Square, try the North Point Shopping Garage at 350 Bay St., where the tab is $1.25 per half hour, $13.50 maximum; or the Ghirardelli Square Garage at 900 North Point, which offers 90 minutes of free parking with validation, otherwise $1.50 per hour, $15 maximum. On Union Street, in the area of high-traffic shopping, try the Cow Hollow Garage at 3060 Fillmore St. for $2 per hour, $10 maximum.

DRIVING RULES California law requires that both drivers and passengers wear seatbelts. You may turn right at a red light (unless otherwise indicated), after yielding to traffic and pedestrians, *and* after making a complete stop. Cable cars, like sailing ships, always have the right-of-way, as do pedestrians at intersections and crosswalks. Pay attention to signs and arrows on the streets and roadways or you may find yourself suddenly in a lane that requires exiting or turning when you really want to go straight ahead. What's more, San Francisco's profusion of one-way streets can create a few small difficulties, but most road maps of the city indicate which way traffic flows.

BY FERRY

The opening of the Golden Gate Bridge in 1937 signaled the end of the ferry service that plied the bay between downtown San Francisco and the Marin shores. But this ferry tale has a happy ending. In August 1970 service resumed, as a result of growing commuter traffic too great for the bridge to bear alone. The **Golden Gate Ferry Service** (tel. 332-6600) fleet dashes back and forth between the San Francisco Ferry Building, at the foot of Market Street, and downtown Sausalito and Larkspur.

To/From Sausalito Service to Sausalito is frequent, departing at reasonable intervals every day of the year except New Year's Day, Thanksgiving Day, and Christmas Day. Phone for exact schedule information. The ride takes a half hour and costs $4 for adults and $3 for young riders aged 6 to 12. Senior and physically disabled passengers ride for $2; children 5 and under ride free.

To/From Larkspur The Larkspur ferry is primarily a commuter service during the week, with frequent departures around the rush hours. Weekend service is offered during the summer only. Boats make the 13-mile trip in about 50 minutes and cost $2.50 for adults, $1.90 for young riders aged 6 to 12, and $1.25 for seniors and physically disabled passengers; on weekends, prices rise to

$4 for adults, $3 for young riders, and $2 for seniors and the physically disabled; children 5 and under ride free.

ON FOOT

San Francisco is a walking city par excellence. The hills can be challenging, but the best way to explore the city is definitely on foot. Most of the main tourist attractions are within easy strolling distance of one another: The downtown shopping district is adjacent to Chinatown, which runs right into North Beach, which, in turn, buffets Fisherman's Wharf. If at any time you become too tired to hoof it, the city's vast and efficient public transportation system can easily whisk you to your destination.

FAST FACTS SAN FRANCISCO

Airport See Section 1, "Orientation," earlier in this chapter.

American Express For travel arrangements, traveler's checks, currency exchange, and other member services, American Express has offices at 2500 Mason Street (tel. 788-3025), near Fisherman's Wharf (open daily 10am to 6pm), and at 455 Market Street (tel. 512-8250) in the Financial District (open Monday through Friday from 9am to 5pm). To report lost or stolen traveler's checks, call toll free 800/221-7282.

Area Code There are two area codes in the San Francisco Bay Area. The city of San Francisco and the entire peninsula are identified by the 415 area code. Oakland, Berkeley, and much of the East Bay use the 510 area code. All phone numbers in this book assume San Francisco's 415 area code, unless otherwise noted.

Babysitters Hotels can often recommend a babysitter or child-care service. If yours can't, try Temporary Tot Tending (tel. 355-7377, or 871-5790 after 6pm), which offers child care by licensed teachers, by the hour or day, for children from three weeks to 12 years of age. It's open Monday through Friday from 6am to 7pm (weekend service is available only during convention times).

Bookstores Chain bookstores can be found in almost every shopping center in the city, including B. Dalton at 2 Embarcadero Center (tel. 982-4278) and Brentano's at Ghirardelli Square (tel. 474-8328) and the San Francisco Shopping Center at Market and Fifth Streets (tel. 543-0933). See Chapter 9, "Shopping from A to Z," for a list of the city's excellent specialty booksellers.

Business Hours Most banks are open Monday through Friday from 9am to 3pm. Several stay open until about 5pm at least one day a week. Many banks also feature ATMs for 24-hour banking (see Section 1, "Information and Money," in Chapter 2).

Most stores are open Monday through Saturday from 10am to 6pm; closed Sunday. But there are exceptions: Stores in Chinatown are generally open daily from 10am to 10pm. Ghirardelli Square and Pier 39 shops are open Monday through Thursday from 10am to 6pm and on Friday and Saturday from 10am to 9pm (later during the summer). San Francisco Shopping Center shops are open Monday through Saturday from 9:30am to 8pm and on Sunday from 11am to 6pm. Large department stores, including Emporium, Macy's, and Nordstrom, keep late hours and are open Sunday.

Most restaurants serve lunch from about 11:30am to 3pm and dinner from 5:30 to 11pm. You can sometimes get served later on weekends. Nightclubs and bars are usually open daily until 2am, when they are legally bound to stop serving alcohol.

Car Rentals   See Section 2, "Getting Around," earlier in this chapter.

Climate   See Section 2, "When to Go—Climate and Events," in Chapter 2.

Convention Center   The Moscone Convention Center, 774 Howard St. (tel. 974-4000), between 3rd and 4th streets, was completed in 1981 and named for slain San Francisco mayor George Moscone. Part of a large revitalization project in the SoMa district, the center contains one of the world's largest column-free exhibition halls.

Currency and Exchange   See "Fast Facts: For the Foreign Traveler" in Chapter 3.

Dentist   In the event of an emergency, see your hotel concierge or contact the San Francisco Dental Society (tel. 421-1435) for 24-hour referral to a specialist. The San Francisco Dental Office, 132 The Embarcadero (tel. 777-5115), between Mission and Howard streets, offers emergency service and comprehensive dental care Monday and Friday from 8am to 4:30pm, Tuesday through Thursday from 10:30am to 7pm.

Doctor   In an emergency, call an ambulance by dialing 911 from any phone; no coins are required. Saint Francis Memorial Hospital, 900 Hyde Street, on Nob Hill (tel. 353-6000), provides urgent-care service 24 hours; no appointment is necessary. The hospital also operates a physician-referral service (tel. 353-6566).

Documents Required   See Section 1, "Preparing for Your Trip," in Chapter 3.

Driving Rules   See Section 2, "Getting Around," earlier in this chapter.

Drugstores   There are Walgreens pharmacies all over town, including one at 135 Powell Street (tel. 391-4433) that's open Monday through Saturday from 8am to midnight and on Sunday from 9am to 9pm. The branch on Divisadero Street at Lombard (tel. 931-6415) is open 24 hours. Merrill's Drug Center, 805 Market St. (tel. 781-1669), is open Monday through Friday from 7am to 10pm and on Saturday and Sunday from 7:30am to 10pm. Both chains accept MasterCard and Visa.

Earthquakes   There will always be earthquakes in California—most of which you'll never notice. However, in case of a significant shaker, there are a few basic precautionary measures you should know. When you are inside a building, seek cover; *do not run outside*. Move toward the center of the building, away from windows. Duck under a large, sturdy piece of furniture or stand against a wall or under a doorway. If you exit the building, use stairwells, not elevators. If you are in your car, pull over to the side of the road and stop—but not until you are away from bridges, overpasses, telephone poles, and power lines. Stay in your car. If you're out walking, stay outside and away from trees, power lines, and the sides of buildings. If you're in an area with tall buildings, find a doorway in which to stand.

Embassies and Consulates   See "Fast Facts: For the Foreign Traveler" in Chapter 3.

Emergencies To reach the police, an ambulance, or the fire department, dial 911 from any phone; no coins are needed. Emergency hotlines include the Poison Control Center (tel. 476-6600), Suicide Prevention (tel. 221-1424), and Rape Crisis (tel. 647-7273).

Eyeglasses For emergency replacement of lost or broken glasses, Lens Crafters, 685 Market St., at Third Street (tel. 896-0680), offers one-hour service. They're open Monday through Friday from 8am to 7pm, Saturday from 10am to 6pm, and Sunday from 11am to 5pm. Pearle Vision Express, 720 Market St. (tel. 677-9701), offers similar services, selections, and prices. It's open Monday through Friday from 10am to 9pm, Saturday and Sunday 11am to 6pm. For top-name brand frames, try Spectacles of Union Square, 177 Maiden La. (tel. 781-8556). They feature one-hour service, in-stock contact lenses, and a full-time staff technician. It's open Monday through Friday from 9am to 5:30pm, Saturday from 11am to 4pm.

Hairdressers and Barbers In addition to haircutters in the top hotels, respected salons include the avant-garde Architects & Heroes, 207 Powell St., at O'Farrell Street (tel. 391-8833); the English coiffeur David Oliver, 3356 Sacramento St., at Presidio Avenue (tel. 563-2044); and the classic Vidal Sassoon, 130 Post St., at Grant Street (tel. 397-5105).

Holidays See Section 2, "When to Go—Climate and Events," in Chapter 2.

Hospitals See "Doctor," above.

Hotlines See "Emergencies," above.

Information See "Tourist Information" in Section 1, "Orientation," earlier in this chapter.

Laundry and Dry Cleaning Laundries abound; ask at your hotel for the closest one. If you want to have some fun while you wash your clothes, visit Brain Wash, 1122 Folsom St., south of Market (tel. 431-WASH). It features dozens of washers and dryers along with a cafe and bar, and live music Tuesday through Thursday. It's open daily from 7:30am to 11pm. Dry cleaning is also available.

Libraries The main branch of the San Francisco Public Library (tel. 557-4400) is located in Civic Center Plaza, just north of Market Street, and houses some 1.2 million volumes. Call for open hours and the location and hours of other branches.

Liquor Laws Liquor and grocery stores, as well as some drugstores, can sell packaged alcoholic beverages between 6am and 2am. Most restaurants, nightclubs, and bars are licensed to serve alcoholic beverages during the same hours. The legal age for purchase and consumption is 21; proof of age is required.

Lost Property If you lose any personal property on the street, it's probably gone for good, but call the local police anyway (tel. 553-0123). If you lose it on a Muni cable car, bus, or Metro streetcar, call the lost-and-found office (tel. 923-6168).

Mail There are dozens of post offices located all around the city. The closest office to Union Square is inside Macy's department store, 121 Stockton St. (tel. 956-3570). You can pick up mail addressed to you, and marked "General Delivery" (Poste Restante), at The Civic Center Post Office Box Unit, P.O. Box 429991, San Francisco, CA 94142-9991.

Maps See Section 1, "Orientation," earlier in this chapter.

Money See Section 1, "Information and Money," in Chapter 2, and "Currency and Exchange" in "Fast Facts: For the Foreign Traveler" in Chapter 3.

Newspapers and Magazines The city's two main dailies are the *San Francisco Chronicle* and the *San Francisco Examiner;* both are distributed throughout the city. The two papers combine for a massive Sunday edition that includes a pink "Datebook" section—an excellent preview of the week's upcoming events. The free weekly *San Francisco Bay Guardian,* a tabloid of news and listings, is indispensable for nightlife information; it's widely distributed through street-corner dispensers and at city cafes and restaurants.

Of the many free tourist-oriented publications, the most widely read are *Key* and *San Francisco Guide.* Both of these handbook-size weeklies contain maps and information on current events. They can be found in most hotels and in shops and restaurants in the major tourist areas.

Photographic Needs Drugstores and supermarkets are probably the cheapest places to purchase film. You'll pay loads more for the same product at specialized kiosks near major tourist attractions. Brooks Cameras, 45 Kearny St., at Maiden Lane (tel. 392-1900), has a complete inventory of cameras and accessories. It also offers an authorized repair service and one-hour photo finishing. It's open Monday through Friday from 8:30am to 6pm and on Saturday from 9:30am to 5:30pm.

Police For emergencies, dial 911 from any phone; no coins are needed. For other matters, call 553-0123.

Post Office See "Mail," above.

Radio About four dozen radio stations can be heard in San Francisco. On the AM dial, 740 (KCBS) and 810 (KGO) are the top picks for news, sports, talk, and information. The best music stations on the FM dial included KQED (88.5) for classical, KSAN (94.9) for country, and KRQR (97.3) and KFOG (104.5) for album-oriented rock; KBLX (102.9) and KUSF (90.3) play dance and alternative rock, respectively.

Religious Services San Francisco has houses of worship for all major faiths, including the following: First Friendship Institutional Baptist Church, 501 Steiner St. (tel. 431-4775); Buddha's Universal Church, 720 Washington St. (tel. 982-6116); Congregation Emanu-El (Jewish), 21 Lake St. (tel. 751-2535); Mission Dolores Basilica (Roman Catholic), 3321 16th St. (tel. 621-8203); Grace Cathedral (Episcopal), 1051 Taylor St. (tel. 776-6611); and New Liberation Presbyterian Church, 1100 Divisadero St. (tel. 929-8881).

Restrooms Only department stores let customers use the restrooms, and many restaurants offer their facilities for customers only. But most malls have bathrooms, as do the ubiquitous fast-food restaurants. Many public beaches and large parks provide toilets, though in some places you have to pay or tip an attendant. If you have the time, look for one of the large hotels; most have well-stocked, clean restrooms in their lobbies.

Safety Innocent tourists are rarely the victims of violent crime. Still, few locals would recommend that you walk alone late at night. The Tenderloin, between Union Square and the Civic Center, is one of San Francisco's most infamous areas. Compared with similar areas in other cities, however, even this section of San Francisco is relatively tranquil. Other areas where you should be particularly alert are the Mission District, around 16th and Mission streets;

the Fillmore area, around lower Haight Street; and the SoMa area south of Market Street. None of these areas is of particular interest to tourists. See Section 3, "Insurance and Safety," in Chapter 2 for additional safety tips.

Shoe Repairs There are dozens of shoe- and leather-repair shops around the city. Check the San Francisco *Yellow Pages* for the location nearest you or visit Jack's Shoe Service, 53 Sutter St., between Montgomery and Sansome streets (tel. 392-7336). It's open Monday through Friday from 7:30am to 5:30pm.

Taxes An 8½% sales tax is added at the register for all goods and services purchased in San Francisco. In restaurants, a 7% tax will be tacked onto your bill. The city hotel tax is a whopping 11%. There is no airport tax.

Taxis See Section 2, "Getting Around," earlier in this chapter.

Television In addition to the cable stations, available in most hotels, all the major networks and several independent stations are represented. They include: Channel 2, KTVU (NBC); Channel 4, KRON (CBS); Channel 5, KPIX (CBS); Channel 7, KGO (ABC); and Channel 9, KQED (PBS).

Time San Francisco, like the entire West Coast, is in the Pacific standard-time zone, which is eight hours behind Greenwich mean time. To find out what time it is, call 767-8900.

Tipping A 15% tip is standard for waiters and waitresses, bartenders, taxi drivers, and hairdressers. Porters should be tipped 50¢ to $1 per bag, and parking valets should be given $1. It's proper to leave a few dollars on your pillow for the hotel maid; lavatory attendants will appreciate whatever change you have.

Transit Information The San Francisco Municipal Railway, better known as Muni, operates the city's cable cars, buses, and Metro streetcars. Information is available 24 hours by calling 673-6864.

Useful Telephone Numbers American Express Global Assist (for cardholders only) (tel. toll free 800/554-2639), tourist information (tel. 391-2001), highway conditions (tel. 557-3755), time (tel. 767-8900).

KFOG Entertainment Line (tel. 777-1045), KJAZ Jazz Entertainment Line (tel. 510/769-4818), KKSF Bay Line—covering movies, theaters, and lectures—(tel. 392-1037), KMEL's Movie Phone Line (tel. 777-FILM), Grateful Dead Hotline (tel. 457-6388), Morrison Planetarium Sky Line (tel. 750-7141).

Weather Call 936-1212 to find out when the next fog bank is rolling in.

3. NETWORKS & RESOURCES

FOR STUDENTS There are dozens of colleges in San Francisco, though most are vocational schools. The largest campuses belong to the University of California, San Francisco (UCSF), and the University of San Francisco (USF). Like many urban schools, these colleges blend into the surrounding community and lack individual academic climates. Both are largely commuter schools, and the stores and shops of the surrounding neighborhoods serve as student hangouts.

UCSF, 513 Parnassus Ave. (tel. 476-9000), is primarily a medical school. It's located above the Haight, overlooking the southeastern corner of Golden Gate Park.

USF (tel. 666-6886) is a private Jesuit university located at Golden Gate and Parker Avenues, near the northeast corner of Golden Gate Park. This compact, attractive campus includes a student center and an excellent sports facility.

FOR GAY MEN & LESBIANS As the gay and lesbian capital of the United States, San Francisco does not disappoint. The Bay City has long been a place where gay men (and, to a lesser extent, women) can enjoy their lifestyle openly. The AIDS crisis has taken an especially heavy toll here, but it has also raised consciousness and reinforced the city's principles of tolerance. Because of AIDS, promiscuity has waned, and the community has become politicized as never before; hardly a week passes without a demonstration by gay-rights activists.

The Castro, an area surrounding Castro Street near Market Street, has traditionally been *the* area for gay men. It is still packed with primarily gay-oriented establishments, but it is no longer isolated; gay clubs and bars are located all over town. Lesbian interests are concentrated primarily in the East Bay, but a significant community resides in the Mission District, around 16th Street.

The San Francisco Visitor Information Center (see "Tourist Information" in Section 1, "Orientation," above) has specialized information on local alternative happenings. Several dedicated publications also have in-depth news, information, and listings of goings-on around town. The *San Francisco Sentinel* features a centerfold map of San Francisco, with listings of events and happenings at area bars and restaurants. The *Bay Area Reporter* has the most comprehensive listings, including a weekly calendar of events: social gatherings, art classes, sports events, community meetings, and the like. Both papers are free and are distributed weekly on Thursday. They can be found stacked at the corner of 18th and Castro streets and at 9th and Harrison streets, as well as in bars, bookshops, and various stores around town.

The **Lesbian/Gay Switchboard** (tel. 510/841-6224) offers 24-hour counseling and advice, as well as activity information and counseling referrals.

FOR WOMEN Women's services are often lumped together in the lesbian category, but there are resources geared toward women without regard to sexuality. The **Bay Area Resource Center,** 318 Leavenworth St. (tel. 474-2400), offers specialized services and city information to women. The **Women's Building,** 3543 18th St. (tel. 431-1180), is a Mission-area space housing feminist art shows and political events. The **Rape Crisis Hotline** (tel. 647-7273) is staffed 24 hours daily.

FOR SENIORS The **Senior Citizen Information Line** (tel. 626-1033) offers advice, referrals, and information on city services. The **Friendship Line for the Elderly** (tel. 752-3778) is a crisis-intervention service. Seniors who are disabled should also see Section 5, "Tips for the Disabled, Seniors, Families, and Students," in Chapter 2.

SAN FRANCISCO ACCOMMODATIONS

San Francisco is well known for its excellent accommodations—from deluxe hotels to modest family establishments. In terms of facilities, services, cleanliness, and courtesy, hotels here represent some of the best values in the world. In addition, the many hostelries appeal to a multiplicity of personalities and pocketbooks. There are over a dozen international luxury-class hotels—remarkable for a city of fewer than a million inhabitants. And a large number of historic buildings, both large and small, have been reconstituted, reworked, and refurbished (most of them successfully) into handsome new hotels. Many are very posh, exuding European elegance, beauty, and charm. Most of the hotels listed below are within easy walking distance of Union Square. This central area is close to both the city's major shops and the Financial District, so it's understandably popular with tourists and businesspeople alike.

Prices listed below do not include state and city taxes, which total a whopping 11%. Be aware that most hotels impose additional charges for parking (with in-and-out privileges, except where noted) and levy heavy surcharges for telephone use. Many have their own on-site health facilities. When they don't, an arrangement has often been made with a nearby club, allowing you to use the club's facilities on a per diem basis. Charges usually run $8 to $15. Inquire about these extras before committing yourself.

Finally, even in the budget categories, all the following listings meet my pretty exacting standards of comfort and cleanliness.

There are so many hotels in San Francisco—in every price range—that few regularly fill to capacity. Even during the height of the tourist season, you can usually drive right into the city and find decent accommodations fairly quickly. But be careful. If you have your sights set on a particular hotel, if you *have* to have a Nob Hill view, or if you want to locate in an area where accommodations are not particularly plentiful, you should book your room in advance.

Hotel-operated toll-free telephone numbers can also help you with your search. These "800" numbers will save you time and money when you're inquiring about rates and availability. When available, toll-free numbers are listed below, under the heading of each hotel. Some of the larger hotel-reservations chains with proper ties in the San Francisco area, as well as toll-free numbers, include: Best Western (tel. 800/528-1234), Days Inn (tel. 800/325-2525),

IMPRESSIONS

In all my travels I have never seen the hospitality of San Francisco equaled anywhere in the world.
—CONRAD HILTON, HOTELIER

Holiday Inn (tel. 800/465-4329), Quality Inn (tel. 800/228-5151), Ramada Inn (tel. 800/272-6232), and TraveLodge (tel. 800/255-3050).

To help you decide on the accommodations option that's best for you, I've classified the hotels below first by area and then by price, using the following guide: **Very Expensive:** more than $160 per night; **Expensive:** $120 to $159 per night; **Moderate:** $80 to $119 per night; and **Budget:** less than $80 per night. These categories reflect the price of an average double room during the high season, which runs approximately from April through September. *Read each of the entries carefully:* Many hotels also offer rooms at rates above and below the price category that they have been assigned in this guidebook.

In general, hotel rates in San Francisco are rather inelastic; they don't vary much during the year, but recent economic sluggishness has seen a small rate reduction throughout the city, and bargains and special packages can be had. Ask about weekend discounts, corporate rates, and family plans.

Bed and Breakfast International, P.O. Box 282910, San Francisco, CA 94128 (tel. 415/696-1690 or toll free 800/872-4500, fax 415/696-1699), specializes in unique accommodation arrangements in San Francisco and the entire Bay Area. The cost of these private B&Bs range from $60 to $150 per night, and there's a two-night minimum. Accommodations vary depending on price, and range from simple rooms in private homes to luxurious, full-service carriage houses, houseboats, and Victorian homes. I have been very impressed with the quality and consistency offered by this established company; keep in mind that they can also help you with arrangements throughout California.

1. UNION SQUARE

VERY EXPENSIVE

CAMPTON PLACE HOTEL, 340 Stockton St., San Francisco, CA 94108. Tel. 415/781-5555, or toll free 800/426-3135. Fax 415/955-5536. 117 rms. 10 suites. A/C MINIBAR TV TEL **Cable Car:** Powell-Hyde and Powell-Mason lines (1 block west). **Bus:** 2, 3, 4, 30, or 45.
$ Rates: $185–$320 single or double; from $395 suite. AE, CB, DC, MC, V. **Parking:** $19.

This intimate hotel between Post and Sutter Streets offers all the luxury of its larger competitors. It occupies the early 20th-century buildings of the former Drake-Wiltshire Hotel and was reopened after $25-million worth of renovations and improvements. The results are terrific—luxurious, modern, and gorgeous.

Guest rooms are beautifully appointed, with extra-large beds, concealed color TVs with remote control, and AM/FM clock radios. Elegant bathrooms have marble floors, brass fixtures, bathrobes, telephone, and goodies like soaps, shampoos, and bath gels.

Dining/Entertainment: The Campton Place Restaurant, which serves three meals a day, is especially popular at lunch. The menu is contemporary American, with dishes like stuffed, braised oxtail and saffron-steamed sea bass, priced from $19 to $30.

Services: 24-hour room service, concierge, overnight shoe shine, morning paper delivered to your door.

Facilities: Access to off-premises health club, jewelry boutique, no-smoking rooms.

DONATELLO, 501 Post St., San Francisco, CA 94102. Tel. 415-441-7100, or toll free 800/227-3184, 800/792-9837 in California. Fax 415/885-8842. 95 rms, 7 suites. A/C TV TEL. **Cable Car:** Powell-Hyde and Powell-Mason lines (2 blocks west). **Bus:** 2, 3, 4, 30, or 45.
$ Rates: $175–$225 single or double; from $295 suite. Additional person $25. Children under 12 stay free in parents' room. AE, CB, DC, DISC, MC, V. **Parking:** $15.

Located at Mason Street, one block west of Union Square, the Donatello boasts some of the largest guest rooms in the city. The hotel's refined atmosphere is apparent the moment you enter the lobby, which is replete with 18th- and 19th-century European antiques, imported Venetian chandeliers, a 17th-century Belgian tapestry, museum-quality lithographs, and Italian marble quarried from the same site where Michelangelo selected the marble for his statue *David*.

The spacious rooms are somewhat plainer and a bit outdated, though they are well decorated with cool colors, tapestries or locally produced art, and live plants. The 14-floor hotel is not as service-oriented as its high prices would lead you to believe, but the in-room amenities are up to par. Besides the traditional amenities, you will still find special touches, such as extra-length beds, remote-control TVs, clock radios, and terry-cloth bathrobes.

Dining/Entertainment: The intimate (54-seat) Ristorante Donatello enjoys a superior reputation, with an à la carte dinner menu featuring classic northern Italian cuisine—crisp duckling with Italian spices, boneless squab, quail, and, of course, pasta. Main

---

 FROMMER'S SMART TRAVELER: HOTELS

1. A hotel room is a perishable commodity; if it's not sold, the revenue is lost forever. Always ask if the hotel has a lower rate, and make it clear that you're shopping around.
2. For the best rates, seek out business-oriented hotels on weekends and in the summer, and tourist-oriented bed-and-breakfasts during the off-season.
3. Ask about summer discounts, corporate rates, and special packages. Most hotel reservations offices don't tell you about promotional rates unless you ask.
4. Always inquire about telephone and parking charges. In San Francisco it could add $25 per night for your car and $1 per local call.

Abigail Hotel **43**
Albion House Inn **13**
Alexander Inn **37**
ANA Hotel San Francisco **46**
Andrews Hotel **32**
AYH Hostel at Union Square **36**
Bedford Hotel **32**
Bed & Breakfast Inn **6**
Beresford Arms **32**
Brady Acres **35**
Campton Place Hotel **29**
Cartwright Hotel **27**
Chelsea Motor Inn **4**
Commodore International **25**
Cornell Hotel **20**
Cow Hollow Motor Inn **3**
Donatello **34**
Edward II Inn & Carriage House **2**
Fairmont Hotel & Tower **15**
The Fitzgerald **32**
Four Seasons Clift **36**
Galleria Park Hotel **30**
Golden Gate Hotel **20**
Grand Hyatt San Francisco
on Union Square **29**
Grant Plaza Hotel **23**
Handerly Union Square Hotel **36**
Hotel Beresford **26**
Hotel Nikko **39**
Hotel Savoy **36**
Hotel Triton **22**
Hotel Union Square **40**
Hotel Vintage Court **21**
Huntington Hotel **15**
Hyatt Regency San Francisco **24**
Inn at the Opera **11**
Juliana Hotel **21**
Kensington Park Hotel **33**
King George Hotel **34**
Lombard Hotel **31**
The Mansions **8**
Mark Hopkins **15**
Miyako Hotel **9**
Monticello Inn **39**
Nob Hill Lambourne Spa **18**
Orchard **27**
Pacific Bay Inn **35**
Parc Fifty-Five **41**
Pensione International **32**
Phoenix Inn **42**

Pied a Terre **7**
Prescott Hotel **34**
Queen Anne Hotel **10**
The Raphael **36**
Red Victorian
Bed & Breakfast **12**
Ritz-Carlton **17**
San Francisco Hilton **37**
San Francisco
International Hostel **1**
San Francisco Marriott **44**
The Shannon Court **36**
Sheehan **26**
Sheraton at
Fisherman's Wharf **14**
Sheraton Palace Hotel **45**
Sir Francis Drake **28**
Stouffer Stanford Court **16**
Union Street Inn **5**
Villa Florence **38**
Westin St. Francis **38**
White Swan Inn **19**

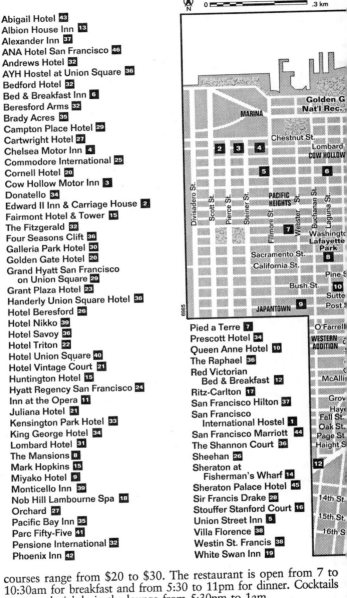

courses range from $20 to $30. The restaurant is open from 7 to 10:30am for breakfast and from 5:30 to 11pm for dinner. Cocktails are served nightly in the lounge from 5:30pm to 1am.

Services: Room service (6am to midnight), concierge, evening turndown, complimentary overnight shoe shine, morning newspaper.

Facilities: Business center.

FOUR SEASONS CLIFT, 495 Geary St., San Francisco, CA 94102. Tel. 415/775-4700, or toll free 800/332-3442. 800/268-6282 in Canada. Fax 415/441-4621. 329 rms, 25 suites. A/C

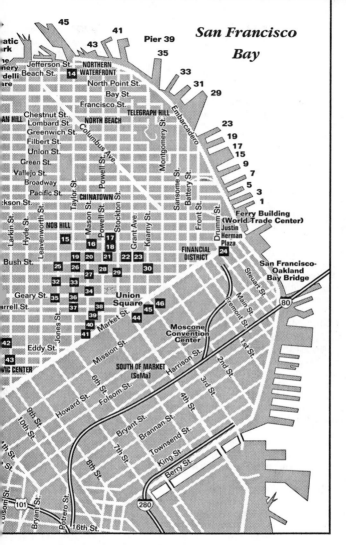

SAN FRANCISCO ACCOMMODATIONS

San Francisco Bay

Pier 39

Jefferson St.
Beach St.
NORTHERN WATERFRONT
North Point St.
Bay St.
Francisco St.

TELEGRAPH HILL

NORTH BEACH

Chestnut St.
Lombard St.
Greenwich St.
Filbert St.
Union St.
Green St.
Vallejo St.
Broadway
Pacific St.
ckson St.

Embarcadero

Columbus Ave.

Montgomery St.

Sansome St.
Battery St.
Front St.

Ferry Building
(World Trade Center)

CHINATOWN

Taylor St.
Powell St.
Mason St.
Stockton St.
Grant Ave.
Kearny St.

Justin Herman Plaza

NOB HILL

Larkin St.
Hyde St.
Leavenworth St.

Bush St.

Drumm St.
FINANCIAL DISTRICT

San Francisco–Oakland Bay Bridge

Geary St.
rrell St.

Union Square

Jones St.

Market St.

Moscone Convention Center

Steuart St.
Main St.
Fremont St.
1st St.

80

Eddy St.

VIC CENTER

Mission St.

SOUTH OF MARKET (SoMa)

Harrison St.

2nd St.
3rd St.

6th St.
Folsom St.

Howard St.

Bryant St.
Brannan St.

4th St.

7th St.

Townsend St.

King St.

8th St.

Berry St.

9th St.
10th St.
th St.

son St.

280

101

Bryant St.

Potrero St.

16th St.

MINIBAR TV TEL **Cable Car:** Powell-Hyde and Powell-Mason lines (2 blocks east). **Bus:** 2, 3, 4, 30, 38, or 45.

$ Rates: $205–$315 single; $205–$345 double; from $355 suite. AE, CB, DC, MC, V. **Parking:** $22.

Few of San Francisco's huge deluxe hotels have the warm elegance, finesse, and sophistication of the Four Seasons Clift, on Geary at Taylor Street, two blocks west of Union Square. Opened in 1915 as the Clift, the property was purchased by Four Seasons in 1974 and was completely restored. Subsequent renovations have left the rooms tastefully and individually decorated with cool color schemes and plush furnishings. Today the hotel sets the city's standard for luxury accommodations and claims an aristocratic clientele.

Guest rooms are spacious, with high ceilings, restored moldings and woodwork, fine Georgian reproductions, and marble bathrooms with everything from hairdryers to plush terry-cloth robes. Thoughtful extras include padded hangers, individual climate controls, two-line telephones, shampoos and bath gels, and a scale in your dressing room.

The Very Important Kids program provides traveling families with baby blankets, teddy bears, Nintendo video games, children's-size robes, and other amenities to help children and their parents feel at home. The hotel also accepts pets.

Dining/Entertainment: The French Room offers breakfast, lunch, and dinner, and specializes in seasonally appropriate California-French cuisine. Dinner might spotlight potato risotto with prosciutto, asparagus, and shaved parmesan; or medallions of venison with roasted pears and bacon. Main courses cost from $25 to $32. More health-conscious "spa-style" meals (like Pinot Noir-poached salmon) are also always available. The hotel's Redwood Room, a true art deco beauty, is one of San Francisco's poshest piano bars; its gorgeous redwood interior was built from a single 2,000-year-old tree. The lobby lounge serves cocktails daily and a traditional English tea Monday through Saturday.

Services: 24-hour room service, concierge, twice-daily maid service, overnight laundry and shoe polishing, evening turndown, complimentary in-room fax and computers.

Facilities: Business center; gift shop; small weight room, stair machines, and stationary bicycles; no-smoking rooms.

GRAND HYATT SAN FRANCISCO ON UNION SQUARE, 345 Stockton St., San Francisco, CA 94108. Tel. 415/ 398-1234, or toll free 800/233-1234. Fax 415/391-1780. 693 rms, 30 suites. A/C MINIBAR TV TEL **Cable Car:** Powell-Hyde and Powell-Mason lines (2 blocks west). **Bus:** 2, 3, 4, 30, 38, or 45.

$ Rates: $149–$220 basic single or double; $185–$245 Regency room; from $350 suite. AE, CB, DC, MC, V. **Parking:** $22.

One of the most enjoyable hotels in town is the conveniently located Grand Hyatt, between Post and Sutter streets. Although not as startlingly innovative as the Hyatt Regency San Francisco (see "Financial District," below), this is a handsome, modern hotel with an elegant old-world courtyard graced by Ruth Asawa's bronze fountain sculpture.

The rooms, renovated in 1990 at a cost of $20 million, are ultramodern, with mirrored walls; beige rugs; and gold, brown, or royal-blue drapes and spreads. Accommodations include such amenities as TVs in both the bedroom and the bath, first-run movies, and a telephone with computer-connection capability. Regency rooms are larger and come with continental breakfast and evening hors d'oeuvres.

Dining/Entertainment: The hotel's signature Plaza Restaurant has floor-to-ceiling windows overlooking Union Square. Breakfast, lunch, and dinner are served in a garden setting created by bamboo furnishings, a fountain, potted palms, and a stained-glass skylight dome. Napper's Deli, an indoor/outdoor bistro, serves custom-cut sandwiches, seasonal salads, soups, and desserts; continental breakfasts are served here on weekends beginning at 8:30am. Club 36, located appropriately on the 36th floor, serves cocktails with live jazz six nights a week.

Services: 24-hour room service, concierge, free weekday morning towncar service to the Financial District.

Facilities: Fitness center, tour desk, car-rental desk, fully equipped business center, no-smoking rooms.

HOTEL NIKKO, 222 Mason St., San Francisco, CA 94102. Tel. 415/394-1111, or toll free 800/645-5687. Fax 415/421-0455. 500 rms, 22 suites. A/C MINIBAR TV TEL

$ Rates: $185–$275 single; $215–$305 double; from $375 suite. AE, CB, DC, MC, V. **Parking:** $23.

Top-of-the-line business standards make Hotel Nikko a reliable choice in the Union Square area. Most rooms have king-sized beds and fantastic floor-to-ceiling windows that overshadow the rooms' plain wall art. Cotton coverings on room furnishings are upgraded to silk on the Concierge Level, where guests also get continental breakfast and evening cocktails. Every room features voice-mail telephones, computer-modem lines and pay-for-view movies. Particularly large marble bathrooms feature separate shower and baths and are outfitted with hairdryers and (sometimes) dual sinks. At $975 per night, the Nikko's Tokyo-priced Japanese-style suites are not cheap. But they offer an indulgence that's not easily replicated in this country. In addition to a Western-style sitting room, Japanese suites include a traditional tatami room, complete with a well for performing the tea ceremony, and a small rock garden overlooking all of San Francisco. Silk-covered futons are unrolled each night.

The Nikko is one of the few hotels in San Francisco to have its own swimming pool, and the entire property is accessible to wheelchair-bound guests.

Dining/Entertainment: The bistro-style Cafe 222 serves California cuisine enlivened with Japanese spices. A new lobby-level sushi bar has all the favorites but is open for lunch only.

Services: 24-hour room service, twice-daily maid service, massage, weight training, business center, concierge.

Facilities: Swimming pool, fitness center, sauna, hot tub, tanning booth, Japanese soaking tubs, gift shop.

HOTEL TRITON, 342 Grant Ave., San Francisco, CA 94108. Tel. 415/394-0500, or toll free 800/433-6611. Fax 415/394-0555. 140 rms, 7 suites. A/C MINIBAR TV TEL **Cable Car:** Powell-Hyde and Powell-Mason lines (2 blocks west).

$ Rates: $169 single or double; $259 suite. AE, DC, DISC, MC, V. **Parking:** $20.

One of San Francisco's newest hotels is also one of the city's most stylish. Located directly across from Chinatown's orange dragon-gate entrance, at Bush Street, the hotel's plain-brick exterior belies a whimsical interior that's designed to make you smile. Playful murals, original art, and Daliesque custom furniture make the lobby look more like a contemporary museum installation. Sapphire theater curtains, colorful original art, and mahogany furniture, designed with geometric shapes, turn guest rooms into veritable artist showcases. It's all done with excellent workmanship and terrific style.

Dining/Entertainment: Café Aïoli, an Italian restaurant and bar, serves breakfast, lunch, and dinner. Home-cured prosciutto and veal carpaccio win raves as the appetizers, while wild boar ravioli, snapper ratatouille, and braised rabbit are some of the more unusual entree selections. None top $16. Complimentary wine is served each evening in the hotel lobby.

Services: Room service, same-day laundry, complimentary morning limousine to the Design District.

Facilities: No-smoking rooms.

PARC FIFTY FIVE, 55 Cyril Magnin St., San Francisco, CA 94012. Tel. 415/392-8000, or toll free 800/338-1338. Fax 415/403-6602. 1,006 rms, 24 suites. A/C TV TEL **Cable Car:** Powell-Hyde and Powell-Mason lines (1 block north). **Bus:** All Market Street buses. **Muni Metro:** All Market Street trams.

$ Rates: $155–$175 basic single; $170–$195 basic double. Concierge Club, $195–$225 single or double; from $340 one-bedroom suite, from $800 two-bedroom suite. Extra person $15. Packages available. AE, CB, DC, DISC, MC, V. **Parking:** $22.

Built in 1984, this palatial hotel occupies an entire city block at Market and North Fifth streets. Inside, two stone lions hold court in the travertine marble lobby, which looks upward into a three-story atrium. In front of you, as you enter, you'll see an imposing seven-panel bas-relief mural of the history of San Francisco by Ruth Asawa.

All the rooms offer bay windows and cable TV, and show a strict attention to detail: king-size beds, bathroom phone, well-lit makeup mirror, shower massage, even French milled soap on the marble vanity. This is largely a business hotel, however, and is somewhat sterile in atmosphere. Windows don't open; fresh air is supplied by air vents.

The Concierge Club occupies the top four floors and offers guests the royal treatment. Personal check-in and concierge service, a continental breakfast, and afternoon hors d'oeuvres are included in the basic charge. Seven of the suites contain private whirlpool baths.

Dining/Entertainment: Located on the second floor is the hotel's premier restaurant, the Veranda. The menu features innovative specialties—perhaps a guacamole omelet for breakfast or a tostada grande with chicken, avocado, tomato, cheese, and refried beans at lunch. Luncheon dishes range from $8 to $15; at dinner they run $12 to $20 (to $30 for lobster). In the atrium you can enjoy a leisurely drink at the Piazza Lounge while listening to contemporary and classical piano music.

Services: 24-hour room service, concierge, foreign-language information desk, currency exchange.

Facilities: Business center, tour desk, car rental, health club, facilities for the handicapped, no-smoking rooms.

PRESCOTT HOTEL, 545 Post St., San Francisco, CA 94102. Tel. 415/563-0303, or toll free 800/283-7322. Fax 415/563-6831. 167 rms, 36 suites. A/C MINIBAR TV TEL **Cable Car:** Powell-Hyde and Powell-Mason lines (1 block west). **Bus:** 2, 3, 4, 30, 38, or 45.

$ Rates: $165 standard single or double: $185 concierge level single or double; from $235 suite. AE, CB, DC, MC, V. **Parking:** $15.

The Prescott, between Mason and Taylor streets, is just one block from Union Square and the Powell Street cable car. It opened in 1989 following a complete renovation of the old Hotel Cecil, built in 1917. This prestigious medium-size, first-class hotel offers elegance and gracious personal service. Each room has a simple neoclassical design and custom-made cherry furnishings—beds with columned headboards, bow-front armoires, and faux-marble bedside lamps. Bedspreads and draperies are beautifully done in hunter green, cerise, purple, and saffron. Amenities include telephone with call waiting and an extra-long cord, color TV with remote control and complimentary HBO, and a digital clock radio, all in a thoroughly sound-proofed environment. Bathrooms are black and taupe and are supplied with terry-cloth robes and hairdryers.

Concierge-level rooms include plusher furnishings, free continental breakfast, evening cocktails, and exercise bicycles or rowing machines brought up to your room on request. Suites have an adjoining parlor with a comfortable overstuffed sofa, upholstered chairs, a coffee table, and an oval dining/desk table; other pleasant touches include a VCR and a whirlpool bathtub.

Dining/Entertainment: Chef Wolfgang' Puck's popular Postrio Restaurant adjoins the Prescott. Make reservations when you book your room. The restaurant serves contemporary San Franciscan cuisine (see Chapter 6, "San Francisco Dining," for complete information).

Services: Complimentary coffee and tea each morning, wine and hors d'oeuvres every evening in the Library, limousine service weekday mornings to the Financial District, concierge, evening turndown, same-day valet/laundry service, overnight shoe shine, room service from the Postrio.

Facilities: Access to off-premises health club, including swimming pool, free weights, and sauna; no-smoking rooms.

SAN FRANCISCO HILTON AND TOWERS, 333 O'Farrell St., San Francisco, CA 94142. Tel. **415/771-1400,** or toll free 800/445-8667. Fax 415/771-6807. 1,900 rms, 180 suites. A/C MINIBAR TV TEL **Cable Car:** Powell-Hyde and Powell-Mason lines (1 block east). **Bus:** 2, 3, 4, 30, 38, or 45.

$ Rates: $175–$240 single; $200–$265 double; from $300 suite. Children stay free in parents' room. AE, CB, DC, DISC, MC, V. **Parking:** $22.

One of the largest hotels on the West Coast is this conveniently situated, first-class hotel on O'Farrell at Mason Street. The San Francisco Hilton is a city within a city, composed of three connecting buildings: the original 19-story main building, a 46-story tower topped by a panoramic restaurant, and a 23-story landmark with an additional 386 luxurious rooms and suites.

After you get past the sweeping grand lobby entrance, you'll find well-proportioned guest rooms competently furnished in typical Hilton style. This is a grand-scale group hotel, with plenty of bus and business traffic. If you can tear yourself away from the memorable floor-to-ceiling view, you'll find a color TV with first-run movies, minibar, radio, and a marble bathroom. There are 40 rooms located poolside.

Dining/Entertainment: Cityscape, on the 46th floor, serves classic California cuisine in a breathtaking setting. The magnificent 360° view encompasses both the Golden Gate Bridge and the Bay Bridge, as well as Sausalito, Telegraph Hill, and the Easy Bay; the retractable skylight exposes the night sky in all its grandeur. Kiku of Tokyo presents authentic Japanese cuisine. The Mason Street Deli serves breakfast and lunch, and Intermezzo, serves Italian-style food to-go. An elegant sidewalk cafe, Café on the Square, provides a lovely spot for spectators to eye the passing parade and the promenade of hotel shops.

Services: Room service (6am to midnight), concierge, laundry, shoe shine.

Facilities: Swimming pool, health club, car rental, tour desk, handicapped-equipped rooms, shopping arcade, no-smoking rooms.

SAN FRANCISCO MARRIOTT, 55 Fourth St., San Francisco, CA 94103. Tel. 415/896-1600, or toll free 800/228-9290. Fax 415/442-0141. 1,500 rms, 134 suites. A/C MINIBAR TV TEL **Cable Car:** Powell-Hyde and Powell-Mason lines (3 blocks west). **Bus:** All Market Street buses. **Muni Metro:** All Market Street trams.

$ Rates: $169–$245 standard single or double; $195–$265 concierge level single or double; from $350 suite. AE, CB, DC, MC, V. **Parking:** $24.

The Marriott has variously been referred to as a giant jukebox, a 40-story robot, and the world's biggest parking meter. Architectural criticisms aside, it is the only hotel than can lay claim to opening its doors during the week of the October 1989 quake. The Marriott is one block from the Moscone Convention Center and the Powell Street cable-car turnaround, and a short stroll from Nordstrom. It's also one of the largest buildings in San Francisco; enter from Fourth Street, between Market and Mission streets, to avoid a long, long trek to the registration area.

Amenities include remote-control color TVs and plush baths. Rooms on the concierge level are more spacious and provide a lengthy list of complimentary services, including continental breakfast, afternoon snacks and beverages, evening hors d'oeuvres and canapés, and an open honor bar.

Dining/Entertainment: The Kinoko is a Japanese teppanyaki restaurant and sushi bar. The Garden Terrace, facing the hotel's central fountain, has a breakfast bar and two buffets that prepare made-to-order omelets, and it serves a varied lunch and dinner menu. As for lounge areas, the Atrium Lounge is on the atrium level, the View Lounge is on the 39th floor and has a truly spectacular view of the bay and Golden Gate Bridge (assuming there's no fog) as well as live entertainment, and Treats serves refreshments in the Golden Gate Foyer.

Services: Room service, concierge.

Facilities: Indoor pool and health club, business center, tour desk, car-rental and airline desk, gift shop, no-smoking rooms.

WESTIN ST. FRANCIS, 335 Powell St., San Francisco, CA 94102. Tel. 415/397-7000, or toll free 800/228-3000. Fax 415/774-0124. 1,200 rms, 83 suites. A/C MINIBAR TV TEL **Cable Car:** Powell-Hyde and Powell-Mason lines (direct stop). **Bus:** 2, 3, 4, 30, 45, or 76.

$ Rates: Main building $150–$195 single; $180–$225 double; from $300 suite. Tower $205–$230 single; $235–$260 double; from $425 suite. Extra person $30. AE, CB, DC, MC, V. **Parking:** $20.

Located in the heart of the city—on verdant Union Square between Geary and Post streets—is the elegant grande dame of San Francisco hotels. The splendid, recently renovated marble-columned lobby extends back to the carpeted foyer of the 32-story tower building, and it's here that the main desk and an open cocktail area are located.

Looking like exotic space capsules, the five outside elevators whisk guests to their rooms. The rooms are attractively furnished and supplied with lots of amenities, such as color TVs with in-room movies and direct-dial phones. The older rooms of the main building vary in size and have more charm than the newer and more expensive tower rooms. But the tower is remarkable for its great views of the city, once you rise above the 18th floor.

Dining/Entertainment: High above the city, on the tower's top floor, are the award-winning Victor's, featuring excellent Californian-cuisine dinners, and the adjoining Oz, one of the city's hottest dance clubs. Additional dining facilities include the Dutch Kitchen, a breakfast restaurant, open from 6 to 11:30am. Fresh seafood, steaks, and other grilled items are offered at the handsome, oak-paneled St. Francis Grill, open daily for dinner. Soup-and-sandwich fare is served daily at the hotel's Dewey's Bar. The Compass Rose is open daily for lunch and high tea, and is the perfect spot for an afternoon drink in a plush, nostalgic setting.

Services: 24-hour room service, babysitting referral, laundry.

Facilities: Health club with exercise bikes and rowing machines, business center, accommodations for the handicapped, tour desk, car rental, barber/beauty salon, gift shop, no-smoking rooms.

EXPENSIVE

CARTWRIGHT HOTEL, 524 Sutter St., San Francisco, CA 94102. Tel. 415/421-2865, or toll free 800/227-3844. Fax 415/421-2865. 114 rms, 5 suites. TV TEL **Cable Car:** Powell-Hyde and Powell-Mason lines (direct stop). **Bus:** 2, 3, 4, 30, or 45.

$ Rates: $119 single; $129 double or twin; $160–$170 family suite sleeping four. AE, CB, DC, DISC, MC, V. **Parking:** $12.

A charming and distinctly cozy establishment at Powell Street, the recently renovated Cartwright is remarkably quiet despite its convenient location near one of the busiest downtown corners. The hotel takes great pride in its reputation for comfort, cleanliness, and efficiency. And it's well earned—reflected in every nook and cranny, from the small, well-groomed lobby to the rooms furnished with antiques and brightened with fresh flowers. Each unit is decorated in a unique, charming style, and no-smoking rooms are available. Although water pressure could be better, baths feature shower massages, thick fluffy towels, and terry-cloth robes. Accommodations with air conditioning or refrigerator are available on request at no additional charge. Special attention is paid to the guests' comfort. In addition to turndown service, there are such extras as irons, hairdryers, and large reading pillows.

Guests have access to a nearby health club. Complimentary tea and cakes are served in a wonderful library adjacent to the lobby from 4 to 6pm, and Teddy's restaurant, located behind the lobby, serves good country breakfasts, including waffles, pancakes, and omelets.

HANDLERY UNION SQUARE HOTEL, 351 Geary St., San Francisco, CA 94102. Tel. 415/781-7800, or toll free 800/843-4343. Fax 415/781-0269. 375 rms, 20 suites. TV TEL **Cable Car:** Powell-Hyde and Powell-Mason lines (direct stop). **Bus:** 2, 3, 4, 30, 38, or 45.

$ Rates: $120–$130 basic single or double; club section, $145 single, $155 double; from $220 suite. Extra person $10. AE, CB, DC, MC, V. **Parking:** $12.50.

This establishment, between Mason and Powell streets, is the attractive offspring of the Handlery Motor Inn and the Hotel Steward, following a $10-million renovation and merger completed in 1989. The shopping, theater, and financial districts are easily accessible from this location, which is half a block from Union Square.

Every room contains a handy safe; 100 rooms have minibars. The club section offers services that one usually expects only from a larger hotel. The rooms are truly large and luxurious, with such frills as electric shoe polishers, coffeemakers, dressing rooms with makeup mirrors, custom bathroom amenities, scales, robes, hairdryers, and two phones. The club section also provides a complimentary morning newspaper and turndown service.

Services: Multilingual concierge staff, same-day laundry, babysitting, complimentary coffee and tea served every morning.

Facilities: Heated outdoor swimming pool and sauna, barber shop, tour desk, gift shop, candy store, art gallery.

JULIANA HOTEL, 590 Bush St., San Francisco, CA 94108. Tel. 415/392-2540, or toll free 800/328-3880. Fax 415/391-8447. 106 rms, 22 suites. A/C MINIBAR TV TEL **Cable Car:** Powell-Hyde and Powell-Mason lines (1 block west). **Bus:** 2, 3, 4, 30, 38, or 45.

$ Rates: $134 single or double; $160 junior suite; $170 suite. Special winter packages available. AE, CB, DC, MC, V. **Parking:** $15.

Another fine European-style hotel—small, comfortable, beautifully done—the Juliana is a charming haven at Stockton Street. The lobby is a commercial beauty, with attractive English prints and working marble fireplace brightened with brass framing.

The rooms are light and spacious and have an elegant country air. Delicate pastel walls and white furnishings flatter the striking floral prints of the drapes, spreads, and comfortably upholstered chairs. Each room has a small stocked refrigerator, individually controlled air conditioning and heat, and remote-control TV with HBO. Other thoughtful touches are reflected in the bath: large makeup bulbs placed strategically around a sizable mirror, and a charming little bird-shaped wicker basket holding soap and other house toiletries. No-smoking rooms are available. Services include complimentary morning coffee and tea, and evening wine served by the fireplace. There's complimentary morning limousine service to the Financial District, and access to an off-premises health club.

MONTICELLO INN, 127 Ellis St., San Francisco, CA 94102. Tel. 415/392-8800, or toll free 800/669-7777. Fax 415/398-2650. 91 rms, 36 suites. A/C MINIBAR TV TEL **Cable Car:** Powell-Hyde and Powell-Mason lines (direct stop), **Muni Metro:** All Market Street metros. **Bus:** All Market Street buses.

$ Rates (including continental breakfast): $120 single; $135 double; $145–$180 suite. AE, CB, DC, DISC, MC, V. **Parking:** $15 weekdays, $25 weekends.

Opened in 1987, between Cyril Magnin and Powell streets, the Monticello is a first-rate addition to the neighborhood. Colonial American charm is the theme, and Thomas Jefferson, whose bust is displayed in the lobby, would have been pleased with the inn's simplicity and elegance. The spacious lobby features Early American reproductions, a Federal-period desk, a stately grandfather clock, fresh floral displays, and a cozy library where you can enjoy a complimentary evening glass of wine by the fireplace. Should you need information, directions, or reservations, the friendly staff is very helpful.

Each soundproofed room is decorated in country-colonial style and features elegant canopied beds, digital clock radios, cable TV, and computer hookups.

Dining/Entertainment: The hotel's restaurant, the Corona Bar & Grill, features southwestern cuisine; it's located next door, at the corner of Ellis and Cyril Magnin streets (see Chapter 6, "San Francisco Dining." for complete information).

Services: Complimentary limousine service to the Financial District, same-day laundry, valet service.

Facilities: Business center, tour desk, no-smoking rooms.

SIR FRANCIS DRAKE, 450 Powell St., San Francisco, CA 94102. Tel. 415/392-7755, or toll free 800/227-5480. Fax 415/677-9341. 417 rms. TV TEL **Cable Car:** Powell-Hyde and Powell-Mason lines (direct stop). **Bus:** 2, 3, 4, 30, 45, or 76.

$ Rates: $140–$180 single/double or twin; from $300 suite. Additional person $20. AE, CB, DC, MC, V. **Parking:** $23.

Reopened in 1994 after a four-month renovation, the hotel is now managed by the Kimton Hotel Group, a privately held company that owns about a dozen other fine properties in the city. The Drake's smallish guest rooms are disappointing, as they lack many of the amenities you'd expect from a top hotel. The single-line telephones are archaic, and undersized bathrooms are equipped with precious few towels and a skimpy selection of toiletries. Air conditioners are fitted into windows that are painted shut, elevators are exceedingly sluggish, and service personnel are, for the most part, both unresponsive and unfriendly. The rush to reopen the Drake was done at the guests' expense, and frankly, the hotel cannot be recommended at this time. With time, however, I hope that this Union Square landmark will achieve the superior status of Kimton's other hotels.

Dining/Entertainment: In Café Espresso the menu features an eclectic range of dishes, all accompanied by San Francisco's famous sourdough bread. On the 21st floor, Harry Denton's Starlite Roof is a popular downtown spot for dancing, complimentary hors d'oeuvres beginning at 4pm, and drinks.

VILLA FLORENCE, 225 Powell St., San Francisco, CA 94102. Tel. 415/397-7700, or toll free 800/553-4411. Fax 415/397-1006. 177 rms, 36 suites. A/C MINIBAR TV TEL **Cable Car:** Powell-Hyde and Powell-Mason lines (direct stop). **Bus:** 2, 3, 4, 30, 38, or 45.

$ Rates: $139–$149 single or double; $159–$169 junior suite; $249 deluxe suite. AE, CB, DC, DISC, MC, V. **Parking:** $16.

If there were nothing more to be said about the Villa Florence, its price and location would make it an exceptional buy. Near Union Square and Geary Street, it's ideal for anyone who wants to be downtown. The hotel is two blocks from the heart of the Financial District, the Moscone Convention Center, and the BART and Muni stations. It's adjacent to Saks Fifth Avenue, Macy's, Neiman-Marcus, and enough specialty shops to satisfy even the most dedicated shopper.

The Villa Florence is the superb result of a $6.5-million renovation of what was the turn-of-the-century Manx Hotel. As soon as you enter, you'll have an idea of the magnificent refurbishing job done throughout: The arched entryway, graceful palms, marble columns, murals of Florence, huge marble fireplace, rich maroon upholstered chairs, Etruscan-style table lamps, giant urns, and fresh flowers all reflect an aura of Italian grandeur.

The beautiful, elegant bedrooms feature pink-and-blue floral chintz drapes and matching spreads, as well as white furnishings. The rooms are a bit small, but the light decor and the high ceilings contribute a feeling of airiness. Modern amenities include color TVs, pull-out writing tables, direct-dial phones, coffeemakers, and well-stocked refrigerators. The bath has makeup-mirror lighting, overhead heat lamps, hairdryers, and hand-milled soap.

Dining/Entertainment: Kuleto's, to the left of the hotel's main lobby, is a gem of a northern Italian restaurant with specialties from Tuscany (see Chapter 6, "San Francisco Dining," for complete information). Caffè Kuleto's is the hotel's new espresso bar, serving pastries, sandwiches, salads, and dessert from 7am to 10:30pm.

Services: Complimentary limousine service to the Financial District 7:20am and 8am Monday through Friday.

WHITE SWAN INN, 845 Bush St., San Francisco, CA 94108. Tel. 415/775-1755. Fax 415/775-5717. 26 rms, 1 suite. MINIBAR TV TEL **Cable Car:** California Street line (1 block north). **Bus:** 1, 2, 3, 4, 27, or 45.
$ **Rates** (including breakfast): $145–$160 single or double; $260 suite. Extra person $15. AE, MC, V. **Parking:** $15.

Just two and a half blocks from Union Square, two blocks from Nob Hill, and one and a half blocks from the Powell Street cable car, the White Swan Inn enjoys an excellent location between Taylor and Mason streets. This tasteful hotel was constructed in the early 1900s and renovated by Four Sisters Inns. The handsome reception area features a cheery fireplace, a carousel horse, and an antique oak breakfront cabinet. With the charm and serenity of an English garden inn, the White Swan still offers service and style to fit the needs of the most discriminating traveler. It's a delightful, romantic discovery.

Each spacious room comes with its own teddy-bear companion. Soft English wallpaper and floral-print bedspreads add to the feeling of warmth and comfort, as do the working fireplaces, fluffy oversized towels, color TVs, and bedside telephones.

Dining/Entertainment: Each morning a generous breakfast is served in a lovely common room just off a tiny garden. Afternoon tea is also served, with hors d'oeuvres, sherry, wine, and home-baked pastries. You can have your sherry in front of the fireplace while you browse through the books in the Library.

Services: Concierge, laundry, evening turndown, morning newspaper, overnight shoe shine.

Facilities: Off-premises health club.

MODERATE

ANDREWS HOTEL, 624 Post St., San Francisco, CA 94109. Tel. 415/563-6877, or toll free 800/926-3739. Fax 415/928-6919. 43 rms, 5 suites. MINIBAR TV TEL **Cable Car:** Powell-Hyde and Powell-Mason lines (3 blocks east). **Bus:** 2, 3, 4, 30, 38, or 45.
$ **Rates** (including continental breakfast and evening glass of California wine): $82–$106 single or double; $119 petite suite. AE, MC, V. **Parking:** $13.

Just two blocks west of Union Square, near Taylor Street, the Andrews offers gracious simplicity amid warm surroundings. The charming rooms evoke the casual atmosphere of an intimate European-style hotel. All rooms have luxurious, custom-made chintz bedspreads with matching pillow shams, coordinated with armchairs, and a white enameled headboard. White lace curtains and fresh flowers in each room add a light touch. Mark Hall is a warm and friendly manager, and the rest of the staff emulates his courtesy.

The adjoining Fino Bar and Ristorante, a new Italian eatery, is open every night.

BEDFORD HOTEL, 761 Post St., San Francisco, CA 94109. Tel. 415/673-6040, or toll free 800/227-5642. Fax 415/563-6739. 144 rms, 7 suites. MINIBAR TV TEL **Cable Car:** Powell-Hyde and Powell-Mason lines (4 blocks east). **Bus:** 2, 3, 4, or 27.
$ Rates: $109–$119 single or double; from $175 suite. AE, CB, DC, MC, V. **Parking:** $15.

A charming European-style hotel in a quiet but convenient location three blocks from Union Square, the Bedford is on the southwestern slope of Nob Hill between Leavenworth and Jones streets. Each room is well furnished with king-size, queen-size, or two double beds, VCR, AM/FM clock radio, writing desk, and armchair. Color schemes are a cheerful pale blue, peach, or yellow; and many rooms have remarkable views of the city. No-smoking rooms are available. The Bedford's staff is enthusiastic, attentive, and very professional.

The hotel's Wedgewood Lounge is a small bar opposite the registration desk. Canvas Cafe, a sunny, warm, and inviting eatery located behind the lobby, is under separate management. Services include room service, valet parking, and complimentary wine in the lobby each evening from 5 to 6pm. There's a video library, and free morning limousine service to the Financial District.

BERESFORD ARMS, 701 Post St., San Francisco, CA 94109. Tel. 415/673-2600, or toll free 800/533-6533. Fax 415/474-0449. 92 rms, 52 suites. MINIBAR TV TEL **Cable Car:** Powell-Hyde line (three blocks east). **Bus:** 2, 3, 4, 27, or 38.
$ Rates: $75 single; $85 double; $105 Jacuzzi suite; $135 parlor suite. Extra person $10. Children under 12 stay free in parents' room. Senior-citizen discount available. AE, CB, DC, DISC, MC, V. **Parking:** $15

Under the same management as the Hotel Beresford (see below), this hostelry at Jones Street has a friendly, helpful staff. All units are equipped with color TV, direct-dial phone, and complete bath. A recent renovation reduced the number of guest rooms and added Jacuzzis to some of the suites, which also have kitchen units or wet bars. Complimentary coffee, tea, and pastries are served in the lobby each morning, and a complimentary tea and wine social is held each afternoon in the lobby.

HOTEL BERESFORD, 635 Sutter St., San Francisco, CA 94102. Tel. 415/673-9900, or toll free 800/533-6533. Fax 415/474-0449. 114 rms. MINIBAR TV TEL **Cable Car:** Powell-Hyde line (1 block east). **Bus:** 2, 3, 4, 30, 38, or 45.
$ Rates (including continental breakfast): $75 single; $85–$94 double. Extra person $5. Children under 12 stay free in parents' room. Senior-citizen discounts available. AE, CB, DC, MC, V. **Parking:** $15.

A small, lively, and delightfully friendly hostelry, the Hotel Beresford, near Mason Street, is a good, moderately priced choice near Union Square.

There is a writing parlor off the lobby, with wicker furniture, desks, a color TV, and a portrait of Lord Beresford. Rooms, which are priced according to occupancy rates, have color-coordinated bedspreads, sparkling white drapes, wall-to-wall carpeting, refrigerators, direct-dial phones, and color TVs. There are health facilities and an Olympic-size swimming pool just across the street.

The White Horse restaurant, an attractive replica of an old English pub, serves a complimentary continental breakfast, as well as lunch and dinner.

THE FITZGERALD, 620 Post St., San Francisco, CA 94109. Tel. 415/775-8100, or toll free 800/334-6835. Fax 415/775-1278. 42 rms, 5 suites. TV TEL **Bus:** 2, 3, 4, or 27.

$ Rates (including continental breakfast): $59–$69 single; $69–$99 double; from $95 suite. Extra person $10. Lower rates in the low season. AE, DISC, MC, V. **Parking:** $15.

One of Union Square's newest moderately priced hotels, the Fitzgerald is also one of the best. The building has been miraculously transformed from a dilapidated welfare hotel into one that's both stylish and modern. A clean, plush little lobby gives way to immaculately maintained guestrooms outfitted with new plumbing and lively decorations that include bright bedspreads and carpets with overly busy designs. Smallish rooms and positively tiny closets are a drawback, but they are fully functional and well maintained. For size, the rooms with queen-size beds are particularly recommended. Suites, some of which are located on no-smoking floors, include an additional sitting room furnished with a foldout couch. The hotel's telephones feature private voice-mail service.

Breakfasts include home-baked breads, scones, muffins, juice, tea, and coffee. A nearby off-premises swimming pool is available free for guests' use. All and all, a good value.

HOTEL SAVOY, 580 Geary St., San Francisco, CA 94102. Tel. 415/441-2700, or toll free 800/227-4223. Fax 415/441-2700. 83 rms, 13 suites. MINIBAR TV TEL **Bus:** 2, 3, 4, 27, or 38.

$ Rates (including continental breakfast): $119–$129 single or double; from $169 suite. AE, CB, DC, DISC, MC, V. **Parking:** $16.

Located between Taylor and Jones streets, the Savoy likes to think of itself as a bit of provincial France in the middle of San Francisco. Completely renovated in 1990, the medium-size rooms are decorated with 18th-century period furnishings and feature feather pillows, remote control color TVs, and hairdryers. The little extras are here, too: triple sheets, turndown service, full-length mirrors, and two-line telephones. No-smoking rooms are available. Guests also enjoy concierge service and overnight shoe-shine services. Rates include complimentary late-afternoon sherry and tea, and continental breakfast, served in the Brasserie Savoy, a seafood restaurant complete with a raw bar.

HOTEL UNION SQUARE, 114 Powell St., San Francisco, CA 94102. Tel. 415/397-3000, or toll free 800/553-1900. Fax 415/399-1874. 131 rms, 7 suites. MINIBAR TV TEL **Muni Metro:** All Market Street metros. **Bus:** All Market Street buses.

$ Rates: $99 single or double; from $129 suite. AE, CB, DC, DISC, MC, V. **Parking:** $16.

At the foot of Powell Street, fronting the cable-car turnaround, the Hotel Union Square is pleasant, friendly, and very well located. It also proudly claims its place in American literary history: In the 1920s, as the Golden West Hotel, it was an occasional stop for then Pinkerton detective Dashiell Hammett, creator of Sam Spade.

The hotel has been renamed and considerably modernized since those days, but it retains its early charm. Its refurbished guest rooms feature art deco decor and soft, floral-print bedspreads and curtains. Shampoos, conditioners, and soaps are supplied in the bathrooms. No-smoking rooms are available. Complimentary coffee, tea, and croissants are served each morning. Weekday newspapers are available. The hotel's penthouse suites come complete with redwood decks and garden patios and are especially nice during sunny weather.

HOTEL VINTAGE COURT, 650 Bush St., San Francisco, CA 94108. Tel. 415/392-4666, or toll free 800/654-1100. Fax 415/433-4065. 106 rms. 1 suite. A/C MINIBAR TV TEL **Cable Car:** Powell-Hyde and Powell-Mason lines (direct stop). **Bus:** 2, 3, 4, 30, 45, or 76.

$ Rates (including continental breakfast): $109–$149 single or double; $250 penthouse suite. AE, CB, DC, DISC, MC, V. **Parking:** $15.

This handsome, European-style hotel, between Powell and Stockton streets, is two blocks from Union Square and half a block from the cable car. Its relatively small size allows for excellent personal service, and it's so popular that you should make reservations at least two or three weeks in advance. Classically comfortable sofas, a lobby fireplace, soft classical music, and the warm tones of the furnishings create an intimate, cozy feeling.

Grape clusters embossed on custom-made bedspreads and draperies are complemented by impressionistic prints of the wine country. Each room has a private refrigerator and minibar stocked daily, and a well-lit writing desk. No-smoking rooms are available. The deluxe two-room penthouse suite includes an original 1912 stained-glass skylight, a wood-burning fireplace, a whirlpool tub, a complete entertainment center, and magnificent views of the city.

The hotel's eatery, Masa's, serving traditional French fare, is one of the top restaurants in San Francisco (see Chapter 6, "San Francisco Dining," for complete information). Complimentary continental breakfast is served daily, and a variety of California wines is poured free in the evening. Services include complimentary morning limousine service to the Financial District, tour desk, and car-rental service. There is also access to an off-premises health club.

KENSINGTON PARK HOTEL, 450 Post St., San Francisco, CA 94102. Tel. 415/788-6400, or toll free 800/553-1900. Fax 415/399-9484. 86 rms. 1 suite. TV TEL **Cable Car:** Powell-Hyde and Powell-Mason lines (2 blocks east).

$ Rates: $115 single or double; $350 suite. 50% discount for post-midnight check-in. Extra person $10. AE, CB, DC, MC, V. **Parking:** $16.

Very well maintained, this cozy choice two blocks from Union Square impresses with its cathedral-like lobby, complete with a hand-painted Gothic ceiling, crystal chandelier, and baby grand piano. Rooms do not disappoint either. Mahogany furnishings highlighted with warm blue and rose accents, and brass-and-marble bathrooms, are comforts usually known only to more expensive hotels. Complimentary coffee and croissants are available on each floor every morning from 7 to 10am. Tea and sherry are served in the lobby each afternoon.

The hotel offers 50% off rack rates to guests who arrive after midnight. (No advance reservations are accepted, and the offer is restricted to a one-night maximum.) Check-out is noon.

Services: Room service, concierge, same-day laundry, morning newspaper, complimentary morning limousine to the Financial District; fax and secretarial services also available.

Facilities: Theater On The Square located in hotel, access to off-premises health club, no-smoking rooms.

KING GEORGE HOTEL, 334 Mason St., San Francisco, CA 94102. Tel. 415/781-5050, or toll free 800/288-6005. Fax 415/391-6976. 139 rms, 2 suites. TV TEL **Cable Car:** Powell-Hyde and Powell-Mason lines (3 blocks west). **Bus:** 2, 3, 4, 30, 38, or 45.

$ Rates: $107 single; $117 double; $185 suite. Special-value packages available seasonally. AE, CB, DC, DISC, MC, V. **Parking:** $15.50.

Full of charm and personality, this particularly beautiful European-style restoration is located just one block from Union Square. The hotel is entered through an elegant lobby with an air of quiet sophistication and a fine collection of European period prints. The rooms have been completely renovated in subtle pastel tones and are equipped with color TVs, direct-dial phones, and private baths. Laundry, valet, and 24-hour room service are available.

On the mezzanine above the lobby, the Bread & Honey Tearoom offers continental breakfast daily from 7 to 10am. Every afternoon (except Sunday) from 3 to 6:30pm the hotel offers proper high tea, complete with scones, trifle, tea sandwiches, and assorted pastries. The hotel also has a comfortable cocktail lounge and piano bar. Services include laundry, concierge, and a business center. Guests have access to an off-premises health club, which includes free weights, bikes, and a swimming pool.

THE ORCHARD, 562 Sutter St., San Francisco, CA 94102. Tel. 415/433-4434, or toll free 800/433-4434. Fax 415/433-3695. 94 rms, 2 suites. MINIBAR TV TEL **Cable Car:** Powell-Hyde and Powell-Mason lines (1 block east). **Bus:** 2, 3, 4, 30, 38, or 45.

$ Rates: $110–$140 single or double; $225 suite. AE, CB, DC, MC, V. **Parking:** $15.

This elegant, meticulously reconstructed historic building is situated near several fine galleries, theaters, and restaurants. The hotel's imported furnishings impart a comfortable European ambience. Armoires have a rich dark-walnut tone, complemented by warm deep-rose carpeting and delicate rose-tone walls and draperies. Suites are luxuriously appointed, with large sitting rooms. The lobby lounge, with its magnificent Austrian crystal chandeliers, French furnishings, and delicate Oriental paintings, is a lovely place to relax. The lobby adjoins the art deco Sutter Garden Restaurant, which serves breakfast, lunch, and cocktails daily.

Services: Room service, concierge, tour desk, and same-day laundry/dry cleaning.

Facilities: Access to an off-premises health club across the street.

THE RAPHAEL, 386 Geary St., San Francisco, CA 94102. Tel. 415/986-2000, or toll free 800/821-5343. Fax 415/397-2447. 152 rms, 2 suites. A/C TV TEL **Cable Car:** Powell-Hyde and Powell-Mason lines (2 blocks east). **Bus:** 2, 3, 4, 30, 38, or 45.

$ Rates: $99–$134 single; $109–$134 double; $145–$195 suite. AE, CB, DC, DISC, MC, V. Weekend discounts available. **Parking:** $15.75.

Billing itself as San Francisco's "little elegant hotel," the Raphael, at Mason Street, one block from Union Square, provides quite luxurious accommodations at moderate prices. Its rooms occupy 12 stories, and the door to each is individually hand-painted, making for very cheerful hallways. Each interior is uniquely attractive. All rooms have two phones, color TVs with pay-per-view movies, AM/FM radios, individually controlled air and heat, clocks, makeup mirrors, hairdryers, and 21-hour room service. No-smoking rooms are available.

THE SHANNON COURT, 550 Geary St., San Francisco, CA 94102. Tel. 415/775-5000, or toll free 800/228-8830. Fax 415/928-6813. 173 rms, 5 suites. TV TEL **Cable Car:** Powell-Hyde and Powell-Mason lines (3 blocks east). **Bus:** 2, 3, 4, 30, 38, or 45.

$ Rates: $110–$115 single; $100–$135 double or twin; from $200 suite. Extra person $10. AE, CB, DC, MC, V. **Parking:** $13.

In 1989 the Shannon Court, between Jones and Taylor streets, underwent a multimillion-dollar refurbishment. Originally constructed in 1929, the historic landmark building has a distinctly Spanish flavor, with gracefully curved arches, white stucco walls, and highly polished brass fixtures. While still retaining the ambience of the original building, the restoration has updated the spacious guest rooms and suites in delicate pastels with a comfortable contemporary look. All rooms have outside exposures and are equipped with color TVs and phones. The hotel's five luxury suites are on the 16th floor; two have rooftop terraces. Complimentary morning coffee and afternoon tea are available in the lobby. Accommodations for the handicapped are available, as are no-smoking rooms.

The City of Paris restaurant and bar is the hotel's latest addition. It's open every day, serving three meals from 7am to midnight, while the bar remains open until 2am. Well-priced lunch and dinner entrees include a half herb-roasted chicken for $9, and seared yellowfin tuna for $15; there's also an oyster bar and a great wine list.

BUDGET

ALEXANDER INN, 415 O'Farrell St., San Francisco, CA 94102. Tel. 415/928-6800, or toll free 800/843-8709. Fax 415/928-3354. 48 rms (all with bath). TV TEL **Cable Car:** Powell-Hyde and Powell-Mason lines (2 blocks east).

$ Rates: $48–$72 single or double; $58–$78 triple; $64–$84 family suite. AE, DC, DISC, MC, V. **Parking:** Available nearby for $12.50.

Far from fancy, but both clean and comfortable, the Alexander gets marks for affordable accommodations in a notoriously high-rent district. Most rooms in this six-floor hotel are twins; special no-smoking units are available. All have extra touches like direct-dial telephones, color TVs, and even coffee/tea makers. Located at Taylor Street, the hotel is just three blocks from Union Square.

AYH HOSTEL AT UNION SQUARE, 312 Mason St., San Francisco, CA 94102. Tel. 415/788-5604. 200 beds. **Cable Car:** Powell-Mason line. **Bus:** 7B, 38.

$ Rates: $14 per person for AYH members, $17 for non-members; half-price for persons under 18 when accompanied by a parent. Maximum stay 6 nights. MC, V.

The city's newest hostel is located right in the middle of the city at Union Square. Occupying five sparsely decorated floors, rooms here are simple and clean, each with two or three beds, its own sink, and a closet. Although most rooms share hallway baths, a few en-suite rooms are reserved for families. Freshly painted hallways are adorned with laminated posters, and there are several common rooms including a reading room, a smoking room, and a large kitchen with lots of tables, chairs, and refrigerator space. There are laundry facilities nearby, and a helpful information desk offering tour reservations and sightseeing trips. The hostel is open 24 hours and reservations are essential.

BRADY ACRES, 649 Jones St., San Francisco, CA 94102. Tel. 415/929-8033, or toll free 800/627-2396. Fax 415/441-8033. 25 rms (all with bath). MINIBAR TV TEL **Bus:** 2, 3, 4, 27, or 38.

$ Rates: $50–$55 single; $60–$75 double. Weekly rates available. MC, V. **Parking:** Garage nearby.

Inside this small, four-story brick building is one of the best budget hotels in the city. Enter through a black-and-gold door, with lamp sconces on either side. Inside, you'll find very clean rooms accessorized with microwave ovens, small refrigerators, radio cassette players, direct-dial phones (with free local calls), answering machines, toasters, and coffee-makers. Baths are newly remodeled, with showers, tubs, and hairdryers. A coin-operated washer and dryer are located in the basement, along with free laundry soap and irons. Resident proprietor Deborah Liane Brady is usually on hand to offer friendly, personal service.

COMMODORE INTERNATIONAL, 825 Sutter St., San Francisco, CA 94109. Tel. 415/923-6800, or toll free 800/338-6848. 113 rms. TV TEL **Bus:** 2, 3, 4, 27, 38, or 76.

$ Rates: $60–$90 single; $70–$100 double or twin. AE, CB, DC, DISC, MC, V. **Parking:** $12.

Located in a six-story 1920 building illuminated by iron lanterns, the Commodore International, at Jones Street, welcomes guests with a warm, old-fashioned lobby, complete with grandfather clock and lots of plaster curlicues on the walls. Rooms have large wardrobes, as well as direct-dial phones and color TVs.

Just off the lobby is a small coffee shop and cocktail lounge, open daily for breakfast and lunch. Some of the city's most famous restaurants are nearby, as the hotel is only four blocks from Union Square and five blocks from Chinatown. During the summer season, reserve far in advance.

CORNELL HOTEL, 715 Bush St., San Francisco, CA 94108. Tel. 415/421-3154, or toll free 800/232-9698. Fax 415/399-1442. 60 rms. TV TEL **Cable Car:** Powell-Hyde and Powell-Mason lines (2 blocks east). **Bus:** 2, 3, 4, 30, or 45.

$ Rates (including breakfast): $65–$75 single; $75–$95 double. Weekly package with seven breakfasts and five dinners, $395 single, $495 double. AE, CB, DC, MC, V. **Parking:** $10.

The Cornell Hotel, located within walking distance of Union Square, near Mason Street, is relaxed, charming, unpretentious, and homey. As you enter you'll see several medieval prints opposite the desk. Upstairs, each floor is dedicated to an artist and is decorated with related reproductions. Rooms are all simple, comfortable, and individually decorated. No smoking is allowed in any of them. Light-blue carpeting gives the rooms a pleasant, warm feeling. Meals are prepared by a French chef and served in the adjoining restaurant, Jeanne d'Arc.

GRANT PLAZA HOTEL, 465 Grant Ave., San Francisco, CA 94108. Tel. 415/434-3883, or toll free 800/472-6899. Fax 415/434-3886. 72 rms (no suites). TV TEL **Cable Car:** Powell-Hyde and Powell-Mason lines (2 blocks west).

$ Rates: $39–$42 single; $42–$65 double. MC, V. **Parking:** $8.50.

Offering basic, clean rooms overlooking Chinatown's main street, the Grant Plaza, at the corner of Pine Street, represents one of the best accommodation deals in San Francisco. The six-story hotel's simple, clean lobby and equally modest rooms are conscientiously cared for by a particularly hospitable Chinese management. Guest rooms, which contain little more than a bed, desk, and chair, are on the small side. Corner rooms on higher floors are both larger and brighter. There are ice and soda machines in the lobby.

Grant Plaza is not for everybody; its motel-quality rooms occupy one of the city's busiest urban corners. But if you're happy with basic accommodations, and relish being right in the heart of the hustle, this hotel is thoroughly recommendable. Rooms in back are quieter. You should also be aware that no visitors are permitted in the rooms after 11pm.

GOLDEN GATE HOTEL, 775 Bush St., San Francisco, CA 94108. Tel. 415/392-3702, or toll free 800/835-1118. Fax 415/392-6202. 23 rms (14 with bath). TV **Cable Car:** Powell-Hyde and Powell-Mason lines (1 block east). **Bus:** 2, 3, 4, 30, 38, or 45.
$ Rates (including continental breakfast): $55–$65 single or double without bath, $89 single or double with bath. AE, CB, DC, MC, V. **Parking:** $14.

Among San Francisco's small, charming hotels born near the turn of the century are some real gems: the Golden Gate Hotel, between Powell and Mason streets, is one. It's two blocks north of Union Square and two blocks down (literally) from the crest of Nob Hill. The cable car stops at the corner for easy access to Fisherman's Wharf and Chinatown. The city's theaters and best restaurants are also within walking distance.

Part of the charm of the Golden Gate is that it is a family-run establishment. John and Renate Kenaston are delightful, hospitable innkeepers who take obvious pleasure in making their guests comfortable. They offer lovely rooms that have been individually redecorated with handsome antique furnishings from the early 1900s. Draperies and spreads with floral prints add to the quaintness and warmth, as do fresh flowers in each room. The antique clawfoot tubs are great for long hot soaks. Most, but not all, rooms have phones, so request one when you make your reservation.

Complimentary afternoon tea is served daily from 4 to 7pm. Concierge services are available and sightseeing tours can be arranged with a pickup at the hotel.

PACIFIC BAY INN, 520 Jones St., San Francisco, CA 94102. Tel. 415/673-0234, or toll free 800/445-2631. Fax 415/673-4781. 84 rms (all with bath). TV TEL **Cable Car:** California Street line (direct stop). **Bus:** 2, 3, 4, 27, or 38.
$ Rates: $45 single; $65 double (ask about special rates). AE, CB, DC, DISC, MC, V. **Parking:** $12.

This pleasant, recently renovated little hotel between Geary and O'Farrell streets, three blocks west of the Powell Street cable car and Union Square, offers no frills to budget-conscious visitors. The inn is easily identified by the international flags flying outside. The lobby has recently been given a comfortable high-tech look, and there's 24-hour desk service.

Cozy and light, accommodations are done in airy peach tones with maroon floral-print spreads and maroon-and-gray carpeting throughout. The rooms have showers only—no tubs–and some rooms are for nonsmokers.

PENSIONE INTERNATIONAL, 875 Post St., San Francisco, CA 94109. Tel. 415/775-3344. 46 rms (15 with bath). **Bus:** 38.
$ Rates (including continental breakfast): $30–$40 single without bath, $40–$55 single with bath; $40–$50 double without bath, $50–$75 double with bath. AE, DISC, MC, V.

Popular with budget-minded Europeans, this small Union Square–area hotel, complete with molded doors, gilded mirrors, and framed art, could easily fit into Rome or Paris. While it's not a fancy place, this pensione offers basic, stylish rooms, located on two floors atop narrow staircases. Accommodations tend to be small, and are outfitted with mismatched furniture and decor. All rooms have sinks and mirrors, and the more expensive ones have TVs and private baths.

THE SHEEHAN, 620 Sutter St., San Francisco, CA 94102. Tel. 415/775-6500, or toll free 800/654-6835. Fax 415/775-3271. 68 rms (51 with bath), 2 suites. TV TEL **Cable Car:** Powell-Hyde and Powell-Mason lines (2 blocks east). **Bus:** 2, 3, 4, 30, 38, or 45.

$ Rates (including continental breakfast): $40–$47 single without bath, $60–$75 single with bath; $50–$57 double without bath, $75–$98 double with bath; $85–$90 suite. AE, CB, DC, MC, V. **Parking:** $12.

Formerly a YWCA hotel, the Sheehan, near Mason Street, is well located just two blocks from Union Square. You can easily walk from here to most places in the downtown area. Mostly remodeled in 1990, the rooms are carpeted, comfortable, clean, and well furnished; some are no-smoking units. In addition to beds, each has a table, chairs, and cableless color TV. The hotel has a clean and pleasant lobby; a comfortable Tea Room, open for light lunches and afternoon tea; and an indoor, heated swimming pool and work-out area—a very good value.

2. NOB HILL

VERY EXPENSIVE

FAIRMONT HOTEL AND TOWER, 950 Mason St., San Francisco, CA 94108. Tel. 415/772-5000, or toll free 800/527-4727. Fax 415/772-5013. 600 rms, 62 suites. A/C MINIBAR TV TEL **Cable Car:** California Street line (direct stop).

$ Rates: Main building $179–$209 single or double; from $450 suite. Tower $239–$300 single or double; from $500 suite. Extra person $30. AE, CB, DC, DISC, MC, V. **Parking:** $25.

Perhaps the most famous hotel in San Francisco, the luxurious Fairmont, atop Nob Hill, is a garish marble palace sheltering hundreds of good-quality rooms, six restaurants, several cocktail lounges, and conveniences ranging from a pharmacy to a full-service bank. The huge lobby, with its marbleized columns, high silver-and-white ceilings, and red-velvet–covered furnishings, is more kitsch than classic and is often full with doctors, lawyers, conventioneers, and red-jacketed bellhops.

In addition to the usual luxuries, guests will appreciate such details as goose-down pillows, electric shoe buffers, hairdryers, bath scales, huge walk-in closets, and multiline telephones with private voice-mail message capability. All suites are also equipped with personal fax machines.

Dining/Entertainment: The Bella Voce Restaurant, open for three meals daily, features Italian cuisine served by a singing staff.

The Crown offers lavish buffet meals and a spectacular view of the Bay Area. The exotic Tonga Restaurant and Hurricane Bar have an extensive selection of Chinese and Polynesian specialties in a lavish South Seas ambience. There are dancing on a boat deck and simulated indoor "thundershowers." Masons serves contemporary California cuisine in a sophisticated atmosphere, with a good view of the cable cars. Afternoon tea is served daily in the hotel's magnificent lobby.

Services: 24-hour room service, evening turndown, concierge, babysitting services, doctor on call, overnight laundry, complimentary morning limousine to the Financial District.

Facilities: Health club, business center, barbershop, beauty salon, pharmacy, travel agency, bank, shopping arcade, no-smoking rooms.

HUNTINGTON HOTEL, 1075 California St., San Francisco, CA 94108. Tel. 415/474-5400, or toll free 800/227-4683, 800/652-1539 in California. Fax 415/474-6227. 140 rms, 40 suites. MINIBAR TV TEL **Cable Car:** California Street line (direct stop). **Bus:** 1.

$ Rates: $165–$215 single; $185–$250 double; from $315 suite. Special packages available. AE, CB, DC, MC, V. **Parking:** $16.50.

Discreet Nob Hill elegance and old-world charm are the hallmarks of the Huntington, between Mason and Taylor Streets. Extra-large rooms offer a view of the city or the bay and overlook Huntington Park and Grace Cathedral.

My top-rated favorite hotel in San Francisco, the Huntington, is not for attention-loving glitterati. The stately hotel's low-key elegance is attractive to "old money" guests who appreciate strict privacy and unintrusive service. From Irish linens and imported silks to Ming Dynasty treasures and signature artwork, each room and suite is individually decorated with custommade and antique furnishings, as well as modern amenities, such as color TVs and hairdryers.

Dining/Entertainment: The Big Four restaurant is one of the city's most handsome cocktail lounges and dining rooms. Named for the Central Pacific Railroad's "big four" tycoons—Huntington, Stanford, Crocker, and Hopkins—the restaurant serves excellent contemporary continental cuisine, with seasonally inspired dinner entrees ranging from $13 to $29. Its walnut-paneled interior showcases an impressive collection of 19th-century photos and memorabilia. There is live piano music in the lounge nightly from 5 to 11:30pm.

Services: Room service, concierge, complimentary limousine to the Financial District and Union Square (8am to 4pm daily), overnight shoe shine, laundry, evening turndown, complimentary morning newspaper, complimentary formal tea or sherry service upon arrival.

Facilities: Access to off-premises health club.

MARK HOPKINS INTERCONTINENTAL, 1 Nob Hill, San Francisco, CA 94108. Tel. 415/392-3434, or toll free 800/327-0200. 390 rms, 27 suites. Fax 415/421-3302. A/C MINIBAR TV TEL **Cable Car:** California Street line (direct stop). **Bus:** 1.

$ Rates: $180–$275 single; $200–$305 double or twin; from $400 suite. AE, CB, DC, MC, V. **Parking:** $20.

The elegant Mark Hopkins, at the crest of Nob Hill, stands 19 stories tall and offers a marvelous view from every one of its gracious rooms. It opened in 1926 on the spot where railroad millionaire Mark Hopkin's turreted monster of a mansion once stood. The hotel gained global fame during World War II, when it was considered de rigeur for Pacific-bound servicemen to toast their good-bye to the States in the Top of the Mark cocktail lounge.

The Mark Hopkins is now a member of the Intercontinental Hotel Group. Guests are still treated to classic decor and excellent service. All the rooms have sumptuous baths, color TVs, alarm clocks, and radios. Suites offer more of the same, and the Jacuzzi Suite has a view of the Golden Gate Bridge from its private terrace. One problem with the hotel is that it has only three guest elevators, making a quick trip up to your room difficult during busy periods.

Dining/Entertainment: In addition to the famous Top of the Mark lounge, the Legends at the Mark serves breakfast, lunch, and dinner daily. Its menu is best described as international with a California flair. The Lower Bar, under a skylight roof, is a delightful setting for cocktails and piano bar entertainment Tuesday through Saturday nights.

Services: 24-hour room service, concierge, evening turndown, overnight shoe shine.

Facilities: Business center, health club, car-rental desk, no-smoking rooms.

RITZ-CARLTON, 600 Stockton St., San Francisco, CA 94108. Tel. 415/296-7465, or toll free 800/241-3333. Fax 415/296-0288. 336 rms. 44 suites. A/C MINIBAR TV TEL **Cable Car:** Powell-Hyde and Powell-Mason lines (direct stop).

$ Rates: $205–$305 standard single, double, or triple; $345 club-level single, double, or triple; from $460 suite. Weekend discounts and packages available. AE, CB, DC, DISC, MC, V. **Parking:** $25.

In April 1991, after a massive 3½-year, multimillion-dollar restoration, the Ritz-Carlton opened in an 83-year-old Nob Hill landmark. The building's majestic facade, with its 17 Ionic columns, rich filigree, winged hourglasses, carvings, and lions' heads, is indeed exquisite. The lobby is less opulent and is sometimes crowded with conventioneers and tour groups.

The new rooms, however, are up to par and, like the rest of the hotel, offer every amenity and service known to the hotel industry: Italian-marble bathrooms, with double sinks, telephone, and namebrand toiletries; remote-control TV; a stocked bar and refrigerator; and plush terry bathrobes. The more expensive rooms take advantage of the hotel's location—the south slope of Nob Hill—and have good views of the city. There is twice-daily maid service, including nightly turndown. Club rooms, located on the eighth and ninth floors, have a dedicated concierge; separate elevator-key access; and continuous complimentary meal presentations, including continental breakfast, afternoon tea, cocktails and hors d'oeuvres, and late-evening cordials and chocolates.

Dining/Entertainment: The Dining Room, the hotel's flagship restaurant, seats 96 people for intimate, elegant dining. Critically acclaimed chef Gary Danko presents his American version of classic French cuisine using strictly seasonal ingredients. The Dining Room is open Tuesday through Saturday for dinner only. The hotel's second eatery—named, simply, The Terrace—is the city's only hotel restaurant offering courtyard seating (weather permitting). Menus offer light or hearty international meals. It's open daily for breakfast, lunch, dinner, and Sunday jazz brunch. The relatively plain lobby lounge offers afternoon tea and cocktails daily, with low-key live entertainment from 3pm to 1am.

Services: Same-day valet, 24-hour room service, concierge, child care, morning newspapers delivered to guest rooms.

Facilities: Business center, fitness center, gift boutique, car-rental desk, VCR and video library, no-smoking rooms. Of the many services and facilities, the most outstanding is the fitness center, which is free to guests. A large, indoor swimming pool and an adjacent whirlpool are complimented by saunas, free weights, and Nautilus machines

STOUFFER STANFORD COURT HOTEL, 905 California St., San Francisco, CA 94108. Tel. 415/989-3500, or toll free 800/227-4736, 800/622-0957 in California. Fax 415/391-0513. 402 rms. 18 suites, A/C TV TEL **Cable Car:** Powell-Hyde and Powell-Mason lines (direct stop). **Bus:** 1.

$ Rates: $195–$295 single; $225–$325 double; from $450 suite. Extra person 18 or over, $30. AE, CB, DC, DISC, MC, V. **Parking:** $22.

The Stouffer Stanford Court stands at the top of Nob Hill (at the corner of Powell Street), and all three cable-car lines pass by its doors. Once the site of the Leland Stanford mansion and the luxurious Stanford Court Apartments, the building was constructed in 1912 and is considered a historic landmark. A lofty, stained-glass dome highlights the entrance of the hotel, and its furnishings consist of antiques and period pieces.

Many of the guest rooms have partially canopied beds, and all have a writing desk with dictionary, marble bedside tables, etchings of Old San Francisco on the walls, and oak armoires that cleverly conceal the TV set. Bathrooms include remote-control TV, telephone, heated towel racks, overhead heat lamps, hand-milled soap, and prethreaded sewing kits.

Dining/Entertainmen: Fournou's Ovens, the hotel's award-winning restaurant, features a massive, tile-faced, European roasting oven and contemporary American cuisine. Dinners here might begin with marinated lobster, scallops, and oysters with buckwheat noodles, and proceed to the likes of roast rack of lamb or grilled salmon. Main courses are $19 to $28, and the menu is often augmented with seasonal specialties. The adjacent International Bar features panoramic views of the city skyline. The Stanford Court wine cellar is truly extensive, featuring a choice of some 20,000 bottles.

Services: Concierge, 24-hour room service, complimentary service to downtown destinations via Mercedes stretch limousine, complimentary morning newspaper and coffee or tea, evening turndown service, complimentary overnight shoe shine, babysitter on call.

Facilities: Business services, including no surcharges for collect and credit-card phone calls; no-smoking rooms.

EXPENSIVE

NOB HILL LAMBOURNE SPA, 725 Pine St., San Francisco, CA 94108. Tel. 415/433-2287. 12 rms, 8 suites. A/C MINIBAR TV TEL **Cable Car:** California Street line (1 block north).

$ Rates (including continental breakfast): $119–$145 single or double; from $199 suite. AE, CB, DC, DISC, MC, V. **Parking:** $13 self, $18 valet.

Ⓕ FROMMER'S COOL FOR KIDS: HOTELS

Donatello (see p. 57) Since the Donatello has some of the biggest rooms in the city, there's plenty of space for romping. The Donatello is not cheap, but children under 12 stay free in their parents' room.

Four Seasons Clift (see p. 58) The hotel's Very Important Kids (VIK) program provides traveling families with baby blankets, teddy bears, Nintendo video games, children-size robes, and other amenities to help kids feel as pampered as their parents.

The Mansions (see p. 83) Furnished with theatrical originality, this hotel will appeal to children's creative fantasies. On-site entertainment includes nightly performances by virtuoso pianist Claudia the Ghost, who is sometimes accompanied by owner Bob Pritikin on the saw.

A small "boutique" hotel, the Lambourne bills itself as an urban spa, offering on-site massages, clay-wraps, body oilings, and yoga lessons. Even without this "hook," the Lambourne deserves a top-of-the-class rating. Sporting one of San Francisco's most-stylish interiors, the hotel flaunts every penny's worth of its recent multimillion-dollar renovation that, happily, has not favored form over function. Top-quality, hand-sewn mattresses and goose-down comforters are complemented by a host of in-room accoutrements that include desktop computers, fax machines, stereos, coffeemakers, and smartly designed contemporary furnishings. Bathrooms contain oversized tubs and hair dryers, as well as an "honor bar" of Neal's Yard–brand pamperings like geranium and orange bath oil, herbal lip balm, and jasmine moisturizer, sold for $6 to $10 each.

Guest rooms are priced according to size, but even those at the top end are relatively small. Suites include an additional sitting room, and all guests are treated to a complimentary ten-minute neck and shoulder massage, offered each afternoon.

Services: Evening turndown, business services, spa treatments.
Facilities: Spa treatment room.

3. FINANCIAL DISTRICT

VERY EXPENSIVE

ANA HOTEL SAN FRANCISCO, 50 Third St., San Francisco, CA 94103. Tel. 415/974-6400, or toll free 800/262-4683. Fax 415/543-8268. 641 rms, 26 suites. A/C MINIBAR TV TEL **Bus:** All Market Street buses. **Muni Metro:** All Market Street trams.
$ Rates: $170–$190 single or double; from $300 suite. AE, MC, V. **Parking:** $22.

Originally known as Le Meridien, this skyscraping hotel received a $28-million facelift along with its name change in 1992, when it was purchased by the company that owns Japan's second-largest airline. The hotel's large number of uniformly decorated rooms and fine location—just one block south of Market Street, and one block from the Moscone Convention Center—makes the ANA attractive to both groups and business travelers. Separate check-in facilities for conventioneers keep the main lobby clear and welcoming for independent guests.

From the outside, the ANA Hotel is an unspectacular glass-and-steel monolith. Inside, the design makes itself understood with dramatic floor-to-ceiling windows that dominate almost every guest room. Packed with accessories, rooms are well outfitted with three telephones (with voice mail), a minibar, and interesting original art work. Corner suites look across the Bay Bridge to Candlestick Park, and Executive Level rooms include continental breakfast and evening hors d'oeuvres.

Specially outfitted "Green Rooms," located on the hotel's third floor, contain air- and water-filtration systems, and environmentally friendly products like facial and bathroom tissues made from recycled paper, pens made from recycled plastics, and all-natural, biodegradable, "cruelty-free" soaps, shampoos, conditioners, and body lotions. Part of the rooms' $10 surcharge is donated to a nonprofit environmental organization.

Dining/Entertainment: Café Fifty-Three serves three meals daily, and a special Sunday brunch. The adjacent Lobby Bar serves cocktails, wine, beer, and appetizers.

Services: Room service, concierge, twice-daily maid service, overnight laundry, and dry cleaning.

Facilities: Fitness center, business center, complimentary use of nearby tennis club, gift shop, no-smoking rooms.

HYATT REGENCY SAN FRANCISCO, 5 Embarcadero Center, San Francisco, CA 94111. Tel. 415/788-1234, or toll free 800/233-1234. Fax 415/398-2567. 803 rms, 44 suites. TV TEL **Muni Metro:** All Market Street trams. **Bus:** All Market Street buses.

$ Rates: $175–$260 single or double; from $350 suite. AE, CB, DC, MC, V. **Parking:** $20.

The architecturally impressive Hyatt Regency rises from the edge of the Embarcadero Center at the foot of Market Street. The structure is shaped like a vertical triangle, with two sides forming a right angle and the stunning third sweeping inward from ground level like the side of an Egyptian pyramid, serrated with long rows of jutting balconies. The hotel was closed for three months in 1993 and reopened after a $27-million renovation that completely redesigned the public areas and updated all the hotel's technology. The stunning lobby, illuminated by museum-quality theater lighting, features flowing water and a simulated environment of California grasslands and wildflowers.

Rooms are comfortably furnished; their rich browns and earth tones are set off by bold splashes of color. Each has a color TV, clock radio, voice-mail telephone, and computer ports for modems. Some rooms have coffee/tea–making facilities, and private fax machines are available free upon request. Rooms with two double beds also include a sofa, easy chair, and cocktail table. The hotel's 16th and 17th floors house the Regency Club, with 102 larger guest rooms, private bar-lounges and games rooms, complimentary continental breakfast, after-dinner cordials, and private concierge.

Dining/Entertainment: The Eclipse Café is an open-air lobby restaurant serving three meals daily; the new Thirteen-Views Bar seats about 200 and is open for morning coffee and evening cocktails. The rooftop Equinox is a revolving lunch, dinner, and cocktail spot that gives you a complete panorama of San Francisco every 45 minutes. But perhaps the most charming place for lunch is the street cafe, where on sunny days you can watch the passing brokers, bankers, secretaries, and artists while listening to street musicians in the Embarcadero Center.

Services: 24-hour room service, concierge, laundry, overnight shoe shine.

Facilities: Business center, access to off-premises health club, swimming pool, tennis courts, and no-smoking rooms.

SHERATON PALACE HOTEL, 2 New Montgomery St., San Francisco, CA 94105. Tel. 415/392-8600, or toll free 800/ 325-3535. Fax 415/543-0671. 550 rms, 32 suites, A/C TV TEL **Muni Metro:** All Market Street trams. **Bus:** All Market Street buses.

$ Rates: $225–$295 single; $255–$315 double; from $500 suite. Additional person $20. Children under 18 sharing existing bedding stay free in parents' room. Weekend rates and packages available. **Parking:** $20.

⭐ Completed in 1875, the original Palace Hotel was one of the world's largest and most luxurious hostelries. After a two-year, $150-million renovation, the hotel reopened in April 1991. Today, behind a relatively unassuming facade, this new Sheraton hides what is without question the most spectacular lobby in San Francisco. It's the Garden Court, a San Francisco landmark, that has been restored to its original 1909 elegance. It is graced by a $7-million dome ceiling of iridescent glass, through which the sun filters, creating an amber glow. The Court is flanked by a double row of massive Italian-marble Ionic columns and is further enhanced by 10 huge chandeliers, valued at $50,000 each. The on-site, fourth-floor health club features a pretty skylight-covered lap pool, whirlpool, sauna, and exercise room.

The nostalgic elegance of every room has been lovingly restored; new coverings bless the original antiques with new life. Each room has a refrigerator, safe, color TV, and radio. In the bathrooms, high ceilings contrast with sparkling fittings, built-in hairdryers, and other contemporary accoutrements.

Dining/Entertainment: The Garden Court serves breakfast daily from 6:30 to 11am, lunch Monday through Saturday from 11:30am to 2pm, and dinner daily from 5:30 to 10pm. It's American cuisine. Afternoon tea is served Monday through Saturday from 2:30 to 5pm, and brunch is served on Sunday from 10:30am to 2pm. The Court is open for drinks Monday through Saturday until 1am.

In Maxfields' Restaurant, a traditional San Francisco grill, guests can enjoy a more intimate meal with turn-of-the-century charm, enhanced by a stained-glass ceiling and mosaic tile floor. Open daily for lunch and dinner.

The Pied Piper Bar, one of the best watering holes in San Francisco, is named for the Maxfield Parrish mural that hangs inside. Valued at approximately $2.5 million, the mural hung in the M. H. de Young Memorial Museum while the hotel underwent restoration.

Services: 24-hour room service, concierge, evening turndown, overnight dry cleaning.

Facilities: Business service center, health club, lobby-level shops, and no-smoking rooms.

EXPENSIVE

GALLERIA PARK HOTEL, 191 Sutter St., San Francisco, CA 94104. Tel. 415/781-3060, or toll free 800/792-9639. Fax 415/433-4409. 177 rms, 15 suites. A/C MINIBAR TV TEL **Muni Metro:** All Market Street trams. **Bus:** All Market Street buses.
$ Rates: $149 single or double; from $185 suite. AE, CB, DC, DISC, MC, V. **Parking:** $14.

From its impressive black-marble facade and stylized lobby—complete with fireplace and crystal skylight—to its beautifully appointed rooms and suites, the Galleria Park, at Kearney Street, has been totally restored in the art nouveau style of its original 1911 construction. A good, upscale business-class hotel, the Galleria Park offers all the expected necessities and some unusual extras, like a rooftop jogging track.

Dining/Entertainment: Bentley's seafood restaurant, on the lobby level, serves fresh seafood specialties, a variety of oysters at a grand-scale raw bar, and a good selection of nonfish dishes. There's also a bar. The adjacent piano lounge features a pianist nightly. Brasserie Chambord is the house French restaurant, serving an inspired country cuisine. Both restaurants are open daily for breakfast, lunch, and dinner.

Services: Room service, concierge.

Facilities: Rooftop running track and park, fitness room, no-smoking rooms.

4. JAPAN CENTER & ENVIRONS

EXPENSIVE

THE MANSIONS, 2220 Sacramento St., San Francisco, CA 94115. Tel. 415/929-9444. 21 rms, 5 suites. TV TEL **Bus:** 1, 3, or 83.
$ Rates (including breakfast): $129–$190 single or double; from $250 suite. AE, DC, DISC, MC, V. **Parking:** $10.

Bob Pritikin's inn, between Laguna and Buchanan streets, is one of San Francisco's most unusual and eclectic hideaways, attracting the likes of Robin Williams and Barbra Streisand. Set in a terraced garden adorned with sculptures, The Mansions are actually two historic buildings, connected by an interior corridor. Their total and often theatrical originality is reflected in Pritikin's philosophy that "The Mansions is only as good as its last performance."

Guests are greeted by a host in Victorian attire and offered a glass of wine or sherry upon check-in. Each room is different, but most rooms look out on a rose or sculpture garden, and all are furnished with well-chosen antiques, brass beds, and Victorian memorabilia. All have fresh flowers, direct-dial phones, and TVs (delivered on request). Each unit is named for a famous San Franciscan—Bufano, Coit, Huntington, or Pritikin—and includes a wall mural depicting that person's story. The ultimate indulgence is the opulent Empress Josephine Room, furnished with priceless antiques. There's even an all-glass Garden Room, partly done in spectacular stained glass.

Dining/Entertainment: Breakfast includes English crumpets, English-style banger sausages, fruit, fresh-squeezed orange juice, coffee, and more. The Victorian Cabaret Theater stages nightly performances by virtuoso pianist Claudia the Ghost, playing requests with invisible fingers. Some nights, she performs extraordinary feats of magic, and Pritikin, "America's foremost saw player," also entertains. There's also a games room with billiard tables.

MIYAKO HOTEL, 1625 Post St., San Francisco, CA 94115. Tel. 415/922-3200, or toll free 800/533-4567. Fax 415/921-0417. 218 rms, 11 suites. A/C TV TEL **Bus:** 38 Geary.

$ Rates: $99–$159 single; $129–$189 double or twin; from $279 suite. Children 18 and under stay free in parents' room. AE, CB, DC, MC, V. **Parking:** $20.

Just a mile from the heart of downtown, the Miyako is located in the Japan Center at Laguna Street, which borders Nihonmachi, the city's Japanese quarter. The center was opened in 1968 and the hotel's 15-story tower and 5-story Garden Wing overlook its fascinating complex of shops and restaurants. From the moment you enter the peaceful lobby, with its beautiful flock of origami birds at the bell desk, you know this is a successful merger of East and West. Bay Area residents often come for the weekend, hire a Japanese suite, settle into the bathtub, and leave it only for forays to Nihonmachi.

Most of the rooms are equipped with American-style beds and chairs, carpets, color TVs, and Japanese baths. Shoji screens slide away to frame views of the city. Two of the luxury suites have their own private redwood saunas and deep-tub Japanese baths. Six of the Miyako's accommodations are done in all-Japanese decor, which means you sleep on a floor laid with tatami mats and spread with huge down futons. A bamboo and rock garden runs the length of the wall and can be contemplated in peace from your sunken bathtub. Four rooms combine Eastern- and Western-style accommodations and are ideal for families.

Dining/Entertainment: The Asuka Brasserie offers continental-Japanese cuisine prepared and presented in a contemporary California garden setting. The restaurant serves breakfast, lunch, and dinner, as well as Sunday brunch, with dinner dishes at $15 to $30. The mezzanine cocktail lounge is open from 10am to 1am daily.

Services: Room service, concierge, evening turndown, overnight shoe shine.

Facilities: Business center, access to an off-premises health club, car-rental desk, and no-smoking rooms.

MODERATE

QUEEN ANNE HOTEL, 1590 Sutter St., San Francisco, CA 94109. Tel. 415/441-2828, or toll free 800/227-3970. Fax 415/775-5212. 49 rms, 4 suites. TV TEL **Bus:** 2, 3, 4, or 38.

$ Rates (including continental breakfast): $99–$150 single or double; from $175 suite. Extra person $10. AE, DC, MC, V. **Parking:** $12.

This handsomely restored Victorian mansion, one mile west of Union Square, at Octavia Street, was Miss Mary Lake's School for Girls at the turn of the century. Later it became a private gentlemen's club, then returned to its original gender as the Girl's friendly Society Lodge. After a complete restoration, it opened as the Queen Anne in 1981.

The pretty English oak-paneled lobby is furnished with antiques; the unique guest rooms preserve a turn-of-the-century atmosphere while providing all-modern conveniences. Each room has been individually decorated: Some have corner turret bay windows that look out on tree-lines streets, as well as separate parlor areas and wet bars; others have cozy reading nooks and fireplaces. All rooms have telephones with extensions in the bathroom and remote-control color TV. The Queen Anne provides complimentary continental breakfast. Services include room service, concierge, morning newspaper, and complimentary afternoon tea and sherry. There's access to an off-premises health club, with lap pool and Nautilus machines. Accommodations for the handicapped are available, as are units for non-smokers.

5. CIVIC CENTER

EXPENSIVE

THE INN AT THE OPERA, 333 Fulton St., San Francisco, CA 94102. Tel. 415/863-8400, or toll free 800/325-2708, 800/423-9610 in California. Fax 415/861-0821. 30 rms, 18 suites. MINIBAR TV TEL **Bus:** 5, 21, 47, or 49.

$ Rates (including continental breakfast): $130–$180 single or double; from $185 suite. Extra person $10. AE, MC, V. **Parking:** $16.

The Inn at the Opera is a small, elegant hotel specializing in luxurious accommodations and attentive, personalized service. This is the city's premier "boutique hotel." Tucked away in the heart of the performing-arts center, the inn has become a hideaway for both performers and patrons of the arts.

The hotel's plain facade belies its handsome interior. The reception area is light and airy, with European furnishings, fresh flowers, and old brass inkwells on the front desk. Rooms, which recently underwent a complete renovation, reflect the same warmth, with subtle pastel shades, opulent furnishings, and huge stuffed pillows. All feature queen-size beds draped with half canopies, fully stocked minibars, fresh flowers, and microwave ovens. Baths include hairdryers, scales, terry-cloth robes, and French milled soaps. The beautifully appointed suites are especially recommended.

Dining/Entertainment: Act IV Restaurant, the hotel's fine dining room, provides an intimate setting, with fireside seating, plush furnishings, original art, and soft piano accompaniment. Executive chef Kenneth Fredsted oversees the preparation of daily special menus of Mediterranean cuisine with California influences. It's open for breakfast, lunch, and dinner, as well as Sunday brunch.

Services: 24-hour room service, concierge, evening turndown, complimentary light pressing and overnight shoe shine, staff physician, complimentary limousine service to the Financial District and morning newspaper.

Facilities: Access to an off-premises health club, no-smoking rooms.

MODERATE

PHOENIX INN, 601 Eddy St., San Francisco, CA 94109. Tel. 415/776-1380, or toll free 800/248-9466. Fax 415/885-3109. 44 rms, 3 suites. TV TEL **Bus:** 19, 31, or 38.

$ Rates (including continental breakfast): $89 single or double; $129–$139 suite. AE, DC, MC, V. **Parking:** Free.

⭐ A stylish, offbeat spot at Larkin Street, the Phoenix is an unusual motel that wouldn't look out of place in the heart of Miami Beach. The fun owners like to think of this gathering place for visiting rock musicians, writers, and filmmakers as a little bit of Los Angeles transplanted to San Francisco. Indeed, the Phoenix is an island of creativity in the middle of a less than prosperous area. And if you'd like to say that you've stayed at the same inn as Linda Ronstadt, Arlo Guthrie, and the Dance Theater of Harlem, this is the place. At the center of this oasis is a small, heated outdoor pool set in a spacious courtyard and modern-sculpture garden.

Rooms are spacious, light, comfortable, and attractively decorated in pastels. Oversize furnishings and chairs are handmade of Philip-pine bamboo. Potted plants and original local art add attractive touches. The high ceilings and overhead lighting, in addition to the usual standing lamps, give an airy outdoor feeling to the rooms. In addition to the usual amenities, the inn's own closed-circuit channel shows films exclusively made in or about San Francisco, among them *The Maltese Falcon*, *Vertigo*, and *Foul Play*.

Miss Pearl's Jam House is the hotel's lobby restaurant (see Chapter 6, "San Francisco Dining," for complete information).

BUDGET

ABIGAIL HOTEL, 246 McAllister St., San Francisco, CA 94102. Tel. 415/861-9728, or toll free 800/243-6510. Fax 415/861-5848. 60 rms, 1 suite. TV TEL **Muni Metro:** All Market Street trams. **Bus:** All Market Street buses.

$ Rates: $79 single or double; $140 suite. Extra person $10. AE, CB, DC, MC, V. **Parking:** $6.

What the Abigail lacks in luxury is more than made up in charm. The handsome white exterior, with its canopy and polished brass, might have been picked up in London and set down two blocks from the San Francisco Opera. In the lobby you'll find a small desk, contemporary furnishings, and a popular cafe.

Guests rooms contain blue floral drapes, white curtains, old prints, down comforters, and an occasional antique table or lamp. Most rooms are light and quiet.

Mama Justice, the Abigail's new restaurant/cafe, is open for breakfast, lunch, and dinner.

ALBION HOUSE INN, 135 Gough St., San Francisco, CA 94102. Tel. 415/621-0896. 9 rms. TEL **Muni Metro:** All Market Street trams. **Bus:** All Market Street buses.

$ Rates (including breakfast): $75–$150 single or double. AE, MC, V. **Parking:** $3.50.

Albion House Inn, at Lily Street, is a delightful example of a successful San Francisco bed-and-breakfast. Built as a small hotel in 1907, it has since been remodeled to reflect the contemporary charm of a moderately priced Northern European bed-and-breakfast. Each room is decorated differently. Sonoma, for example, evokes images of the Wine Country with a double-size brass bed and floral prints; and Cypress, inspired by the Lone Cypress in

Carmel, is decorated in tans and furnished with a queen-size bed. All rooms have telephones and private baths; some rooms have color TVs.

The heart of the Albion House Inn is the common room, a large living room decorated in cool pinks, with exposed redwood beams and a fireplace. A full breakfast is served here each morning, set on china and silver service. Coffee and tea are available throughout the day, and complimentary brandy or wine is served each evening. There is evening turndown service.

6. COW HOLLOW

EXPENSIVE

UNION STREET INN, 2229 Union St., San Francisco, CA 94123. Tel. 415/346-0424. 5 rms (all with bath). 1 cottage. TV TEL **Bus:** 22, 41, 45, or 47.

$ Rates (including continental breakfast): $125–$175 standard single or double; $225 cottage. AE, MC, V. **Parking:** $10.

Helen Steward's Union Street Inn is a renovated Victorian-era beauty, located between Fillmore and Steiner streets. Its six rooms are well furnished with carefully selected antiques. Downstairs is a beautiful, homey parlor with apricot velvet walls, a velvet sofa, and a fireplace.

Rooms are fancifully named (Wildrose, Holly, Golden Gate, English Garden, New Yorker) and charmingly decorated. They have canopied or brass beds with polished cotton spreads, well-chosen art on the walls, a table and chairs, live plants and beautifully arranged flowers, and magazines to read. All have private baths, multipaned bay windows, and garden views. TVs are available on request, and no smoking is allowed in any of the rooms. The Cottage is similarly decorated, nuzzles up against the garden, and has a Jacuzzi in its own huge bathroom. You can have breakfast (fresh-baked croissants, with Helen's homemade kiwi or plum jam, fresh-squeezed orange juice, fruit, and coffee) in the parlor, in your room, or on an outdoor terrace overlooking a lovely garden with its own lemon tree.

MODERATE

CHELSEA MOTOR INN, 2095 Lombard St., San Francisco, CA 94123. Tel. 415/563-5600. Fax 415/346-9127. 60 rms. A/C TV TEL **Bus:** 22, 28, 30, or 76.

$ Rates: $73–$85 single; $78–$95 double. AE, CB, DC, MC, V. **Parking:** Free.

An attractive establishment on the "motel strip" that stretches from the Golden Gate Bridge to Van Ness Avenue, the Chelsea Motor Inn, at Fillmore Street, is perfectly located for a stroll along Union Street. Rooms are very comfortable and pleasantly decorated in shades of rose, blue, or brown.

BUDGET

BED & BREAKFAST INN, 4 Charlton Court, San Francisco, CA 94123. Tel. 415/921-9784. 11 rms (7 with bath), 2 suites. TV TEL **Bus:** 41 or 45.

$ Rates (including continental breakfast): $70–$90 single or double without bath, $115–$140 single or double with bath; $190–$215 suite. No credit cards. **Parking:** $7.50 a day at nearby garage.

Located in a charming courtyard just off Union Street between Buchanan and Laguna Streets, this B&B is Bob and Marily Kavanaugh's noteworthy addition to the Bay Area's hostelries. The Bed & Breakfast Inn offers exquisite accommodations, with a good level of luxury and personal service. Guests are greeted by name and introduced to each other. There's a library for guests, furnished with a writing desk, TV, and pay phone.

Rooms are located in three Victorian houses that pre-date the 1906 earthquake by several decades. Each room is uniquely and charmingly decorated—perhaps in a Casablanca motif with a peacock chair and a ceiling fan, perhaps with a Victorian or brass bed. All are wonderfully cozy and contain cherished family antiques, original art, plants and fresh flowers, fruit, a thermos of ice water, clocks, down pillows, and a selection of quality books and magazines. All the rooms with private baths also have color TVs and direct-dial telephones. Those rooms without baths have doors leading to the lovely enclosed garden out back. The Mayfair Suite, formerly the Kavanaughs' flat, has a latticed terrace and a private garden. The largest room is the Garden Suite with a full kitchen, two fireplaces, a Jacuzzi, two bedrooms, a study, and French doors leading out into the garden. Breakfast (freshly baked croissants; orange juice; and coffee, fancy teas, or cocoa) is either brought to your room on a tray with flowers and a morning newspaper or served in a sunny Victorian breakfast room with antique china. Sherry is available at all times.

COW HOLLOW MOTOR INN & SUITES, 2190 Lombard St., San Francisco, CA 94123. Tel. 415/921-5800. Fax 415/922-8515. 117 rms, 12 suites (all with bath). A/C TV TEL **Bus:** 28, 43, or 76.

$ Rates: $73 single; $78–$86 double; from $175 suite. Extra person $10. AE, DC, MC, V. **Parking:** Free.

Located at Steiner Street, this modest brick hotel comes loaded with such amenities as cable TV, free local phone calls, no-smoking rooms, free covered parking, and in-room coffeemakers. The inn is well run by hospitable co-managers Warren and Catherine Murphy.

EDWARD II INN & CARRIAGE HOUSE, 3155 Scott St., San Francisco, CA 94123. Tel. 415/922-3000, or toll free 800/473-2846. Fax 415/931-5784. 31 rms (20 with bath), 6 suites. TV TEL **Bus:** 28, 30, 43, or 76.

$ Rates (including continental breakfast): $67 single or double without bath, $85 single or double with bath; $150–$200 suite. Rates reduced Jan–Feb from Sun–Thurs. AE, MC, V. **Parking:** $9.

At Lombard Street, the well-appointed, and well-priced, Edward II was originally built in 1914 for the Pan-Pacific Exposition. It has since been transformed into a smoothly run European-style bed-and-breakfast. Guest rooms are simple and charming, with quilted bedspreads, antique and English-country rattan dressers, and white plantation shutters. All rooms have color TVs with cable hookups.

Each of the suites is different, but all, beautifully furnished, represent some of the best values in San Francisco. Four have whirlpool Jacuzzi baths and wet bars, while others have full kitchens and living rooms. They're highly recommended.

7. HAIGHT-ASHBURY

RED VICTORIAN BED AND BREAKFAST INN, 1665 Haight St., San Francisco, CA 94117. Tel. 415/864-1978. 18 rms (4 with bath), 1 suite. TEL **Muni Metro:** N line. **Bus:** 7, 66, 71, or 73.

$ Rates (including continental breakfast and afternoon tea): $60–$75 single without bath; $65–$80 double without bath, $95–$125 double with bath; $135 suite. Extra person $15. MC, V. **Parking:** Guarded lot nearby.

Owner Sami Sunchild, a confessed former flower child, runs one of the most unusual hotels in the city. Rooms with names like Japanese Tea Garden, Flower Child, and Summer of Love are inspired by San Francisco's sights and history, and are decorated accordingly. Charlotte, the house cat, has access to the Cat's Cradle room via her own cat door, and the Teddy Bear room is filled with stuffed animals. Four guest rooms have private baths; the remaining accommodations share four bathrooms down the hall, including the Aquarium Bathroom, which has guests guessing what happens to the goldfish when they flush the toilet. The unusual Peacock Suite is decorated with a Persian temple light, small shrine, and turn-of-the-century electric fireplace, and is large enough to accommodate four adults. In general, rooms and baths are clean, and the furnishings are pleasant, if a bit eccentric. No smoking is allowed in the rooms.

A continental breakfast is served every morning in the Inn's Global Village Center and Gallery, a storefront gift shop.

STANYAN PARK HOTEL, 750 Stanyan St., San Francisco, CA 94117. Tel. 415/751-1000. Fax 415/668-5454. 36 rms (all with bath), 6 suites. TV TEL **Muni Metro:** N line. **Bus:** 7, 33, 71, or 73.

$ Rates (including continental breakfast): $78–$96 single or double; from $130 suite. Extra person $20. AE, CB, DC, DISC, MC, V. **Parking:** $5.

Another inn-style hostelry is the Stanyan Park, at Waller Street, across from Golden Gate Park. It has operated as a hotel under a variety of names since 1904. In its current incarnation, it's a charming, three-story establishment decorated with antique-style furnishings; Victorian wallpaper; and pastel quilts, curtains, and carpets. Modern amenities include color TVs, direct-dial phones, and tub/shower baths, complete with massaging shower head and shampoos and fancy soaps.

There are one-bedroom and two-bedroom suites. Each has a full kitchen, and formal dining and living rooms, and can sleep up to six comfortably; they're ideal for families. Complimentary tea and cookies are served each afternoon.

8. AROUND TOWN

EXPENSIVE

THE SHERATON AT FISHERMAN'S WHARF, 2500 Mason St., San Francisco, CA 94133. Tel. 415/362-5500, or toll free 800/325-3535. Fax 415/956-5275. 525 rms, 6 suites. A/C TV TEL **Cable Car:** Powell-Mason line (1 block east, two blocks south). **Bus:** 15, 32, or 42.

$ Rates: $139–$190 single or double; from $275 suite. Extra person $20. AE, CB, DC, DISC, MC, V. **Parking:** $12.

Built in the mid-1970s, this modernistic, three-story stucco hotel is not architecturally outstanding but, as a Sheraton, it offers some of the most reliably comfortable rooms in the touristy Fisherman's Wharf area. The no-bones business-hotel interior features attractive, though nondescript, guest rooms, outfitted in soft pastels. The hotel is located near the water, at Beech Street; its relatively high tariff is a reflection of its fine location.

Dining/Entertainment: The Mason Beach Grill serves breakfast, lunch, and dinner daily. The menu is heavy on seafood. Chanen's Lounge is a Victorian-style piano bar offering live jazz several nights a week, along with cocktails and assorted appetizers.

Services: 24-hour room service, concierge, evening turndown.

Facilities: Outdoor heated swimming pool, access to nearby health club, business center, hair salon, car-rental desk, travel desk, no-smoking rooms.

PIED A TERRE, 2424 Washington St., San Francisco, CA. Tel. 415/929-8033, or toll free 800/627-2396. 2 apts. A/C TV TEL

$ Rates: $150–$200 double. Weekly rates available. **Parking:** On street only.

If you want to live like the locals—the rich locals—then I can make no better suggestion than the Pied à Terre apartments. The fully equipped rentals are superbly located in Pacific Heights, between Alta Plaza and Lafayette parks, just a block from the upper Fillmore shopping area. Each apartment has two bedrooms, a living room, two fireplaces, and a gourmet kitchen complete with stylish dishwasher, gas range, large refrigerator, and microwave oven. Adjacent dining areas have room enough for up to eight guests, and laundry facilities are available.

MODERATE

THE ARCHBISHOP'S MANSION, 1000 Fulton St., San Francisco, CA 94117. Tel. 415/563-7872, or toll free 800/543-5820. 10 rms, 5 suites. A/C TEL TV **Bus:** 19, 31, or 38.

$ Rates (including continental breakfast): $115–$207 single or double; from $289 suite. AE, MC, V. **Parking:** Free.

Built in 1904 for the archbishop of San Francisco, this authentic turn-of-the-century parkfront mansion is one of the city's most unusual upscale bed-and-breakfasts. A historic landmark, the mansion's elegant rooms are each unique in character, color, shape, and size. Furnishings include oversize four-poster and canopied beds, copious antiques, and embroidered linens, which in suites extend to private sitting areas. Most rooms have working fireplaces, as well as large old-fashioned bathtubs or Jacuzzis. The home's interior is decorated with polished redwood paneling, beam ceilings, and a magnificent, palatial staircase.

The mansion's considerable size and sturdy wall construction provide guests at this B&B with more privacy than most. The tradeoff is lost intimacy, as well as a lack of services and facilities that can be expected at most similarly priced hotels.

Facilities: Breakfast is served each morning in guests' rooms.

Services: Complimentary morning newspaper and afternoon wine.

LOMBARD HOTEL, 1015 Geary St., San Francisco, CA 94109. Tel. 415/673-5232, or toll free 800/777-3210. 100 rms (all with bath). TV TEL **Bus:** 2, 3, 4, 19, or 38.

$ Rates: $83–$89 single or double. Extra person $10. Children under 12 stay free in parents' room. AE, CB, DC, DISC, MC, V. **Parking:** $10.

The Lombard Hotel, at Polk Street, is the kind of hostelry you might expect to find on a fashionable London street. It's about six blocks west of Union Square and half a dozen blocks north of the Civic Center. Most rooms feature queen-size beds; all have private baths with tubs and/or showers. There are a billiards room and sun deck, plus complimentary morning limousine service to the Financial District.

The marble-floored lobby boasts a grand piano and fireplace and is perfect for tea or sherry, which is served each afternoon. Also in the lobby is the small Gray Derby restaurant, where breakfast is served.

BUDGET

SAN FRANCISCO INTERNATIONAL HOSTEL, Building 240, Fort Mason, San Francisco, CA 94123. Tel. 415/771-7277. 156 beds. **Bus:** 19, 30, 42, 47, or 49.

$ Rates: $13 per person. Maximum stay 5 nights. MC, V (to hold reservation only).

Some of the cheapest accommodations in San Francisco are these well-located dormitory rooms, inside a park between the Golden Gate Bridge and Fisherman's Wharf. Anyone can use the dormitory, regardless of age, and the facility is handicapped accessible. For families or compatible couples, there are three rooms with four bunks, obviously in great demand. Kitchen facilities are available, as are lockers, laundry facilities, snack-vending machines, and several community rooms with fireplaces, stereo, piano, and a wide selection of books. You'll also find several bulletin boards with information on tours and places to go during your stay. Rooms are closed to guests from 11am to 1pm. Call to find out if there's space, from 7am until midnight.

CHAPTER 6

SAN FRANCISCO DINING

According to San Francisco columnist-laureate Herb Caen, "A city has to be a place where you can get blinis and caviar, fisherman's spaghetti, white figs and prosciutto, a '45 Mouton Rothschild, or a movie in any one of six languages. . . ." San Francisco is such a city—and more. You can also get Moroccan couscous, Szechuan shrimp, Indonesian rijstaffel, and a decent pastrami on rye—all within walking distance of one another.

Ethnic flavors have a solid history here. Spanish and Mexican cuisines were established in the Bay Area long before the Anglos arrived. Scores of Chinese, French, and Germans who arrived for the Gold Rush remained in the city to cook. They were followed by Russians, Italians, Basques, Filipinos, Japanese, Greeks, and Scandinavians, most of whom started by catering to their own compatriots. Vietnamese and Thai immigrants have added the newest culinary options.

With the exception of New York and Los Angeles, San Francisco is quite possibly the most cuisine-conscious city in the United States. Its citizens take food seriously. One reason might be the wine—San Francisco is within minutes of some of the world's finest vineyards. The vast majority of city restaurants offer a good selection of California wines, including house table wines that are often served from unlabeled bottles—French rural style.

No matter what you want to eat, you will be able to find it in San Francisco. And happily, there are also a fair number of moderately priced establishments to choose from. In this chapter, I have tried to include a selection of restaurants in each price category to cover the gamut from Continental to California, hamburgers to hummus.

Restaurants below are divided first by area, then by price, using the following guide: **Expensive,** more than $40 per person; **Moderate,** $20 to $40 per person; **Inexpensive,** $10 to $20 per person; and **Budget,** less than $10 per person.

These categories reflect the price of the majority of dinner menu items and include an appetizer, main course, coffee, dessert, tax, and tip.

1. UNION SQUARE

EXPENSIVE

FLEUR DE LYS, 777 Sutter St., at Jones St. Tel. 673-7779.

Cuisine: FRENCH. **Reservations:** Recommended. **Bus:** 2, 3, 4, 27, or 38.

$ Prices: Appetizers $8–$20; main courses $25–$30; five-course tasting menu $62.50; four-course vegetarian menu $50. AE, CB, DC, MC, V.

Open: Dinner only, Mon–Thurs 6–10pm, Fri–Sat 5:30–10:30pm.

⭐ Visually and gastronomically delightful, Fleur de Lys is one of the city's most celebrated and romantic dining spots. The lovely interior, designed by the late Michael Taylor, elegantly captures a feeling of the French countryside. Tables are set under an immense, burgundy color garden tent made of locally hand-printed fabric, evoking an autumnal, rustic mood.

Host Maurice Rouas and executive chef Hubert Keller are also the restaurant's co-owners, ensuring perfect preparations and top service to each patron. Chef Keller has distinguished himself by serving under such great French masters as Roger Verge, Paul Haeberlin, and Paul Bocuse. The Provençal fare includes such appetizers as foie gras salad, venison with black chanterelle sauce, and crispy sweetbreads with rock shrimp mousse and citrus peppercorn vinaigrette. Main courses include grilled swordfish with whole-grain mustard and spinach-wrapped lamb with garlic and truffle oil. In addition to the impressive à la carte menu, a five-course tasting menu is offered, featuring daily market selections. A four-course vegetarian menu is also available. An appropriately extensive wine list features both French and California vintages.

MASA'S, in the Hotel Vintage Court, 648 Bush St., at Stockton St. Tel. 989-7154.

Cuisine: FRENCH. **Reservations:** Required; accepted up to 21 days in advance. **Cable Car:** Mason and Hyde. **Bus:** 2, 3, 4, 30, or 45.

$ Prices: Appetizers $11.50–$19; main courses $30–$38.50; fixed-price dinner $68–$75. AE, CB, DC, DISC, MC, V.

Open: Dinner only, Tues–Sat 6–9:30pm. **Closed:** First week in Jan and July 4th week.

After the death of founder Masataha Kobayashi in 1984, local gourmets questioned the future of Masa's—but no more. Chef Julian Serrano's brilliant cuisine and the elegant but simple decor have solidified the restaurant's reputation as one of the country's great French outposts.

Either fixed price or à la carte, dinner is a memorable experience from start to finish. You might begin with fresh foie gras smothered in pan juices, cognac, and black truffles. The sautéed médaillons of venison, served with a rich brown sauce, are also recommended, as are any of the game-bird dishes. The wine list includes some excellent older French wines as well as an impressive cache of California bottles. No smoking is allowed.

IMPRESSIONS

[San Francisco is] the city that knows how.
—PRESIDENT WILLIAM HOWARD TAFT

[San Francisco is] the city that knows chow.
—TRADER VIC, RESTAURATEUR

POSTRIO, 545 Post St. Tel. 776-7825.
Cuisine: AMERICAN. **Reservations:** Required. **Cable Car:** Mason and Hyde. **Bus:** 2, 3, 4, or 38.
$ Prices: Appetizers and pastas $8–$15; main courses $18–$25; breakfast $6–$15. AE, CB, DC, DISC, MC, V.
Open: Breakfast Mon–Fri 7–10am; lunch daily 11:30am–2pm; dinner daily 5:30–10:30pm; brunch Sat–Sun 9am–2pm; bar daily 11:30am–2am.

Celebrity chef Wolfgang Puck has brought his fame and formula to San Francisco in the form of this trendy eatery on Post Street at Mason Street, adjacent to the Prescott Hotel. Best known for his Los Angeles restaurant Spago, Puck presides over Postrio with two other executive chefs, Anne and David Gingrass.

The dramatic art-gallery interior is as creative as the cuisine. Breakfast here means cinnamon-raisin French toast with strawberry jam and maple syrup; or a trio of salmon, sturgeon, and whitefish served on homemade bagels.

Lunchtime pastas can be ordered as appetizer or main-course portions. Whimsical concoctions include clam-filled dumplings with angel hair pasta, and crispy, grilled sweetbreads with pumpkin ravioli. Spago won fame for its designer pizzas, many of which have been imported here. Toppings like smoked salmon, crème fraîche, and golden caviar have never even been imagined in Naples.

The gloves come off at dinner when elegant first courses include home-smoked sturgeon with potato pancakes, and crabcakes served with smoked red-pepper sauce. Selecting just one main course is equally frustrating. Possibilities may include roast dungeness crab with spicy curry risotto, crispy Wolf Ranch quail with spicy pineapple sauce, or grilled squab with noodle cakes and blackberry sauce. An exceptionally diverse wine selection spans the globe and deserves special attention. Gourmet pizzas are served at the bar well into the night, pleasing a see-and-be-seen crowd. Reservations are essential, as this is one of the hottest restaurants in the city.

MODERATE

CAFE CLAUDE, 7 Claude Lane. Tel. 392-3505.
Cuisine: FRENCH. **Reservations:** Accepted. **Cable Car:** Powell-Hyde and Powell-Mason lines.
$ Prices: Appetizers $3–$7; main courses $5–$9.50. AE, MC, V.
Open: Mon–Thurs 8:30am–9:30pm, Fri–Sat 8:30am–10pm.

Crammed and crazy, Café Claude, situated on a quaint little lane near Union Square, is San Francisco's most authentic Parisian bistro. Seemingly everything—every table, every spoon, every salt-shaker, and every waiter—is imported from France. A tin *Buvez Pepsi* sign attracts young trendies who create a fun, lively atmosphere. There is usually live jazz on weekends, and, with prices topping out at about $9 for entrees like pan-fried sturgeon, Café Claude is a terrific value.

ICHIRIN, 330 Mason St., at O'Farrell St. Tel. 956-6085.

Cuisine: JAPANESE. **Reservations:** Accepted. **Cable Car:** Mason and Hyde. **Bus:** 27, 38, or any Market Street bus. **Muni Metro:** All Market Street trams.

$ Prices: Appetizers $3–$8; main courses $15–$20. AE, DC, MC, V.

Open: Dinner daily 5–10:30pm.

First-rate food and service sets Ichirin apart from other local Japanese joints. In addition to a full sushi bar, the restaurant specializes in shabu shabu—thinly sliced beef, vegetables, and tofu, cooked tableside by kimono-clad waitresses. Some 28 appetizers include gyoza, deep-fried chicken wings, and marinated broiled beef wrapped with green onion. Fixed-price lunches are a chef's choice of appetizer, main course, and dessert, in traditional Japanese fashion. Private tatami rooms are available.

JOHN'S GRILL, 63 Ellis St., at Stockton St. Tel. 986-DASH.

Cuisine: AMERICAN. **Reservations:** Accepted. **Cable Car:** Mason and Hyde. **Bus:** 38, or any Market Street bus. **Muni Metro:** All Market Street trams.

$ Prices: Appetizers $5–$10; main courses $12–$25. AE, DC, DISC, MC, V.

Open: Mon–Sat 11am–10pm, Sun 5–10pm.

John's was one of Dashiell Hammett's regular hangouts in the 1920s, and the restaurant has been cashing in on that connection ever since. You may recall that in *The Maltese Falcon,* Sam Spade stops here for chops, a baked potato, and sliced tomatoes, before setting out on a wild-goose chase after the mysterious Brigid O'Shaughnessy. Say you don't recall? Well, it's a nice place anyway.

The wood-and-leather dining room and ground-floor bar are fitted with glass chandeliers and white-clothed tables. The like-themed menu features "Sam Spade's Chops," a re-creation of the detective's *Maltese Falcon* meal, as well as straightforward American dishes like chicken Jerusalem, with fresh artichokes, mushrooms, and white wine; oysters Wellington; and shrimp- and crab-stuffed filet of sole, baked in lemon-and-butter sauce. Jack LaLanne's reputed favorite is the salad of crab, shrimp, avocado, mushrooms, chopped egg, and tomato. Specialty drinks are also available, including Bloody Brigid

---

**FROMMER'S SMART TRAVELER:
RESTAURANTS**

1. Go ethnic. The city has some great, inexpensive ethnic dining.
2. Eat your main meal at lunch, when prices are lower; you can sample gourmet hot spots for a fraction of the prices charged at dinner.
3. Watch the liquor; it can add greatly to the cost of any meal.
4. Look for fixed-price menus, two-for-one specials, and coupons in local newspapers and magazines.

(O'Shaughnessy), a mix of vodka, soda, fresh pineapple, lime, grenadine, and the like, served in a souvenir glass that you can take home with you. Despite the hype, the food here is really good.

KULETO'S, 221 Powell St., at Geary St. Tel. 397-7720.
   Cuisine: NORTHERN ITALIAN. **Reservations:** Recommended.
   Cable Car: Mason and Hyde. **Bus:** 2, 3, 4, or 38.
$ **Prices:** Breakfast $3–$8; appetizers $4–$9; main courses $8–$17. AE, CB, DC, DISC, MC, V.
   Open: Breakfast Mon–Fri 7–10:30am, Sat and Sun 8–10:30am; lunch/dinner daily 11:30am–11pm.

S There are hundreds of Italian restaurants in the city, but exceptionally good food, unusual preparations, a comfortable setting, and moderate prices make Kuleto's hard to beat. For the full effect, enter through the Powell Street bar. Between yesteryear's high ceilings and the black-and-white–marble tile floors, over a magnificently long mahogany bar, hang strings of dried peppers and garlic. Kuleto's is the familiar, friendly restaurant you've known for years—even if you've never been here before.

The same extensive northern Italian menu filled with Tuscan specialties is offered at both lunch and dinner. Antipasti include calamari fritti, and roasted garlic, meant to be squeezed and spread over the crusty Italian bread. For a main dish the management suggests sausage and peppers with Parmesan polenta, or roast duck with grappa-soaked cherries. But go with what you like, as I favor the fresh fish, which is grilled over the hardwoods, The well-selected wine list includes some fine champagnes.

MARRAKECH, 419 O'Farrell St., at Taylor St. Tel. 776-6717.
   Cuisine: MOROCCAN. **Reservations:** Recommended. **Cable Car:** Mason and Hyde. **Bus:** 38, or any Market Street bus. **Muni Metro:** All Market Street trams.
$ **Prices:** Appetizers $3–$7; main courses $9–$17; fixed-price dinner $20–$24. AE, MC, V.
   Open: Dinner only, daily 6–10pm.

Both a belly and an eye full, a meal at Marrakech is a ritual feast. The restaurant itself is a sumptuous regal palace. Enter past a marble pool, and take your place on a goatskin ottoman atop high-quality Oriental rugs. At once you are served by waiters in kaftans, who wash and dry your hands while a belly dancer weaves her way between the tables.

Choose from four award-winning multiple-course, fixed-price menus, each of which includes a piquant Moroccan salad, meant to be scooped up with chunks of homemade bread; and b'stila, a mixture of chicken, egg, and almonds, encased in phyllo dough. Next, choose among chicken with lemons, lamb with honey, lamb with onions, and hare with paprika, all eaten by hand. Couscous follows, itself preceded by fruit and mint tea.

BUDGET

THE FAMILY INN COFFEE SHOP, 505 Jones St., at Geary St. Tel. 771-5995.
   Cuisine: AMERICAN. **Reservations:** Not accepted. **Cable Car:** Mason and Taylor. **Bus:** 2, 3, 4, or 38.
$ **Prices:** Appetizers $1–$3; main courses $4–$6. No credit cards.
   Open: Tues–Fri 7am–6pm; Sat 7am–4:30pm.

If you want a really inexpensive, hearty meal, it's hard to top the Family Inn. The menu varies daily, but homemade soups are featured at lunch, along with a special so cheap they're practically giving it away—a main course served with mashed potatoes, a vegetable, bread, and dessert costs less than $5. It's not the least bit fancy—just counter seats in front of a hard-working kitchen—but the food is wholesome, good, and the price is right.

SALMAGUNDI, 442 Geary St., at Taylor St. Tel. 441-0894.
Cuisine: AMERICAN SOUP. **Reservations:** Not accepted.
Cable Car: Mason and Taylor. **Bus:** 2, 3, 4, or 38.
$ Prices: Soups and salads $3–$8. AE, MC, V.
Open: Tues–Sat 11am–11pm, Sun–Mon 11am–9pm.

Modern, bright, and pleasant, Salmagundi is a casual soupery, offering three unusual varieties daily. Among the possibilities are English country Cheddar, Hungarian goulash, North Beach minestrone, Barbary Coast bouillabaisse, and Ukrainian beef borscht. Sandwiches and salads are also available.

The atmosphere is pleasant, clean, and casual. Highly polished wood floors are topped with Formica tables and bentwood chairs. Seats in the rear look out onto a tiny garden.

2. FINANCIAL DISTRICT

EXPENSIVE

HARBOR VILLAGE, 4 Embarcadero Center, Lobby level, at Sacramento St. Tel. 781-8833.
Cuisine: CHINESE. **Reservations:** Recommended. **Bus:** 15, 45, or 76.
$ Prices: Appetizers $8–$14; main courses $9–$30. AE, DC, MC, V.
Open: Lunch Mon–Fri 11am–2:30pm. Sat 10:30am–2:30pm, Sun 10am–2:30pm; dinner daily 5:30–9:30pm.

One of the city's most upscale Chinese restaurants, Harbor Village claims to have introduced Imperial cuisine—the classical Cantonese cuisine of Hong Kong—to this country. Five hand-picked, imported specialty chefs work under the direction of executive chef Andy Wai. And though most of the dishes are steadfastly Cantonese, the kitchen seems equally at home with spicy Szechuan dishes and such popular "northern" specialties as crackling Peking duck. Crystal chandeliers, porcelain place settings, and delicate engraved chopsticks aren't chop suey either. Nor are the six opulent private dining rooms, each laid with Chinese antiquities and teak furnishings.

An uncharacteristically courteous staff can guide you through the extensive menu, which includes some 30 seafood dishes alone. Unique appetizers include shredded spicy chicken and minced squab in lettuce cups. Stir-fried garlic prawns and sizzling beef in black-pepper sauce are excellent main-course choices. Among several wine selections, the house chardonnay is especially drinkable, at about $14 a bottle.

The restaurant offers free validated parking at all the Embarcadero Center garages (located at the foot of Clay Street) after 5pm Monday through Friday and all day on Saturday, Sunday, and holidays.

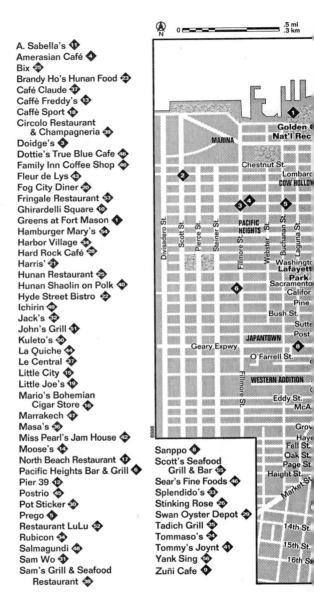

SCOTT'S SEAFOOD GRILL & BAR, 3 Embarcadero Center, 3rd Floor. Tel. 981-0622.

Cuisine: SEAFOOD. **Reservations:** Recommended.

$ Prices: Appetizers $3–11; lunch $9–19; main courses $11–$28. AE, CB, DC, DISC, MC, V.

Open: Mon–Thurs 11am–10pm, Fri–Sat 11am–11pm. Sun 4:30–9:30pm.

Although there are several Scott's Seafood Grills around California, this is no corporate-style chain eatery. The restaurants chefs and

SAN FRANCISCO DINING

San Francisco Bay

managers are encouraged to experiment and create an environment that's appropriate to their location. This Scott's, located in the heart of San Francisco's Financial District, had earned an excellent reputation for its seafood dishes, prepared with lots of fresh herbs and spices and served in a modern country-French setting. White-clothed tables, each topped with a small hurricane lamp and separated by massive gray-stone pillars and brass railings, front floor-to-ceiling windows. During warm weather, diners can choose to eat al fresco, on a terrace under large green umbrellas.

Creamy clam chowder, seafood salads, and pan-fried sole are Scott's signature lunch dishes. Dinners are more exotic and include local sand dabs, Cajun-style fried oyster pasta, and a selection of fresh fish that changes daily. There is a good wine list available by the glass, as well as an unusual wheat beer.

JACK'S, 615 Sacramento St., at Montgomery St. Tel. 986-9854.

Cuisine: CONTINENTAL. **Reservations:** Recommended. **Bus:** 15 or 41.

$ Prices: Appetizers $2.50–$9; main courses $9–$22; fixed-price dinner $19. AE.

Open: Mon–Fri 11:30am–9:30pm, Sat 5–9:30pm.

Founded in 1864, this venerated San Francisco institution at Montgomery Street, claims a fanatically faithful following. The wooden Thonet chairs, worn tile floors, and sure-footed waiters all look as they might have a century ago. Despite all appearances, this is a relatively fancy place, and jackets are suggested for men.

Choices run the gamut from cheese blintzes to Thanksgiving-style roast-turkey dinners, but the real specialty here is the rex sole. Fixed-price dinners are served from 5 to 9pm only, and are usually a particularly good buy.

LE CENTRAL, 453 Bush St. Tel. 391-2233.

Cuisine: FRENCH/CALIFORNIA. **Reservations:** Recommended. **Bus:** 15, 45, or 76.

$ Prices: Appetizers $5–$9; main courses $12–$20. AE, DISC, MC, V.

Open: Mon–Sat 11:30am–10:30pm.

Since 1974, Le Central, on Bush Street between Kearny Street and Grant Avenue, has been one of San Francisco's best versions of a classic Parisian bistro. A pair of long and narrow, mirrored dining rooms are lined with simple tables. The food is equally simple and very good. The day's specials are chalked on a small board, though you probably will want to order the cassoulet which, as the sign says, has been simmering on the stove since opening. Roast chicken and rack of lamb are also good bets, primarily because of the crispy pommes frites that accompany them. Even with a reservation, there can be a wait on the weekends.

SAM'S GRILL AND SEAFOOD RESTAURANT, 374 Bush St. Tel. 421-0594.

Cuisine: SEAFOOD. **Reservations:** Accepted only for parties of six or more. **Bus:** 15, 45, or 76.

$ Prices: Appetizers $4–$13; main courses $7–$20. AE, DC, MC, V.

Open: Mon–Fri 11am–8:30pm.

Power-lunching at Sam's is a San Francisco tradition, and they've been doing a brisk business with Financial District types for more than 40 years. The entry, which holds a lovingly polished, small mahogany bar, opens onto a main dining room where most of the seating is in booths with shoulder-high partitions. It's pretty noisy at midday, but if privacy is your primary concern, choose one of the individually curtained booths that line the corridor to the left of the main dining room.

For lunch, consider the clam chowder, charcoal-broiled filet of fish, and a dessert of French pancakes anisette. Luncheon specials might include bones rex sole à la Sam, or fresh crab au gratin. The restaurant is located near Kearny Street.

🄵 FROMMER'S COOL FOR KIDS: RESTAURANTS

Hard Rock Café *(see p. 115)* Touristy but fun, the famous Hard Rock chain flips one of the best burgers in town.

Little Joe's *(see p. 105)* Although it's often busy, Joe's is not cramped—it's fun. Children will like the convivial atmosphere, as well as the simple pasta and meat dishes.

Marrakech *(see p. 96)* Whose children wouldn't like to eat with their hands in a fancy restaurant? Marrakech is dining entertainment, complete with music, dancing, and a totally themed environment. For adventurous children only.

SPLENDIDO'S, 4 Embarcadero Center. Tel. 986-3222.
 Cuisine: MEDITERRANEAN/AMERICAN. **Reservations:** Accepted. **Bus:** 15, 45, or 76.
$ Prices: Appetizers $5–$10; main courses $7–$14 at lunch, $10–$23 at dinner. AE, DC, DISC, MC, V.
 Open: Lunch Mon–Fri 11:30am–2:30pm; dinner daily 5:30–10pm.

⭐ It's difficult to believe that the feel of a small, old-world Mediterranean village could be captured within such an architecturally sophisticated building, but designer Pat Kuleto (who also worked magic on Postrio) has done just that, using 200-year-old olivewood doors, Moorish arches, rustic French stone walls, Italian tiles, Spanish wrought-iron banisters, and a Portuguese pewter-topped bar. Stone pillars, huge hand-hewn beams, wormwood cabinetry, and soft rose lighting are used to create intimate dining areas. When the weather is pleasant you can eat under a canopy on the outdoor patio, or choose the exhibition seating in front of the full-display kitchen, complete with an open grill and wood-burning pizza oven.

And then there's the food. Beautifully presented starters might include curry soup with spiced chicken; or ravioli of prosciutto, mascarpone, and shallots. Main courses may feature pan-roasted quail with lemon and herb dumplings; sautéed sweetbreads with pancetta vinaigrette, wild mushrooms, and chestnuts; or grilled loin of lamb with white-bean/garlic flan. The dessert creations of pastry chef Cameron Ryan are surely procured from somewhere beyond the pearly gates. The list may include polenta cake with fresh strawberry sauce; a frozen terrine of pears, chocolate, Armagnac, and prunes; tiramisù with chocolate pinenut bark; or my favorite, pistachio crème brûlée. Like the pasta and baked goods, all the desserts are prepared fresh daily in the restaurants hard-working bakery. An excellent wine list is especially notable for its good selection of wines by the glass. The restaurant is located between Clay and Drum streets.

TADICH GRILL, 240 California St. Tel 391-1849.
 Cuisine: SEAFOOD. **Reservations:** Not accepted. **Bus:** All Market Street buses. **Muni Metro:** All Market Street trams.
$ Prices: Appetizers $7–$13; main courses $12–$25. MC, V.
 Open: Mon–Fri 11am–9pm, Sat 11:30am–9pm.

The famous, venerated old California institution that is the Tadich Grill arrived with the Gold Rush in 1849, and maintains the handsome dignity of the successful survivor it is. Tradition is honored by an ageless mahogany bar that extends the entire length of the restaurant. No-nonsense white-linen–draped tables are topped with big plates of sourdough bread. Power-lunchers get one of the seven enclosed private booths.

Tadich's claims to be the very first to broil seafood over mesquite-hardwood charcoal, back in the early 1920s. Then it was known simply as charcoal broiling. Their reputation was immediately solidified, and it continues to be fantastic. For a light meal you might try one of the delicious seafood salads, like shrimp or prawn Louis, with a glass of wine, fresh sourdough bread, and butter. Hot dishes include baked avocado with shrimp diablo, baked casserole of stuffed turbot with crab and shrimp à la Newburg, and mesquite-charcoal–broiled petrale sole with butter sauce—a local favorite. Anyone who's anyone gets a side order of big, tasty french fries. The restaurant is located between Battery and Front streets.

INEXPENSIVE

YANK SING, 49 Stevenson St. Tel. 541-4949.

Cuisine: CHINESE. **Reservations:** Not accepted. **Bus:** 5, 6, or 38. **Muni Metro:** All Market Street trams.

$ Prices: Dim sum $2–$4 per plate. AE, MC, V.

Open: Mon–Fri 11am–3pm.

Loosely translated as "a delight of the heart," dim sum are any number of Chinese appetizers traditionally served around brunch time. Most dim sum are dumplings, filled with tasty concoctions of pork, beef, fish, or vegetables. Congees (porridges), spareribs, stuffed crab claws, scallion pancakes, shrimp balls, pork buns, and other palate pleasers complete the menu. Like most good dim sum meals, at Yank Sing you get to choose the small dishes from a cart that's continually wheeled around the dining room and reloaded in the kitchen. Whether you're a novice or veteran dim sum eater, Yank Sing is heartily recommended. A good fill will cost about $15. The restaurant is located a block south of Market Street, at First Street.

A second restaurant is at 427 Battery St. (tel. 362-1640), in the Financial District.

BUDGET

HUNAN RESTAURANT, 924 Sansome St. Tel. 956-7727.

Cuisine: CHINESE. **Reservations:** Accepted. **Bus:** 15, 45, or 76.

$ Prices: Appetizers $4–$7; main courses $7–$11. AE, DC, DISC, MC, V.

Open: Daily 11am–9:30pm.

It's not much to look at, even by Chinese-restaurant standards, but even noted food critic Craig Claiborne has sung the praises of this restaurant, near Broadway. Regulars choose either the onion cakes or the dumplings (often called pot stickers) as an appetizer, then move on to hot-and-sour beef, chef Henry Chung's special chicken, or bean curd (tofu) with pickled vegetables. There are a number of spicy dishes, but the kitchen does their best to accommodate delicate palates.

3. NORTH BEACH

EXPENSIVE

BIX, 56 Gold St. Tel. 433-6300.

Cuisine: CALIFORNIA. **Reservations:** Recommended. **Bus:** 15, 30, 41, or 45.

$ Prices: Appetizers $5–$10, main courses $11–$25; lunch $5–$12. AE, CB, DC, DISC, MC, V.

Open: Mon–Thurs 11:30am–11pm, Fri–Sat 11:30am–midnight, Sun 6–10pm.

Located in the middle of a narrow alley near Columbus Avenue, BIX looks and smells very much like an upscale 1930s-era speakeasy. A small, dimly lit dining room, taller than it is wide, is overlooked by a second seating area on a wraparound balcony. Clubby tables are topped with shaded candles that cast shadows on the room's dark redwood walls and ornately capitaled columns. Perfectly suited to the see-and-be-seen set, the restaurant offers good sightlines, and a particularly busy bar. A singer usually sits at a grand piano, though it's hard to hear him over the din of the crowd.

BIX is not the place to rush through a meal; diners linger for the night, and table turnover is low. Consequently food is expensive; but happily, it's worth it. Lobster-bisque pasta is especially recommended, as are the potato and leek pancakes wrapped around smoked salmon, with caviar and crème fraîche. Entrees, which are heavy on seafood, include sand dabs with asparagus, and salmon with aïoli and fried capers. Grilled meats include pork and lamb chops, and thick-cut steaks. At lunch, smaller portions are offered at smaller prices.

CAFFE SPORT, 574 Green St. Tel. 981-1251.

Cuisine: ITALIAN. **Reservations:** Accepted only for parties of four or more. **Bus:** 15, 30, 41, or 45.

$ Prices: Appetizers $5–$9; main courses $14–$29. AE, DC, MC, V.

Open: Lunch Tues–Thurs noon–2pm, Fri–Sat noon–2:30pm. Dinner Tues–Thurs seatings at 5, 6:30, 8:30, and 10pm; Fri–Sat at 6:30, 8:30, and 10pm.

You either love or hate this robust Sicilian eatery between Grant and Columbus avenues. The dining room is a clutter of hanging hams and sausages, fishnets, decorative plates, dolls, and mirrors. Artful tables and chairs are hand-painted and colorfully collaged. The restaurant is better known for its surly staff and eclectic ambience than for its fine food. Owner/chef/artiste Antonion Latona serves up healthy portions of attitude along with garlic-laden pasta dishes and is happy to report that this former Mayor Diane Feinstein's favorite eatery.

Lunch is less hectic; at dinner the Sport is mobbed and lively. Disregard the framed menu that sits on each table and accept the waiter's "suggestions." Whatever arrives—whether it be a dish of calamari, mussels, and shrimp in tomato-garlic sauce, or pasta in pesto sauce—it will be delicious. Bring a huge appetite, but above all, don't be late if you have a reservation.

MOOSE'S, 1652 Stockton St. Tel. 989-7800.

Cuisine: CONTINENTAL. **Reservations:** Recommended. **Bus:** 15, 30, 41, or 45.

$ Prices: Appetizers $5–$11, main courses $8–$25, lunch $7–$14. AE, CB, DC, MC, V.

Open: Sun–Thurs 11:30am–11pm, Fri–Sat 11:30am–midnight. (Bar stays open later.)

Overlooking Washington Square Park, a big, blue, stylized neon moose beckons diners into the restaurant's two huge dining rooms enlivened with blown-glass chandeliers and Romanesque archways. Most of the herd that grazes there are well-dressed locals who are very much a part of the young establishment scene. Nicely lit, Moose's is small enough to feel intimate, yet big enough to get a table, even on busy nights.

An open kitchen turns out creative continental meals with a quasi-Mediterranean flair. Menus, which change weekly, might include Dungeness crabcakes with vanilla bean coleslaw; goat cheese, roasted peppers, and garlic-stuffed calzone; pan-roasted fish; or grilled veal marinated in port wine and served with a potato–onion tart. Similar meals, with smaller portions and prices, are served at lunch.

The bar, separated from the main dining room by a low, frosted-glass partition, remains busy long after the kitchen closes.

RUBICON, 558 Sacramento St. Tel. 434-4100.

Cuisine: CONTINENTAL. **Reservations:** Recommended.

$ Prices: Appetizers $7–$14, main courses $17–$23. AE, MC, V.

Open: Lunch Mon–Fri 11:30am–2:30pm. Dinner Mon–Thurs 5:30–10:30pm, Fri–Sat 5:30–11pm.

Debuting in 1994, Rubicon won instant publicity from the fame of its owners, film director Francis Ford Coppola and actor Robert De Niro—both of whom are part of the Myriad investment group that opened Tribeca Grill and Montrachet in New York. Named for Coppola's Napa Valley wine, Rubicon, located on the corner of Leidesdorff Street, features a contemporarily conservative dining room that feels like the proper place for an expensive dinner.

The menu is short and to the point, offering favorite delicacies like sautéed foie gras with rhubarb, and house-cured salmon with crisp potato cakes. Equally opulent entrees like rabbit or tuna are accompanied by creamy corn, polenta, or chick pea pancakes with tomato confit.

MODERATE

LITTLE CITY, 673 Union St., at Powell St. Tel. 434-2900.

Cuisine: MEDITERRANEAN/ITALIAN. **Reservations:** Accepted only for parties of six or more. **Cable Car:** Mason Street. **Bus:** 15, 30, 41, or 45.

$ Prices: Appetizers $5–$9; main courses $10–$16. AE, MC, V.

Open: Daily 11:30am–midnight (bar 11:30am–2am).

Once one of the most fashionable restaurants in San Francisco, Little City now attracts upscale young people with jobs. Colorful prints and paintings line the exposed brick walls, while brass fans whirl slowly overhead. Burgundy cafe curtains frame the large windows, and white-linen napkins sit upon heavy, dark-wood tables, which are spread over two levels.

The excellent food is what originally attracted the trendies, and it still never disappoints. The menu is heavy on antipasti—you'd do well to circumvent the main course entirely and make a meal of the appetizers. Among the best choices are grilled sausage and polenta, baked brie with roasted garlic (served with plenty of bread), Manila clams, and prawns borracho (marinated in tequila, chiles, garlic, and lime). The best pasta is covered with a sauce of Gorgonzola, walnuts, and sun-dried tomatoes. If you must, other dishes (which change daily) include fresh fish, pot roast, and osso buco. The sacripantina is a must—rum-soaked sponge cake, layered with zabaglione ($4, and worth it). The limited wine list is acceptable; the Scotch and grappa selections are exceptional.

LITTLE JOE'S, 523 Broadway, near Columbus Ave. Tel. 433-4343.

> **Cuisine:** ITALIAN. **Reservations:** Not accepted. **Bus:** 15, 30, 41, or 45.
>
> **$ Prices:** Appetizers $2–$3; main courses $8–$12. MC, V.
>
> **Open:** Mon–Thurs 11am–10pm, Fri–Sat 11am–11pm, Sun noon–10pm.

Little Joe's is a real San Francisco experience. It's a wide-open grill room, completely without pretension. Joe's gets busy, so tables are shared with other patrons, and that's part of the fun. Portions are huge, and preparations are straightforward. The menu is heavy on veal and chicken, both prepared in several styles—parmigiana, piccata, saltimbocca, scaloppine. A half-dozen pastas, with at least as many sauces, are also available. But the specialty here is cacciucco, a stew of clams, cod, crab, mussels, and prawns, cooked in a tomato-and-garlic sauce. The gamberone (prawns) are also recommended, and are served over a big plate of spaghetti.

NORTH BEACH RESTAURANT, 1512 Stockton St., between Union and Green Sts. Tel. 392-1587.

> **Cuisine:** ITALIAN. **Reservations:** Accepted only for parties of three or more. **Bus:** 15, 30, 41, or 45.
>
> **$ Prices:** Appetizers $5–$8; main courses $12–$30; fixed-price dinner $25–$35. AE, DC, MC, V.
>
> **Open:** Daily 11:30am–11:45pm.

Highest praise goes to chef Bruno Orsi for the first-rate *cucina Toscana* at this bistro. The unpretentious decor includes white cloths, tabletop candles in red holders, hanging plants, and the requisite braids of garlic suspended overhead. The atmosphere also is flamboyantly Italian, marked by robust conversation, charming waiters and attentive service. Dining here is something of an occasion.

The top appetizer is easily melon with home-cured prosciutto, and along with a side order of homemade pasta, it makes a great light meal. In addition to a choice of cooked-to-order dishes like cioppino, eggplant parmigiana, and veal scaloppine marsala, full seven-course fixed-price dinners include an enormous antipasto, salad, soup, fresh vegetable, and pasta with prosciutto sauce. A la carte choices include a selection of 22 homemade pasta dishes. Desserts range from an excellent zabaglione to a tray of cheese, walnuts, apples, and figs. You'll want to order a bottle of wine from the excellent cellar.

STINKING ROSE, 325 Columbus Ave. Tel. 781-7673.
> **Cuisine:** ITALIAN/INTERNATIONAL. **Reservations:** Accepted.
> **Bus:** 15, 30, 41, or 45.
> **$ Prices:** Appetizers $4–$10, main courses $8–$18; lunch about half price. AE, MC, V.
> **Open:** Sun–Thurs 11am–11pm, Fri–Sat 11am–midnight.

Garlic, of course, is the "flower" from which this restaurant gets its name. From soup to ice cream, the supposedly healthful herb is a star ingredient in most every dish. From a strictly gourmet point of view, the Stinking Rose is nothing special—pizzas, pastas, and meats smothered in simple, overpowering garlic sauces are tasty, but memorable only for their singular garlicky intensity. That said, this is a fun place; the restaurant's lively atmosphere and themed menu is good entertainment. Several casually decorated dining areas are floored with black and white checkerboard linoleum topped with gray marble tables. Large windows overlooking the enviable Columbus Avenue block between Vallejo and Broadway put passersby on display. The best dishes here include garlic steamed clams and mussels, garlic pizza, and 40-clove garlic chicken (served with garlic mashed potatoes).

So what if tourists are the restaurant's "regulars"? It's a gimmick, to be sure, but it works.

TOMMASO'S, 1042 Kearny St., at Pacific Ave. Tel. 398-9696.
> **Cuisine:** ITALIAN. **Reservations:** Not accepted. **Bus:** 15 or 41.
> **$ Prices:** Appetizers $4–$8.50; pasta and pizza $8–$17; meat and fish courses $10–$17. MC, V.
> **Open:** Tues–Sat 5–10:30pm; Sun 4–9:30pm. **Closed:** Dec 15–Jan 15.

Partitioned dining areas are on either side of a boisterous dining room decorated with the usual murals of the Neapolitan countryside. The center of attention is Mama Crotti, who continuously tosses huge hunks of garlic and mozzarella onto pizzas before sliding them into the oak-burning brick oven. Pizza is the dish of choice here, even though dishes like veal marsala and chicken cacciatore are also brick-oven baked. Half bottles of house wines are available, as are homemade cannoli and Italian-roast coffee.

INEXPENSIVE

CAFFE FREDDY'S, 901 Columbus Ave. Tel. 922-0151.
> **Cuisine:** CONTINENTAL. **Reservations:** Accepted.
> **$ Prices:** Appetizers $3–$7; lunch $4–$7; main courses $5–$8; brunch $2–$8. MC, V.
> **Open:** Mon, lunch only, 11:30am–3pm; Wed–Fri 11:30am–10pm, Sat 9am–10pm, Sun 9am–9pm.

Recognizable by the large, painted palms, which frame the doorway, Caffè Freddy's, at the corner of Lombard Street, is a good-looking Italian-American diner with large, storefront windows overlooking Columbus Avenue. Inside, under an exceptionally high ceiling, are large modern prints, lots of small matte-black tables, and a few gray booths.

It would take several pages to mention all of the different offerings that are prepared in this restaurant's open kitchen. Those with smaller appetites might opt for one of the many sandwiches or salads (like warm cabbage with goat cheese, currants, walnuts, rosemary, and spinach) available in full or half orders. The large assortment of appetizers includes an antipasti plate of bruschetta, fresh melon, ham, sun-dried tomatoes, and pesto. One of the restaurant's specialties is grilled polenta (corn meal) topped with one or more ingredients that may include salmon, a variety of cheeses, and assorted vegetables. Gourmet pizzas and creative pastas are topped with everything from grilled chicken to green beans, red onions, lemon, garlic, bread crumbs, and Parmesan cheese.

BUDGET

MARIO'S BOHEMIAN CIGAR STORE, 566 Columbus Ave. Tel. 362-0536.

Cuisine: ITALIAN. **Bus:** 15, 30, 41, or 45.
$ **Prices:** Sandwiches $5–$6. No credit cards..
Open: Mon 10am–midnight, Sun 10am–11pm. **Closed:** Dec 24–Jan 1.

⭐ Catercorner to Washington Square is North Beach's friendliest neighborhood joint. Mario's is best known for its focaccia sandwiches, like meatball or eggplant—they're great. Wash it all down with an excellent cappuccino or a house Campari, and watch the tourists stroll by.

4. CHINATOWN

One of the best things about eating in Chinatown is strolling the streets and deciding on a place to eat. There are hundreds of restaurants to choose from, but it's nice to know that you can always rely on these following suggestions:

MODERATE

BRANDY HO'S HUNAN FOOD, 217 Columbus Ave., at Pacific Ave. Tel. 788-7527.

Cuisine: CHINESE. **Reservations:** Accepted. **Bus:** 15 or 41.
$ **Prices:** Appetizers $4–$9; main courses $8–$13. AE, DC, DISC, MC, V.
Open: Sun–Thurs 11:30am–11pm, Fri–Sat 11:30am–midnight.

⭐ Because it offers great food in a down-to-earth atmosphere, Brandy Ho's is one of my hippest friends' favorite restaurants. The simple and pleasant interior features black-and-white granite tabletops and a large, open kitchen.

Fried dumplings with sweet-and-sour sauce make a good starter, as do several uncommon soups, including moo shu soup with eggs, pork, vegetables, and tree-ear mushrooms; and fish-ball soup with spinach, bamboo shoots, noodles, and other goodies. The best main course is Three Delicacies, a combination of scallops, shrimp, and chicken with onion, bell pepper, and bamboo shoots, seasoned with ginger, garlic, and wine and served with black-bean sauce. Most dishes here are quite hot and spicy, but the kitchen will adjust the level to meet your specifications. There is a small selection of wines and beers, including plum wine and saké.

BUDGET

POT STICKER, 150 Waverly Place. Tel. 397-9985.
   Cuisine: CHINESE. **Reservations:** Not accepted. **Bus:** 15, 30, 41, or 45.
$ Prices: Appetizers $3–$6; main courses $7–$11. AE, MC, V.
   Open: Daily 11:30am–9:45pm.

It's nice to know about a simple, quite, untouristed Chinatown oasis patronized largely by locals in-the-know. Pot stickers are this restaurant's specialty, an appetizer of pan-fried or steamed, thin-skinned dumplings stuffed with seasoned meat or vegetables. These are staples of Mandarin cooking and do just what their name suggests—stick to the pot they're cooked in. The full menu of authentic standards reads like a survey of Chinese cooking. Moo shu pork, Mongolian beef, General Tsao's chicken, and other specialties are traditionally prepared by extremely experienced hands. The restaurant is located just east of Grant Avenue, between Clay and Washington streets.

5. CIVIC CENTER

EXPENSIVE

ZUÑI CAFE, 1658 Market St. Tel. 552-2522.
   Cuisine: MEDITERRANEAN. **Reservations:** Recommended. **Bus:** 6, 7, 71, or 75. **Muni Metro:** All Market Street trams.
$ Prices: Appetizers $6–$10; main courses $17–$23. AE, MC, V.
   Open: Tues–Sat 7:30am–midnight, Sun 7am–11pm.

This wedge-shaped restaurant near the corner of Page Street is a festival of angles, attracting one of the most eclectic crowds in the city. The common denominators between diners in black leather and those in pinstripes are good looks, success, and a taste for a good martini. Perpetually packed, regulars come for the scene as much as for the food. The changing menu always includes meat, like New York steak with Belgian endive gratin, but the fish is best—either grilled or braised in the kitchen's brick oven. Whatever you do, be sure to order the shoestring potatoes, the best in the world. A separate foot-long oyster menu has half a dozen or so varieties on hand at all times. The restaurant is located three blocks south of the Opera House.

MODERATE

MISS PEARL'S JAM HOUSE, 601 Eddy St., at Larkin St. Tel. 775-5267.
   Cuisine: CARIBBEAN. **Reservations:** Accepted. **Bus:** 19, 31, or 38.
$ Prices: Appetizers $3–$7; small plates $5–$10; main courses $15–$17. DC, MC, V.
   Open: Lunch Tues–Fri 11:30am–2:30pm; dinner Tues–Thurs 6–10pm, Fri–Sat 6–11pm, Sun 5:30–9:30pm; brunch Sun 11am–2:30pm (bar open until 2am).

Popular with a young, artistic, gold-card crowd, Miss Pearl's is a wacky, lively restaurant and bar with a ridiculous Caribbean-inspired "Gilligan's Island" interior. It adjoins the Phoenix Inn, an equally esoteric motel (see Chapter 5, "San Francisco Accommodations").

Starters may include blackeyed-pea fritters or catfish fingers with Trinidadian pepper and cilantro pesto. Salads include hearts of palm and jicama, and cold calamari with ginger, chiles, lime, and peppers. Blackened fish, "jerked" chicken, and rock shrimp quesadillas often make the list of main courses. The dinner menu also includes a terrific selection of small plates (*tapas*) that can be combined into a fulfilling meal. Grilled tequila-marinated prawns might complement chicken-mango sausage or eggplant with wild mushroom risotto. The restaurant has a full bar and a limited selection of California wines. On weekends, stick around after dinner for drinks and dancing to steel drums and other island sounds. The restaurant is located four blocks north of the Civic Center.

6. JAPAN CENTER & ENVIRONS

MODERATE

PACIFIC HEIGHTS BAR & GRILL, 2001 Fillmore St., at Pine St. Tel. 567-5226.
   Cuisine: SEAFOOD. **Reservations:** Recommended for dinner. **Bus:** 2, 3, or 22.
$ **Prices:** Appetizers $5–$8; main courses $6–$17. AE, CB, DC, MC, V.
   Open: Lunch Wed–Sun 11:30am–2:30pm; Dinner Sun –Thurs 5:30–9:30pm; Fri–Sat 5:30–10:30pm; brunch Sun 10:30am–2:30pm.

Handsome and spacious, this friendly spot enjoys a warm neighborhood patronage. A long oak bar fronts comfortable lounge chairs, arranged around small cocktail tables. The dining room is dominated by a broad front window, which puts every diner on display. Pictureless frames decorate an entire wall, while color is provided by fresh flowers and a lively clientele.

The menu changes nightly, but always includes 12 to 16 varieties of oysters—including Belon, jumbo Blue Point, and Portuguese. Clams and mussels are also available on the half shell. Prices average $1.10 to $1.30 each, or $6.50 to $7.50 per half dozen. From amberjack to sturgeon, fresh fish is the house specialty, followed by seafood stews, paella, and cioppino. Understandably, the selection changes daily, and a good selection of Californian wines is available by the glass.

INEXPENSIVE

SANPPO, 1702 Post St., at Laguna St. Tel. 346-3486.
   Cuisine: JAPANESE. **Reservations:** Not accepted. **Bus:** 2, 3, 4, or 38.
$ **Prices:** Appetizers $3–$6; main courses $6–$13; combination dishes $10–$17. MC, V.
   Open: Tues–Sat 11:45am–10pm, Sun 3–10pm.

Simple and unpretentious though it is, Sanppo, across from the Japan Center, serves excellent, down-home Japanese food. You may be asked to share one of the few tables that surround a square counter in the small dining room. Lunches and dinners all include miso soup, rice, and pickled vegetables. At lunch you might have an order of fresh, thick-cut sashimi, teriyaki, tempura, beef donburi, or an order of gyoza (dumplings filled with savory meat and herbs) for $6 to $12. The same items are available at dinner for about $1 additional. Combination dishes, like tempura, shasimi, and gyoza, or tempura and teriyaki, are also available. Beer, wine, and saké are served.

7. UNION STREET

MODERATE

PREGO, 2000 Union St., at Buchanan St. Tel. 563-3305.
   Cuisine: ITALIAN. **Reservations:** Accepted. **Bus:** 41 or 45.
$ Prices: Appetizers $3–$7; pasta and pizza $6–$12; meat and fish courses $10–$18. AE, CB, DC, MC, V.
   Open: Daily 11:30am–midnight.
A light and airy trattoria, Prego is pretty and pleasant, with a veritable garden of seasonal flowers blossoming in the windows. Pasta is the house specialty, but competently prepared meat, fowl, and fish dishes are also designed to please. Spit-roasted free-range chickens are prepared on a rotisserie, and served with potatoes and vegetables. Did I mention the crusty pizzas that emerge from the oak-fired brick ovens? A good selection of wines is also available by the glass or bottle.

AMERASIAN CAFE, 2165 Union St. Tel. 963-9638.
   Cuisine: CHINESE. **Reservations:** Not accepted. **Bus:** 22, 41, 45, or 57.
$ Prices: Appetizers $2–$6, main courses $5–$8; sandwiches $4–$6. AE.
   Open: Mon–Sat 11am–10pm, Sun 10:30am–7pm.
Occupying a small storefront in the middle of the Union Street shopping district, Amerasian Café serves upwardly mobile California cuisine in a decidedly down-home dining room. Order at the counter that separates the kitchen from the ten-table dining area, then take a seat and wait for your hamburger, potstickers, or kung pao chicken to arrive. Asian chefs preparing a wholly à la carte menu are as adept at grilling chicken as they are stir-frying vegetables.

8. HAIGHT-ASHBURY

MODERATE

CHA CHA CHA, 1805 Haight St., at Schrader St. Tel. 386-5758.
   Cuisine: CARIBBEAN. **Reservations:** Not accepted. **Bus:** 6, 7, 66, 71, or 73. **Muni Metro:** N line.
$ Prices: Small plates $4–$7; main courses $9–$13. No credit cards.
   Open: Lunch Mon–Fri 11:30am–3pm, Sat–Sun 10am–4pm; dinner Mon–Thurs 5–11pm. Fri–Sun 5–11:30pm.

⭐ I hesitate to recommend this culinary party because the line is already long enough. But this is the restaurant I dream about when I'm away, and the wait is well worth it.

Colorful booths and tables sit under Créole shrines, while small plates (tapas) of out-of-this-world delights are served by an unpretentious, friendly young staff. The chicken paillard is to die for. Sangría is served by the pitcher, and is particularly potent. Squeeze in with the hip Haight Street crowd and have some drinks while you wait an hour or more.

BUDGET

ZONA ROSA, 1797 Haight St. Tel. 668-7717.
   Cuisine: MEXICAN. **Reservations:** Not accepted. **Bus:** 6, 7, 66, 71, or 73. **Muni Metro:** N line.
$ **Prices:** Burritos $3–$4. No credit cards.
   Open: Daily 11am–11pm.

Zona Rosa, on Haight at the corner of Shrader, has absolutely the best burritos in the world. Period. Don't argue—just walk up to the counter, choose your ingredients of beans, rice, cheese, salsa, steak, and chicken, and watch your guacamole dreams be rolled right before your eyes. It's pretty nice for a dive. You can sit on a stool at the window or at one of five colorful interior tables. Zona Rosa is cheap *and* it's one of the best meals around. It's located in the Haight, two blocks from Golden Gate Park.

9. MISSION DISTRICT

FLYING SAUCER, 1000 Guerrero St. Tel. 641-9955.
   Cuisine: INTERNATIONAL. **Reservations:** Recommended.
$ **Prices:** Appetizers $7–$17, main courses $15–$24. No credit cards.
   Open: Tues–Sat 5:30–9:30pm.

Never have I seen food so outrageously and artfully presented. Not in Hong Kong, New York, nor Japan. Peering into the open kitchen, diners can catch chefs leaning over plates, carefully standing a jumbo prawn on its head, atop a baked column of potato polenta, which is itself a centerpiece amid a commotion of food art. Fish, beef, and fowl dishes are competently grilled, baked, or flamed before being surrounded by a flurry of sauces and accoutrements. While the pricey food is flavorful, the overwhelming sense at this restaurant is visual. The party extends from the plate to the decor, where toy plastic flying saucers mingle with colorful murals and creative lighting. The menu changes frequently, and there are almost always specials. If you ask your waiter to bring you the chef's most flamboyant-*looking* offering, you won't be disappointed.

One word of warning. The restaurant is located in the Mission District, at 22nd Street. This is not the city's safest neighborhood, and you may wish to take a cab.

VAL 21, 995 Valencia St. Tel. 821-6622.
   Cuisine: CALIFORNIA. **Reservations:** Recommended. **Muni Metro:** J line to 16th Street Station.
$ **Prices:** Appetizers $4–$10, main courses $8–$18. AE, MC, V.
   Open: Sun–Thurs 11am–11pm, Fri–Sat 11am–midnight.

In this dining age—when New San Franciscan cuisine also usually means high-tech lighting, Kenneth Cole shoes, and smoked pesto pizzas—Val 21, a Mission District standout, proves refreshingly different. Located at 21st Street, the restaurant's dining room is contemporarily stylish, yet not too opulent, nor too trendy. The food is top quality, although you never know what will be on the menu, a drawback for some. Inspired meals depend on the availability of fresh and wholesome ingredients. Wonderfully spiced chicken and fish dishes arrive with surprise accompaniments, like black beans or fried plantains. While preparations are somewhat exotic, they are far from obscure, and well within the realm of this kitchen's capabilities. Breads and portions are ample, and appetizers are truly tray-sized.

10. AROUND TOWN

EXPENSIVE

A. SABELLA'S, Fisherman's Wharf, 2766 Taylor St., 3rd Floor. Tel. 771-6775.

Cuisine: ITALIAN/SEAFOOD. **Reservations:** Accepted.

$ Prices: Appetizers $7–$10; main courses $16–$38. AE, DC, MC, V.

Open: Lunch daily 11:30am–3pm; dinner daily 5–11pm.

The Sabella family has been serving seafood in San Francisco since the turn of the century, and have operated A. Sabella's restaurant on the Wharf continuously since 1920. Today, the traditionally creative kitchen is under the direction of fourth-generation chef Michael Sabella, a graduate from New York's Culinary Institute of America.

The freshest local and imported fish, crab, shrimp, and other seafoods are served cooked or in cocktails, as well as on top of pastas. The restaurant's dedicated sous chefs also make steak, veal, and other "turf" dishes special. The truly special wine list is particularly strong with selections from Napa and other California regions.

HARRIS', 2100 Van Ness Ave. Tel. 673-1888.

Cuisine: AMERICAN. **Reservations:** Recommended.

$ Prices: Appetizers $6–$10; main courses $16–$25. AE, CB, DC, DISC, MC, V.

Open: Dinner only, Mon–Fri 6–11pm, Sat–Sun 5–11pm.

Every great city has a great steak restaurant, and in San Francisco, it's Harris'. Proprietor Ann Lee Harris knows steaks; she grew up on a cattle ranch, and married the owner of the largest feedlot in California. In 1976 the couple opened the Harris Ranch Restaurant on Interstate 5 in central California, where they built a rock-solid reputation up and down the coast. Harris' well-marbled, corn-fed Midwestern steaks tempt diners through a glass-walled aging room. They are cut thick—either New York–style or T-bone—and are served with a baked potato and seasonal vegetables.

For those who like to visit steakhouses and order something else, Harris' offers roast duckling in a light orange sauce, lamb chops, pork tenderloin with peppercorn sauce, and fresh fish and lobster. My friends who like brains rave about the restaurant's sautéed brains in brown butter.

Harris' light, brick-walled dining room, upholstered in muted florals, is more casual than the restaurant's tie-and-jacket dress code would suggest.

MODERATE

FOG CITY DINER, 1300 Battery St. Tel. 982-2000.

Cuisine: AMERICAN. **Reservations:** Accepted.

$ Prices: Appetizers $2–$9, main courses $11–$14. CB, DC, DISC, MC, V.

Open: Sat–Thurs 11:30am–11pm, Fri 11:30am–midnight.

Looking like a dressed-up diner—but smelling like a bar—Fog City Diner is a good pick South of Market. Made famous by a Visa credit-card commercial, the restaurant looks like a genuine American metallic diner—but only from the outside. Inside, dark polished woods, inspired lighting, and a well-stocked raw bar tell you this is no hash-slinger.

Dressed-up diner dishes include gourmet chili dogs, salads, pork chops, and pot roast. Fancier fish and meat meals include grilled catches of the day and thick-cut steaks. Lighter eaters can make a meal out of the long list of "small plates" that include sautéed mushrooms with garlic custard, and seasoned walnuts; and quesadilla with chili peppers and almonds.

FRINGALE RESTAURANT, 570 Fourth St. Tel. 543-0573.

Cuisine: FRENCH. **Reservations:** Recommended.

$ Prices: Appetizers $4–$10, main courses $8–$18; lunch $4–$12. AE, MC, V.

Open: Lunch Mon–Fri 11:30am–2:30pm; dinner Mon–Sat 5:30–10:30pm.

A celebrated newcomer, Fringale, which is French for "urge to eat," is an upscale bistro-style restaurant with an ebullient owner and fine food. The cozy, low-key South of Market dining room can only accommodate about 15 tables, all of which are usually in service.

French-Basque cuisine means starters like onion pie with Roquefort, prosciutto, and walnuts; and cucumber salad with smoked salmon and crème fraîche. Main courses like sautéed sea scallops Basquaise with shaved fennel, or veal scallops with wild mushrooms, are equally adventuresome—and well within the chef's substantial range. Roquefort ravioli with basis and pine nuts, and roasted lamb and eggplant sandwiches are added to the lunch menu. Serious wine drinkers will appreciate the restaurant's long, well-chosen list of domestic and international selections.

GREENS RESTAURANT, FORT MASON, in Building A, Fort Mason Center. Tel. 771-6222.

Cuisine: VEGETARIAN. **Reservations:** Recommended two weeks in advance. **Bus:** 30.

$ Prices: Appetizers $5–$7; main courses $10–$12; fixed-priced dinner $36; brunch $8–$10. DISC, MC, V.

Open: Lunch Tues–Thurs 11:30am–2pm, Fri–Sat 11:30am–2:30pm; dinner Mon–Thurs 5:30–9:30pm, Fri–Sat 6–9:30pm; brunch Sun 10am–2pm (bakery, Tues–Sat 9:30am–4:30pm, Sun 10am–3pm).

Knowledgeable locals swear by Greens, one of natural food's best ambassadors. Located in an old warehouse, with enormous windows overlooking the marina and the bay, the restaurant is both a pioneer and a legend. Haute vegetarian cuisine includes North African vegetable stew, packed with a garden of greens and served with raisin-almond couscous; pizza with shiitake and porcini mushrooms, Gruyère and fontana cheeses, tomatoes, and thyme; and marinated, mesquite-grilled tofu and vegetables, with wild rice pilaf. Appetizers and soups are equally as adventuresome, as are fresh desserts like polenta cake with strawberry-rhubarb compote, and cherry-almond biscotti. Dinner is served à la carte Tuesday through Thursday. Friday and Saturday nights are particularly clubby, when a single, fixed-price dinner menu is offered exclusively.

Lunch and brunch are somewhat simpler, but equally as inventive. Lunch offerings include overstuffed pita sandwiches, designer lettuce salads, chili, soup, and specials like spinach frittata and grilled tofu on potato bread. Brunch encompasses a variety of breads, muffins, omelets, and sandwiches. An extensive wine list is always available.

Like the restaurant, the adjacent bakery is also operated by the Zen Center. It sells homemade breads, sandwiches, and pastries to take home. Enter Fort Mason opposite the Safeway at Buchanan and Marina streets.

HYDE STREET BISTRO, 1521 Hyde St. Tel. 441-7778.

Cuisine: NORTHERN ITALIAN. **Reservations:** Recommended. **Cable Car:** Mason and Hyde.
$ Prices: Appetizers $5–$7; main courses $12–$16. MC, V.
Open: Daily 5:30–10:30pm.

Chef/owner Albert Rainer combines his Austrian background with California style to create consistently good dishes like strudel filled with a mélange of vegetables, and a roasted Sonoma chicken with a potato pancake and vegetables. Pasta dishes are particularly abundant. Chef Rainer recommends ravioli with wild mushroom sauce, or penne with sausage, peppers, tomato, and eggplant.

Hyde Street Bistro is exceptionally romantic. Despite the business, the small European dining room feels singular and special. Albert greets diners personally at the door, making you feel pampered and special. The prices are exceptionally reasonable for food of such high caliber. The restaurant is located on the northwestern slope of Nob Hill, between Pacific and Jackson streets.

RESTAURANT LULU, 816 Folsom St. Tel. 495-5775.

Cuisine: CONTINENTAL. **Reservations:** Recommended. **Bus:** 15, 30, 32, 42, or 45.
$ Prices: Appetizers $5–$8, main courses $9–$18; lunch $7–$17. AE, MC, V.
Open: Mon–Sat 11:30am–10:30pm, Sun 5:30–10:30pm.

Lulu's excellent food, upscale casual surroundings, and pulsing town-meeting atmosphere combine to make this South of Market newcomer one of San Francisco's most terrific bargains. Enormous windows and warehouse-high ceilings represent the current local style. The single, large dining room suffers from such high decibel levels that the cooks must wear headsets with microphones in order to communicate with each other.

The restaurant's not-to-be-missed roasted mussels arrive at the table piled high on an iron skillet. While you might skip the rather ordinary pastas and gourmet pizzas, meats from the wood-fired rotisserie are simply delicious. Included in this recommendation are leg of lamb, rosemary chicken, and pork loin. Sandwiches, like fresh tuna with sweet pepper, and roasted chicken, are served at lunchtime. Lulu's wine list is particularly interesting, including an excellent selection of rare and oversize bottles ranging from California's Clos du Val Cabernet Sauvignon, 1983 ($50) to France's Vieux Telegraphe Chateauneuf du Pape, 1990 ($500).

INEXPENSIVE

HAMBURGER MARY'S, 1582 Folsom St., at 12th St. Tel. 626-5767.

    Cuisine: AMERICAN. **Reservations:** Recommended. **Bus:** 9, 12, 42, or 47.

$ Prices: Breakfast $5–$9; lunch/dinner $5–$11. AE, MC, V.

    Open: Tues–Thurs 11am–1am, Fri 11:30am–2am, Sat 10am–2am, Sun 10am–1am.

Easily the hippest burger joint in San Francisco, Hamburger Mary's is popular with an ever trendy crowd of South of Market dance clubbers. The restaurant's kitsch decor includes thrift-shop floral wallpaper, family photos, garage-sale prints, stained glass, religious drawings, and Oriental screens. You'll get to know the bar well—it's where you'll stand with the masses while you wait for a table. Don't despair. They mix a good drink, and hanging out is what you're here for anyway.

Best of all, Hamburger Mary's serves some of the best burgers in town. Top it with grilled mushrooms, avocado spread, salsa, blue cheese, or a swamp of chili and cheese. Order home fries instead of french fries any day.

You have no reason to be anywhere near here come breakfast, but if you are, it's a good stop for a three-egg omelet, banana bread, or French or Hawaiian toast.

HARD ROCK CAFE, 1699 Van Ness Ave., at Sacramento St. Tel. 885-1699.

    Cuisine: AMERICAN. **Reservations:** Not accepted. **Cable Car:** California. **Bus:** 1.

$ Prices: Appetizers $3–$6; main courses $4.50–$13. AE, MC, V.

    Open: Sun–Thurs 11am–11:30pm, Fri–Sat 11am–midnight.

What can I say about one of the most popular tourist-oriented eateries ever to gimmick the public out of hard-earned vacation money? Like its affiliated restaurants around the world, this loud, nostalgia-laden place is the home of the guaranteed wait. Don't arrive hungry, especially on weekend nights, when the line can run down the block.

Formerly an auto showroom, the cafe is decorated with gold records, historic front pages, and the usual "Save the Planet" clutter. It's a convention center with ceiling fans. Despite the hype, the menu is decent, prices are moderate, and this place flips a pretty good burger. Baby back ribs, grilled fish, and chicken are also available, as are salads and sandwiches. The restaurant is located about six blocks west of Nob Hill's summit.

SWAN OYSTER DEPOT, 1516 Polk St. Tel. 673-1101.

    Cuisine: OYSTER BAR. **Reservations:** Not accepted. **Bus:** 27.

$ Prices: Seafood cocktails $5–$8, clams and oysters on the half shell $6–$7.50 per half dozen. No credit cards.

    Open: Mon–Sat 8am–5:30pm.

Almost 85 years old and looking even older, Swan Oyster Depot is classic San Francisco. Opened in 1912, this tiny hole-in-the-wall with the city's friendliest servers is little more than a narrow fish market that decided to slap down some stools. There are only twenty or so seats here, chairs jammed toe-to-toe along a long marble bar. Most patrons come for a quick cup of chowder or a plate of half-shelled oysters that arrive chilling on crushed ice. Indeed, there's little more than that available here. The menu is limited to fresh crab, shrimp, oyster and clam cocktails, Maine lobster, and Boston-style clam chowder. Fish is only available raw and to go.

BUDGET

HUNAN SHAOLIN ON POLK, 1150 Polk St. Tel. 771-6888.

Cuisine: CHINESE. **Reservations:** Not accepted. **Bus:** 2, 3, or 4.

$ Prices: Appetizers $2–$5; main courses $5–$9; fixed-price lunch about $4. AE, CB, DC, DISC, MC, V.

Open: Daily 11am–10pm.

Some of the city's best Chinese restaurants lie outside Chinatown, and Hunan Shaolin, smack in the middle of "Polk Gulch," between Sutter and Post streets, proves it. Pink-plastic–covered tablecloths, bentwood chairs, an odd assortment of lighting fixtures, and cheap Asian art surely must mean that the food is good. Indeed, the hot and sour soup is one of the best in the city. Of the main courses, I highly recommend the iron-platter specials (sizzling prawns, for one). Traditional dishes such as cashew chicken are also available. Lunch specials, offered weekdays from 11:30am to 2:30pm, are particularly a bargain at about $5. The restaurant is located seven blocks west of Union Square.

MARCELLO'S, 420 Castro. Tel. 863-3900.

Cuisine: PIZZA. **Muni Metro:** J line to Castro Street Station.

$ Prices: Pizza slices $1.50–$2.50; pies $10–$15.

Open: Mon–Fri 11am–2pm, Sat–Sun 11am–1pm.

Marcello's is not a fancy place, just a traditional pizza joint with a couple of tables and pizza by the slice. But, hey, this New Yorker thinks it's pretty good.

THE METRO, 3600 16th St. Tel. 703-9750.

Cuisine: CHINESE. **Reservations:** Accepted only for parties of four or more. **Bus:** 8. **Muni Metro:** K, L, or M line.

$ Prices: Appetizers $3–$7; main courses $5–$10. AE, MC, V.

Open: Nightly 5:30–11pm (bar, daily 3:30pm–2am).

Located on 16th at Market and Noe streets, the Metro is an outstanding dinner selection in the Castro district. Touched here and there with slim gold lines, the black lacquer restaurant sports a stylish art deco, Parisian decor.

The lively Hunan menu is varied enough and includes many items not commonly seen in your neighborhood Chinese restaurant (unless, of course, you live in San Francisco). Among the beef and lamb dishes is a first-rate hot braised beef and delicious lamb curry. The list of seafood choices is lengthy, but you can always rely on scallops with black mushrooms. And the bean curd with garlic-braised eggplant and black mushrooms in oyster sauce is great whether or not you're a vegetable aficionado.

TOMMY'S JOYNT, 1109 Geary St., at Van Ness Ave. Tel. 775-4216.

Cuisine: AMERICAN. **Reservations:** Not accepted. **Bus:** 2, 3, 4, or 38.

$ Prices: Appetizers $1.50–$3; main courses $4–$7. MC, V.

Open: Daily 11am–2am (bar, daily 10am–2am).

Tommy's colorful carnival entrance is unmistakable—it's like a huge paint warehouse gone mad. The interior is equally wild, jammed with suspended hockey sticks, bamboo poles with attached stuffed birds, a mounted buffalo head, an ancient piano, rusty firearms, fading prints, a beer-guzzling lion, and Santa Claus masks. There's an immense mahogany bar on one side, a buffet counter on the other, and chairs and tables in the middle. Get the picture?

The restaurant serves cafeteria style and is most famous for buffalo stew, which is always on hand. More traditional meats are also on the menu. Best of all, almost 100 varieties of beer are served, including some impressive bottles you've probably never heard of.

11. SPECIALTY DINING

DINING COMPLEXES
GHIRARDELLI SQUARE

This outdoor shopping complex encompasses several good restaurants, most of which have great views of the water. Below are the best:

GAYLORD'S, 900 North Point St., Ghirardelli Square. Tel. 771-8822.
   Cuisine: INDIAN. **Reservations:** Recommended. **Cable Car:** Hyde Street line. **Bus:** 19, 42, 47, or 49.
$ **Prices:** Appetizers $4–$8; main courses $12–$19; fixed-price meals $14–$18 at lunch, $22–$28 at dinner. AE, CB, DC, DISC, MC, V.
   Open: Lunch Mon–Sat 11:45am–1:45pm, Sun noon–2:45pm; dinner daily 5–10:45pm.

With branches in London, New York, Beverly Hills, and New Delhi, this far-flung chain may be the most successful Indian restaurant in the world. Opened in 1976, San Francisco's Gaylord's has earned its reputation by serving an accessible North Indian haute cuisine in stunning surroundings. The warm, candlelit interior is spiced with superb bay views from almost every seat.

A la carte selections are available, but the fixed-price dinners are the most sensible choice. Most everything on the menu is offered, including soup, tandoori chicken, lamb kebabs, chicken tikka, Indian breads, saffron rice, dessert, and tea or coffee. Lunch is a choice of fixed-price menus only. Dining here is not cheap—a moderate dinner could house a Bangladeshi family for a month. But Gaylord's is good. Trust that most Indians don't eat like this.

A second Gaylord's is located at One Embarcadero Center (tel. 397-7775).

THE MANDARIN, 900 North Point St., Ghirardelli Square. Tel. 673-8812.
   Cuisine: CHINESE. **Reservations:** Accepted. **Cable Car:** Hyde Street line. **Bus:** 19, 30, 42, 47, or 49.
$ **Prices:** Appetizers $5–$12; main courses $15–$38; fixed-price dinners $22, $25, $28, and $38. AE, CB, DC, MC, V.
   Open: Daily 11:30am–11:30pm.

Created by Madame Cecilia Chiang in 1968, The Mandarin is meant to feel like a cultured northern Chinese home and features beamed twig ceilings, fine furnishings, silk-covered walls, and good-quality Asian art. Tables are spaced comfortably apart, and the better of two softly lit dining rooms offers matchless views of the bay.

True to its name, The Mandarin offers exceptional Peking-style cookery. Dinner might start with sizzling-rice soup, a chicken broth with shrimp, mushrooms, and fried rice that actually sizzles as it goes into the bowl. Unusual dishes include walnut chicken, minced squab, tangerine beef, Szechuan string beans, and smoked tea duck. Dim sum are served daily from 11:30am to 3pm.

PIER 39

Seafood restaurants are the Pier's specialty. While none of the restaurants below rates among the city's best, most are atmospheric and well located, and have good bay views. Good choices include the art nouveau **Chic's Place** (tel. 421-2442), a seafood bar and grill with a particularly good wine selection.

The two-level **Dante's Italian Seafood Restaurant** (tel. 421-5778) is also very art nouveau, with a plush living room–style cocktail lounge upstairs, an exquisite food display up front, and incredible bay views. Charcoal-broiled seafood and steaks, pasta, generous drinks, and sumptuous deserts are featured.

A bit of Old San Francisco can be found a the **Eagle Café** (tel. 433-3689). The cafeteria style is perfect because you share space at long tables. It's open for breakfast, lunch, and dinner.

Then there's **Vannelli's** (tel. 421-7261), with its gorgeous mahogany bar and a large variety of seafood dishes and wines.

Non-seafood samplings include a branch of **Yet Wah** (tel. 434-4430), a very popular San Francisco Chinese restaurant with first-rate Mandarin and terrific views.

Another Bay Area tradition, **Swiss Louis** (tel. 421-2913), moved to the Pier from Broadway, where it had been located for more than 40 years. It's not Swiss, by the way—it's Italian.

If you do want Swiss fare (French Swiss, actually), you can have it in the homey and charming **Old Swiss House** (tel. 434-0432), complete with alpine-style carved chairs, lace-curtained windows, and a blazing fireplace in the cocktail lounge.

Most Pier restaurants open for lunch at 11:30am and serve food until 10:30 or 11pm nightly. Call for specific information.

BREAKFAST/BRUNCH

If I could choose to be in any city in the world come breakfast time, I'd choose San Francisco. This city has no peer when it comes to honest, filling, American morning food. Go out for breakfast in San Francisco, even if you have to go to bed early in order to wake up in time.

DOIDGE'S, 2217 Union St. Tel. 921-2149.

> **Cuisine:** AMERICAN. **Reservations:** Accepted; necessary Sat–Sun. **Bus:** 41 or 45.
>
> **$ Prices:** Breakfast $5–$10; lunch $5–$8. MC, V.
>
> **Open:** Mon–Fri 8am–1:45pm, Sat–Sun 8am–2:45pm.

Started in 1971 with counter service and six tables, Doidge's has quickly become *the* quintessential breakfast joint. The restaurant has since expanded to include a comfortable dining room that sports a distinctly French look: fresh table flowers, oak sideboards, and so on. But seats at the original mahogany counter are still the most coveted by locals, who like to be close to the coffee pots.

Doidge's fame lies in the eggs Benedict, quite possibly the best you've ever tasted. The eggs Florentine runs a close second, prepared with thinly sliced Motherlode ham. Loggers and other hearty eaters would do well to order breakfast casserole, a medley of ham or Italian sausage, potato, onion, and tomato, baked with cheese, and topped with a poached egg. French toast, fresh fruits, and buttermilk pancakes are offered along with an extensive list of omelets for the wide-eyed. Champagne and mimosas are also available.

DOTTIE'S TRUE BLUE CAFE, 522 Jones St. Tel. 885-2767.

Cuisine: BREAKFAST. **Reservations:** Not accepted. **Cable Car:** California Street Line.

$ Prices: $2–$6. No credit cards.

Open: Daily 7:30am–2pm.

This family-owned breakfast restaurant in the Pacific Bay Inn has only ten tables and a handful of counter stools. A traditional coffeeshop, Dottie's serves standard American morning fare (French toast, pancakes, bacon and eggs, omelets, and the like) delivered to blue-and-white checkerboard tablecloths on rugged, diner-quality plates. Whatever you order, include bread, muffins, or scones, all of which are made on the premises.

PORK STORE CAFE, 1451 Haight St. Tel. 864-6981.

Cuisine: AMERICAN. **Reservations:** Not accepted. **Bus:** 6, 7, 66, 71, or 73. **Muni Metro:** N line.

$ Prices: Breakfast dishes $3–$6. No credit cards.

Open: Mon–Fri 7am–3pm, Sat–Sun 8am–4pm.

⭐ Despite its unappealing, carnivorous name, the Pork Store serves the Haight's best breakfast, and everybody knows it. The usual omelet-and-pancake fare is supplemented by good oatmeal, great biscuits, and heaps of crunchy, mushy home fries. If possible, avoid weekends, when everyone who couldn't get up early enough during the week is here.

SEARS FINE FOODS, 439 Powell St., at Sutter St. Tel. 986-1160.

Cuisine: AMERICAN. **Reservations:** Not accepted. **Bus:** All Market Street buses. **Muni Metro:** All Market Street trams.

$ Prices: Meals $5–$10. No credit cards.

Open: Wed–Sun 6:30am–3:30pm.

⭐ Sears would be the perfect place to breakfast on the way to work, but you can't always guarantee you'll get in the door before 9am. It's not just a diner, it's an institution, famous locally for its luscious, dark-brown waffles, light sourdough French toast, and unbelievably delicious pancakes. Be prepared to wait, especially during rush hour.

AFTERNOON TEA

FAIRMONT HOTEL, 950 Mason St. Tel. 772-5000.

Cuisine: TEA. **Reservations:** Accepted. **Cable Car:** California Street line (direct stop).

$ Prices: $15 set tea; à la carte available.

Tea served: Mon–Sat 3–6pm, Sun 1–6pm.

Served in Connoisseur's Corner, away from the hotel's usually busy lobby, this serene lounge offers plush, red velvet chairs and plentiful sandwiches and pastries along with hot tea and cider.

FOUR SEASONS CLIFT HOTEL, 495 Geary St. Tel. 775-4700.

Cuisine: TEA. **Reservations:** Accepted. **Cable Car:** Powell-Hyde and Powell-Mason lines (2 blocks east). **Bus:** 2, 3, 4, 30, 38, or 45.

$ Prices: $10 light tea; à la carte available.

Tea served: Mon–Sat 3–5pm.

The Clift's lobby bar is one of the coziest tea rooms in the city. Diners relax on comfortable chairs and love seats while tea is served on a small, lace-draped tables.

NEIMAN-MARCUS, 150 Stockton St., Union Square. Tel. 362-3900.
  Cuisine: TEA. **Reservations:** Accepted. **Cable Car:** Powell-Hyde and Powell-Mason lines (1 block west). **Bus:** 2, 3, 4, 30, 38, or 45.
$ Prices: $9 set tea; à la carte available.
Tea served: Mon–Sat 3–5pm.
The Rotunda Restaurant has long offered fine dining under the department store's famous turn-of-the-century glass dome. During tea time, finger sandwiches, scones, and pastries are brought to your table on a silver tiered tray. Sadly, however, tea here is brewed from bags.

SHERATON PALACE HOTEL, 2 New Montgomery St. Tel. 392-8600.
  Cuisine: TEA. **Reservations:** Accepted. **Muni Metro:** All Market Street trams. **Bus:** All Market Street buses.
$ Prices: $16 set tea; $20 with champagne.
Tea served: Daily 2:30–5pm.
It's hard to beat this grand hotel's fantastic glass-roofed Garden Court, especially at tea time, when changing sunlight and moody clouds turn the room into a dramatic light show. A harpist, or other lone musician adds a theatrical score.

LATE-NIGHT DINING

SAM WO, 813 Washington St., by Grant Ave. Tel. 982-0596.
  Cuisine: CHINESE. **Reservations:** Not accepted. **Bus:** 15, 30, 41, or 45.
$ Prices: Appetizers $2–$3; main courses $4–$5. No credit cards.
  Open: Mon–Sat 11am–3am, Sun 12:30–9:30pm.
Very handy for late-nighters, Sam's is a total dive that's well known and often packed. The restaurant's two pocket-size dining rooms are located on top of each other, on the second and third floors—take the stairs past the first-floor kitchen. You'll have to share a table, but this place is for mingling almost as much as for eating.
The house specialty is *jook* (known as *congee* in its native Hong Kong)—a disgustingly thick rice gruel flavored with fish, shrimp, chicken, beef, or pork; the best is Sampan, made with rice and seafood. Several other dishes you've never seen are just as famous. Try sweet-and-sour port rice, wonton soup with duck, or a roast-pork/rice-noodle roll. Chinese doughnuts sell for 50¢ per hole.

WHAT TO SEE & DO IN SAN FRANCISCO

San Francisco is an outdoor city; it's meant to be strolled in, climbed, gazed at, and admired. Accordingly, the best sights are outdoors—bridges, monuments, vantage points, and neighborhoods. Of course, San Francisco has terrific museums and galleries, but somehow, when you think about sightseeing in this city, you think about the beauty of the bay, the history of Alcatraz, the whimsy of Lombard Street, the exotic bustle of Chinatown, the toylike cable cars, and a leisurely stroll along Fisherman's Wharf.

SUGGESTED ITINERARIES

IF YOU HAVE ONE DAY Put on your walking shoes for a hearty stroll from Union Square to Fisherman's Wharf. From Union Square, head north along Chinatown's Grant Avenue and continue to Columbus Avenue. Take your time to explore exotic side streets or stop for a dim sum lunch (see Chapter 6, "San Francisco Dining"). At Columbus Avenue, turn left and you'll be heading straight through the heart of North Beach. Again, don't rush. Stop for a rest in Washington Square Park or for a cappuccino in one of the many area cafes (see Chapter 6, "San Francisco Dining"). Look left down Lombard and you'll see the "crookedest street in the world." If you feel hardy, turn right on Lombard and climb to the top of Telegraph Hill for a magnificent view from Coit Tower. Columbus Avenue ends near the waterfront, where you can take in the delicious smells of boiled crab and explore Fisherman's Wharf, Pier 39, the Cannery, and Ghirardelli Square.

For dinner, walk back to a restaurant in North Beach or Chinatown, or better yet, hop in a cable car to your dinner destination. After dinner, head back to the Union Square area for a show or drinks, or taxi over to the South of Market area and spend the night dancing in one of the city's hippest clubs (see Chapter 10, "San Francisco Nights").

IF YOU HAVE TWO DAYS On your first day, follow the itinerary above. You can easily split the previous day's sightseeing into two parts and take more time in Chinatown or North Beach (see

? DID YOU KNOW...?

- More than 5,000 gallons of paint are used annually on the Golden Gate Bridge.
- The city's cable cars, along with New Orleans' St. Charles streetcar, are the only moving Historical Landmarks in the United States.
- Twenty-six foghorns blast in the bay.
- Most of the city rests on a foundation of sandstone, shale, and volcanic rock.
- There are 43 hills in San Francisco.
- "I Left My Heart in San Francisco" is the city's official ballad.
- There are almost 3 million annual hotel guests in this city of fewer than 750,000 inhabitants.
- Mission Dolores, dedicated on August 2, 1791, is the city's oldest extant structure.

Chapter 8, "Walking and Driving Around San Francisco").

On your second day, spend some time shopping around Union Square, Union Street, or Haight Street (see Chapter 9, "Shopping from A to Z"). Alternatively, head into Golden Gate Park and go boating or take in a museum or two (see Chapter 8, "Walking and Driving Around San Francisco"). When evening rolls around, make your way to the Golden Gate Park and eye the city at twilight. At night, take a North Beach bar crawl or explore that area's great cafe culture.

IF YOU HAVE THREE DAYS Take a boat trip to Alcatraz and tour the island. Afterward, visit the Exploratorium or one of the city's small, specialized museums. If you have kids in tow, you might want to visit the zoo or take a tour of the submarine U.S.S. *Pampanito,* docked at Fisherman's Wharf. After an early dinner, go to a baseball or basketball game or savor the city's rich cultural life by taking in a show or by going to the opera, symphony, or ballet.

IF YOU HAVE FIVE DAYS OR MORE It's unlikely that you've exhausted all the opportunities of interest to you in the city, but if you can, try to take a boat trip across the bay to Sausalito or Larkspur. Better still, drive to the Wine Country or to Muir Woods. It's amazing how, just across the Golden Gate Bridge, you are suddenly in the country, surrounded by trees and vineyards. Hike through the Marin Headlands or take a day trip to Sonoma or Napa.

1. THE TOP ATTRACTIONS

ALCATRAZ ISLAND, San Francisco Bay. Tel. 546-2700.

⭐ Spanish explorer Juan Manuel de Ayala sighted this oblong chunk of rock in 1775 and christened it "Isla de los Alcatraces," or Island of the Pelicans, after the thousands of birds that made their home there. American settlers drove the birds off and successively transformed the island into a fortress, an army prison, and finally a maximum-security prison. The last incarnation occurred in 1934, at the peak of America's gangster scare, when tough guys like John Dillinger and "Pretty Boy" Floyd seemed to bust out of ordinary jails with toothpicks. An alarmed public demanded an escape-proof "tiger cage"—and the federal government fingered Alcatraz for the part.

The choice seemed ideal. The Rock, as it became known, is ringed by strongly swirling, bone-chilling water, enough to defeat even the strongest swimmer. At great cost, the old army cages were made into tiers of tiny, toolproof, one-man cells, guarded by machine-gun turrets, high walls, steel panels, and electronic metal detectors called "snitch boxes." Even more forbidding than the walls were the prison rules: No talking, no newspapers, no canteen, no playing cards, and no inducement to good behavior—merely punishment for bad.

The Rock resembled a gigantic, absolutely spotless tomb with the hush of death upon it. Into that living cemetery went most of the criminal big shots who let themselves be taken alive—Al Capone, "Machine Gun Kelly," "Doc" Barker, "Creepy" Karpis, and dozens more. All were broken by Alcatraz . . . except those who died while trying to escape from it.

While, in some respects, Alcatraz seemed a macabre success, it was a huge white elephant from the start. Its cells were designed to hold 300 convicts, but there simply weren't that many top torpedoes in captivity. Consequently, more and more small fry were added just to maintain the population, which eventually included ordinary car thieves, forgers, and burglars—tin-pot crooks who could just as well have been jailed elsewhere. Yet the cost of maintaining the prison was colossal (drinking water, for instance, had to be ferried across in tank boats), and by the 1950s the money required to keep a single inmate on The Rock could have housed him in a luxury hotel suite. When three men seemed to have staged a successful escape from Alcatraz in June 1962, the federal government took the opportunity to order the prison "phased out"—closed. I say "seemed" because it's far from certain whether the trio actually did get away. They may have drowned while swimming for shore (like several others), but their bodies were never recovered—a good mystery for modern tourists.

In the decade that followed, Alcatraz was abandoned, a rock without a purpose. The only tenants were a caretaker, his wife, and an assistant. In 1969 a group of protesters occupied the island with the intention of establishing a Native American cultural center; they left in 1971.

Once a major colony for thousands of seabirds, the island's wildlife population dwindled during federal prison days. The birds were frightened away by guard dogs, and the island's flora was kept trim to reduce the number of hiding places. Since Alcatraz joined the Golden Gate National Recreation Area in 1972, rangers have noticed birds returning—the black-crowned night-heron and western gulls both nest here in abundance. You can take a ranger-guided nature tour (schedules are posted at the dock) or buy a self-guided walking-trail map (25¢).

Today great numbers of visitors explore the island's grim cells and fortifications on tours conducted by the U.S. National Parks Service—fascinating accounts by park rangers on the island's history, an award-winning audio tour in the prison cell house, and a slide show.

A trip to Alcatraz is a popular excursion, and space is limited. Try to make reservations as far in advance as possible. Tours and tickets are available through **Red and White Fleet** (tel. 415/546-2700, or toll free 800/229-2784 in California) and can be charged to your American Express, MasterCard, or Visa card. You can also purchase tickets on the day of sailing from the Red and White Fleet ticket office on Pier 41.

Ⓕ FROMMER'S FAVORITE SAN FRANCISCO EXPERIENCES

Riding the Cable Cars Roller-coasting over the city's hills, and hanging on tightly on curves, is understandably one of San Francisco's top tourist draws.

Walking Across the Golden Gate Bridge It might be windy and cold, but nothing matches the thrill of viewing San Francisco's spectacular stalactites from the world's most famous suspension bridge.

Eating in North Beach or Chinatown If you had only one meal in the city, it would be tough to choose where to eat it. These two colorful neighborhoods are adjacent to one another, making restaurant window-shopping a breeze.

Shopping Along Haight Street The chain stores are moving in, but there are still plenty of outrageous boutiques in America's most-famous psychedelic neighborhood.

Dancing in a South-of-Market Club Even if you've forgotten your black clothes, you're guaranteed a good time hanging out with the trendies in up-and-coming SoMa.

Cruising to Alcatraz Beautiful, scary, fun, and fascinating, Alcatraz is one of the best sightseeing attractions to be found anywhere.

Be sure to wear comfortable shoes and take a heavy sweater or windbreaker. Even if the sun is shining when you embark, the bay can turn bitterly cold in minutes. You should know that hiking around the island is not easy; there's a steep rise, and you have to climb several flights of stairs. The National Parks Service advises those with heart or respiratory conditions to reconsider taking the tour if climbing stairs leaves them short of breath.

For those who want to get a closer look at Alcatraz without all the hiking, two boat-tour operators offer short circumnavigations of the island. (See Section 5, "Organized Tours," below, for complete information.)

Admission: Tours, $8.75 adults, $7.75 seniors 62 and older, $4.25 children 5–11.

Open: Winter, daily 9:30am–2:45pm; summer, daily 9:15am–4:15pm. Ferries depart from Pier 41 by Fisherman's Wharf every half hour, at 15 and 45 minutes after the hour. Arrive at least 20 minutes prior to sailing time.

CABLE CARS. Tel. 673-6864.

✪ Although they may not be San Francisco's most practical means of transportation, cable cars are the best loved. Designated official historic landmarks by the National Parks

Service in 1964, these rolling symbols continuously cross the city like mobile museum pieces.

Cable cars owe their existence to the soft heart and mechanical genius of London-born engineer Andrew Hallidie. It all started in 1869, when Hallidie was watching a team of overworked horses haul a heavily laden carriage up a steep San Francisco slope. One horse slipped and the car rolled back, dragging the other tired beasts with it. Right then and there then engineer decided to invent a mechanical contraption to replace horses, and just four years later, in 1873, the first cable car made its maiden run from the top of Clay Street. Promptly ridiculed as "Hallidie's Folly," the cars were slow to gain acceptance. One early onlooker voiced general opinion by exclaiming: "I don't believe it—the damned thing works!"

Even today a good many visitors have difficulty believing that these vehicles work. The cable cars' basic design hasn't changed in over a century—and still they have no engines! Each weighing about six tons, the cars are hauled along by a steel cable, enclosed under the street in a center rail. You can't see the cable unless you peer straight down into the crack, but you'll hear its characteristic clanking sound whenever you're nearby.

The cars move when the gripper (not driver) pulls back a lever that closes a pincerlike "grip" on the cable. The speed of the car therefore is the speed of the cable; a constant 9½ m.p.h.—never more or less. This may strike you as a snail's pace, but it doesn't feel that way when you're cresting an almost perpendicular hill and look down at what seems like a bobsled dive straight into the ocean. And when you're slamming around a horseshoe curve you'd swear you're on two wheels. But in spite of the nerve tingles they can produce, cable cars are eminently safe. They have four separate braking devices, and most of the crew's time is spent applying them. The gripper operates the wheel brakes and the track brakes. The conductor frequently helps him by turning the hand lever of the rear brakes on the rear platform. And in real emergencies, there's a lever that rams a metal wedge into the cable slot, stopping the car so effectively that it takes a welding crew to dislodge it.

The two types of cable cars in use hold, respectively, a maximum of 90 and 100 passengers and the limits are rigidly enforced. The best views are had from the outer running boards, where you have to hold on tightly when taking curves. Everyone, it seems prefers to ride on the running boards. It's quite a sight to see a beehivelike cluster of people inching uphill, with a cable car tucked away somewhere in their midst. Because some of the cars have only one-way controls, they have to be reversed manually on a turntable by their crews. Cable-car crews may be hardworking, but they're an elite corps—the marines of Muni. They're also an integral part of the show, ringing the famous bell and hollering "*Heeeeere* we go!" and, at the appropriate moments, "Hold on tight for the curve!" Conductors and grippers positively bask in the admiration of local

---

IMPRESSIONS

It's an odd thing that anyone who disappears was said to be seen in San Francisco. It must be a delightful city and possess all the attractions of the next world.
—OSCAR WILDE

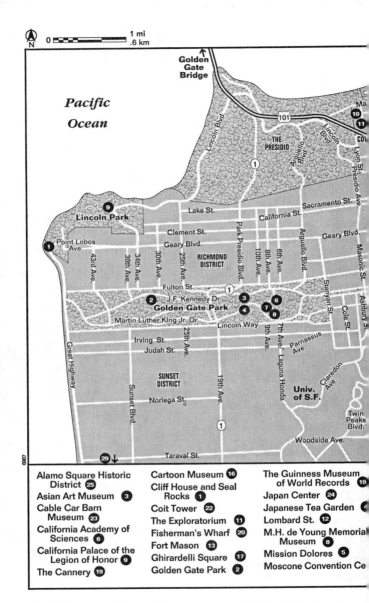

kids and tourists alike, and never cease polishing their image as "characters."

By the turn of the century, Hallidie's cable cars were running in most parts of the globe. Since then, they have been scrapped, one by one, in favor of more "modern" forms of transportation—Melbourne, Australia, was among the last cities to give up their trolleys. On several occasions the San Francisco municipality wanted to follow suit. But each time it encountered so much opposition that, in 1955, the cable car's perpetuation was written into the city

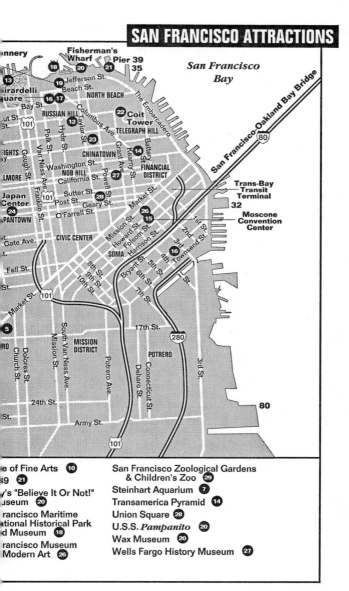

SAN FRANCISCO ATTRACTIONS

San Francisco Bay

San Francisco-Oakland Bay Bridge

Cannery
Fisherman's Wharf
Pier 39 35
Jefferson St.
Beach St.
NORTH BEACH
Girardelli Square
Bay St.
RUSSIAN HILL
Columbus Ave.
Coit Tower
TELEGRAPH HILL
CHINATOWN
FINANCIAL DISTRICT
NOB HILL
California St.
Japan Center
JAPANTOWN
CIVIC CENTER
SOMA
Market St.
Trans-Bay Transit Terminal
Moscone Convention Center
MISSION DISTRICT
POTRERO

e of Fine Arts ⑩	San Francisco Zoological Gardens
39 ㉑	& Children's Zoo ㉙
y's "Believe It Or Not!" Museum ⑳	Steinhart Aquarium ⑦
rancisco Maritime ational Historical Park d Museum ⑱	Transamerica Pyramid ⑭
	Union Square ㉘
	U.S.S. *Pampanito* ⑳
rancisco Museum Modern Art ㉖	Wax Museum ⑳
	Wells Fargo History Museum ㉗

charter. This mandate cannot be revoked without the approval of a majority of voters—a prospect that is not soon coming.

San Francisco's three existing lines comprise the world's only surviving system of cable cars. For complete information on riding them, see Section 2, "Getting Around," in Chapter 4.

Fares: $2; $1 for seniors from 9pm–midnight and 6–7am.

COIT TOWER, atop Telegraph Hill. Tel. 362-0808.

In a city known for its great views and vantage points, Coit Tower is tops. Located atop Telegraph Hill, just east of North

IMPRESSIONS

When San Franciscans set out to do something, I think they do it better than anybody else in the world.
PRESIDENT FRANKLIN D. ROOSEVELT, TALKING ABOUT THE 1939 FAIR ON TREASURE ISLAND

Beach, the round, stone tower offers magnificent 360° views of San Francisco.

Completed in 1933, the tower is the legacy of Lillie Hitchcock Coit, a wealthy eccentric who left San Francisco a $125,000 bequest "for the purpose of adding beauty to the city I have always loved." Inside the base are some colorful murals titled *Life in California, 1934.* Commissioned by the Public Works of Art Project, under President Franklin D. Roosevelt's New Deal program, the recently restored frescoed paintings are a curious mélange of art and politics—a social realist's vision of America and Americans during the Great Depression.

Admission: Base free; tower $2 adults and students, $1 children 6–12.

Open: Daily 10am–7pm. **Bus:** 39 ("Coit").

THE EXPLORATORIUM, in the Palace of Fine Arts, 3601 Lyon St. Tel. 563-7337, or 561-0360 for recorded information.

The only museum to make this "Top Attractions" list is the thoroughly mind-boggling Exploratorium, on Lyon Street at Marina Boulevard. This fun, hands-on science fair is a participatory venture, where you use all your senses and stretch them to new dimensions. More than 650 permanent exhibits explore everything from color theory to Einstein's Theory of Relativity. Optics are demonstrated in booths where you can see a bust of a statue in three dimensions—but when you try to touch it, you discover it isn't there! The same surreal experience occurs with an image of yourself: When you stretch your hand forward, a hand comes out to touch you, and the hands pass in midair. Every exhibit is designed to be used. You can whisper into a concave reflector and have a friend hear you 60 feet away, or you can design your own animated abstract art—using sound.

The museum is located on one of the prettiest parcels in the city, in the only building left standing from the Panama-Pacific Exposition of 1915, which celebrated the opening of the Panama Canal. The adjoining lagoon is home to ducks, swans, seagulls, and sawgrass.

Admission: $8 adults, $6 senior citizens, $4 children 6–17, free for children under 6; free for everyone first Wed of each month.

Open: Memorial Day–Labor Day and holidays, Mon–Tues and Thurs–Sun 10am–5pm, Wed 10am–9:30pm; the rest of the year, Tues and Thurs–Sun 10am–5pm, Wed 10am–9:30pm. **Closed:** Mon from Labor Day to Memorial Day (except holidays), Thanksgiving Day, and Christmas Day. **Bus:** 30 from Stockton Street to the Marina stop. **Directions:** If driving, from U.S. 101 north, take the last exit before the bridge.

FISHERMAN'S WHARF AND VICINITY.

City sights often exploit their pasts for tourist dollars, but few are as adept at wholesaling their history as Fisherman's Wharf. Not only would you be hard-pressed to find any fishermen left here, but there's not even much around to remind visitors that this dock

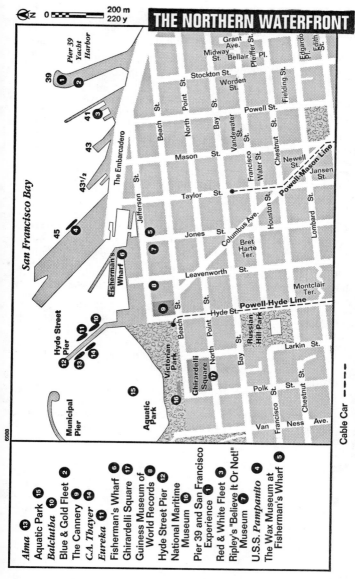

San Francisco Bay

Pier 39 Yacht Harbor

The Embarcadero

Fisherman's Wharf

Hyde Street Pier

Municipal Pier

Aquatic Park

Victorian Park

Ghirardelli Square

Russian Hill Park

Powell-Mason Line

Powell-Hyde Line

Cable Car - - - -

Alma 13
Aquatic Park 15
Balclutha 10
Blue & Gold Fleet 2
The Cannery 9
C.A. Thayer 14
Eureka 11
Fisherman's Wharf 6
Ghirardelli Square 17
Guiness Museum of World Records 8
Hyde Street Pier 12
National Maritime Museum 16
Pier 39 and San Francisco Experience 1
Red & White Fleet 3
Ripley's "Believe It Or Not!" Museum 7
U.S.S. Pampanito 4
The Wax Museum at Fisherman's Wharf 5

was once theirs. Today, Fisherman's Wharf and the festive area surrounding it pulsates like a nonstop carnival. Sidewalks are jammed with strollers, who come down to the water to eat, shop, browse, and people-watch. Crowds jostle for space around street performers, consisting of frozen mannequins, mimes, puppeteers, magicians, musicians, and the like.

Originally called Meigg's Wharf, this bustling strip of waterfront got its present moniker from generations of fishermen who used to base their boats here. Chinese shrimpers, sailing high-prowed junks, were the first fishers on the wharf, followed by Genovese feluccas and southern Italian trawlers. Upon landing, the fishermen sold their catch—crab, herring, salmon, shrimp, abalone, perch, squid, sand dabs, sea bass, mackerel, and cod—fresh off the boat to homemakers and restaurateurs. Small stands then sprouted where the fresh fish were cooked to order for curious passersby.

The bay has become polluted with toxins, and bright yellow placards warn against eating fish from these waters every day—and against pregnant women eating them at all. According to the environmental group Citizens for a Better Environment, several Silicon Valley–based companies that ring the southern end of the bay dump some 30,000 tons of toxic waste there annually.

Today, fish are still caught offshore, but Fisherman's Wharf has become too popular, and the bulk of the fishing industry has moved elsewhere. There are now scores of seafood restaurants and stalls, as well as dozens of stores, selling everything from original art to cans of "San Francisco Fog," and innumerable street hawkers and tourist traps. You can buy a caricature of yourself (drawn in three minutes) or visit the Wax Museum's Chamber of Horrors (see Section 3, "Cool for Kids," below). T-shirt hawkers and balloon vendors abound, along with the usual cluster of tourist-oriented paraphernalia shops.

Fisherman's Wharf is only one part of a long, strollable strip of shopping arcades and restaurant plazas—all along the waterfront on Jefferson Street. The nearby complexes of Pier 39, the Cannery, and Ghirardelli Square are discussed in detail under "Markets" in Section 2, "More Attractions," below and "Shopping Centers and Complexes" in Chapter 9, "Shopping from A to Z." Cruises to Alcatraz Island and around the bay also leave from this area (see "Alcatraz Island," above, and Section 5, "Organized Tours," below, for information on these aquatic excursions).

Admission: Free.

Open: The Wharf, daily 24 hours; most area shops, daily 11am–8pm (later during the summer); most restaurants, Sun–Thurs 10am–midnight, Fri–Sat 10am–2am. **Cable Car:** Powell-Mason line (it climbs to Nob Hill, swings around Chinatown, and descends through North Beach to its terminus near the east end of Fisherman's Wharf—a great ride!).

GOLDEN GATE BRIDGE. Tel. 921-5858.

The year 1995 marks the 58th birthday of what is possibly the most beautiful—certainly the most photographed—bridge in the world. Often half-veiled by the city's trademark rolling fog, San Francisco's Golden Gate spans tidal currents, ocean waves, and battering winds to connect the "City by the Bay" with the "Redwood Empire" to the north.

With its gracefully swung single span, spidery bracing cables and sky-zooming twin towers, the bridge looks more like a work of abstract art than the practical engineering feat that it is—among the greatest of this century. Construction began in May 1937 and was completed at the then-colossal cost of $35 million. Contrary to pessimistic predictions, the bridge neither collapsed in a gale or earthquake nor proved to be a white elephant. A symbol of hope when the country was afflicted with widespread joblessness, the Golden Gate single-handedly changed the Bay Area's economic life, encouraging the development of areas north of San Francisco.

The mile-long steel link, which reaches a towering height of 746 feet above the water, is an awesome bridge to cross. Traffic usually moves quickly, so **crossing by car** won't give you too much time to see the sights. If you drive ($3 toll, payable southbound), park in the lot at the foot of the bridge (on the city side; when approaching the bridge, drive slowly, stay in the right-hand lane, and exit into the lot at the base of the bridge) and make the crossing by foot. Back in your car, continue to Marin's Vista Point, by making the first left turn at the bridge's northern end. Look back and you'll be rewarded with one of the greatest views of San Francisco.

Millions of pedestrians **walk across the bridge** each year, gazing up at the tall red towers, out at the vistas of San Francisco and Marin County, and down into the stacks of oceangoing liners. You can walk out onto the span from either end. But be prepared: It's usually windy and cold, and the bridge vibrates. Still, walking even a short way is one of the best ways to experience the immense scale of the structure.

Bus: Bridge-bound Golden Gate Transit buses (tel. 332-6600) depart every half hour during the day for Marin County, starting from the Transbay Terminal at Mission and First streets and making convenient stops at Market and Seventh streets, at the Civic Center, and along Van Ness Avenue and Lombard Street. Consult the route map in the *Yellow Pages* of the telephone directory or phone for schedule information.

LOMBARD STREET, between Hyde and Leavenworth Sts.

Known as the "crookedest street in the world," the whimsically winding block of Lombard Street, between Hyde Street and Leavenworth Street, puts smiles on the faces of thousands of visitors each year. The elevation is so dramatic that the road has to snake back and forth to make a descent possible. The street zigzags around bright flower gardens that explode with color during warmer months. This short stretch of Lombard Street is one way, downhill, and great fun to drive. Take the curves slowly and in low gear. Save your photographing for the bottom, where you can find a parking space and gaze to your heart's content. You can also walk the block, either up or down, via staircases (without curves) on either side of the street.

THE NAMES PROJECT, 2362 Market St. Tel. 863-1966.

The NAMES Project began in 1987 as a memorial for people who have died from Acquired Immune Deficiency Syndrome (AIDS). The idea was to direct grief into positive action and help the world understand the devastating impact of AIDS. Sewing machines and fabric were acquired, and the public was invited to make coffin-sized panels for a giant memorial quilt. More than 26,000 individual panels now commemorate the lives of individuals who have died of complications related to AIDS. Each has been uniquely designed and sewn by the victims' friends, lovers, and family members.

The quilt, which would cover ten football fields if laid out end to end, was first displayed on the Capitol Mall in Washington, D.C., during a 1987 national march on Washington for Lesbian and Gay Rights. Although the quilt is often on tour in pieces throughout the world, portions of the heart-wrenching art project are on display here. A sewing machine and fabrics are also available here, free, for your use.

Open: Mon noon–6:30pm, Tues–Wed, and Fri noon–7pm, Sat–Sun noon–5pm. **Muni Metro:** J line to Castro Street Station.

2. MORE ATTRACTIONS

ARCHITECTURAL HIGHLIGHTS

ALAMO SQUARE HISTORIC DISTRICT.

San Francisco's plethora of beautiful Victorian homes is one of the city's greatest assets. Most of the 14,000 extant structures date from the second half of the 19th century and are private residences. Spread throughout the city, many have been beautifully restored and ornately painted by residents, who are proud of their city's heritage. The small area bordered by Divisadero Street on the west, Golden Gate Avenue on the north, Webster Street on the east, and Fell Street on the south—about ten blocks west of the Civic Center—has one of the city's greatest concentrations of these "Painted Ladies." One of the most famous views of San Francisco—seen on postcards and posters all around the city—depicts sharp Financial District skyscrapers behind a row of delicate Victorians. This fantastic juxtaposition is the view from Alamo Square, a small picnic-quality park in the center of this historic district, at Fulton and Steiner streets.

San Francisco's traditionally designed Victorian homes have little to do with the British queen after whom they're named. They were built en masse, in developments, and were designed to thrive in the Bay Area's climate and topography. Almost uniformly tall and narrow, many of these houses share common walls. They are called "Victorian" only because they were built during the reign of Queen Victoria.

HAAS-LILIENTHAL HOUSE, 2007 Franklin St. Tel. 441-3004.

Of the city's many gingerbread Victorians, this handsome Queen Anne house at Washington Street is one of the most flamboyant. The 1886 structure features all the architectural frills of the period, including dormer windows, flying cupolas, ornate trim, and wistful turrets. The elaborately styled house is now a museum; its rooms are fully furnished with period pieces. The house is maintained by the Foundation for San Francisco's Architectural Heritage, which offers tours two days a week, every half hour.

Admission: $4 adults, $2 children 6–12, $3 seniors.

Open: Wed noon–3:15pm, Sun 11am–4:15pm. **Cable Car:** California Street line.

THE GARDEN COURT, in the Sheraton Palace Hotel, 2 New Montgomery St. Tel. 392-8600.

This spectacular enclosed courtyard is topped by a lofty, iridescent glass roof supported by 16 Doric columns. Rebuilt in 1909 after the Great Earthquake, the elegant court has been painstakingly restored, with marble floors, crystal chandeliers, and a leaded-glass ceiling. The hotel, situated between Market and Third streets, reopened in 1991. Even if you are not staying here (see Chapter 5, "San Francisco Accommodations"), it's definitely worth a look.

Admission: Free.

Open: Daily 24 hours. **Muni Metro:** All Market Street trams. **Bus:** All Market Street buses.

TRANSAMERICA PYRAMID, 600 Montgomery St.

The tallest structure in San Francisco's skyline is this corporate headquarters between Clay and Washington streets. The building's unique white wedge is 48 stories tall, capped by a 212-foot spire. It was completed in 1972.

Muni Metro: All Market Street trams. **Bus:** All Market Street buses.

BANK OF AMERICA WORLD HEADQUARTERS, 555 California St.

This carnelian-marble-covered building dates from 1969. Its 52 stories are topped by a panoramic restaurant and bar, the Carnelian Room (see Chapter 10, "San Francisco Nights," for complete information). The focal point of the building's formal plaza is an abstract black granite sculpture, known locally as the "Banker's Heart." It was designed by Japanese architect Masayuki Nagare.

Muni Metro: All Market Street trams. **Bus:** All Market Street buses.

SAN FRANCISCO–OAKLAND BAY BRIDGE. Tel. 510/464-1148.

Although it's visually less appealing than the nearby Golden Gate, the Bay Bridge is in many ways more spectacular. The silvery giant that links San Francisco with Oakland has a total length of 8¼ miles and is one of the world's longest steel bridges. The San Francisco–Oakland Bay Bridge opened in 1936, six months before the Golden Gate. Each of its two decks contains five automobile lanes. The Bay Bridge is not a single bridge at all but a superbly dovetailed series of spans joined in midbay—at Yerba Buena Island—by one of the world's largest (in diameter) tunnels. To the west of Yerba Buena, the bridge is really two separate suspension bridges, joined at a central anchorage. East of the island is a 1,400-foot cantilever span, followed by a succession of truss bridges. And it looks even more complex than it sounds.

Transportation: You can drive across the bridge (the toll is $1, paid westbound), or you can catch a bus at the Transbay Terminal (Mission at First Street) and ride to downtown Oakland.

CHURCHES

MISSION DOLORES, 16th St. at Dolores St. Tel. 621-8203.

In 1776, at the behest of Franciscan Missionary Junípero Serra, Father Francisco Palou came to the Bay Area to found the sixth in a series of missions that dotted California's howling wilderness. From these humble beginnings grew what was to become the city of San Francisco. Surrounded by a four-foot-thick wall, the adobe Mission Dolores is the oldest structure in the city. The mission's small, simple chapel was built by Native Americans who were converted to Christianity. Its interior is a curious mixture of native construction methods and Spanish-colonial style. A statue of Father Serra stands in the mission garden, though the portrait looks somewhat more contemplative, and less energetic, than he must have been in real life. Lovingly preserved by the Roman Catholic diocese, the mission is a relatively tranquil oasis in a funky part of town. Even when tour buses are not lined up out front, the mission's walls are an interesting, calm counterpoint to the busy neighborhood that surrounds them.

Admission: $1.

Open: May–Oct daily 9am–4:30pm; Nov–Apr daily 9am–4pm; Good Fri 10am–noon. **Closed:** Thanksgiving Day and Christmas Day. **Muni Metro:** J line, down Market Street to the corner of Church and 16th streets.

GLIDE MEMORIAL UNITED METHODIST CHURCH, 330 Ellis St. Tel. 771-6300.

There would be nothing so special about this plain Tenderloin-area church if it weren't for its exhilarating pastor Cecil Williams. Williams's enthusiastic and uplifting preaching and singing with homeless and poor people of the neighborhood has attracted nationwide fame. Last year, during the pastor's 30th anniversary celebrations, singers Angela Bofill and Bobby McFerrin joined with comedian Robin Williams, author Maya Angelou, and talk-show queen Oprah Winfrey to honor him publicly. Williams's non-dogmatic, fun Sunday services attract a diverse audience that crosses all socioeconomic boundaries.

Services held: Sun 9am and 11am.

MARKETS

In addition to Fisherman's Wharf, three market complexes front the bay on or near Jefferson Street:

GHIRARDELLI SQUARE, 900 North Point St. Tel. 775-5500.

The Ghirardelli complex, at Polk and Larkin streets, dates back to 1864 when it served as a factory making Civil War uniforms. But it's best known as the former chocolate-and-spice factory of Domingo Ghirardelli. Saved from demolition in 1962, the factory is now a ten-level streamlined mall that is a beehive of terraces, shops, theaters, cafes, restaurant, and exhibitions—and one of the city's most popular rendezvous spots. The largely unchanged exterior still retains lots of historic charm. Inside are some 50 stores, retailing everything from clothing and family coats-of-arms to hand-cut lead crystal. (Many of these shops are described in Chapter 9, "Shopping from A to Z.") Ghirardelli Square also boasts the best restaurants of any of the malls on the waterfront. Close to 20 eateries, in all price categories, can satisfy almost any craving. So if you're exploring the entire wharf area, plan to end up here at mealtime. (See Chapter 6, "San Francisco Dining," for specific recommendations.) Scheduled street performers—including mimes, magicians, and puppeteers—play regularly in the West Plaza. Each is handpicked for talent. The whole complex is crowned by a charming clock tower, an exact replica of the one at France's Château de Blois. Inside the tower, on the mall's plaza level, is the Ghirardelli soda fountain, where small amounts of chocolate are still made and are available for purchase, along with other candy and ice cream. A free map and guide to the mall is available from the information booth, located in Ghirardelli's center courtyard. Illustrated with photographs, it contains a history of the square and details all the shops, restaurants, and attractions.

Incidentally, the Ghirardelli Chocolate Manufactory still turns out magnificent chocolate, but in a lower-rent district in the East Bay.

Admission: Free.

Open: Shops, Memorial Day–Labor Day, Mon–Sat 10am–9pm, Sun 10am–6pm; the rest of the year, Mon–Thurs 10am–7pm,

Fri–Sat 10am–9pm, Sun 10am–6pm. Restaurant hours vary; see the individual listings in Chapter 6, "San Francisco Dining," for complete information. **Cable Car:** Powell-Hyde line to Aquatic Park.

THE CANNERY, 2801 Leavenworth St. Tel. 771-3112.

Built in 1894 as a fruit-canning plant for the Del Monte company, the structure was abandoned in 1963 and acquired by developer Leonard V. Martin. Inspired by the chocolate factory-cum-shopping mall up the street, Martin left the red-brick exterior intact and transformed the structure into a vaguely Florentine three-story shopping, eating, and entertainment complex. Divided by a zigzagging alley, the mall is lined with arcades, spanned by bridges, and fitted with elevators and escalators. There are about a dozen eateries here and more than 50 shops, many of which are detailed in Chapter 9, "Shopping from A to Z." In the courtyard, amid a grove of century-old olive trees, are vendors' stalls and sidewalk cafes. On summer weekends some of the city's best street talents perform here.

The Museum of the City of San Francisco (tel. 928-0289) recently opened on the third floor. Dedicated solely to the city's history, the museum outlines the city's chronological development with displays and artifacts that include the head of the 22-foot *Goddess of Progress* statue that topped City Hall until it was demolished in 1909. The museum is free and is open Wednesday through Sunday from 10am to 4pm.

Admission: Free.

Open: Winter, Mon–Sat 10am–6pm, Sun 11am–6pm; summer and holidays, Mon–Sat 10am–8pm, Sun 11am–8pm. **Cable Car:** Powell-Hyde line to Aquatic Park.

PIER 39, on the waterfront at Embarcadero and Beach St. Tel. 981-7437.

This $54-million, 4½-acre waterfront complex, a few blocks east of Fisherman's Wharf, is San Francisco's latest tourist-oriented bayside conversion—it even has parking for 1,000 cars. Constructed on an abandoned cargo pier, it is, ostensibly, a re-creation of a turn-of-the-century street scene. The walkways are built of aged and weathered wood salvaged from demolished piers, but don't expect a slice of old-time maritime life. This is the busiest mall of the bunch, drawing visitors with its shops, restaurants, and usual assortment of jugglers, mimes, musicians, and other street entertainers. There are more than 100 shops, selling games, toys, jewelry, luggage, trinkets, mugs, and kites, among a plethora of other items (see Chapter 9, "Shopping from A to Z," for information on specific stores). To please the palate, there are ten restaurants of varying quality, cuisine, ambience, and price, some of them with great views of the bay. In addition, over a dozen nosheries serve everything from clam chowder to Mexican pastries.

Two marinas—which, combined, accommodate more than 350 boats—flank the pier and house the Blue and Gold bay sightseeing fleet. In recent years some 600 California sea lions have taken up residence on the adjacent floating docks. They arrived without warning and may abandon their new resting ground just as fast. But, for now, the silent sunning and playful yelping of these cute, blubbery creatures creates one of the best diversions in the entire city.

Admission: Free.

Open: Shops, daily 10:30am–8:30pm; restaurants, daily 11:30am–11:30pm; bars, daily until 2am. **Cable Car:** Powell-Mason line to Bay Street.

JAPAN CENTER, Post and Buchanan Sts. Tel. 922-6776.

The immense Japan Center is an Asian-oriented shopping mall located in San Francisco's revitalized Japantown, about a mile west of Union Square. At its center is a serenely noble five-tiered Peace Pagoda, designed by world-famous Japanese architect Yoshiro Taniguchi "to convey the friendship and goodwill of the Japanese to the people of the United States." Surrounding the pagoda, in a network of arcades, squares, and bridges, are dozens of shops and showrooms featuring everything from cameras and transistor radios to pearls, bonsai (dwarf trees), and kimonos. When it opened, with fanfare, in 1968, the complex seemed as modern as a jumbo jet. Today the aging concrete structure seems less impressive, but it still holds some interesting surprises. The renowned **Kabuki Hot Spring,** 1750 Geary Blvd. (tel. 922-6000), is the center's most famous tenant. The Kabuki is an authentic traditional Japanese bathhouse with deep ceramic communal tubs, as well as private baths. In addition to steaming water and restful rooms, the Kabuki features Japanese-style shiatsu finger-pressure massages. Facilities include a *furo* (hot bath) and *mizoburo* (cold bath), dry-heat saunas, a steam room, steam cabinets, and a Japanese-style sit-down showers. Appointments are required. The Japan Center also houses several restaurants (including sushi bars) and teahouses, the AMC Kabuki 8 cinema, and the luxurious 14-story Miyako Hotel (see Chapter 5, "San Francisco Accommodations," for complete information).

There is often live entertainment on summer weekends, including Japanese music and dance performances, tea ceremonies, flower-arranging demonstrations, martial-arts presentations, and other cultural events. Japanese festivals are celebrated here four times a year: the Northern California **Cherry Blossom festival** (Sakura Matsuri) in April, the **Buddhist Bon festival** in July, the **Nihonmachi Street Fair** in August, and an **Autumn festival** (Aki Matsuri) in September or October. Each is a colorful occasion, complete with beautiful costumes and traditional Japanese music and dance.

Japantown, or Nihonmachi, San Francisco's Japanese quarter, stretches for seven square blocks directly north of the Japan Center. Though less exotic and colorful than Chinatown, this area is notable for some interesting gift stores and several good Japanese restaurants. In the Buchanan Mall, between Post and Sutter streets, is a cobblestone walkway designed to resemble a meandering stream. It is lined on either side with flowering cherry and plum trees, and contains two origami-inspired fountains by Ruth Asawa.

Admission: Free.

Open: Mon–Fri 10am–10pm, Sat–Sun 9am–10pm. **Bus:** 2, 3, or 4 (exit on Buchanan and Sutter streets); 22 or 38 (exit on the northeast corner of Geary Boulevard and Fillmore Street).

MULTIMEDIA SHOWS

THE SAN FRANCISCO EXPERIENCE, at Pier 39, on the waterfront at Embarcadero and Beach St. Tel. 982-7394, or 982-7550 for recorded information.
388-6037

Two centuries of San Francisco history are condensed into about 30 minutes in this multimedia show that lets you see, hear, and even feel events from the city's past. From the city's founding to the Gold Rush, the Great Earthquake, and the Summer of Love, the life and times of San Francisco are neatly pieced together for a lightly informative and highly entertaining look at the forces that made the Bay City what it is today. Three film and 32 slide projectors coordinate their images in an extraordinarily fast-paced presentation on a 70- by 35-foot screen. In addition, famous historical events and conditions unique to the city are simulated by many three-dimensional surprises, including a San Francisco "fog" that really rolls in.

Admission: $7 adults, $6 seniors over 55, $4 children 5–16.
Open: Jan–Mar, shows daily (every half hour) 10am–8:30pm; the rest of the year, shows daily (every half hour) 10am–9:30pm.

MUSEUMS

SAN FRANCISCO MUSEUM OF MODERN ART, 151 Third St. Tel. 537-4000.

Scheduled to move into its new home in early 1995, the Museum of Modern Art originally opened in 1935 as the first collection on the West Coast to be devoted solely to 20th-century art. International in scope, the permanent collection consists of more than 4,000 paintings, sculptures, and works on paper, as well as a selection of objects relating to architecture, design, and the media arts.

The museum is strong on American abstract expressionism and other major schools of the 20th century. Rotating displays regularly include works by Clyfford Still, Jackson Pollock, Mark Rothko, and Willem de Kooning. It also has a strong representation of German expressionism, fauvism, Mexican painting, and local art. It stands out as one of the first major galleries to recognize photography as a serious art form. The collection of approximately 8,000 photographs includes works by Alfred Stieglitz, Ansel Adams, and Edward Weston, as well as good examples of 1920s German avant-garde and 1930s European surrealist photographers.

Temporary exhibits cover a broad spectrum of styles and media. Past shows included a major Alberto Giacometti retrospective, the paintings of New York artist Julian Schnabel, a survey of turn-of-the-century Chicago architecture, and the drawings of the celebrated Californian artist Richard Diebenkorn.

The new, red-colored museum building, designed by Mario Botto, is a funky, futuristic construction combining simple primary shapes. It's located two blocks south of Market Street in a revitalized neighborhood newly named Yerba Buena Gardens.

Docent tours are offered daily at 1:15pm and on Thursday at 7:15 and 7:45pm. In addition, the museum regularly organizes special artistic events, lectures, concerts, dance performances, poetry readings, conceptual art events, and special activities for children. Phone for current details.

Admission: $7 adults, $3.50 students 14–18 and seniors, free for children 13 and under; half price for everyone Thurs 5–9pm, and free for everyone the first Tues of each month.
Open: Tues–Wed and Fri–Sun 11am–6pm, Thurs 11am–9pm. **Closed:** Mondays and holidays. **Muni Metro:** J, K, L, M to Montgomery Station. **Bus:** 15, 30, or 45.

M. H. DE YOUNG MEMORIAL MUSEUM, in Golden Gate Park near 10th Ave. and Fulton St. Tel. 750-3600, or 863-3330 for recorded information.

One of the city's oldest museums, the de Young is also the most diversified, housing a hodgepodge of art that spans continents and centuries. Located on the Music Concourse of Golden Gate Park, the museum is best known for its American art, from colonial times to the 20th century, and includes paintings, sculptures, furniture, and decorative arts by Paul Revere, Winslow Homer, John Singer Sargent, and Georgia O'Keeffe. Special note should be taken of the American landscapes, as well as the fun trompe-l'oeil and still-life works from the turn of the century.

Named for the late-19th-century publisher of the *San Francisco Chronicle*, the museum also possesses an important textile collection, with primary emphasis on rugs from central Asia and the Near East. Other collections on view include ancient art from Egypt, Greece, and Rome; decorative art from Africa, Oceania, and the Americas; and British art by Gainsborough, Reynolds, Lawrence, Raeburn, and others. Major traveling exhibitions are equally eclectic, including everything from ancient rugs to great Dutch paintings. Call the museum to find out what's on. Docent tours are offered daily; call for times.

The museum's eatery, Café de Young, is an exceptional cafeteria serving rotating specials that include Peruvian stew, Chinese chicken salad, and Italian vegetables in tomato-basil sauce. In summer, dining is in the garden, among bronze statuary. The cafe is open Wednesday through Sunday from 10am to 4pm.

Admission (including the Asian Art Museum and California Palace of the Legion of Honor): $5 adults, $3 seniors over 65, $2 youths 12–17, free for children 11 and under (fees may be higher for special exhibitions); reduced admission for everyone the first Wed and first Sat of each month.

Open: Wed 10am–8:45pm, Thurs–Sun 10am–5pm. **Bus:** 44.

ASIAN ART MUSEUM, in Golden Gate Park near 10th Ave. and Fulton St. Tel. 668-8921, (752-2635 for the hearing impaired).

Adjacent to the M. H. de Young Museum and the Japanese Tea Garden, this exhibition space, opened in 1966, contains an academically oriented array of art and artifacts from the entire Asian continent. Only about 1,800 pieces from the museum's vast collection of 12,000 are shown at any one time. About half of the works on display are in the ground-floor Chinese and Korean galleries and include sculptures, paintings, bronzes, ceramics, jades, and decorative objects. There is also a wide range of exhibits from Pakistan, India, Tibet, Japan, and Southeast Asia, including the world's oldest-known, dated Chinese Buddha. The museum's daily guided tours are highly informative and sincerely recommended. Call for times.

Admission (including the M. H. de Young Memorial Museum and California Palace of the Legion of Honor): $5 adults, $3 seniors 65 and over, $2 youth 12–17, free for children 11 and under (fees may be higher for special exhibitions); reduced admission for everyone the first Wed and first Sat of each month.

Open: Wed–Sun 10am–5pm. **Bus:** 44.

CALIFORNIA PALACE OF THE LEGION OF HONOR, Lincoln Park. Tel. 750-3600, or 863-3330 for recorded information.

The white architectural sculpture that rises unexpectedly from a green hilltop above the bay is San Francisco's most beautiful

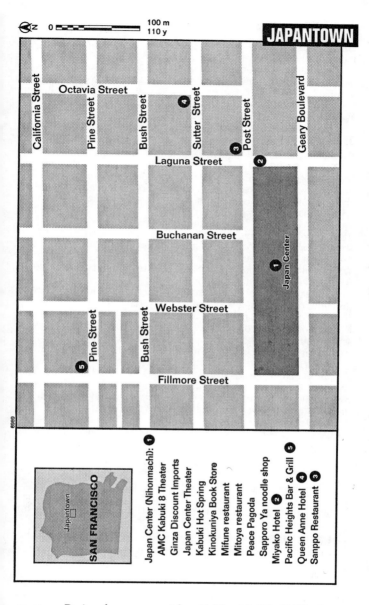

JAPANTOWN

100 m
110 y

Octavia Street
California Street
Pine Street
Bush Street
Sutter Street
Post Street
Geary Boulevard
Laguna Street
Buchanan Street
Japan Center
Webster Street
Pine Street
Bush Street
Fillmore Street

SAN FRANCISCO
Japantown

Japan Center (Nihonmachi): ❶
AMC Kabuki 8 Theater
Ginza Discount Imports
Japan Center Theater
Kabuki Hot Spring
Kinokuniya Book Store
Mifune restaurant
Mitoya restaurant
Peace Pagoda
Sapporo Ya noodle shop
Miyako Hotel ❷
Pacific Heights Bar & Grill ❺
Queen Anne Hotel ❹
Sanppo Restaurant ❸

museum. Designed as a memorial to California's World War I casualties, the neoclassical structure is an exact replica of the Legion of Honor Palace in Paris, right down to the inscription HONNEUR ET PATRIE above the portal.

Scheduled to open in late 1995 after a two-year, $29-million renovation and seismic upgrading project that was stalled by the discovery of almost 300 turn-of-the-century coffins, the museum's collection is based on paintings, sculpture, and decorative arts from Europe, as well as international tapestries, prints, and drawings. The chronological display of more than 800 years of European art includes one of the world's finest collections of Rodin sculpture.

Admission (including the Asian Art Museum and M. H. de Young Memorial Museum): $5 adults, $3 seniors 65 and over, $2 youths 12–17, free for children 11 and under (fees may be higher for special exhibitions); reduced admission for everyone the first Wed and first Sat of each month.

Open: Hours were not set at press time; phone for details. **Bus:** 38 or 18.

CABLE CAR BARN MUSEUM, Washington and Mason Sts. Tel. 474-1887.

Of course you wonder how the cable cars work; everyone does, and this museum explains it all to you. Yes, this is a museum, but the Cable Car Barn is no stuffed shirt. It's the living powerhouse, repair shop, and storage place of the cable car system and is in full workaday operation. Built for the Ferries & Cliff House Railway in 1887, the building underwent an $18-million reconstruction to restore its original gaslight look, install a spectators' gallery, and add a museum of San Francisco transit history. The exposed machinery, which pulls the cables under San Francisco's streets, looks like a Rube Goldberg invention.

You can stand in the mezzanine gallery and watch the massive groaning and vibrating winders as they thread the cable that hauls the cars through a huge figure-8 and back into the system via slack-absorbing tension wheels. Don't miss going through the room where you can see the cables operating underground.

On display here is one of the first grip cars developed by Andrew S. Hallidie and operated for the first time on Clay Street on August 2, 1873. Other displays include an antique grip car and trailer that operated on Pacific Avenue until 1929 and dozens of exact-scale models of cars used on the various city lines. There's also a shop where you can buy a variety of cable-car gifts.

Admission: Free.

Open: Apr–Oct, daily 10am–6pm; Nov–Mar, daily 10am–5pm.

Cable Car: Both Powell Street lines stop by the museum.

PARKS & GARDENS

In addition to Golden Gate Park (see Chapter 8, "Walking and Driving Around San Francisco"), San Francisco boasts more than 2,000 additional acres of city park, most of which are perfect for picnicking.

AQUATIC PARK, at the foot of Hyde St. Tel. 556-2904.

Adjacent to Ghirardelli Square, three blocks west of Fisherman's Wharf, this green lawn and protected marina was built in 1937 as a project of the federal Works Progress Administration. It's popular with sunbathers as well as strollers, who walk out on the long pier. The large, white building fronting the water is the National Maritime Museum (see Section 3, "Cool for Kids," below).

Cable Car: Powell-Hyde line to Aquatic Park.

FORT MASON, Bay and Franklin Sts. Tel. 441-5706.

Aquatic Park quickly gives way to the expansive waterfront grounds of Fort Mason. A former military installation and headquarters for the Pacific Fleet in World War II, the park now contains the Fort Mason Center, a complex of buildings housing theaters, galleries, and various arts programs. More than 1,000

activities are held here monthly, including concerts and fairs on the adjacent piers.
Bus: 30.

MARIN HEADLANDS, across the Golden Gate Bridge. Tel. 331-1540.

Administered by the Golden Gate National Recreation Area, the headland's 70,000 acres encompass ocean beaches, wildlife sanctuaries, and more than 100 miles of trails. Protected by a 1972 act of Congress, the rolling hills of this expansive park start just across the Golden Gate Bridge, where an excellent view can be had of the entire city.

Bus: Bridge-bound Golden Gate Transit buses (tel. 332-6600) depart every half hour during the day for Marin County, starting from the Transbay Terminal at Mission and First streets and making convenient stops at Market and Seventh streets, at the Civic Center, and along Van Ness Avenue and Lombard Street. Consult the route map in the *Yellow Pages* of the telephone directory or call for schedule information.

JUSTIN HERMAN PLAZA, at the foot of Market St.

More of a landscaped concrete plaza than a park, this square in the Financial District is popular with office workers at lunchtime. At its center is Vaillancourt Fountain, a free-form water sculpture that was designed to be walked through. The surrounding sidewalks are dotted with cafes and stalls selling leather goods, jewelry, pottery, paintings, and sculpture. The plaza is particularly packed on sunny weekday afternoons.

Muni Metro: All Market Street trams. **Bus:** All Market Street buses.

LINCOLN PARK, Clement St. and 34th Ave.

One of my personal favorites is this 270-acre green on the northeastern side of the city. The California Palace of the Legion of Honor is here (see "Museums," above), as is a scenic 18-hole municipal golf course (see Section 6, "Sports and Recreation," below). But the best things about this park are the 200-foot cliffs that overlook the Golden Gate Bridge and San Francisco Bay.

Bus: 38 from Union Square to 33rd and Geary streets, then transfer to Bus 18 into the park.

PRESIDIO OF SAN FRANCISCO, at the foot of Golden Gate Bridge. Tel. 415/556-3111.

After more than 200 years as a military stronghold guarding the entrance to the Golden Gate and San Francisco Bay, the Presidio Army base is being decommissioned and transferred to the National Park Service's Golden Gate National Recreation Area. The 1,400-acre waterfront park has its own golf course, water system, and more than 800 buildings, over half of which are of historical significance. One of America's most wonderful products of the "peace divided," the Presidio is resplendent with natural treasures that include a forest of windblown cypress trees and the only free-flowing stream left in the city. Among the park's habitats are coastal scrub, sand dunes, and prairie grasslands that contain many rare plants. In addition, there are about 170 species of birds, some 50 of which nest here.

Planning for the new Presidio is still underway, and debate rages about the park's future. An environmental learning center is in the works; at least some of the historic homes will be opened to the public; and park officials are projecting annual visitor rates in excess of 20 million. The Presidio will have a visitor center, food service, trails, public transportation within the park, historical programs, and traditional military ceremonies. For a free 16-page summary of the proposed Presidio plan, write to Presidio Information Center, Fort Mason Building 201, San Francisco 94123, or phone the number above.

3. COOL FOR KIDS

With few exceptions, most of the major sights in San Francisco are just as cool for adults as they are for kids. Windy Lombard Street, the majestic Golden Gate Bridge, Golden Gate Park's Japanese Tea Garden, Alcatraz Island—they're all fun destinations. Which is why San Francisco is one of America's favorite cities. For all its vaunted sophistication, the Bay City is a kid's paradise. Children usually take one look at the cable cars and decide they want to take them home. The whole of the Fisherman's Wharf is like one gigantic playground, and children are just as enthralled as adults by the view from Coit Tower and the excitement of Chinatown.

In addition to those sights listed above, the following attractions are of particular interest to kids. A few of them, at least, are bound to capture yours as well.

WELLS FARGO HISTORY MUSEUM, 420 Montgomery St., at California St. Tel. 396-2619.

Wells Fargo, one of California's largest banks, got its start in the Wild West. Its history museum, at the bank's head office, houses hundreds of genuine relics—pistols, photographs, early banking articles, posters, and mining equipment—from the company's whip and six-shooter days.

In the center of the main room stands a genuine Concord stagecoach, probably the most celebrated vehicle in American history. This was the 2,500-pound buggy that opened the West as surely as the Winchester and the iron horse. The interior seems cramped even when empty; it's hard to believe that it could hold nine passengers "passing comfortably"—with six more perched on the roof. That's not counting the "knight of the whip," who drove the six-horse team, and the essential "shotgun rider" beside him.

On the mezzanine, you can take an imaginary ride in a replica stagecoach or send a telegraph message in code using telegraph key and the codebooks, just the way the Wells Fargo agents did more than a century ago. The Wiltsee Collection of western stamps and postal franks will interest collectors. In addition, there are samples of the treasure that Wells Fargo carried—gold nuggets and coins from the fabulous Mother Lode mines—and mementos of the men who were after it. Chief among them was "Black Bart," a verse-writing humorist who robbed 27 stages single-handedly. Identified by a laundry mark on his handkerchief, he was captured in 1883 by Wells Fargo's top detective, James B. Hume.

Admission: Free.
Open: Mon–Fri 9am–5pm. **Closed:** Bank holidays. **Muni Metro:** Montgomery Street. **Bus:** Any to Market Street.

SAN FRANCISCO NATIONAL MARITIME HISTORICAL PARK AND MUSEUM, at the foot of Polk St. Tel. 929-0202.

Shaped like an art deco ship and located near Fisherman's Wharf, the National Maritime Museum is a treasure trove of sailing, whaling, and fishing lore. Remarkably good exhibits include intricate model craft, scrimshaw, and a terrific collection of shipwreck photographs and historic marine scenes, including an 1851 snapshot of hundreds of abandoned ships, deserted en masse by crews rushing off to participate in the largest gold strike. The museum's walls are lined with beautifully carved, high-busted, brightly painted wooden figureheads from old windjammers.

Two blocks east, on Aquatic Park's Hyde Street Pier, are several museum-operated historic ships, now moored and open to the public.

The **Balclutha,** one of the last surviving square-riggers and the handsomest vessel in San Francisco Bay, was built in Glasgow, Scotland, in 1886 and used to carry grain from California at a near-record speed of 300 miles a day. The *Balclutha* was one of the legendary "Cape Horners" of the windjammer age; it rounded the treacherous cape 17 times in its career. It survived a near wreck off the coast of Alaska and was refitted in 1906. The ship is now completely restored. Visitors are invited to spin the wheel, squint at the compass, and imagine they're weathering a mighty blow. Kids can climb into the bunking quarters, visit the "slop chest" (galley to you, matey), and read the sea chanties (clean ones only) that decorate the walls.

The 1890 **Eureka** still carries a cargo of nostalgia for San Franciscans. It was the last of 50 paddle-wheeled ferries that regularly plied the bay; it made its final trip in 1957. Restored to its original splendor at the height of the ferryboat era, the side-wheeler is loaded with deck cargo, including antique cars and trucks.

The "steam schooner" **Wapama,** built in 1915, is a good example of shipping in the Industrial Revolution. Originally built as a sailing ship, it was later fitted with a steam engine, after the technology became available.

The black-hulled, three-masted **C. A. Thayer,** built in 1895, was crafted for the lumber trade and carried logs felled in the Pacific Northwest to the carpentry shops of California.

Other historic ships docked here include the tiny two-masted **Alma,** one of the last scow schooners to bring hay to the horses of San Francisco; the **Hercules,** a huge 1907 oceangoing steam tug; and the **Eppleton Hall,** a side-wheeled tugboat built in England in 1914 to operate on London's River Thames.

At the pier's small-boat shop, visitors can follow the restoration progress of historic boats from the museum's collection. It's located behind the maritime bookstore on your right as you approach the ships.

Admission: Museum, free; ships, $3 adults, $1 children 11–17, free for children under 11 and seniors over 62.

Open: Museum, daily 10am–5pm. Hyde Street Pier, Apr–Oct, daily 10am–6pm, the rest of the year, daily 9:30am–5pm. **Closed:** Thanksgiving Day, Christmas Day, and New Year's Day. **Cable Car:** Hyde Street line to the last stop. **Bus:** 19, 30, 32, 42, or 47.

CALIFORNIA ACADEMY OF SCIENCES, on the Music Concourse of Golden Gate Park. Tel. 221-5100, or 750-7145 for recorded information.

This group of related museums and exhibitions is clustered around the Music Concourse in Golden Gate Park.

The **Steinhart Aquarium** houses one of the largest and most-diverse collections of aquatic life in the nation. Some 14,000 specimens call Steinhart home, including amphibians, reptiles, marine mammals, and penguins. The aquarium contains a California tidepool and a "hands-on" area where children can touch starfish and sea urchins. Their living coral reef is the largest display of its kind in the country and the only one in the West. In the Fish Roundabout—a unique, 100,000-gallon tank—visitors are surrounded by fast-swimming schools of open-ocean fish. Seals and dolphins are fed every two hours, beginning at 10:30am; the penguins are fed at 11:30am and 4pm.

The **Morrison Planetarium** is northern California's largest indoor theater of the outdoors. Its awesome sky shows are projected onto a 65-foot domed ceiling. Approximately four major exhibits, with titles such as *Star Death: The Birth of Black Holes* and *The Universe Unveiled,* are presented each year. Related cosmos' exhibits are located in the adjacent Earth and Space Hall. Call for show schedules and information.

In the **Earth and Space Hall** you can weigh yourself as if on other planets, see a real moon rock, experience one of San Francisco's infamous earthquakes on the "Safe Quake," and learn about the rotation of our planet at a replica of Foucault's Pendulum (the real one is in Paris).

In **Meyer Hall,** the "Wild California" exhibition includes a 14,000-gallon aquarium and seabird rookery, life-size battling elephant seals, and two larger-than-life views of microscopic life forms. There's also a poisonous, twin-headed snake.

In **McBean-Peterson Hall,** visitors are encouraged to "walk through time" as they are presented with evidence of evolution. This massive exhibit walks you through 3.5 billion years of history, from the earliest life forms to the present day.

Admission: Aquarium and science exhibits, $7 adults, $4 students 12–17 and seniors 65 and over, $1.50 children 6–11, free for children under 6; free for everyone the first Wed of every month. Planetarium shows, $2.50 adults, $1.25 children under 18 and seniors 65 and over. Show a valid Muni transfer for $2 off the admission price.

Open: Labor Day–July 4, daily 10am–5pm; July 4–Labor Day, daily 10am–7pm; first Wed of every month 10am–9pm. **Muni Metro:** N line ("Judah") to Golden Gate Park. **Bus:** 5 ("Fulton"), 71 ("Haight-Noriega"), or 44 ("O'Shaughnessy").

SAN FRANCISCO ZOOLOGICAL GARDENS AND CHILDREN'S ZOO, Sloat Blvd. and 45th Ave. Tel. 753-7080, or 753-7083 for recorded information.

Located between the Pacific Ocean and Lake Merced, in the southwest corner of the city, the San Francisco Zoo is among America's highest-rated animal parks. Begun in 1889 with a grizzly bear named Monarch donated by the *San Francisco Examiner,* the zoo now sprawls over 65 acres and is growing. It attracts more than a million visitors each year. Most of the 1,000-plus inhabitants are contained in realistically landscaped enclosures guarded by cunningly concealed moats. The innovative Primate Discovery Center is particularly noteworthy for its many rare and endangered species. Soaring outdoor atriums, sprawling meadows, and a midnight world for exotic nocturnal primates house a speedy Patas monkey that can run up to 35 miles per hour and the Senegal bush baby, a pint-size primate that can jump up four feet.

Other highlights include Koala Crossing, patterned after an Australian outback station; Gorilla World, one of the world's largest exhibits of these gentle giants; and Penguin Island, home to a large breeding colony of Magellanic penguins. Musk Ox Meadow is a 2½-acre habitat for a herd of rare white-fronted musk oxen brought from Alaska. And the Lion House is home to four species of cats, including Prince Charles, a rare white tiger (you can watch them being fed at 2pm daily except Monday.)

The **Children's Zoo,** adjacent to the main park, allows both kids and adults to get close to animals, including zoo babies being tended in the nursery. The barnyard is alive with strokable, cuddly baby animals. And then there's my personal favorite, the fascinating Insect Zoo—the only one in the western United States and one of only three such exhibits in the country. Over 6,000 specimens include a colony of velvet ants, honey bees, scorpions, and several hissing cockroaches. On weekends at 2:30pm you can see the popular show *Amazing Insects in Action,* which gives an intimate look at live insects through a "macro" video system.

A free, informal walking tour of the zoo leaves from Koala Crossing at 12:30 and 2:30pm on weekends. The *Zebra Zephyr* train tour takes visitors on a 20-minute "safari" daily (in winter, only on weekends). The tour is $2.50 for adults, $1.50 for children 15 and under and seniors.

Admission: Main zoo, $6.50 adults, $3 seniors and youths 12–15, $1 for children 6–11, and free for children under 5 if accompanied by an adult; children's zoo, $1, free for children under 3.

Open: Main zoo, daily 10am–5pm; children's zoo, daily 11am–4pm. **Muni Metro:** L line from downtown Market Street to the end of the line.

KIDS' FAVORITES AT FISHERMAN'S WHARF

The following sights are all clustered on or near Fisherman's Wharf. To reach this area **by cable car,** take the Mason line to the last stop and walk to the Wharf; **by bus,** take no. 30 ("Stockton"), 42 ("Downtown Loop"), or 32 ("Embarcadero"). If you're arriving **by car,** park on adjacent streets or on the Wharf between Taylor and Jones streets.

U.S.S. *PAMPANITO,* **Pier 45, Fisherman's Wharf. Tel. 441-5819.**

This popular battle-scarred World War II fleet submarine saw plenty of action in the Pacific. It has been completely restored, and visitors are free to crawl around inside. An audio tour is available.

Admission: $4 adults, $3 students 12–17, $2 children 6–11 and seniors 65 and over, free for children under 6.

Open: May–Oct, daily 9am–8pm; Nov–Apr, daily 9am–6pm.

RIPLEY'S "BELIEVE IT OR NOT!" MUSEUM, 175 Jefferson St. Tel. 771-6188.

Believe it or not, this amazing and silly "museum" is still open. A bizarre collection of wax figures, photos, and models depicts natural oddities from Robert LeRoy Ripley's infamous arsenal.

There's a one-third-scale matchstick replica of a cable car, a dinosaur made of old car bumpers, and the usual freak-show assortment of midgets, sword swallowers, and the like. Some examples from the collection of "humorous" gravestone epitaphs can be seen at the door, including such gems as "HERE LIES JONATHAN BLAKE, STEPPED ON THE GAS, INSTEAD OF THE BRAKE."

Admission: $7.75 adults, $6.25 teens 13–17 and seniors over 60, $4.75 children 5–12, free for children under 5.

Open: June 15–Labor Day, daily 9am–11pm; the rest of the year, Sun–Thurs 10am–10pm, Fri–Sat 10am–midnight.

WAX MUSEUM, 145 Jefferson St. Tel. 202-0400.

Conceived and executed in the Madame Tussaud mold, San Francisco's wax museum features more than 250 eerily lifelike figures of the rich and famous. The "museum" donates the lion's share of its space to images of modern superstars like singer Michael Jackson and political figures like former president George Bush. Tableaux include "Royalty," "Great Humanitarians," "Wickedest Ladies," "World Religions," and "Feared Leaders," the last including Fidel Castro, Nikita Krushchev, Benito Mussolini, and Adolf Hitler. The Chamber of Horrors—which features Dracula, Frankenstein, and a werewolf, along with bloody victims hanging from meathooks—is the stuff tourist traps are made of. It may also scare younger children.

Admission: $8.95 adults, $6.95 seniors over 60, $4.95 children 6–12, free for children under 6.

Open: Summer, Sun–Thurs 9am–11:30pm, Fri–Sat 9am–midnight; winter, Sun–Thurs 9am–10pm, Fri–Sat 9am–11pm.

THE HAUNTED GOLD MINE, 113 Jefferson St. Tel. 202-0400.

Under the same ownership as the Wax Museum, the Haunted Gold Mine is a fun house complete with mazes, a hall of mirrors, spatial-disorientation tricks, wind tunnels, and animated ghouls. Even very young children will probably not find it too scary, but it's fun.

Admission: $4.95 adults, $3.95 seniors, $2.95 children 6–12, free for children under 6.

Open: Summer, Sun–Thurs 9am–11pm, Fri–Sat 9am–midnight; winter, Sun–Thurs 9am–10pm, Fri–Sat 9am–11pm.

GUINNESS MUSEUM OF WORLD RECORDS, 235 Jefferson St. Tel. 771-9890.

You've read the book, now see the displays! Kids—and they only—will enjoy this large collection of superlatives opened in 1980. Your arms won't reach around a plastic replica of the world's fattest man; he tipped the scales at 1,069 pounds! You can march over to the participation area and try to break records of your own! There are also movies and videotapes of record-breaking events—like the world's largest domino tumble! And artifacts such as the world's smallest camera! Or most expensive shoes!

Admission: $6.50 adults, $5.25 students, $5.50 seniors 60 and over, $3.50 children $5–12, free for children under 5.

Open: Summer, Sun–Thurs 10am–11pm, Fri–Sat 10am–midnight; the rest of the year, Sun–Thurs 10am–10pm, Fri–Sat 10am–midnight.

CHILDREN'S PLAYGROUNDS

COW HOLLOW PLAYGROUND, Baker St., between Green-wich and Filbert Sts.

Surrounded by apartment buildings on three of four sides, this lushly gardened ground features a bi-level play area fitted with well-conceived, colorful play structures including a tunnel, slides, swings, and a miniature cable car.

HUNTINGTON PARK, Taylor St., between Sacramento and California Sts.

Atop Nob Hill, this tony play area contains several small play structures that are particularly well suited to children under five.

JULIUS KAHN PLAYGROUND, West Pacific Ave., at Spruce St.

A popular playground, Julius Kahn is situated inside San Francisco's great Presidio park. Larger play structures and pretty, forested surroundings make this ground attractive to children and adults alike.

4. SPECIAL-INTEREST SIGHTSEEING

FOR HISTORY BUFFS

OCTAGON HOUSE, 2645 Gough St. Tel. 441-7512.

Located at Union Street, this unusual, eight-sided, cupola-topped house dates from 1861 and is maintained by the National Society of Colonial Dames of America. Inside, you'll find furniture, silverware, and American pewter from the Colonial and Federal periods. There are also some historic documents, including signatures of 54 of the 56 singers of the Declaration of Independence. Even if you're not able to visit during opening hours, this strange structure is work a look.

Admission: Free (donation requested).

Open: On the second Sun and second and fourth Thurs of each month noon–3pm. **Closed:** Jan and holidays.

FOR RAPID-TRANSIT LOVERS

BAY AREA RAPID TRANSIT [BART], 800 Madison St., Oakland. Tel. 788-BART, 510/465-BART in Oakland.

One of the world's best commuter systems, BART's 71 miles of rail link eight San Francisco stations with Daly City to the south and 25 stations in the East Bay. Under the bay, BART runs through one of the longest underwater transit tubes in the world. This link opened in September 1974, two years behind schedule and six months after the general manager resigned under fire. The train cars are 70 feet long and are designed to represent the last word in public transport luxury. Twenty years later they no longer seem futuristic, but they're still attractively modern, with carpeted floors, tinted picture windows, automatic air conditioning, and

ng. The trains can hit a top speed of 80 miles per
uterized control system monitors and adjusts their

he people who run BART think so highly of their
trains   itions that they sell a $2.60 "Excursion Ticket," which
allows you, in effect, to "sightsee" the BART system. Tour as much
as you like, then exit from the same station you entered. If this is
your idea of fun, you can buck the system and save some money
by buying an 80¢ ticket at any station, then riding as much as you
like before exiting three blocks away at an adjacent station.

5. ORGANIZED TOURS

WALKING TOURS

WOK WIZ CHINATOWN WALKING TOURS, 750 Kearny St., Suite 800, San Francisco, CA 94108. Tel. 415/355-9657.

⭐ San Francisco's Chinatown is always fascinating, but for
many visitors with limited time it's hard to know where to
search out the "nontouristy" shops, restaurants, and historical spots in this magnificent microcosm of Chinese culture. Founded
by author, TV personality, cooking instructor, and restaurant critic
Shirley Fong-Torres, Wok Wiz tours take you into nooks and cran-
nies not usually seen by tourists. Each of her guides is Chinese,
speaks fluent Cantonese or Mandarin, and is intimately acquainted
with all of Chinatown's backways, alleys, and small enterprises,
which are generally known only to those who live here. You'll
learn about dim sum (a "delight of the heart") and the Chinese tea
ceremony; meet a Chinese herbalist; stop at a pastry shop to watch
rice noodles being made (noodles and other pasta forms originated
in China, not Italy); watch the famous Chinese artist Y. K. Lau do
his delicate brush painting; learn about *jook,* a traditional Chinese
breakfast; stop in at a fortune-cooking factory; and visit a Chinese
produce market and learn about the very unusual vegetables you
may never identify at lunch or dinner.

All in all, you'll learn more about Chinatown than you'll ever
remember. And you'll also learn enough to return on your own because you'll know that there's more to Chinatown than just the
Grant Avenue gift shops.

Wok Wiz Chinatown Walking Tours are conducted daily from
10am to 1:30pm and include a complete Chinese lunch. The tour
begins in the lobby of the Chinatown Holiday Inn at 750 Kearny
St. (between Washington and Clay streets). It's an easy walk, fun
and fascinating, and you're bound to make new friends. Groups are
generally held to a maximum of 12, and reservations are essential.

Prices (including lunch): $35 adults, $33 seniors 60 and older,
$25 children under 12.

CRUISIN' THE CASTRO, 375 Lexington St., San Fran-cisco, CA 94110. Tel. 415/550-8110.

This fascinating, fun, and informative historical tour of San
Francisco's most famous gay quarter will give you a totally new in-
sight into the contribution of the gay community to the political
maturity, growth, and beauty of San Francisco.

Tours are personally conducted by Ms. Trevor Hailey, who was part of the development of the Castro in the 1970s and knew Harvey Milk—the first openly gay politician elected to office in the United States. You'll learn about Milk's rise from shopkeeper to city supervisor and visit Harvey Milk Plaza, where most marches, rallies, and protests begin. Then there are the beautifully restored Victorian homes on the Castro's side streets. The area is also rich in community pride. It is filled with unusual gift shops, bookstores, restaurants, and businesses, and Ms. Hailey knows most of the local business owners personally.

Tours are conducted Tuesday through Saturday, from 10am to 1:30pm, and begin at Harvey Milk Plaza, atop the Castro Street Muni station. The cost includes brunch at the historic Elephant Walk Restaurant. Reservations are required.

Prices (including brunch): $30 adults, $25 seniors 62 and older and children 16 and under.

BUS TOURS

GRAY LINE, Transbay Terminal, First and Mission Sts. Tel. 558-9400, or toll free 800/826-0202.

San Francisco's largest bus-tour operator offers several itineraries on a daily basis. There is a free pickup and return service between centrally located hotels and departure locations. Reservations are required for most tours.

The one-hour **Motorized Cable Car Tour** continuously loops around the city's downtown, passing Union Square, Nob Hill, Chinatown, North Beach, and Fisherman's Wharf. Passengers ride aboard an authentic cable car–cum–bus. You can get off the bus at either Union Square or Pier 39 and board again later. Tickets cost $12 for adults, $6 for children 5 to 11. Buses depart from Union Square, at the corner of Powell and Geary streets; or from Pier 39. No reservations are required.

The company's 3½-hour **Deluxe City Tour** is a panoramic ride past the city's major sights. You pass by the Opera House, visit Golden Gate Park, and cross the Golden Gate Bridge for the magnificent view from Vista Point (see Section 1, "The Top Attractions," earlier in this chapter). Stops include Mission Dolores, the Japanese Tea Garden, and Cliff House. All tours are led by a driver/guide. Tours cost $25 for adults, $12.50 for children 5 to 11. Buses depart from the Transbay Terminal, at First and Mission streets, daily at 9, 10, and 11am, and 1:30 and 2:30pm; from May 4 to September 30 there's an additional departure at 3:30pm.

The three-hour **San Francisco by Night Tour** starts with a bus ride to the glittering lights of Ghirardelli Square, the Cannery, and Fisherman's Wharf. Then it's on to a walking tour of Chinatown with an Asian guide to point out the Painted Balconies, the Dragon Lanterns, and the Tongs. Tours cost $25 for adults, $12.50 for children 5 to 11. Buses depart nightly at 7pm from Union Square, at Powell and Geary streets.

THREE BABES AND A BUS. Tel. 552-2582.

Perhaps the world's hippest scheduled tour operator, this unique company runs regular nightclub trips for out-of-towners and locals who want to brush up on San Francisco's loudest sights. Although their 3½-hour roller-coaster ride through trendy SoMa and adjacent regions begins a little early for the most hardened clubbers, there is no lack of black clothes on the bus. The

Babes' ever-changing itinerary waltzes into four different clubs per night, cutting in front of every line with priority entry. The party continues en route, when the Babes entertain. Their bus departs on weekends only, at locations throughout the city. Phone for complete information and reservations.

Prices: $30, including club entrances.
Tours: Fri and Sat nights only, from 9:30pm to 1:30am.

BOAT TOURS

One of the best ways to look at San Francisco is from a boat bobbing on the bay. There are several cruises to choose from, many of which start from Fisherman's Wharf. Two companies are:

RED AND WHITE FLEET, Pier 41, Fisherman's Wharf. Tel. 546-2700, or toll free 800/229-2784 in California.

The city's largest boat-tour operator offers more than half a dozen itineraries on the bay. The fleet's primary ships are two-toned double- and triple-deckers, capable of holding 150 to 500 passengers. You can't miss the observation-tower ticket booths, at Pier 43½, located next to the Franciscan Restaurant.

The **Golden Gate Bay Cruise** is a 45-minute cruise by the Golden Gate Bridge, Angel Island, and Alcatraz Island. Tours cost $15 for adults, $12 for juniors 12 to 18 and seniors 55 and older, $8 for children 5 to 11. Tour prices include audio narration in six languages: English, French, German, Japanese, Mandarin, and Spanish. They depart from Pier 41 and Pier 43½ daily, every hour and a half from 10:45am to 3:45pm.

BLUE AND GOLD FLEET, Pier 39, Fisherman's Wharf. Tel. 705-5444.

Blue and Gold's **Bay Cruise** tours the bay year round in a sleek, 400-passenger sightseeing boat, complete with food-and-beverage facilities. The fully narrated 1¼-hour cruise passes beneath the Golden Gate and Bay bridges, and comes within yards of Alcatraz Island. Frequent daily departures from Pier 39's West Marina begin at 10am during summer and 11am in winter. Tickets cost $15 for adults, $7 for juniors 5 to 18 and seniors over 62; children under 5 sail free.

CAR TOURS

A beautiful **49-Mile Scenic Drive** follows a rough circle around the city and passes virtually all the best-known sights. Originally designed for the benefit of visitors to San Francisco's 1939–40 Golden Gate International Exposition, the route of this self-guided driving tour is marked with blue-and-white seagull signs. The drive guides you along some of the city's most colorful streets and past the prettiest vantage points for views of the city, bay, and ocean. Although it makes an excellent half-day tour, this mini-excursion can easily take longer if you decide, for example, to stop to walk across the Golden Gate Bridge or to have tea in Golden Gate Park's Japanese Tea Garden.

The San Francisco Visitor Information Center, at Powell and Market streets (see "Tourist Information" in Section 1, "Orientation," in Chapter 4), distributes free route maps. Since a few of the Scenic Drive marker signs are missing, the map will come in handy. Try to avoid the downtown area during the weekday rush hours from 7 to 9am and 4 to 6pm.

6. SPORTS & RECREATION

SPECTATOR SPORTS

The Bay Area's good sports scene includes several major professional franchises, including football, baseball, and basketball. Check the local newspapers' sports sections for daily listings of local events.

BASEBALL

SAN FRANCISCO GIANTS, Candlestick Park, Giants Dr. and Gilman Ave. Tel. 467-8000.

From April through October the National League Giants play their home games at Candlestick Park, off U.S. 101 about eight miles south of downtown. Tickets are usually available up until game time, but seats can be dreadfully far from the action. Tickets may be obtained at Candlestick Park; from Giants Dugout, 170 Grant Ave. (tel. 982-9400); or by phone through BASS Ticketmaster (tel. 510/762-2277). Special $4 express bus service is available from Market Street on game days; call Muni (tel. 673-6864) for pickup points and schedule information. Bring a coat, as this 60,000-seat stadium is known for chilly winds.

OAKLAND ATHLETICS, Oakland Coliseum Complex, at the Hegenberger Rd. exit from I-880, in Oakland. Tel. 510/430-8020.

The 1989 world-champion A's play across the bay in the Oakland Coliseum Stadium. Part of the Oakland Coliseum Complex, the stadium holds close to 50,000 spectators and serviced by BART's Coliseum station. Tickets are available from the Coliseum Box Office or by phone through BASS Ticketmaster (tel. 510/762-2277).

BASKETBALL

GOLDEN STATE WARRIORS, Oakland Coliseum Complex, at the Hegenberger Rd. exit from I-880, in Oakland. Tel. 510/638-6300.

The NBA Warriors play basketball in the 15,025-seat Oakland Coliseum Arena. The season runs from November through April, and most games are played at 7:30pm. Tickets are available at the arena, and by phone through BASS Ticketmaster (tel. 510/762-2277).

FOOTBALL

SAN FRANCISCO 49ERS, Candlestick Park, Giants Dr. and Gilman Ave. Tel. 468-2249.

The football 49ers call Candlestick Park home. The stadium is off U.S. 101 about eight miles south of downtown. Games are played on Sunday from August through December; kickoff is usually at 1pm. Tickets sell out early in the season, but are available at higher prices through ticket agents beforehand and from scalpers at the gate. Ask your hotel concierge or visit City Box Office, 141 Kearny St. (tel. 392-4400). Special $4 express bus service is available from Market Street on game days; call Muni (tel. 673-6864) for pickup points and schedule information.

UNIVERSITY OF CALIFORNIA GOLDEN BEARS, 61 Harmon Gym, University of California, Berkeley. Tel. 642-5150, or toll free 800/GO-BEARS.

The Berkeley Bears play their home games in Memorial Stadium, on the university campus across the bay. Tickets are usually available at game time. Phone for schedules and information.

HORSE RACING

GOLDEN GATE FIELDS, Gilman St., off I-80, in Albany. Tel. 510/559-7300.

Scenic thoroughbred races are held here from January to June. The park is located on the seashore, ten miles northeast of San Francisco. Call for admission prices and post times.

BAY MEADOWS, 2600 S. Delaware St., off U.S. 101, in San Mateo. Tel. 574-7223.

The nearest autumn racing is at this thoroughbred and quarter-horse track on the peninsula. Located about 20 miles south of downtown San Francisco, the course hosts races four or five days each week from September through January. Call for admission and post times.

RECREATION

While San Francisco's climate is not perfectly suited to outdoor recreation, the city does offer a good deal of terrific activities when the sun does shine.

BALLOONING

More than a dozen hot-air-ballooning companies will take you up for a silent flight over the nearby Wine Country.

ADVENTURES ALOFT, P.O. Box 2500, Vintage 1870, Yountville, CA 94599. Tel. 707/944-4408, or toll free 800/367-6272.

The Napa Valley's oldest hot-air-balloon company is staffed with full-time professional pilots. Groups are small, and the flight will last about an hour. The cost of $165 per person includes a preflight continental breakfast, a postadventure champagne brunch, and a framed "first-flight" certificate. Flights are daily between 6 and 8am.

ONCE IN A LIFETIME BALLOON CO., P.O. Box 795, Calistoga, CA 94515. Tel. 707/942-6541, or toll free 800/659-9915 in California.

Daily launches are made between 6 and 8am. The one-hour balloon flight is followed by a gourmet champagne brunch. The cost of $175 per person includes a photo and flight certificate.

BEACHES

Ocean Beach, at the end of Golden Gate Park, on the westernmost side of the city, is San Francisco's prettiest beach. Just offshore, in front of Cliff House, are the jagged Seal Rocks. These dangerous-looking formations are usually inhabited by various shore birds and a large colony of barking sea lions. Bring binoculars if you can. Ocean Beach is great for strolling or sunning, but don't swim here—tides are tricky, and each year bathers drown in the rough surf.

Hike up the hill to explore the ruins of Sutro Baths. These magnificent baths were once the largest indoor pools in the world.

BICYCLING

Two city-designated bike routes are maintained by the Recreation and Parks Department. One tours 7½ miles through Golden Gate Park to Lake Merced; the other traverses the city, starting in the south, and follows a route over the Golden Gate Bridge. These routes are not dedicated to bicyclists, and care must be taken to avoid cars. Helmets are recommended. A bike map is available from the San Francisco Visitor Information Center, at Powell and Mason streets (see "Tourist Information" in Section 1, "Orientation," in Chapter 4), and from bicycle shops all around town.

A massive new seawall, constructed to buffer Ocean Beach from storm-driven waves, doubles as an attractive public walk and bike way along five waterfront blocks of the Great Highway between Noriega and Santiago streets. It's an easy ride from Cliff House or Golden Gate Park.

PARK CYCLERY, 1865 Haight St. Tel. 221-3777.

This is one of two shops in the Haight Street/Stanyan Street area that rent bikes to day trippers. Located next to Golden Gate Park, the Cyclery rents mountain bikes exclusively, along with helmets, locks, and accessories. The charge is $5 per hour, and it's open daily from 9:30am to 5:30pm.

BOATING

GOLDEN GATE PARK BOAT HOUSE, at Stow Lake. Tel. 752-0347.

At Stow Lake, the park's largest body of water, you can rent a rowboat or pedalboat by the hour and steer over to Strawberry Hill, a large, round island in the middle of the lake, for lunch. There's usually a line on weekends.

Open: June–Sept. daily 9am–4pm; the rest of the year, Tues–Sun 9am–4pm.

CASS'S MARINA, 1702 Bridgeway, Sausalito. Tel. 332-6789, or toll free 800/472-4595.

Sailboats measuring 22 to 101 feet are available for rent on San Francisco Bay. Sail under the Golden Gate Bridge on your own or with a licensed skipper. In addition, large sailing yachts leave from Sausalito on a regularly scheduled basis. Call for schedules, prices, and availability of sailboats.

Open: Daily 9am–sunset.

CITY STAIR-CLIMBING

Many U.S. health clubs now have stair-climbing machines and step classes, but in San Francisco, you need only to go outside. The following city stair climbs will not only provide you with a good workout, but with great sightseeing too.

FILBERT STREET STEPS, between Sansome St. and Telegraph Hill.

Scaling the sheer eastern face of Telegraph Hill, this 377-step climb from Sansome and Filbert streets wends its way through verdant flower gardens and charming 19th-century cottages. Napier Lane, a narrow wooden plank walkway, leads to Montgomery Street. Turn right, and follow the path to the end of the cul-de-sac where another stairway continues to Telegraph's panoramic summit.

LYON STREET STEPS, between Green St. and Broadway.

Built in 1916, this historic stairway street contains four steep sets of stairs totaling 288 steps in all. Begin at Green Street and climb all the way up, past manicured hedges and flower gardens, to an iron gate that opens into the Presidio. A block east, on Baker Street, another set of 369 steps descends to Green Street.

CROQUET

The San Francisco Croquet Club (tel. 776-4104) offers public lessons from 11am to 2pm on the first Saturday of each month (or anytime by reservation for parties of four or more). The game is taught according to international six-wicket rules at the croquet lawns in Stern Grove, at 19th Avenue and Wawona Street. Players over 60 years of age can play free from 1 to 4pm on the first and third Wednesdays of each month.

FISHING

NEW EASY RIDER SPORT FISHING, 561 Prentiss St. Tel. 285-2000.

From June to October, Easy Rider makes daily salmon runs from Fisherman's Wharf. Fishing equipment is available; the cost of $47 per person includes bait. Reservations are required. Departures are daily at 6am, returning at 2pm; from June through October there's a second daily departure at 3pm, returning at dusk.

SEA BREEZE SPORTFISHING AT FISHERMAN'S WHARF, P.O. Box 713, Mill Valley, CA 94942. Tel. 381-FISH, or 474-7748.

Salmon-fishing trips depart from Fisherman's Wharf daily at 6am, returning at 2pm. Equipment is available, and reservations are required. The cost is $45 per person.

GOLF

GOLDEN GATE PARK COURSE, 47th Ave. and Fulton St. Tel. 751-8987.

This small 9-hole course covers 1,357 yards and is par 27. All holes are par 3, tightly set, and well trapped with small greens. Greens fees are very reasonable: $8 per person Monday through Friday, $11 on Saturday and Sunday. The course is open daily from 9am to dusk.

LINCOLN PARK GOLF COURSE, 34th Ave. and Clement St. Tel. 221-9911.

San Francisco's prettiest municipal course has terrific views and fairways lined with Monterey cypress trees. Its 18 holes encompass 5,081 yards, for a par 68. This is the oldest course in the city and one of the oldest in the West. Greens fees are $21 per person Monday through Friday, $25 on Saturday and Sunday. The course is open daily from 9am to dusk.

HANDBALL

The city's best handball courts are in Golden Gate Park, opposite Seventh Avenue, south of Middle Drive East. Courts are available free, on a first-come, first-served basis.

RUNNING

The **San Francisco Marathon,** held annually in the middle of July, is one of the largest in the world. For entry information, contact **Pamakid Runners Club** (tel. 681-2322). At other times of the year, call 543-RACE for up-to-date running-event information.

SKATING

Although people skate in Golden Gate Park all week long, Sunday is best, when John F. Kennedy Drive, between Kezar Drive and Transverse Road, is closed to automobiles. A smooth "skate pad" is located on your right, just past the Conservatory.

SKATES ON HAIGHT, 1818 Haight St. Tel. 752-8376.
   The best place to rent either in-line or conventional skates is at this well-stocked shop one block from the park. Although protective wrist guards and knee pads are included free, inexperienced skaters should walk past the cars to the park before lacing up their skates. The cost is $7 per hour for in-line Rollerblades, $6 per hour for "conventionals." Major credit card and ID deposit are required. The shop is open Monday to Friday from 11:30am to 6:30pm, and Saturday and Sunday from 10am to 6pm.

TENNIS

More than 100 courts throughout the city are maintained by the San Francisco Recreation and Parks department (tel. 753-7001). All are available free, on a first-come, first-served basis. The exception are the 21 courts in Golden Gate Park; a nominal fee is charged for their use, and courts must be reserved in advance for weekend play. Call the number above on Wednesday from 7 to 9pm, or on Thursday and Friday from 9am to 5pm.

CHAPTER 8

WALKING & DRIVING AROUND SAN FRANCISCO

1. **WALKING TOUR 1—CHINATOWN**
2. **WALKING TOUR 2—NORTH BEACH**
3. **WALKING (OR DRIVING) TOUR 3—GOLDEN GATE PARK**

The Bay City is a stroller's paradise to the same extent as Los Angeles is a motorist's metropolis. The three tours listed here are unique in their dissimilarity to one another. They are also special for their authenticity, which hasn't yet succumbed to Main Street uniformity.

GUIDED WALKS In addition to the guided walking tours listed in "Organized Tours" in Chapter 7, you should know about the free walking tours of historic areas sponsored by the **Friends of the San Francisco Public Library** (tel. 558-3857). Volunteers conduct these informative tours from May through October. A recorded schedule of the day's tours can be obtained by calling 558-3981. The walks usually last about 1½ hours, and reservations are not required. Tour destinations include City Hall, Coit Tower, North Beach, Victorian Houses of Pacific Heights, and Japantown.

49-MILE SCENIC DRIVE If you want a self-guided tour of the scenic and historic spots of San Francisco and have access to a car, there is no better way to see the city than to follow the blue-and-white seagull signs of the beautiful 40-mile Scenic Drive. Virtually all the best-known sights are on this tour, as well as some great views of the bay and ocean.

In theory, this mini-excursion can be done in half a day, but if you stop to walk across the Golden Gate Bridge or have tea in the Japanese Tea Garden in Golden Gate Park, or enjoy many of the panoramic views, you'll spend the better part of a day.

The Convention and Visitors Bureau's Information Center at Powell and Market streets can supply you with a map of the route. The seagull signs along the way will direct you counterclockwise, but since a few are missing, the map will be especially useful. Try to avoid the downtown area during weekday rush hours from 7 to 9am and 4 to 6pm.

WALKING TOUR 1 — CHINATOWN

Start: Grant Avenue and Bush Street.
Finish: Grant and Columbus avenues.
Time: 1½ hours, not counting food stops.
Best Times: Daily from 11am to 9pm, when the streets are in full swing.
Worst Times: Very early or very late, when shops are closed and the quarter is not at its most cluttered.

The first Chinese immigrants reached San Francisco during the Gold Rush of 1849. They called the collection of huts around the bay somewhat optimistically Gum San Dai Foo—"Great City of the Golden Hill." The Chinese were not concentrated here entirely by choice—they were segregated by anti-Asian prejudice. Chinatown was a cramped, hideously overcrowded ghetto. The opium trade and child prostitution flourished here, as did disease, poverty, and hunger.

Conditions worsened until the Great Earthquake and subsequent fire wiped out the area in 1906. After it was rebuilt, Chinatown became the renowned commercial and culinary quarter that it is today. The seven-block-long, three-block-wide district is now one of the largest Chinese settlements outside Asia—and growing.

Start at the corner of Grant Avenue and Bush Street. You'll know you're at the right place when you spot the:

1. **Chinatown Arch,** a two-story, green-tiled, dragon-topped gate. This pretty Chinese portal is the main entrance to San Francisco's Chinatown. Erected in 1969, it was a gift from the Republic of China (Taiwan).

    Walk uphill, under the arch, and you are strolling on:

2. **Grant Avenue,** the eight-block-long main stem of Chinatown. This primary thoroughfare is a multiethnic parade every day of the year. The shops are crammed with goods, ranging from ordinary utility wares to exotic treasures and—of course—mountains of "souvenirs." Some of it is pure junk, not even of Chinese origin.

    Walk two blocks up Grant Avenue, just past the corner of California Street. On your right you'll see:

3. **Old St. Mary's Church** (tel. 986-4388). Built largely with Chinese labor, Old St. Mary's was the city's first cathedral, dedicated on Christmas Day 1854. A survivor of the 1906 earthquake, the balconied church was constructed from brick brought around Cape Horn and a granite cornerstone quarried in China. Its Gothic lines look oddly out of place amid the surrounding Asian-style structures. Actively serving its perish, the church is open to visitors most days. You can attend services here, too, or go to one of the free concerts, held on Tuesday at 12:30pm.

    Turn right on California Street and walk half a block to:

4. **St. Mary's Square.** The heart of Chinatown's raucous red-light district before the 1906 earthquake, the square is now a placid, flower-filled park. Its centerpiece is the:

5. **Statue of Dr. Sun Yat-sen,** founder of the Chinese Republic. Scultped by Beniamino Bufano, the statue's most-outstanding feature is its stainless-steel cloak. A second monument in the square honors the Chinese-American victims of the two world wars.

    Return to Grant Avenue and turn right. Almost immediately you'll see the:

6. **Canton Bazaar,** 616 Grant Ave. (tel. 362-5750). Among a terrific variety of handcrafts you'll find an excellent selection of rattan and carved furniture, cloisonné enamelwork, rose Canton chinaware, glassware, carved jade, embroideries, jewelry, and antiques from mainland China.

    Half a block ahead, on the corner of Sacramento Street, is the:

7. **Bank of America,** 701 Grant Ave. This pretty building, an imitation of Chinese architecture, has gold dragons ornamenting its front doors and entwining its columns. Some 60 dragon

medallions line its facade.

Turn right on Sacramento Street. Half a block down is the:

8. **Chinese Chamber of Commerce,** 730 Sacramento St. (tel. 982-3000), where the famous dragon resides when it's not parading around the streets during the New Year celebration. You can also stop in for specialized information on Chinatown's shops and services, and the city's Chinese community in general. The office is open Monday through Friday from 9am to 5pm.

Return to Grant Avenue and walk to the:

9. **Chinatown Kite Shop,** (717 Grant Ave. tel. 989-5182). This shop's astonishing assortment of flying objects includes attractive fish kites, windsock kites in nylon or cotton, hand-painted Chinese paper kites, wood-and-paper biplanes, and pentagonal kites—all of which make great souvenirs or decorations. Computer-designed stunt kites have two control lines to manipulate loops and dives.

REFUELING STOP　Opened in 1924, **Eastern Bakery,** at Commercial Street, is the oldest Chinese-American bakery in San Francisco. Stop for some fermented soybean cakes, almond cookies, mooncakes, and other Oriental sweets that will probably take some getting used to.

Turn right down Commercial Street, and walk two blocks to the:

10. **Chinese Historical Society Museum,** 650 Commercial St. (tel. 391-1188). This pocket-size museum traces the history of Chinese immigrants in California through Gold Rush relics, photos, and artifacts.

Return to Grant Avenue, turn right, and walk half a block to the corner of Clay Street. At this corner once stood the:

11. **First House in San Francisco.** Constructed in 1836 when the fledgling town was called Yerba Buena, the house was built by a merchant named Jacob Leese, next to the tent then occupied by Captain Richardson, the settlement's first harbormaster.

Turn right down Clay Street. A few steps down on your left is:

12. **Portsmouth Square,** a quiet little park atop a parking garage. This was the birthplace of Yerba Buena—the central plaza around which grew the city of San Francisco. It was also a favorite contemplation spot for Jack London, Rudyard Kipling, and Robert Louis Stevenson. Today this grassy slope is not the most restful park in the city, but is interesting as the gathering place for Chinatown's old men, who perform tai chi, gamble over games of mahjong and Chinese cards, and chat with each other. The wooden pagoda-style structures were placed here only in 1990.

Cross the hideously ugly footbridge over Kearny Street into the:

13. **Chinese Culture Center,** 750 Kearny St. (tel. 986-1822), inside the Finincial District Holiday Inn. Pass display cases of antique puppets into a gallery presenting changing exhibits on Chinese history and culture. Depending on what's on, it can be very interesting. It's open Tuesday through Saturday from 10am to 4pm; admission is free.

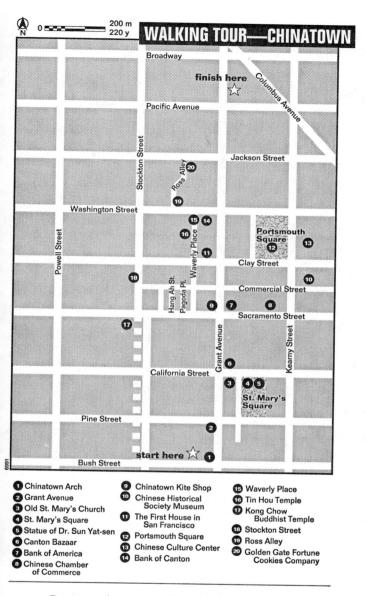

WALKING TOUR—CHINATOWN

❶ Chinatown Arch	❾ Chinatown Kite Shop	⓯ Waverly Place
❷ Grant Avenue	❿ Chinese Historical Society Museum	⓰ Tin Hou Temple
❸ Old St. Mary's Church	⓫ The First House in San Francisco	⓱ Kong Chow Buddhist Temple
❹ St. Mary's Square		⓲ Stockton Street
❺ Statue of Dr. Sun Yat-sen	⓬ Portsmouth Square	⓳ Ross Alley
❻ Canton Bazaar	⓭ Chinese Culture Center	⓴ Golden Gate Fortune Cookies Company
❼ Bank of America	⓮ Bank of Canton	
❽ Chinese Chamber of Commerce		

Return to the park, walk to the far end, and turn right on the path, toward Washington Street. Before you exit the green, notice the statue of Robert Louis Stevenson that stands on your left in the park's northwest corner. Turn left onto Washington Street, back toward Grant Avenue. Here you'll see the:

14. Bank of Canton, 743 Washington St., which boasts the oldest (1909) Asian-style edifice in Chinatown. This three-tiered temple-style building once housed the China Telephone Exchange, known as "China-5" until 1945; operators spoke five dialects, and were famous for their phenomenal memories.

Operators reputedly knew every subscriber by name and would often correct a caller—"No, that's not Mrs. Wu's number; you're calling Mr. Chang."

Cross Grant Avenue, walk half a block, and turn left onto:

15. Waverly Place, the best-known of Chinatown's side streets. This small street is popular because of its especially colorful architecture. Most of the balconied buildings that line this thoroughfare are private family associations and temples, few of which are open to the public. An exception is the:

16. Tin Hou Temple, 125 Waverly Place. Accessible via a narrow stairway, this incense-laden sanctuary is decorated in traditional black, red, and gold lacquered woods. Chinese Buddhists don't attend scheduled services—they enter temples to pray, meditate, and send offerings to their ancestors. You are welcome to visit, but do so unobtrusively. It's customary to drop a dollar in the offering box, or to buy a bundle of stick incense.

REFUELING STOP If you're ready for a snack, try **Pot Sticker,** 150 Waverly Place (tel. 397-9985), a simple, quiet oasis, patronized largely by locals in-the-know. The name comes from its specialty: pot stickers—pan-fried, thin-skinned dumplings stuffed with seasoned meat or vegetables, a staple of Mandarin cooking.

Back on the street, continue for just a few steps and turn right on Clay Street. Walk one block and turn left onto Stockton Street. On the right-hand side, above the post office, you'll find the:

17. Kong Chow Buddhist Temple, 855 Stockton St., fourth floor. This is the oldest and prettiest of Chinatown's many temples. Feel free to take a look, but have respect for those who have come to pray. Exit the temple and backtrack up:

18. Stockton Street. This stretch of Stockton is the center of the Chinese food-market district, an unusual conglomeration of glazed ducks, bamboo shoots, sharks' fins, ginger roots, fish, and chickens.

Walk one block and turn right onto Washington Street. After half a block, turn left onto the small:

19. Ross Alley, a passage connecting Washington and Jackson streets. Along the left-hand side of this alley are a number of Chinese sweatshops, hiding behind boarded-up screen doors— an eerie reminder of the bad old days.

Toward the end of the block is the:

20. Golden Gate Fortune Cookies Company, 56 Ross Alley (tel. 781-3956). It's a tiny place where only one woman sits at the end of a conveyer belt and folds messages into the warm cookies. The manager will try to sell you a big bag of cookies. X-rated fortunes are their specialty.

Turn right at the end of Ross Alley, walk half a block, then turn left and you're back on Grant Avenue. Chinatown terminates at Columbus Avenue, where it fades into strip joints and the beginning of North Beach. Turn around and explore Chinatown on your own, or turn left, up Columbus Avenue, and take a tour of North Beach, San Francisco's Italian quarter (see Walking Tour 2, below).

A FINAL REFUELING STOP   Turn right on Columbus and walk half a block to: **Brandy Ho's Hunan Food,** 217 Columbus Ave. (tel. 788-7527). This down-to-earth place with great food is one of my favorite restaurants in Chinatown. See Chapter 6, "San Francisco Dining," for complete information.

WALKING TOUR 2 — NORTH BEACH

Start: On Columbus Avenue, at the intersection of Pacific Avenue.
Finish: Coit Tower.
Time: 1½ hours, not including cafe stops.
Best Times: 11am to dusk, when stores, restaurants, and cafes are open and well lit.
Worst Times: After dark, when the neighborhood bustles, but it's hard to see the shops and street names.

Along with Chinatown, North Beach is one of the city's oldest neighborhoods. Originally settled by Italians, the area evolved into a tight-knit ethnic community, before evolving into a "beat generation" bedroom, and subsequently a pricey, upscale neighborhood. The current lively mix of cultures has made North Beach San Francisco's equivalent of New York's Greenwich Village, London's Soho, Paris's Left Bank, and Hamburg's Reeperbahn. Despite the changes, Italians are still significant here, and San Francisco's "Little Italy" is Italian with a vengeance. Except for its relative cleanliness, Washington Square, opposite the Church of Saints Peter and Paul, looks as if it could have been transplanted from, say, Genoa or Bologna. The signs above the shopfronts announce themselves as Farmacia, Panetteria, and Fiorista, while markets are crammed with ricotta, mozzarella, mortadella, provolone, and prosciutto. Best of all, espresso machines in this quarter are operated by people who really know how to use them. By the way, North Beach's beach is no more—the area was filled in the 1800s to accommodate a growing population.

With your back to the Transamerica Pyramid, start walking up:
1. **Columbus Avenue.** This busy street sort of separates North Beach from Chinatown and is the Latin Quarter's main thoroughfare. Among the strip joints and hot-dog palaces are a glittering ribbon of restaurants, cafes, and shops.
   The copper-green building on your left, at the corner of Kearny Street, is the:
2. **Sentinel Building,** a 1907 flatiron beauty that is now home to Francis Ford Coppola's Zoetrope Studios.
   Walk about half a block and turn right on tiny Saroyan Place. Here is:
3. **Specs' Adler Museum Café,** 12 Saroyan Place (tel. 421-4112), one of the area's liveliest bars. Inside this small wooden pub you'll find maritime flags, exposed brick walls, and one of the city's friendliest crowds. The tiny bar's small street is named for William Saroyan, who penned *The Time of Your Life,* which describes a 1930s dive somewhat like this bar.
   Just across Columbus Avenue is:
4. **Vesuvio,** 255 Columbus Ave. (tel. 362-3370), North Beach's most-revered cafe. Reminiscent of a left-bank bistro, this

hangout has been popular with writers, poets, and nonliterary "beats" since it opened in 1948 as a bar. Not so curiously, it's also popular with cab drivers, sailors, and tourists. See "The Bar Scene" in Chapter 10 for complete information.

Next door you'll find the:

5. **City Lights Book Store,** 261 Columbus Ave. (tel. 362-8193), the most celebrated literary stop in San Francisco. Owned by Lawrence Ferlinghetti, the renowned "beat generation" poet, this excellent three-level bookshop prides itself on a comprehensive collection of art, poetry, and political paperbacks, as well as more mainstream books. It has a Beat Section Poetry Room, and publishes its own avant-garde contemporary works.

Half a block ahead, at the intersection of Broadway, is the:

6. **Condor Club,** 300 Columbus Ave., one of the city's most famous strip clubs. The plethora of seedy strip joints around this intersection is a relic of the 1960s, when topless entertainment surfaced in San Francisco. Carol Doda, the city's best-known stripper, won fame for the Condor when she danced here on the opening night of the 1964 Republican National Convention, almost single-handedly kicking off the sexual revolution.

REFUELING STOP Turn right on Broadway and walk down several doors to **Little Joe's,** 523 Broadway (tel. 433-4343), a wide-open grill room known for its shellfish dishes, huge portions, and lack of pretension. The specialty here is cacciucco, a stew of clams, cod, crab, mussels, and prawns, cooked in a tomato-and-garlic sauce.

Back on the main street, Columbus Avenue is intersected by:

7. **Grant Avenue,** a chameleon of a street that changes its color, texture, and character three times in its barely 1½ mile length. At its origin at Market Street, it's a typical downtown shopping street. After Bush Street, it becomes the city's Asian main drag. Then, after crossing Pacific Avenue, it suddenly turns into North Beach's bohemian strip of art stores, coffeehouses, and offbeat bars.

Continue up Columbus Avenue to:

8. **Biordi Art Imports,** 412 Columbus Ave. (tel. 392-8096), which sells colorful hand-painted ceramic bowls, tiles, vases, and pasta dishes. Since 1946, Biordi has been stocked with pottery painted with the lively gold, red, blue, and brown hues of the southern Italian towns in which they are made.

Almost next door you'll find:

9. **Caffè Greco,** 423 Columbus Ave. (tel. 397-6261), one of the most recent additions to North Beach's cafe culture. Opened about eight years ago, the Greco quickly became one of the best places to linger. Sophisticated and relaxed, it serves beer, wine, and a good selection of coffee drinks.

Half a block ahead, at the corner of Vallejo, is the:

10. **Caffè Trieste,** 601 Vallejo St. (tel. 392-6739), an Italian outpost since 1957. Opera is always on the jukebox at this classic beatnik North Beach coffeehouse. Jack Kerouac and Allen Ginsberg used to give readings here, and Francis Ford Coppola reportedly wrote most of *The Godfather* script here. It's somehow provincial European feel is augmented by live arias sung by the owners, the Giotta family, on Saturday afternoon.

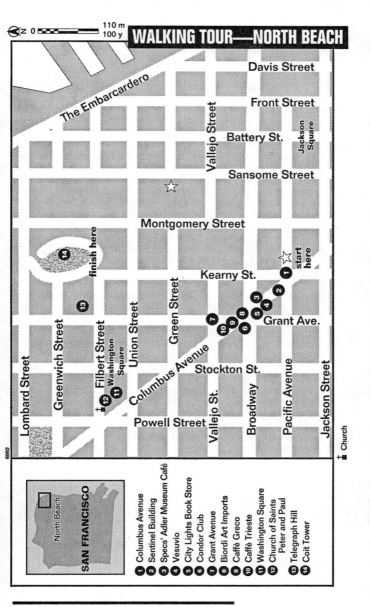

WALKING TOUR—NORTH BEACH

Davis Street
Front Street
Battery St.
Jackson Square
Sansome Street
Montgomery Street
The Embarcardero
Vallejo Street
Kearny St.
Green Street
finish here
Grant Ave.
Union Street
Filbert Street
Washington Square
Columbus Avenue
Stockton St.
Vallejo St.
Broadway
Pacific Avenue
Jackson Street
Greenwich Street
Lombard Street
Powell Street
start here
† Church

① Columbus Avenue
② Sentinel Building
③ Specs' Adler Museum Café
④ Vesuvio
⑤ City Lights Book Store
⑥ Condor Club
⑦ Grant Avenue
⑧ Biordi Art Imports
⑨ Caffè Greco
⑩ Caffè Trieste
⑪ Washington Square
⑫ Church of Saints Peter and Paul
⑬ Telegraph Hill
⑭ Coit Tower

SAN FRANCISCO
North Beach

REFUELING STOP At 566 Columbus Ave. is **Mario's Bohemian Cigar Store** (tel. 362-0536), a terrific hole-in-the-wall renowned for its meatball and eggplant focaccia sandwiches. Seating is at half a dozen tables and a simple linoleum-topped bar. Even if you're not hungry, stop in for a cappucino or Campari with the locals, and watch the unknowing tourists stroll on by.

Across from Mario's is:

11. **Washington Square,** a pentagonal park piazza with plenty of grass and benches. This is North Beach's hub, both geographically and culturally. Like Portsmouth Square in Chinatown (see Walking Tour 1), this pretty parcel is a popular meeting place for the neighborhood's older men. The Colonial American statue that adorns this space is not of America's first president, but of Benjamin Franklin. Looming over the park is the:

12. **Church of Saints Peter and Paul.** Once catering to the Italian community exclusively, the church now offers mass in Italian, English, and Cantonese.

Turn right on Union Street and meander uphill through the center of North Beach's residential area. Turn left up Montgomery Street and climb the steps up:

13. **Telegraph Hill,** a region of narrow alleys and small frame houses perched on alpine inclines. This entrancing, quiet area was once solidly Italian. Rents were low, and in the 1920s and 1930s a more diverse crowd, which included many artists and writers, moved in to take advantage of the cheap housing. The beatniks arrived in the 1950s. They brought fame to North Beach, and made this area desirable for today's younger, upwardly mobile residents. Now, rents have skyrocketed, and many of the quarter's old houses have been transformed into ultrachic apartments.

When you reach the top of the hill, you reach:

14. **Coit Tower,** which stands over North Beach like a big candle, or an upright Leaning Tower of Pisa. In a city known for its great views and vantage points, Coit Tower is tops. Completed in 1933, the tower is the legacy of Lillie Hitchcock Coit, a wealthy eccentric who left the city a $125,000 bequest "for the purpose of adding beauty to the city I have always loved." Inside the base are some colorful murals titled *Life in California, 1934.* Commissioned by the Public Works of Art Project, under the Roosevelt New Deal, the frescoed paintings, which have been recently restored, are a social realist's vision of America in the midst of the Great Depression.

WALKING (OR DRIVING) TOUR 3 — GOLDEN GATE PARK

Start: On Stanyan Street, at the park's easternmost end.
Finish: At the Pacific Ocean, at the park's westernmost end.
Time: 2 hours walking or 1 hour driving, not including picnicking.
Best Times: 11am to dusk, when the museums are open.
Worst Times: Rainy days.

One of the best and largest urban parks in America, San Francisco's Golden Gate Park (tel. 666-7201) is an integral part of the city. Three miles long and half a mile wide, the strip of green that runs east-west from Stanyan Street to the Pacific Ocean is a big source of pride among local residents—even if they rarely visit it. Golden Gate Park is not only huge, it changes with each step, and offers an outstanding variety of settings and attractions,

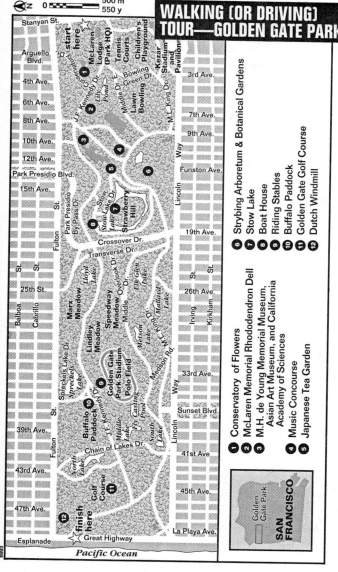

0 _____ 500 m
_____ 550 y

6 Strybing Arboretum & Botanical Gardens
7 Stow Lake
8 Boat House
9 Riding Stables
10 Buffalo Paddock
11 Golden Gate Golf Course
12 Dutch Windmill

1 Conservatory of Flowers
2 McLaren Memorial Rhododendron Dell
3 M.H. de Young Memorial Museum, Asian Art Museum, and California Academy of Sciences
4 Music Concourse
5 Japanese Tea Garden

SAN FRANCISCO

Golden Gate Park

including museums, bowling greens, boccie-ball and tennis courts, a polo and a football field, checker pavilions, baseball diamonds, riding stables, a bandstand, and some 27 miles of footpaths. What's more, you can picnic anyplace you please. Free guided walking tours of the park are offered every weekend from May through October by **Friends of Recreation and Parks** (tel. 221-1311). Call for information and reservations.

San Francisco's most important green was not so much built as wrested from the wasteland of rolling dunes that was purchased by the city in 1868. The existence of the park is something of a horticultural miracle, the result of a hard-fought war with nature by the park's first superintendent, John McLaren. During a record 56 years in office, McLaren relentless planted soil-holding trees and shrubs to tame the shifting sands. By the time he died, in 1943, the lush park was thriving with grassy picnic areas, miles of walking trails, a small chain of lakes, and areas for bicycling, skating, golfing, and playing tennis. In many ways McLaren's triumph was more political than agricultural. He successfully secured the confidence of local politicians, whose idea of a "park" was a stone desert of monuments, parking lots, and driveways. It's ironic, because this park would now be one of the world's best if it were not for the maze of fast-moving roadways that crisscross it, a relatively recent intrusion that has ostensibly turned Golden Gate into a series of little parks.

Now a "drive-thru" park, it is possible to pass most of the major sights without getting out of your car. You'll want to stop, however, to sightsee, stroll, and partake of the park's many wonderful offerings.

Entering from Fell Street, on the park's east side, keep right and walk or drive along John F. Kennedy Drive. Especially busy during the week, this road is closed to traffic on Sunday, when residents and visitors reclaim the greenery on bikes and skates.

Almost immediately on your right, you'll see the:

1. **Conservatory of Flowers** (tel. 666-7017), a fantastic glass Victorian greenhouse, built in Ireland and shipped in pieces around Cape Horn. Fronted by tall palms and manicured flower beds, the Conservatory is both architecturally stunning and horticulturally fascinating. Inside, hundreds of tropical trees and rare orchids stage a brilliant nonstop botanical show. It's open daily from 9am to 5pm; admission is $1.50 for adults and 75¢ for seniors and children 12 to 17.

   Across from the Conservatory is the 20-acre:

2. **McLaren Memorial Rhododendron Dell,** an otherworldly grove of trees that's definitely worth a look, especially in spring and early summer. A statue here honors the former park superintendent.

   Continue on Kennedy Drive for several blocks and turn left at the MUSEUM signs, where the:

3. **M. H. de Young Memorial Museum, Asian Art Museum, and California Academy of Sciences** (see Chapter 7, "What to See and Do in San Fransisco," for complete information) surround the sunken concrete, which is the park's:

4. **Music Concourse,** where free band concerts are staged on sunny summer Sundays. Just beyond the museums is the famed:

5. **Japanese Tea Garden** (tel. 752-1171), an enchanting patch of exotic artistry that mimics Kyoto's quietest corner. The garden was built, strangely enough, by an expatriate Australian named George Turner Marsh. As one of the backers of the 1894 Exposition, and a connoisseur of Japanese landscape gardening, Marsh offered the Japanese garden as an added fair attraction. Built with imported Japanese labor and materials, the "Japanese Village" proved so successful that the Park Commission retained it permanently.

   Visitors enter through an ornately hand-carved gateway toward reflecting pools alive with goldfish. The five-acre glen shines with the deep-green and gray tones of moss-covered rockeries. Pools are spanned by arched bridges and flanked by dwarf trees as dainty as nursery decorations. As you stroll along the bamboo-railed paths, you'll see traditional stone lanterns; a bronze Buddha, cast in Japan in 1790; and the brooding torii statues that guard Shinto shrines. There is also a small, busy open-air teahouse, where kimono-clad waitresses serve traditional green tea. If you're fortunate enough to visit during cherry-blossom time—in late March or early April—you'll be treated to a beautiful display rivaled only in Japan and Washington, D.C. The garden is open daily from 9am to 6:30pm; admission is $3 for adults, $1 for seniors and children 12to 17.

South of the Japanese Tea Garden is the:

6. Strybing Arboretum & Botanical Gardens (tel. 753-7089), with its main entrance at Ninth Avenue and Lincoln Way. Encompassing 70 acres of nature trails and formal gardens, the Strybing nurtures some 6,000 varieties of flowers and plants, including a cluster of native California redwoods. A Garden of Fragrance is designed for the visually impaired. It's open Monday through Friday from 8am to 4:30pm, and on Saturday, Sunday, and holidays from 10am to 5pm. Admission is free.

Back on Kennedy Drive, the roadway curves around:

7. Stow Lake, the park's largest body of water. Signs point to the:

8. Boat House (tel. 752-0347), where you can rent a rowboat or pedalboat, and float over to Strawberry Hill, a large, round island in the middle of the lake. Boat rentals are available year-round. There's usually a line on weekends.

The next mile of Kennedy Drive bisects a series of open meadows where weekend loungers sunbathe and barbecue. You also may see horses from the:

9. Riding Stables, located off to your left. Unfortunately, however, there are no rentals here. On your right-hand side you will encounter the:

10. Buffalo Paddock, a large, fenced bowl containing a small herd of bison. Stop and take a peek at these strange-looking behemoths, kept here by tradition since the 1890s.

West of the paddock is the:

11. Golden Gate Golf Course (tel. 751-8987), a nine-hole course with a short but tricky layout. Greens fees are $8 during the week, $11 on the weekends.

At the golf course, Kennedy Drive doglegs right and continues northwest for several blocks to the Pacific Ocean. Just before exiting the park, you'll see a:

12. Dutch Windmill that was once used to irrigate the park. Built in 1902 and restored in 1981, it is surrounded by a blazing bed of tulips. A second windmill stands near the park's southwest corner.

CHAPTER 9

SHOPPING FROM A TO Z

I f New York and Chicago are department-store cities, then San Francisco is a boutique town. Sure, there are plenty of large emporiums here, but this city's main shopping attractions are small, smart specialty shops, selling distinctive and unusual clothes, crafts, books, antiques, jewelry, and gifts. It is relevant that San Francisco is a great walking city, making it both fun and easy to stroll and shop along the many fashionable streets.

GREAT SHOPPING AREAS San Francisco has many shopping areas, but the following are among the best:

Union Square and Environs San Francisco's downtown, centered around Union Square and enclosed by Bush, Taylor, Market, and Montgomery Streets, contains several fashionable department stores, many high-end specialty shops, and some of the most respected names in retailing. **Maiden Lane,** a tree-lined walk that runs east from Union Square, is lined with some of the most elegant showcases in town. From Market Street, running north, the first four blocks of **Grant Avenue** contain several top-name shops, including Tiffany & Co., Shreve & Co., and Brooks Brothers. **Post Street,** which marks Union Square's northern perimeter, is another chic shopping strip, most densely packed with prestigious shops between Kearny and Taylor Streets.

Chinatown In many ways, Chinatown is the antithesis of Union Square, selling an exceptional variety of cheap goods, T-shirts, knockoffs, and innumerable tourist-oriented trinkets. The best shops in this crowded area are the colorful bazaars, crammed with an eclectic assortment of unrelated objects, from postcards and water pipes to Chinese tableware and plastic toys. Grant Avenue is the area's main thoroughfare, and side streets between Bush Street and Columbus Avenue are full of restaurants, markets, and interesting shops. Walking is best, since traffic through this area is slow and parking next to impossible. Most of the stores in Chinatown are open daily from 10am to 10pm.

Union Street Real San Franciscans are those who know the difference between Union *Square* and Union *Street*. Although they are similarly named, these two shopping areas are located far away from one another. The Cow Hollow section of this trendy street, between Van Ness Avenue and Steiner Street, is an "in" stretch for antiques, handcrafts, hip fashions, and deluxe glassware. A stroll along Union Street, poking through the many boutiques and highly original stores, makes for a very pleasant afternoon. Several excellent eateries are also worth the trip. The area is serviced by bus lines 41 and 45.

Haight Street The neighborhood known as Haight-Ashbury is most famous as a spawning ground for hippies in the

1960s. Although there are no longer so many flower children here, the Haight still has an active street scene and is home to a good number of writers and musicians as well as younger, upwardly mobile types. The six blocks of upper Haight Street, between Central Avenue and Stanyan Street, is the best place in the city to shop for trendy street styles from Europe and America. Along this thoroughfare is a healthy mix of boutiques, secondhand shops, and inexpensive restaurants. Bus lines 7, 66, 71, and 73 run the length of Haight Street.

The Muni metro line N stops at Waller Street and at Cole Street.

Fisherman's Wharf and Environs The nonstop strip of waterfront malls that runs along Jefferson Street includes hundreds of shops, restaurants, and attractions. Ghirardelli Square, Pier 39, the Cannery, and the Anchorage are all outlined under "Shopping Centers and Complexes," below.

HOURS, TAXES & SHIPPING Store hours are generally Monday through Saturday from 10am to 6pm and on Sunday from noon to 5pm. Most department stores stay open later, as do shops around Fisherman's Wharf—the most heavily touristed area.

Sales tax in San Francisco is 8½%, added on at the register for all goods and services purchased.

Most of the city's shops can wrap your purchase and ship it anywhere in the world via United Parcel Service (UPS). If they can't, you can send it yourself, either through UPS (tel. 952-5200) or through the U.S. mail (see "Fast Facts: San Francisco" in Chapter 4).

ANTIQUES

Jackson Square, a historic district just north of the Financial District's Embarcadero Center, is the place to go for the top names in high-end furniture and fine art. There are also a lot of Asian art dealers here. Over a dozen dealers on the two blocks between Columbus and Sansome streets specialize in European furnishings from the 17th to the 19th century. Most shops here are open Monday through Friday from 9am to 5pm and on Saturday from 11am to 4pm.

FUMIKI FINE ASIAN ARTS, 2001 Union St. Tel. 922-0573.

Specializing in fine Asian art and antiques, including Japanese baskets and Chinese artifacts and embroidery, the shop has one of the largest collections of antique Japanese Imari and Korean and Japanese tansus in the country. Open Monday through Saturday from 10am to 6pm and on Sunday from noon to 5pm.

ART

The **San Francisco Gallery Guide,** a comprehensive, bimonthly publication listing the city's current shows, is available free of charge from the William Sawyer Gallery, 3045 Clay St., San Francisco, CA 94115 (tel. 921-1600). Most of the city's major art galleries are clustered downtown, in the Union Square area. Below is a select list of the city's most interesting offerings. All the shops host changing exhibitions. Call for current information.

IMPRESSIONS

Paris is the San Francisco of Europe.
—CHINESE FORTUNE COOKIE

ATELIER DORE, 771 Bush St. Tel. 391-2423.
Atelier Dore features American and European painting from the 19th and 20th centuries, including some WPA art. Open Tuesday through Saturday from 11am to 5pm.

COBRA FINE ART, 580 Sutter St. Tel. 397-2195.
This is primarily a showcase for expressionist drawings, paintings, sculptures, and monotype by highly acclaimed international contemporary artists. Open Monday through Saturday from 10am to 6pm, and Sunday by appointment.

ELEONORE AUSTERER, 540 Sutter St. Tel. 986-2244.
Limited-edition graphics by modern masters like Braque, Matisse, Miró, Picasso, Calder, Man Ray, and Hockney are the offerings at Eleonore Austerer. The gallery, located in a beautiful old building near Union Square, is open Monday through Saturday from 10am to 6pm.

ERIKA MEYEROVICH, 231 Grant Ave. Tel. 421-9997.
Contemporary exhibitions of Warhol, Haring, Lichtenstein, Hockney, and others are sold alongside works by Picasso, Matisse, Chagall, Miró, and others. Open Monday through Friday from 10am to 5pm and on Saturday from 11am to 5pm.

FRAENKEL GALLERY, 49 Geary St. Tel. 981-2661.
This photography gallery features works by contemporary American and European artists. Excellent shows change frequently. Open Tuesday through Friday from 10:30am to 5:30pm and on Saturday from 11am to 5pm.

HARCOURTS MODERN AND CONTEMPORARY ART, 460 Bush St. Tel. 421-3428.
This is an international contemporary gallery featuring works on paper as well as a variety of other media. Open Tuesday through Saturday from 10am to 5:30pm.

IMAGES OF THE NORTH, 1782 Union St. Tel. 673-1273.
The highlight here is one of the most extensive collections of Inuit art—Canadian and Alaskan—in the United States. There's also a fine collection of Native American masks and jewelry. Open Monday through Saturday from 11am to 5:30pm and on Sunday from noon to 4pm.

MAXWELL GALLERIES, 551 Sutter St. Tel. 421-5193.
The specialty at Maxwell Galleries is 19th- and 20th-century European and American sculpture and paintings, including works by Raphael and Butler. Open Tuesday through Friday from 9:30am to 5:15pm and on Saturday from 11am to 5pm.

BOOKS

THE BOOKSMITH, 1644 Haight St. Tel. 863-8688.
Haight Street's best selection of new books is housed in this large, well-maintained shop. It carries all the top titles, along with

works from smaller presses, and over 1,000 different magazines. Open Monday through Saturday from 10am to 9pm and on Sunday from 10am to 6pm.

CHARLOTTE'S WEB, 2278 Union St. Tel. 441-4700.

A terrific children's bookstore, Charlotte's Web is notable for its particularly knowledgeable owner, who sells everything from cloth books for babies to histories and poetry for young adults. Nonliterary items include music cassettes, videos, posters, and cards. Open Monday through Saturday from 10am to 6pm, and Sunday from 10am to 5pm.

A CLEAN WELL-LIGHTED PLACE, 601 Van Ness Ave. Tel. 441-6670.

A really good general bookstore, this independently owned shop sells a wide variety of titles, and has an educated staff that knows about them. Open Monday through Saturday from 10am to 7pm, and Sunday from noon to 5pm.

CITY LIGHTS BOOK STORE, 261 Columbus Ave. Tel. 362-8193.

Owned by Lawrence Ferlinghetti, the renowned beat-generation poet, this excellent three-level bookshop prides itself on a comprehensive collection of art, poetry, and political paperbacks, as well as more mainstream books. Open daily from 10am to 11:45pm.

EASTWIND BOOKS & ARTS, 1435A Stockton St. Tel. 772-5877.

The emphasis here is on Asian-American and Chinese books, including fiction, medicine, history, and language. Open Monday through Saturday from 10am to 6pm and on Sunday from noon to 5pm.

MARKUS BOOKS, 1721 Fillmore St. Tel. 346-4222.

Markus has the Bay Area's best selection of books relating to African-American and African culture. In addition to a good collection of children's books, there are titles on fiction, history, politics, art, and biography. Open Monday through Saturday from 10am to 7pm, and Sunday from noon to 5pm.

MCDONALD'S BOOKSHOP, 48 Turk St. Tel. 673-2235.

San Francisco's biggest used-book shop claims to stock over a million volumes, including out-of-print, esoteric, and hard-to-find books in all categories and languages. As a birthday novelty, they'll find a copy of *Life* magazine from the month and year in which you were born. It's quite a shop. Open Monday, Tuesday, and Thursday from 10am to 6pm and Wednesday, Friday, and Saturday from 10:30am to 6:30pm.

RAND-MCNALLY MAP AND TRAVEL, 595 Market St. Tel. 777-3131.

Hands down the best travel bookstore in the city, this corner shop features maps, atlases, and travel guides to all destinations. Open Monday through Friday from 9am to 6:30pm and on Saturday from 10am to 6pm.

STACEYS, 581 Market St. Tel. 421-4687.

Although they are widely known for their technical, computer, and business sections, Staceys is equally well stocked with fiction and trade books. Open Monday through Friday from 9am to 6:30pm and on Saturday from 10am to 6pm.

CHINA, SILVER & GLASS

THE ENCHANTED CRYSTAL, 1895 Union St. Tel. 885-1335.

This shop has an extensive collection of fine crystal, art glass, jewelry, and one-of-a-kind decorative art, including one of the largest crystal balls in the world (from Madagascar). Open Monday through Saturday from 10am to 6pm and on Sunday from noon to 5pm.

GUMP'S, 250 Post St. Tel. 982-1616.

San Francisco's most impressive museum/store is located between Grant Avenue and Stockton Street. Founded more than a century ago, this supremely elegant establishment offers beautiful objects ranging from Asian antiques and porcelain to Steuben glass and Baccarat and Lalique crystal. It also claims to have the largest collection of freshwater pearls in the United States, and designs and manufactures much of its own jewelry. If you're in the market for a family of hand-carved Chilean lapis-lazuli penguins or for a Venetian opaline glass vase, then Gump's is the place. The store also encompasses an art gallery, a scent shop, and an interior-design salon. Open Monday through Saturday from 10am to 5:30pm.

CRAFTS

THE CANTON BAZAAR, 616 Grant Ave. Tel. 362-5750.

Amid a terrific variety of handcrafts you'll find an excellent selection of rattan and carved furniture, cloisonné enamelwork, rose Canton chinaware, glassware, carved jade, embroideries, jewelry, and antiques from mainland China. Open daily from 10am to 10pm.

THE NEW UNIQUE COMPANY, 838 Grant Ave. Tel. 981-2036.

Primarily a calligraphy and watercolor supplies store, the shop also has a good assortment of books relating to these topics. In addition, there is a wide selection of carved stones for use as seals on letters and documents. The store will carve seals to order should you want a special design or group of initials. Open daily from 10am to 10pm.

SILKROUTE INTERNATIONAL, 3119 Fillmore St. Tel. 563-4936.

Owned and operated by an Afghan who offers fascinating wares, old and new, from his native country, the shop sells needlework, clothing, brass and copperware, jewelry, and even antique guns. In addition, there are lots of Oriental carpets, tribal rugs, and tapestries, as well as Afghan dhurries. Open Monday through Friday from 11am to 7pm, on Saturday from 11am to 6pm, and on Sunday by appointment.

YANKEE DOODLE DANDY, 1974 Union St. Tel. 346-0346, or 346-3337.

This shop features America's largest collection of pre-1935 quilts, many more than 100 years old. In addition, there are folk-art carvings, contemporary primitive paintings, and handmade collector teddy bears. Everything in this country-style store is unique and intriguing, beautiful, or cuddly. Open Monday through Saturday from 10:30am to 5:30pm and on Sunday from noon to 5pm.

DEPARTMENT STORES

EMPORIUM, 835 Market St. Tel. 764-2222.

Located between Fourth and Fifth streets, adjacent to the San Francisco Shopping Centre (see "Shopping Centers and Complexes," below), Emporium is one of northern California's major chains. This is a full-line department store, including fashions, kitchenware, home furnishings, and electronics. Open Monday through Friday from 9:30am to 8pm, on Saturday from 9:30am to 6pm, and on Sunday from 11am to 6pm.

I. MAGNIN, Union Square. Tel. 362-2100.

Founded in 1876, this is one of the city's oldest businesses and the flagship shop in the I. Magnin chain. Ten upscale floors merchandise the finest fashions for women, men, and children. The store's Estée Lauder skin-care spa is almost as famous as its opulent ladies' powder room. Open Monday, Tuesday, and Friday from 10am to 8pm; on Thursday and Wednesday from 10am to 6pm; Saturday from 10am to 7pm; and on Sunday from 11am to 6pm.

MACY'S, Stockton and O'Farrell Sts., Union Square. Tel. 397-3333.

One of the largest stores in San Francisco, Macy's is divided into two distinct buildings. The seven-story Macy's West features contemporary fashions for women and juniors, including jewelry, fragrances, cosmetics, and accessories. The top floors contain home furnishings, while the Cellar sells kitchenware and gourmet foods. Across the street, Macy's East has five floors of men's and children's fashions, as well as one of the best electronics departments in the city. Open Monday through Saturday from 10am to 8pm, and on Sunday from 11am to 7pm.

NEIMAN-MARCUS, 150 Stockton St., Union Square. Tel. 362-3900.

Famous for its classic rotunda, this unit of the Texas-based chain features upscale men's and women's clothes, precious gems, and conservative formal wear. Other departments sell cosmetics, gourmet foods, and gifts. The Rotunda Restaurant, on the top floor, is a beautiful, relaxing place for lunch. Open Monday, Thursday, and Friday from 10am to 8pm; Tuesday, Wednesday, and Saturday from 10am to 6pm; and on Sunday from noon to 6pm.

NORDSTROM, in the San Francisco Shopping Centre, 865 Market St. Tel. 243-8500.

Renowned for its personalized service, this is the largest member of the Seattle-based fashion department-store chain. Nordstrom occupies the top five floors of the San Francisco Shopping Centre (see "Shopping Centers and Complexes," below) and is that mall's primary anchor. Equally devoted to women's and men's fashions, the store has one of the best shoe selections in the city, and thousands of suits in stock. The Nordstrom Café, on the top floor, has a terrific view and is a great place for an inexpensive lunch or light snack. Open Monday through Saturday from 9:30am to 9pm, and on Sunday from 11am to 7pm.

SAKS FIFTH AVENUE, 384 Post St. Tel. 986-4300.

San Francisco's branch of this famous New York–based shop is as opulent as any. Saks sells fashions and gifts for men, women, and children, and has a well-regarded restaurant on the top floor. Open Monday, Thursday, and Friday from 10am to 8pm; Tuesday,

Wednesday, and Saturday from 10am to 6:30pm; and on Sunday from noon to 5pm.

FASHIONS

BURBERRY'S, 225 Post St. Tel. 392-2200.

One of the biggest names in traditional fashions is most famous for its plaid-lined trenchcoat. Luggage, accessories, and other clothes items can also be found in Burberry plaid. Open Monday through Saturday from 9:30am to 6pm and on Sunday from noon to 5pm.

CABLE CAR CLOTHIERS, 1 Grant Ave. Tel. 397-4740.

Inside a beautiful landmark building at the corner of Market Street, this fine clothier features Aquascutum coats, English Church's shoes, McGeorge sweaters, Countess Mara neckwear, and other top fashions. Open Monday through Saturday from 9:30am to 5:30pm.

EDDIE BAUER, 220 Post St. Tel. 986-7600.

One of the first to use goose down in outdoor clothing, Eddie Bauer is known for its high-quality mail-order goods. There's an especially good fishing department. Open Monday through Saturday from 9:30am to 7pm and on Sunday from 11am to 5pm.

GUCCI AMERICA, INC., 200 Stockton St. Tel. 392-2808.

An elegant selection of apparel for men and women is offered by one of the best-known and most prestigious names in international fashion. In addition to shoes, leather goods, and scarves beautiful enough for framing, the shop offers pricey accessories such as a $7,000 handmade crocodile bag. Open Monday through Saturday from 10am to 6pm and on Sunday from noon to 5pm.

POLO/RALPH LAUREN, 90 Post St. Tel. 567-7656.

This beautifully assembled, multilevel store at Kearney Street is a tribute to the elegance and taste of its namesake designer. It features the entire collection of Polo apparel, from casual and roughwear to couture clothing, footwear, and accessories. Open Monday through Saturday from 10am to 6pm.

THREE BAGS FULL, 2181 Union St. Tel. 567-5753.

Knowledgeable locals come here for exquisite sweaters and knitwear. Many of the goods are handmade and one of a kind. Open Monday through Saturday from 11am to 6pm and on Sunday from noon to 5pm. Other city locations are 500 Sutter Street and 3314 Sacramento Street.

MEN'S FASHIONS

ALL AMERICAN BOY, 463 Castro St. Tel. 861-0444.

Long known for setting the mainstream style for gay men, All American Boy is the quintessential Castro clothing shop. Open Monday to Saturday from 10am to 8pm, and Sunday 11am to 7pm.

BOLLA, 1764 Haight St. Tel. 386-3290.

The beautiful wooden floors of this Haight Street shop are topped with metal racks displaying trendy English-style clothes. Women's fashions are available, but the best offerings here are men's dress shirts, ties, belts, socks, watches, and accessories. Open Monday through Saturday from 11am to 7pm and on Sunday from noon to 6:30pm.

BROOKS BROTHERS, 201 Post St. Tel. 397-4500.

In San Francisco, this bulwark of tradition is located near Grant Avenue, one block east of Union Square. Brooks Brothers introduced the button-down collar and single-handedly changed the standard of the well-dressed businessman. The multilevel shop also sells traditional casual wear, including sportswear, sweaters, and shirts. Open Monday through Saturday from 9:30am to 6pm and on Sunday from noon to 5pm.

CITIZEN CLOTHING, 536 Castro St. Tel. 558-9429.

The Castro has some of America's best men's casual clothing stores, and this is one of them. Stylish, but not faddish, pants, tops, and accessories are sold. Open daily from 10am to 8pm.

CULOT OF SAN FRANCISCO, 1969в Union St. Tel. 931-2413.

Specializing in men's undergarments and accessories, Culot sells high-quality underwear in a variety of styles, as well as cufflinks, suspenders, and tie clips. Open daily from 10:30am to 6:30pm.

WOMEN'S FASHIONS

THE CHANEL BOUTIQUE, 151 Maiden Lane. Tel. 981-1550.

The entire elegant Chanel line is under one roof and includes clothing, accessories, scents, cosmetics, and jewelry. Open Monday through Friday from 10am to 6:30pm, Saturday from 10am to 6pm, and on Sunday from 10am to 5pm.

THE DINOSTORE, 1553 Haight St. Tel. 861-3933.

In this great Haight Street boutique for women's shoes and hip, contemporary fashions, cute summer dresses, skirts, and tops are complemented by bustiers, scarves, and accessories. Look for the small green dinosaur out front. Open Monday through Saturday from 11am to 7pm and on Sunday from noon to 6pm.

IMPERIAL FASHION, 838 Grant Ave. Tel. 362-0981.

Near Washington Street you'll find some of the most attractive merchandise in Chinatown, most of it from mainland China—silk blouses, jackets, and kimonos, and also silk fabrics that can be custom-tailored especially for you. Beautiful embroideries, handkerchiefs, and linens are also available. Open daily from 10am to 9:30pm.

JAEGER INTERNATIONAL, 272 Post St. Tel. 421-3714.

Jaeger, near Stockton Street, has an international reputation for conservative designs and superb fabrics, especially lightweight wools. No one has ever accused this place of being on the cutting edge; it specializes in classic cuts in women's jackets, sweaters, pants, and skirts. Open Monday through Saturday from 9:30am to 5:30pm.

SOLO FASHION, 1599 Haight St. Tel. 621-0342.

One of my favorite shops in the Haight for original women's fashions, Solo offers a good selection of upbeat, contemporary English-style street wear, along with a collection of dresses designed exclusively for this shop. Open daily from 11am to 7pm.

CHILDREN'S FASHIONS

KIDS ONLY, 1608 Haight St. Tel. 552-5445.

Among more ordinary and conservative children's clothes can be found a small selection of funky outfits that sport the Haight Street look. Tie-dyed fabrics are sold, along with Nature's Wear brands that are made from all-natural, dye-free cloths. Open Monday through Saturday from 10am to 6pm, and Sunday from 11am to 5pm.

MINIS BY PROFILI, 2042 Union St. Tel. 567-9537.

Christina Profili, a San Franciscan clothing maker who used to design for The Gap, opened this children's clothing store in 1994 to sell her wonderful line of pint-sized pants, shirts, and dresses. Everything Profili designs matches with everything else—the colors and fabrics in every outfit in the store perfectly correspond with one another. A small toy corner includes storybooks that are sold with matching dolls. Open Monday through Thursday from 11:30am to 5:30pm, Saturday from 10am to 5:30pm, and Sunday from noon to 5:30pm.

SECONDHAND CLOTHING

AARDVARK'S, 1501 Haight St. Tel. 621-3141.

One of San Francisco's largest secondhand clothing dealers, Aardvark's has seemingly endless racks of shirts, pants, dresses, skirts, and hats from the last 30 years. Open daily from 11am to 7pm.

BUFFALO EXCHANGE, 1555 Haight St. Tel. 431-7733.

This large storefront on upper Haight Street is crammed with racks of antique and new fashions from the 1960s, '70s, and '90s. It stocks everything from suits and dresses to neckties, hats, handbags, and jewelry. Buffalo Exchange anticipates some of the hottest new street fashions. Open Monday through Saturday from 11am to 7pm, Sunday from noon to 6pm. A second shop is located at 1800 Polk St. (tel. 346-5741).

LA ROSA, 1711 Haight St. Tel. 668-3744.

On a street packed with vintage clothing shops, this is the most upscale, featuring a very good selection of high-quality secondhand goods. Formal suits and dresses are its specialty, but you'll also find sport coats, slacks, and shoes. Open Monday through Saturday from noon to 7pm, Sunday from noon to 6pm.

WASTELAND, 1660 Haight St. Tel. 863-3150.

The enormous art-filled exterior fronts a large collection of vintage and contemporary clothes for men and women. Leathers, natural fibers, and dark colors predominate. Grandma's furniture is also for sale. Open daily from 11am to 7pm.

FACTORY OUTLETS

There are many factory-outlet stores in San Francisco, selling overstocked and discontinued fashions at very good prices. All the following shops are located south of Market Street, in the city's warehouse district.

ESPRIT OUTLET STORE, 499 Illinois St. Tel. 957-2550.

All the Esprit collections and Susie Tompkins merchandise are available here at 30% or more off regular prices. In addition to clothes, the store sells accessories, shoes, and assorted other items. The bargain bins at the back of the store are especially appealing. Open Monday through Friday from 10am to 8pm, Saturday from 10am to 7pm, and Sunday from 11am to 5pm.

GLASSER DESIGNS, 32 Otis St. Tel. 552-3188.

The beautiful soft-leather handbags, totes, and business bags sold here are all handmade in San Francisco. The outlet is located half a block west of Mission Street and South Van Ness Avenue. Open Monday through Friday from 9am to 5:30pm, on Saturday from noon to 5pm.

THE NORTH FACE, 1325 Howard St., at Ninth St. Tel. 626-6444.

Well known for its sporting, camping, and hiking equipment, this off-price outlet carries a good selection of high-quality skiwear, boots, sweaters, and goods such as tents, packs, and sleeping bags. The North Face makes heavy use of Gore-Tex, down, and other durable lightweight materials. Open Monday through Saturday from 10am to 6pm.

FOOD

BEPPLES PIE SHOP AND RESTAURANT, 1934 Union St. Tel. 931-6225.

One of the most celebrated shops on Union Street is this mouth-watering noshery selling soups, muffins, breads, and pies. Open Monday through Wednesday from 7am to 11:30pm, on Thursday from 7am to midnight, on Friday from 7am to 2am, on Saturday from 9am to 2am, and on Sunday from 9am to 10:30pm.

GOLDEN GATE FORTUNE COOKIES CO., 56 Ross Alley. Tel. 781-3956.

This tiny, touristy factory sells fortune cookies hot off the press. You can purchase them in small bags or in bulk, and if your order is large enough, you may even be able to negotiate your own message. Even if you're not buying, stop in to see how these sugary treats are made. Open Monday through Friday from 10am to 7pm.

TEN REN TEA COMPANY, 949 Grant Ave. Tel. 362-0656.

At the Ten Ren Tea Company, between Jackson and Washington streets, you will be offered a steaming cup of roselle tea, made of black tea and hibiscus. In addition to a selection of almost 50 traditional and herbal teas, the company stocks related paraphernalia, such as pots, cups, and infusers. If you can't make up your mind, take home a mail-order form. Open daily from 9:30am to 9pm.

GIFTS

ART OF CHINA, 829–843 Grant Ave. Tel. 981-1602.

Amid a wide variety of collectibles, this shop features exquisite, hand-carved Chinese figurines. You'll also find a lovely assortment of ivory beads, bracelets, necklaces, and earrings. Pink-quartz dogs, jade figurines, porcelain vases, cachepots, and blue-and-white barrels suitable for use as table bases are just some of the many collectibles on offer. Open daily from 10am to 6pm.

AUD'S, 1980 Union St. Tel. 931-7765.

Located inside one of the street's most beautiful Victorians, the shop sells one-of-a-kind "fun things," including toys and wearable art. The jewelry is priced from $10 to $60; the shop's proceeds benefit Bay Area artists. Open daily from 10:30am to 6:30pm.

BABUSHKA, 333 Jefferson St. Tel. 673-6740.

Located near Fisherman's Wharf, adjacent to the Anchorage Shopping Center, Babushka sells exclusively Russian products, most of which are wooden or paper mâché nesting dolls. Open daily from 10am to 10pm.

BODY TIME, 2072 Union St. Tel. 922-4076.

All the oils, lotions, soaps, and pamperings sold here are biodegradable and not tested on animals. Soaps come in over 30 scents, including China Lily, Rain, Pikaki, and Black Rose. And if you don't find the fragrance you want, the shop will create it to your specifications. Other items include aloe vera fresheners, clay masks, and cleansing grains. Body Time also has related application utensils, such as sponges and bath brushes. Open Monday through Saturday from 10am to 6:30pm and on Sunday from 11am to 6pm.

DISTRACTIONS, 552 Haight St. Tel. 252-8751.

This is the best of the Haight Street shops selling pseudo-sixties psychedelia. Retro hippie clothes, pipes, toys, and stickers are liberally intermixed with tie-dyed Grateful Dead paraphernalia and lots of cool stuff to look at. Open Monday through Saturday from 11am to 6:45pm and Sunday from 11am to 6pm.

THE DOLLS AND BEARS OF CHARLTON COURT, 1957 Union St. Tel. 775-3740.

A pint-sized shop cluttered with bears and dolls in all sizes, Charlton Court is not a toy shop, but a collector's emporium, crammed with antique Raggedy Anns and teddys of all sizes. The store is located in a tiny alleyway off Union Street. Open Monday through Saturday from 10:30am to 3pm.

EXPLORATORIUM STORE, in the Palace of Fine Arts, 3601 Lyon St. Tel. 561-0390.

The best museum gift shop in the city is this fanciful store inside a terrific, hands-on science museum (see Chapter 7, "What to See and Do in San Francisco"). Gifts include Space Age Super Balls, high-bouncing rubber balls that never seem to slow down; chime earrings and magnets; and other gizmos and gadgets. Open daily from 10am to 5:30pm, until 9pm on Wednesday. Closed Monday.

FORMA, 1715 Haight St. Tel. 751-0545.

Perhaps the most unusual store in San Francisco is this celebration of urban kitsch between Cole and Shrader streets. In addition to colorful handmade dioramas, you'll find voodoo dolls, ant farms, sea monkeys, Rocky and Bullwinkle toys, Elvis toilet seats, and games such as Lite-Brite and Twister. Open Monday through Saturday from noon to 7pm and on Sunday from noon to 6pm.

OGGETTI, INC., 1846 Union St. Tel. 346-0631.

This fascinating Florentine shop specializes in objects decorated with marbleized paper. The decorative marbleizing technique was invented in the 17th century by Mace Ruette, the royal bookbinder to Louis XIII. Oggetti continues this elegant tradition, featuring covered frames, jewelry boxes, pencils, pencil boxes, and blank books, among other lovely objects. About 95% of Oggetti's items are imported from Italy and are exclusive to the store. Open Monday through Saturday from 10am to 6pm and on Sunday from 11am to 6pm.

PLANETWEAVERS TREASURES STORE, 1573 Haight St. Tel. 864-4415.

There truly are real treasures here; a huge selection of unusual arts and collectibles including drums, dolls, incense, cards, and clothing from around the world. Proceeds from the shop go directly to the United Nations' UNICEF fund that helps save children worldwide from the harmful effects of disease and malnutrition. Open daily 11am to 7pm.

REVIVAL OF THE FITTEST, 1701 Haight St. Tel. 751-8857.

On the corner of Cole Street, this window-wrapped shop sells retro and contemporary clocks, candleholders, picture frames, stemware, dinnerware, telephones, and collectibles. It also carries a good selection of silver and surgical steel jewelry, as well as art postcards. Open Monday through Saturday from 11am to 7pm and on Sunday from noon to 6pm.

SMILE, 500 Sutter St. Tel. 362-3436.

The shop is a treasure trove of unique, contemporary sculpture and gifts, all made by craftspeople with a sense of humor. A must-see. Open Monday through Saturday from 9:30am to 5:30pm.

UNION STREET MUSIC BOX CO., 2201 Union St. Tel. 563-5181.

Although these dust-collectors aren't for everybody, memento collectors will love this shop full of wind-up and electric music boxes. If your experience with these novelties is limited to twirling ballerinas, come check out the miniature cable car that climbs a hill, then turns around and descends it. Open daily from 10am to 7pm.

HOUSEWARES

THE WOK SHOP, 718 Grant Ave. Tel. 989-3797.

This shop, at Clay Street, has every conceivable implement for Chinese cooking, including woks, brushes, cleavers, circular chopping blocks, dishes, oyster knives, bamboo steamers, strainers—you name it. The shop also sells a wide range of kitchen utensils, baskets, handmade linens from China, and aprons. Open Sunday through Friday from 10am to 6pm, Saturday from 10am to 10pm.

Z GALLERIE, 2071 Union St. Tel. 346-9000.

A California-based chain, selling a good selection of poster art, along with unusual gifts, and matte black furnishings and kitchenware. Other stores are located in the San Francisco Shopping Centre (see "Shopping Centers and Complexes," below) and at 1465 Haight St. (tel. 863-7466). Open Monday through Thursday and Sunday from 10am to 7pm, Friday and Saturday from 10am to 11pm.

IMPORTS

COST PLUS IMPORTS, 2552 Taylor St. Tel. 928-6200.

Between Bay Street and North Point, at the Fisherman's Wharf cable-car turntable, Cost Plus is a vast warehouse crammed to the rafters with Chinese baskets, Indian camel bells, Malaysian batik scarves, and innumerable other items from Algeria to Zanzibar. More than 20,000 items from 40 nations are purchased directly from their country of origin and packed into this well-priced warehouse. Open Monday through Saturday from 9am to 9pm and on Sunday from 10am to 8pm.

JEWELRY

CARTIER, INC. 231 Post St. Tel. 397-3180.

One of the most respected names in jewelery and luxury goods operates its San Francisco shop between Grant Avenue and Stockton Street. The boutique's setting is as elegant as the beautifully designed jewelry, watches, crystal, and accessories it sells. Open Monday through Saturday from 10am to 5:30pm.

JERUSALEM SHOPPE, 531 Castro St. Tel. 626-7906.

Known for its fine collection of funky silver jewelry, this small shop in the middle of Castro Street also sells unusual amber pieces. Open Monday through Thursday from 10am to 8pm, Friday and Saturday from 10am to 8:30pm, and Sunday from 10am to 6pm.

OLD & NEW ESTATES, 2181A Union St. Tel. 346-7525.

Top-of-the-line antiques including pendants, diamond rings, necklaces, bracelets, watches, and natural pearls make this San Francisco's best jewelry museum. Bring your checkbook. Open Monday through Saturday from 11:30am to 6pm, Sunday noon to 5pm.

PEARL EMPIRE, 127 Geary St. Tel. 362-0606.

Located between Stockton Street and Grant Avenue, the Pearl Empire has been importing jewelry directly from Asia since 1957. They are specialists in unusual pearls and jade, and offer restringing on the premises. Open Monday through Saturday from 9:30am to 5:30pm.

UNION STREET GOLDSMITH, 1909 Union St. Tel. 776-8048.

A showcase for Bay Area goldsmiths, this exquisite shop sells custom-designed jewelry in all karats. Many pieces emphasize colored stones in their settings. Open Monday through Saturday from 11am to 5:45pm and on Sunday from noon to 4:45pm.

LEATHER

MARK CROSS, 170 Post St. Tel. 391-7770.

For more than 100 years this store has been known for the quality and beauty of its workmanship. All leather goods are hand-constructed and classically styled of calfskin, pigskin, ostrich, and lizard. The store will emboss your purchase with gold initials, free of charge. Open Monday through Saturday from 10am to 6pm, Sunday from noon to 5pm.

NORTH BEACH LEATHER, 1365 Columbus Ave. Tel. 441-3208.

Primarily selling leather jackets and dresses, this shop has up-to-the-minute fashions at high prices. Other leather items from casual to elegant are sold. A second shop is located at 190 Geary St. (tel. 362-8300). Open Monday through Thursday from 10am to 7pm, Friday and Saturday from 10am to 8pm, and on Sunday from noon to 6pm.

OVERLAND SHEEPSKIN CO., 21 Grant Ave. Tel. 296-9180.

Inside this pretty, wooden Southwestern-style shop, just off Market Street, are beautiful sheepskin hats, jackets, booties, and bears.

They stock some of the nicest sheep styles I've ever seen. Open daily from 8am to 8pm.

LINGERIE

BACKSEAT BETTY, 1584 Haight St. Tel. 431-8393.

This is San Francisco's best intimate-apparel shop. Their eclectic collection of synthetic, cotton, and rubber goods makes Victoria's Secret seem tame. Sexy dresses, skirts, and assorted outerwear are also sold, beneath a shrine to Cher. Open daily from 11am to 7pm.

CAROL DODA'S CHAMPAGNE & LACE LINGERIE BOUTIQUE, 1850 Union St. Tel. 776-6900.

Carol Doda, one of the country's most famous strippers, won fame at the Condor in North Beach, when she danced on the opening night of the 1964 Republican National Convention. Today she runs a shop in a Union Street courtyard. Lingerie and bodywear for men and women include bras, bustiers, and teddys (and G-strings for men). Open daily from 11am to 7pm.

UNDER COVER, 535 Castro St. Tel. 864-0505.

This Castro shop sells men's underwear, exercise wear, robes, Lycra shorts, and mini-tops. Check out the dozens of Polaroids of porn stars affixed to the wall behind the cash register. Open Monday through Friday from 11am to 8pm, Saturday from 10am to 8pm, and Sunday from 11am to 7pm.

RECORDS

RECYCLED RECORDS, 1377 Haight St. Tel. 626-4075.

Easily one of the best used-record stores in the city, this loud shop in the Haight has a good selection of promotional CDs and cases of used "classic" rock LPs. Sheet music, tour programs, and old *TV Guides* are sold. Open daily from 10am to 10pm.

ROUGH TRADE RECORDS, 1529 Haight St. Tel. 621-4395.

Both mainstream and alternative (new and used) CDs, tapes, and vinyl are sold in this well-stocked shop. Some local bands and hard-to-find international titles are available. Open Monday through Saturday from 10am to 11pm and on Sunday from 10am to 8pm.

STREETLIGHT RECORDS, 3979 24th St. Tel. 282-3550.

Overstuffed with used music in all three formats, this place is best known for its records and excellent CD collection. Rock music is cheap here, and a money-back guarantee guards against defects. Open Monday through Saturday from 10am to 10pm and on Sunday from 11am to 8pm.

SHOPPING CENTERS & COMPLEXES

Like any city, San Francisco's malls are filled with carbon-copy chain stores, but they are also dotted with a good selection of local specialty shops, and a taste of the avant garde.

THE ANCHORAGE, 2800 Leavenworth St., at Beach and Jefferson Sts., Fisherman's Wharf. Tel. 775-6000.

The newest of the waterfront complexes, The Anchorage offers still more shopping and dining near Fisherman's Wharf. The mall is fronted by an impressive two-story anchor sculpture, and continues the nautical theme throughout its outdoor promenades and decks. Close to 50 units offer everything from music boxes to home furnishings. **The Incredible Christmas Store** (tel. 928-5700) sells holiday items year round. There is also a fair assortment of restaurants and specialty food shops. In the courtyard, musicians, mimes, jugglers, and other street performers entertain. Open in summer daily from 10am to 9pm; the rest of the year, daily from 10am to 6pm.

THE CANNERY, 2801 Leavenworth St., at Jefferson St. Tel. 771-3112.

Once a Del Monte fruit-canning plant, this complex is now occupied by a score or two of shops, restaurants, and nightspots. Mercifully, there are few chain stores here. Shops include **Gourmet Market** (tel. 673-0400), selling international foods, coffees, and teas; **The Print Store** (tel. 771-3576), offering a well-chosen selection of fine art prints and local original art; and the **Basic Brown Bear Factory** (tel. 931-6670), where you can stuff your own teddy bear.

Cobb's Comedy Club (see Chapter 10, "Evening Entertainment") is also here, along with several restaurants.

The Museum of the City of San Francisco (tel. 928-0289) recently opened here; it is dedicated to the city's history and is open Monday through Sunday from 10am to 4pm.

The Cannery is open daily 10am to 6pm; extended hours during the summer and on holidays.

CROCKER GALLERIA, 50 Post St. Tel. 393-1505.

Modeled after Milan's Galleria Vittorio Emanuele, this glass-domed, three-level pavilion, about three blocks east of Union Square, features about 40 high-end shops. Fashions include Stephane Kelian designs, Nicole Miller, Gianni Versace, and Polo. Restaurants and gift and specialty shops round out the offerings. Open Monday through Friday from 9:30am to 6pm and on Saturday from 10am to 5pm.

GHIRARDELLI SQUARE, 900 North Point. Tel. 775-5500.

This former chocolate factory is one of the city's largest malls and most popular landmarks. Many chain stores are located here, including the women's clothier **Ann Taylor** (tel. 775-2872), **Crabtree & Evelyn** (tel. 474-5547) for earth-related gifts, and **The Sharper Image** (tel. 776-1443) for unique, upscale electronics and designs.

Many good restaurants are located here, too. See "Dining Complexes" in Section 11, "Specialty Dining," in Chapter 6 for complete information.

The complex is open daily from 10am to 6pm. Main plaza shops are open Monday through Thursday from 10am to 6pm, Friday and Saturday from 10am to 9pm, and on Sunday from 11am to 6pm; extended hours during the summer. Restaurant hours vary.

PIER 39. Tel. 981-8030.

This abandoned cargo pier is now one of the most popular tourist destinations in San Francisco. Occupying two levels adjacent to Fisherman's Wharf, this waterfront complex offers almost as many shops as Ghirardelli and the Cannery combined.

Some of the most interesting stores include **Designs in Motion** (tel. 397-5050), which claims the largest collection of kinetic sculpture in the city produced by local artists; **Puppets on the Pier** (tel. 781-4435), selling all kinds of manipulable puppets; and **Ready Teddy** (tel. 781-1255) for bears, bears, and more bears. You can watch wood carvers at work at **Whittler's Mother** (tel. 433-3010); and at **Kite Flight** (tel. 956-3181) you can buy a fanciful creation to fly in the breezes off the bay. At **Left Hand World** (tel. 433-3547), southpaws can stock up on scissors, potholders, watches, and corkscrews, all made for "lefties"; and at the **House of Magic** (tel. 346-2218), tricksters can find rubber chickens, fake blood and scars, and unusual masks.

Several Pier restaurants offer great views of the bay. See "Dining Complexes" in Section 11, "Specialty Dining," in Chapter 6 for complete information.

Open daily from 10:30am to 8:30pm; extended hours during the summer; restaurant hours vary.

SAN FRANCISCO SHOPPING CENTRE, 865 Market St. Tel. 495-5656.

Opened in 1988, this $140-million complex is one of the few vertical malls in the United States. Its most stunning features are the four-story spiral escalators that circle their way up to Nordstrom, the center's primary anchor and the largest unit in the Seattle-based fashion specialty chain (see "Department Stores," above). More than 90 specialty shops and restaurants include designer clothiers Adrienne Vittadini, Ann Taylor, Bebe, and Mondi. Lower-fashion outlets include Benetton, Footlocker, J. Crew, and Victoria's Secret. The mall's nine-story atrium is covered by a retractable skylight. Open Monday through Saturday from 9:30am to 8pm and on Sunday from 11am to 6pm; holiday hours may vary.

SHOES

BIRKENSTOCK NATURAL FOOTWEAR, 1815 Polk St. Tel. 776-5225.

Located at Washington Street, this relaxed store is known for its California-style form-fitting sandals. Other orthopedically correct bands are also available, including Finn Comforts, ECCO, and Reikers. Open daily from 10:30am to 6pm.

KENNETH COLE, in the San Francisco Shopping Centre, 865 Market St. Tel. 227-4536.

High-fashion footwear for men and women is sold at this trendy shop. There is also an innovative collection of handbags and small leather goods and accessories. A second shop is located at 2078 Union St. (tel. 346-2161). Open Monday through Saturday from 9:30am to 8pm and on Sunday from 11am to 6pm.

TAMING OF THE SHOE, 1736 Haight St. Tel. 221-4453.

For both men and women, this contemporary shoe and boot shop is filled with the hippest names from America and Europe. It also sells many original styles under its own name, and vintage footwear from the '50s, '60s, and '70s. Open Monday through Saturday from 11am to 7pm, and on Sunday from 11am to 5pm.

TOBACCO

ALFRED DUNHILL OF LONDON, 290 Post St. Tel. 781-3368.

This tobacconist near Stockton Street has been specializing in custom-blended tobacco since the turn of the century. Accessories have been added more recently—Dunhill lighters are among the most elegantly designed and consistently functional. Today the mark also covers an exquisite line of men's clothing, including sweaters, jackets, and shirts. Leather goods and luggage are also of Dunhill quality. Open Monday through Saturday from 9:30am to 6pm and on Sunday from noon to 5pm.

TOYS

THE CHINATOWN KITE SHOP, 717 Grant Ave. Tel. 989-5182.

This shop's astonishing assortment of flying objects includes attractive fish kites, wind socks in nylon or cotton, hand-painted Chinese paper kites, wood-and-paper biplanes, and pentagonal kites—all of which make great souvenirs or decorations. Computer-designed stunt kites have two control lines to manipulate loops and dives. Open daily from 10am to 9pm.

F.A.O. SCHWARZ, 48 Stockton St. Tel. 394-8700.

The world's greatest toy store for both children and adults is filled with every imaginable plaything, from hand-carved, custom-painted carousel rocking horses, dolls, and stuffed animals, to gas-powered cars, train sets, and hobby supplies. At the entrance is a singing 22-foot clock tower with 1,000 different moving parts. If you're with kids and don't want to buy, tell them it's a museum. Open Monday through Wednesday and Friday and Saturday from 10am to 6:30pm; Thursday from 10am to 8pm; and on Sunday from 11am to 6pm.

TRAVEL GOODS

ON THE ROAD AGAIN, Pier 39. Tel. 434-0106.

In addition to lightweight luggage, this smart shop sells toiletry kits, travel bottles, travel-size items, and a good selection of other related goods. Open daily from 10am to 8:30pm.

THOMAS BROTHERS MAPS, 550 Jackson St. Tel. 981-7520, or toll free 800/969-3072.

The best map shop in the city, Thomas Brothers sells street, topographic, and hiking maps depicting San Francisco, California, and the world. A selection of travel-related books is also sold. Open Monday through Friday from 9:30am to 5:30pm.

WINES

THE NAPA VALLEY WINERY EXCHANGE, 415 Taylor St. Tel. 771-2887, or toll free 800/653-9463.

Situated in the heart of downtown, between Geary and O'Farrell streets, this is a convenient place to shop for California wines and champagnes. The selection is excellent, encompassing varieties from every region in the state. Major wineries as well as smaller, limited-release vintners are represented (about 250 different brands in all). The staff is expert at packing wines for travel or shipping. They take phone orders and credit cards are accepted. Open Monday through Saturday from 10am to 7pm.

CHAPTER 10

SAN FRANCISCO NIGHTS

1. THE PERFORMING ARTS

2. THE CLUB & MUSIC SCENE

3. THE BAR SCENE

4. MORE ENTERTAINMENT

As the West Coast's cultural capital, San Francisco does not disappoint. The city's opera is justifiably world-renowned, the ballet is respected, and the theater is high in both quantity and quality. Dozens of piano bars and top-notch drinking rooms are augmented by one of the best dance-club cultures this side of New York. For a city with fewer than a million inhabitants, San Francisco's overall artistic enterprise is nothing short of phenomenal. In fact, the only U.S. city to better it is New York—which is more than ten times its size.

For up-to-date nightlife information, turn to the **San Francisco Weekly** and the **San Francisco Bay Guardian,** both excellent guides to current activities around the city, with comprehensive listings. They are available free at bars and restaurants, and from street-corner boxes all around the city. **Key,** a free touristy monthly, also has information on programs and performance times; it's available in hotels and around the major tourist sights. The local daily newspapers also have good previews of upcoming events. The Sunday edition of the *San Francisco Examiner and Chronicle,* for example, features a **"Datebook"** section, printed on pink paper, with information and listings on the week's upcoming events.

1. THE PERFORMING ARTS

Tix Bay Area (tel. 433-7827) sells half-price tickets to theater, dance, and music performances on the day of the show only; tickets for Sunday and Monday events, if available, are sold on Saturday. They also sell advance, full-price tickets for most performance halls, sporting events, concerts, and clubs. A service charge, ranging from $1 to $3, is levied on each ticket. Only cash or traveler's checks are accepted for half-price tickets; Visa and MasterCard are accepted for full-price tickets. Tix is located on Stockton Street, on the east side of Union Square (opposite Maiden Lane). It's open Tuesday through Saturday from noon to 7:30pm.

Tickets to most theater and dance events can also be obtained through **City Box Office,** Sherman Clay & Co., 141 Kearny St. (tel. 392-4400).

BASS Ticketmaster (tel. 510/762-2277) sells computer-generated tickets to concerts, sporting events, plays, and special events. Downtown BASS Ticketmaster ticketing offices include Tix

IMPRESSIONS

If you are alive, you can't be bored in San Francisco.
—WILLIAM SAROYAN

Bay Area (see above) and the Emporium Department Store, 835 Market St.

Special concerts and performances are staged in San Francisco year round. **San Francisco Performances,** 500 Sutter St., Suite 710 (tel. 398-6449), has been bringing acclaimed artists to the Bay Area for more than a dozen years. Shows run the gamut from classical to dance and jazz, and sometimes include ethnic and other styles. Performances are staged all around town, including the city's Performing Arts Center, Davies Hall, and Herbst Theatre, with occasional productions at the Cowell Theater at Fort Mason. The season lasts from October through May. Tickets cost $12 to $47, and are available through City Box Office (tel. 392-4400). There is also a 6pm Thursday after-work concert series at the EC Cabaret, 3 Embarcadero Center in fall and winter, $6 admission at the door. Call 398-6449 for information.

Other festivals and events are especially heavy during the summer, when workers are on vacation and the tourist season is in full swing. One of the best, and longest-running, summer programs is the free **Stern Grove Midsummer Music Festival** (tel. 398-6551), held every Sunday at 2pm in Golden Gate Park. The first concert is traditionally offered by the San Francisco Symphony Orchestra; other performances include ballet, jazz, and theater. For more than 50 years the festival has run from mid-June through August. Stern Grove is located near 19th Avenue and Sloat Boulevard; arrive early for a good view, and bring a picnic.

THE MAJOR PERFORMING ARTS COMPANIES

CLASSICAL MUSIC

PHILHARMONIA BAROQUE ORCHESTRA, 57 Post St., Ste. 705. Tel. 391-5252.

Acclaimed by the *New York Times* as "the country's leading early-music orchestra," Philharmonia Baroque performs in San Francisco and all around the Bay Area. The season lasts from September to April. In the city, they play at Herbst Theatre. Tickets run $20 to $29.

SAN FRANCISCO CONTEMPORARY MUSIC PLAYERS, 44 Page St., #604A. Tel. 252-6235.

The Contemporary Music Players feature modern chamber works by international artists. Free, informal pre-concert discussions begin at 7pm and are held in the Green Room of the San Francisco War Memorial Building, Van Ness Avenue and McAllister Street. Phone for dates and programs. Tickets cost $14 for adults, $10 for seniors 65 and older, and $6 for students.

SAN FRANCISCO SYMPHONY, Louise M. Davies Hall, 201 Van Ness Ave., at Grove St. Tel. 431-5400.

Founded in 1911, the internationally respected San Francisco Symphony has long been in important part of this city's cultural life. Led by music director Herbert Blomstedt and music director designate Michael Tilson Thomas, the symphony moved to

---

THE MAJOR CONCERT/PERFORMANCE HALLS

Cow Palace, Geneva and Santos Sts., Daly City (tel. 469-6065).

Louise M. Davies Symphony Hall, 201 Van Ness Ave., at Grove LSt. (tel. 431-5400).

The Great American Music Hall (GAMH), 859 O'Farrell St. (tel. 885-0750).

Herbst Theatre, 401 Van Ness Ave. (tel. 392-4400).

Theatre Artaud, 450 Florida St. (tel. 621-7797).

War Memorial Opera House, 301 Van Ness Ave. (tel. 864-3330).

Zephyr Theatre, 25 Van Ness Ave. (tel. (441-6655).

---

the acoustically superior Davies Hall in 1980. The long season runs from September to May and is always packed with internationally acclaimed guest artists. Summer symphony activities include a Composer Festival, a Summer Pops series, and a presentation in concert with the Joffrey Ballet. Tickets range from $8 to $65.

WOMEN'S PHILHARMONIC, 330 Townsend St., Suite 218. Tel. 543-2297.

For more than ten years, this specialist orchestra has been playing works by historical and contemporary women composers. Most performances are held at the First Congregational Church, Post and Mason streets. Phone for dates, programs, and ticket prices.

OPERA

POCKET OPERA, 333 Kearny St., Suite 703. Tel. 989-1855.

From March through June, this comic company stages farcical performances of well-known operas. The setting is intimate and informal, almost always devoid of pricey costumes and sets. The cast ranges from 3 to 16 players, and is supported by a similarly numbered orchestra. The rich repertoire includes such works as *The Merry Widow* and *Così Fan Tutte,* all translated into English. Performances are on Saturday or Sunday. Call for complete information and show times. Tickets cost $18 to $22.

SAN FRANCISCO OPERA, War Memorial Opera House, 301 Van Ness Ave. Tel. 864-3330.

The San Francisco Opera was the United States' first municipal opera, and is one of the cultural bastions that has given this city such a good artistic reputation. A brilliantly balanced cast features celebrated stars like Frederica Von Stade and Placido Domingo, along with promising newcomers for whom this is often the greatest break of their careers. Staging and direction are a wonderful blend of traditional effects and "avant-garde" innovations. All productions have English supertitles.

The opera season starts in September and lasts just 14 weeks. Performances are held most evenings, except Monday, with matinees on Sundays. Performances are considered social as well as artistic events and, unfortunately, tickets are not cheap ($20 to $130, or $8 for standing room, sold after 10:30am on the day of the performance) or easy to acquire. Tickets go on sale as early as August, and the best seats quickly sell out. Unless Pavarotti or Domingo is in town, less-coveted views are usually available until curtain time.

THEATER COMPANIES

AMERICAN CONSERVATORY THEATER [ACT], Stage Door Theater, 440 Mason St. Tel. 749-2228.

The American Conservatory Theater (ACT) made its debut in 1967 and quickly established itself as the city's premier resident theater group. The troupe is so venerated that ACT has been compared to the superb British National Theatre, the Berliner Ensemble, and the Comédie Françiase. ACT offers solid, well-staged, and brilliantly acted theater, and performs both classical drama and new and experimental works. It won a Tony Award for excellence in repertory theater and actor training in 1979. Whatever's on, the repertoire is always exciting and upbeat. The ACT season runs from October through May. Performances are held at various venues around the city, including the Stage Door Theatre, Theatre on the Square, and the Orpheum Theater. Specific locations and transit information can be obtained from the box office. Tickets run $12 to $38.

EUREKA THEATRE COMPANY, 2730 16th St. Tel. 243-9899.

Eureka produces a number of outstanding, award-winning plays in its own 200-seat facility near Harrison Street, south of Market Street. Productions are both contemporary and classical, and usually deal with political or social issues. Eureka's season runs from September to June and performances are usually presented Wednesday through Sunday. Tickets cost $13 to $25, half price for students and seniors ten minutes prior to the performance.

LORRAINE HANSBERRY THEATRE, 620 Sutter St. Tel. 474-8800.

San Francisco's top African-American troupe performs in a 300-seat theater off the lobby of the Sheehan Hotel, near Mason Street. Special adaptations from literature are performed along with contemporary dramas, reworked classics, and world premieres. Phone for dates, programs, and ticket prices.

THE MAGIC THEATRE, Building D, Fort Mason, Laguna St. Tel. 441-8822.

A highly acclaimed resident company, the Magic Theatre is best known for adventuresome, often controversial, works by emerging and established contemporary playwrights. Sam Shepard's Pulitzer Prize–winning play *Buried Child* premiered here. More recent productions have included Jon Robin Baitz's *The End of the Day* and *Temptation*, a play by Czech president Václav Havel. The season usually runs from October to July; performances are offered Wednesday through Sunday. Tickets cost $12 to $21; $12 for students, children, and seniors.

THEATRE RHINOCEROS, 2926 16th St. Tel. 861-5079.

Founded in 1977, this was America's first (and still the foremost) theater ensemble devoted solely to works addressing gay and lesbian issues. The company presents two dozen fully mounted productions of new and classic works each year. The theater is located one block east of the 16th Street/Mission BART station. Phone for dates, programs, and ticket prices.

DANCE COMPANIES

In addition to the local companies, top traveling troupes like the Joffrey Ballet and American Ballet Theatre make regular appearances. Primary modern dance spaces include the **Theatre Artaud,** 450 Florida St. (tel. 621-7797); the **Cowell Theater,** at Fort Mason Center (tel. 441-5706); **Dancer's Group/Footwork,** 3221 22nd St., at Mission (tel. 824-5044); and the **New Performance Gallery,** 3153 17th St. (tel. 863-9834). Check the local papers for schedules or contact the theater box offices directly.

SAN FRANCISCO BALLET, 455 Franklin St. Tel. 861-5600, or 703-9400.

The San Francisco Ballet has won the highest possible praise from around the world, even from London critics, who are notoriously spoiled by their own superlative Royal Ballet company and accept only the Russians and the Danes as equals. This city's troupe, founded in 1933, is the oldest permanent ballet company in the United States, and is widely regarded as one of the best. Under the artistic direction of Helgi Tomasson, former choreographer and principal dancer with the New York City Ballet, the San Francisco Ballet performs classics and world premieres in equal parts. The season usually lasts from January to May, with short gaps in between. Performances are staged at the War Memorial Opera House, Van Ness Avenue and Grove Street, almost nightly (except Monday). *The Nutcracker,* performed in December of every year, is one annual tradition worth supporting. Tickets are $10 to $75.

MAJOR CONCERT HALLS & AUDITORIUMS

COW PALACE, Geneva and Santos Sts., Daly City. Tel. 469-6065.

Located about ten miles south of downtown, this 14,500-seat multipurpose facility features a plethora of concerts, exhibits, conventions, trade shows, and sporting events. In addition to top-name musicians like Van Halen and Neil Diamond, the palace hosts Disney's World on Ice, the Grand National Rodeo, the San Francisco Sports and Boat Show, and the Ringling Bros. and Barnum & Bailey Circus. Tickets are usually available through BASS Ticketmaster (see above), as well as the Cow Palace box office. Prices vary depending on the event.

LOUISE M. DAVIES SYMPHONY HALL, 201 Van Ness Ave., at Grove St. Tel. 431-5400.

This Civic Center hall, having undergone a recent renovation, is the premier concert space for the San Francisco Symphony, classical, pop, and jazz musicians, and top traveling orchestras. The auditorium features an 8,000-pipe Ruffatti organ. Symphony tickets run $8 to $65; tickets to other shows depend on the performance.

THE GREAT AMERICAN MUSIC HALL (GAMH), 859 O'Farrell St. Tel. 885-0750.

From the exterior, this 1907 building looks as though it could house anything from a restaurant to an insurance company, and over the years it probably has. The charming interior sports carved plaster cupids on the ceiling, while huge marble pillars support gilded mezzanine boxes. The hall's eclectic and adventurous booking policy intersperses top names like Etta James, Wynton Marsalis, B. B. King, and Carmen McRae, with rising stars, a capella groups, satirical comedy, and rock-and-roll and swing dance bands. Light meals, snacks, and drinks are available. It's located between Polk and Larkin streets. Tickets cost $5 to $30, depending on the performer.

HERBST THEATRE, 401 Van Ness Ave. Tel. 392-4400.

Opened in 1932 as the Veterans Auditorium and rechristened the Herbst after its 1978 renovation, it has become the city's top hall for local and visiting musicians and artists; the stage is lit almost every night of the year. The 928-seat auditorium was the site of the 1945 signing of the United Nations Charter. Its walls are hung with eight paintings commissioned for the 1915 Panama Pacific International Exposition, created by renowned muralist Frank Brangwyn. Tickets range from $10 to $50, depending on the performance.

THEATRE ARTAUD, 450 Florida St. Tel. 621-7797.

This 300-seat theater, located in the former American Can Company building, is an innovative showplace for dance, music, and drama performances. Tickets run $5 to $25, depending on the performance.

WAR MEMORIAL OPERA HOUSE, 301 Van Ness Ave. Tel. 864-3330.

This magnificent 3,252-seat European-style opera house, on Van Ness Avenue at Grove Street, opened in 1932. It is a terrific example of Beaux Arts architecture. As the premier city stage for top opera and ballet, the auditorium offers good sightlines and superior acoustics. Ballet tickets cost $5 to $75; opera tickets, $20 to $130; and other shows vary depending on the performance.

ZEPHYR THEATRE, 25 Van Ness Ave. Tel. 441-6655.

Three separate theaters are housed in this renovated Masonic Temple, a San Francisco landmark. A busy stage schedule is filled by everything from poetry readings to dance, theater, and music. Ticket prices vary depending on the performance.

THEATERS

Most of San Francisco's stages are clustered together, on the blocks just east of Union Square. This semi-official "theater district" is the closest thing San Francisco has to a Broadway or West End. The city's theater offerings—known for solid staging and acting—are easily the best in the West. The high quality of performances matches the unusual quantity of productions, a result of the large number of artists who have made the Bay Area their home.

While attending the theater in San Francisco is not particularly cheap, it is substantially less expensive than comparable productions in New York or London. Expect to pay $20–$50 per ticket for Broadway-size shows, $5–$15 per ticket for smaller productions.

CLIMATE, 252 Ninth St., at Folsom St. Tel. 626-9196.

After eight successful years, Climate is still going strong, showcasing avant-garde and experimental works in a casual and intimate atmosphere.

CURRAN THEATRE, 445 Geary St. Tel. 474-3800 for information.

Erected in the 1920s, the Curran was one of the last great theaters to be built in San Francisco. Although it once hosted operas, plays, and ballets, the Curran now specializes in big-name Broadway musicals and comedies, usually with major stars, like Judd Hirsch in *I'm Not Rappaport*, James Earl Jones in *Fences*, Lily Tomlin in *The Search for Signs of Intelligent Life in the Universe*, and *Les Miserables*.

GOLDEN GATE THEATER, 1 Taylor St. Tel. 474-3800 for information.

Lavishly appointed, the theater was built in 1922 and has hosted many famous acts, from the Marx Brothers to Carmen Miranda. The original building was so plush that it included a lounge and library solely for orchestra members. Reopened in 1979 after a massive restoration that revealed its original grandeur, the theater once again features marble floors, gilt trimmings, French carpeting, and rococo ceilings. The immense size of the house forces its owners to book popular Broadway-style musicals almost exclusively. It's located at Market Street and Golden Gate Avenue.

LIFE ON THE WATER, Building B, Fort Mason. Tel. 776-8999.

Easily the most innovative stage in the city for avant-garde performances of all kinds, Life on the Water is a must-see for anyone interested in alternative theater and performance art.

MARINE'S MEMORIAL THEATRE, 609 Sutter St. Tel. 771-6900.

Located in the Marines Memorial Association building at Sutter and Mason streets, this stage features shows running the gamut from one-act performance-art prices to full-blown Broadway musicals.

THE ORPHEUM, 1192 Market St. Tel. 474-3800 for information.

This handsomely refurbished vaudeville palace is architecturally patterned after a cathedral in Spain. Located on Market at 8th Street, the theater primarily features Broadway revivals starring top names. Productions have included *Man of La Mancha* and *Secret Garden*. Concerts with stars like Shirley Maclaine and Linda Ronstadt are also featured.

THEATRE ON THE SQUARE, 450 Post St. Tel. 433-6461; box office 433-9500.

Comedies, musicals, and dramas are all staged in this 750-seat, Gothic-Mediterranean–style, second-floor theater. Prepackaged productions are booked here almost exclusively, and most take full advantage of the flexible seating and close contact with the audience. It's located near Union Square, inside the Kensington Park Hotel, between Powell and Mason streets.

2. THE CLUB & MUSIC SCENE

Always a pioneer in arts and entertainment, San Francisco is well known for its liberal policies and alternative culture. The city is credited with popularizing topless entertainment in the early 1960s, and made headlines in the 1970s for its particularly promiscuous gay nightlife. Today, most of the city's strip clubs are rather seedy places, and the AIDS crisis has curtailed the gay party scene. Like other major American metropolitan areas, San Francisco offers a good variety of dance clubs and live-music venues. The hippest dance places are located South of Market Street (SoMa), in former warehouses. The city's most popular music and cafe culture is still centered around North Beach; a walk along Columbus Avenue any night of the week will be rewarded with a number of exciting finds. Check the local papers for the latest.

CABARET & COMEDY

BAY AREA THEATRESPORTS, 450 Geary Blvd. Tel. 824-8220.

Combining comedic improvisation with competitive spirit, Bay Area Theatresports (BATS) is comprised of several four-player teams who take on challenges formed with audience suggestions. Judges then flash scorecards good-naturedly, or honk a horn—Gong Show style—for scenes that just aren't working. Shows are staged on Mondays only. Phone for reservations.

Admission: $10.

BEACH BLANKET BABYLON, at Club Fugazi, 678 Green St. Tel. 421-4222.

Now a San Francisco tradition, Beach Blanket Babylon evolved from Steve Silver's Rent-a-Freak service—a group of party-givers extraordinaire who hired themselves out as a "cast of characters" to entertain, complete with fabulous costumes and sets, props, and gags. After their act caught on, it was moved into the Savoy-Tivoli, a North Beach bar. By 1974 the audience had grown too large for the facility, and Beach Blanket has been at the 400-seat Club Fugazi ever since.

Tiny tables now face the medium-size stage, where one of the most delightful, funny, and original productions is staged nightly. Beach Blanket is a comedic musical send-up that is best known for its outrageous costumes and oversize headdresses. It's been playing almost 20 years now and almost every performance still sells out. The show is updated with enough regularity that it still draws a fair number of locals along with the hordes of tourists. Persons under 21 are welcome at Sunday matinees at 3pm when no alcohol is served; photo ID is required for evening performances. It's wise to write for tickets at least three weeks in advance, or obtain them through TIX (see above). *Note:* When you purchase tickets, they will be within a specific section depending upon price; however, seating is still first-come/first-seated within that section. Performances are given on Wednesday and Thursday at 8pm, on Friday and Saturday at 7 and 10pm, and on Sunday at 3 and 7pm.

Admission: Tickets $17–$40.

COBB'S COMEDY CLUB, 2801 Leavenworth St. Tel. 928-4320.

Located in the Cannery at Fisherman's Wharf, Cobbs attracts an upscale audience with national headliners such as George Wallace, Emo Philips, and Jake Johannsen. There is comedy every night, including a 13-comedian All-Pro Monday showcase (a three-hour marathon). Cobb's is open to those 18 and over, as well as kids aged 16 and 17 if they are accompanied by a parent or legal guardian. Shows are Tuesday through Thursday and Sunday at 9pm, and Friday and Saturday at 9 and 11pm.

Admission: Tues–Sun $8–$15, plus a two-beverage minimum nightly.

FINOCCHIO'S, 506 Broadway. Tel. 982-9388.

For more than 50 years this family-run cabaret club, on Broadway at Kearny Street, has showcased the best female impersonators. This funny, kitschy establishment sets the standard to which all others should strive. There are three different lavish reviews nightly (usually staged Thursday through Saturday at 8:30, 10, and 11:30pm), and a single admission charge is good for the entire evening. Parking available next door at the Flying Dutchman.

Admission: $12, no drink minimum.

HOLY CITY ZOO, 408 Clement St. Tel. 386-4242.

Holy City Zoo, on Clement Street between Fifth and Sixth avenues, is San Francisco's longest-running comedy club. This intimate space is home to many comics, and has helped launch numerous stars, most notably Robin Williams, who used to tend bar here when he wasn't performing. Sunday and Monday are "open-mike" nights, which means that anybody—amateaur or pro—can drop in and do a routine. Tuesday nights are the All-Pro Comedy Showcases. Wednesday is improvisation night, featuring local improv artists. Thursday through Saturday nights headline the best local and national comedic talents. Shows are Sunday through Thursday at 8:30pm and on Friday and Saturday at 8:30 and 10:30pm.

Admission: $5–$10 (depending on the performers), plus a two-drink minimum.

PUNCH LINE, 444 Battery St., plaza level. Tel. 397-4337, or 397-7573 for recorded information.

Between Washington and Clay streets, adjacent to the Embarcadero One office building, this is the largest comedy nightclub in the city. The Punch Line has been San Francisco's premier comedy club since 1978, showcasing top talent plus up-and-coming comedians. Three-person shows with top national and local talent are featured Tuesday through Saturday. Showcase night is on Sunday with 15 to 20 rising stars. There's an all-star showcase or a special event on Monday nights. It's advisable to buy tickets in advance if you don't want to wait in line; advance tickets are available through BASS outlets (tel. 762-2277). Shows are Sunday through Thursday at 9pm, on Friday at 9 and 11pm, and on Saturday at 7, 9, and 11pm.

Admission: Sun $5, Mon–Thurs $7–$10, Fri–Sat $12, plus a two-drink minimum nightly.

ROCK & BLUES CLUBS

In addition to the following listings, see "Dance Clubs," below, for (usually) live danceable rock.

THE FILLMORE, 1805 Geary St. (at Fillmore). Tel. 346-6000.

Reopened after years of neglect, The Fillmore, made famous by promoter Bill Graham in the 1960s, is once again attracting big names. Check the local listings magazines, or call the theater for information on upcoming events.

GRANT AND GREEN, 1371 Grant Ave. Tel. 956-9605.

The atmosphere at this North Beach dive rockery is not that special, but the local bands are pretty good. Look for daytime shows on the weekends. Open daily from 1pm to 2am.

Admission: Fri–Sat $3.

I-BEAM, 1748 Haight St. Tel. 668-6023, or 668-6006 for recorded information.

⭐ Except for the line out front, you'd hardly know that above Haight Street's hippest storefronts is one of the largest and loudest clubs in the city. Live, struggling local and national bands perform almost nightly, while a DJ spins dance discs between sets. There's a lot of new metal here, along with a healthy dose of post-punk, and traditional rock. Sunday is gay tea dance night—where bell-bottoms and platform shoes are still in fashion. Open Monday through Saturday from 8pm to 2am and on Sunday from 5pm to 2am.

Admission: Mon–Sat free–$20, depending on the night and performer; Sun $5–$7.

LOST & FOUND SALOON, 1353 Grant Ave. Tel. 397-3751.
Beer is the main drink at this North Beach blues bar. Leave your tie at home. Open daily from 6am to 2am.

Admission: $3.

THE SALOON, 1232 Grant Ave. Tel. 989-7666.

⭐ An authentic gold rush survivor, this North Beach dive is the oldest extant bar in the city—and smells like it. Popular with both bikers and daytime pin-stripers, there's live blues several nights a week. Drinks run $3 to $5. It's open daily from noon to 2am.

Admission: Fri–Sat $3–$5.

SLIM'S, 333 11th St. Tel. 621-3330.
New Orleans–style Slims is co-owned by musician Boz Scaggs, who sometimes takes the stage under the name "Presidio Slim." Located south of Market Street (SoMa), at Folsom Street, this shiny, slightly overpriced restaurant/bar seats 300, services California cuisine, and specializes in excellent American music—home-grown rock, jazz, and blues—almost nightly. Open Tuesday through Sunday from 8pm to 2am.

Admission: $10–$20, plus a two-drink minimum.

JAZZ & LATIN CLUBS

BAHIA TROPICAL, 1600 Market St. Tel. 861-8657.
Now three years old, this tropical Brazilian club opened with the lambada craze. But it's not cheesy—this is the real McCoy. Excellent bands are featured nightly, and samba dancers often perform. The music starts at 9pm, and there's a dance floor show every weekend at 11:30pm. Open daily from 8pm to 2am.

Admission: $5–$10.

CESAR'S LATIN PALACE, 3140 Mission St. Tel. 648-6611.

⭐ Live Latin bands perform to a very mixed crowd—ethnically, economically, and generationally. There's plenty of dancing and drinking in this ultra-fun club. Open Wednesday through Sunday from 9pm to 2am.

Admission: $4–$8.

JAZZ AT PEARL'S, 256 Columbus Ave. Tel. 291-8255.
Behind large windows directly on North Beach's busy Columbus Avenue, Pearl's is a large, soft, classy restaurant specializing in ribs, chicken, and jazz. The live jams last until 2am nightly. Open daily from 5pm to 2am.

Admission: Free, but there's a two-drink minimum.

KIMBALL'S, 300 Grove St. Tel. 861-5555.

In addition to being a popular pre-theater restaurant, Kimball's has become one of the city's top jazz clubs. It's located right across the street from Davies Symphony Hall and the Opera House, at Franklin Street, inside a particularly handsome old brick building. The cavernous interior encompasses two levels, and attracts top names like Ahmad Jamal, along with superior local talent. Food is served daily from 5pm to midnight or so, and live music is offered Wednesday through Sunday. Call for prices and information before setting out. Open Wednesday through Sunday from 5pm to 1am.

Admission: $12–$15, depending on the performer.

THE MASON STREET WINE BAR, 342 Mason St. Tel. 391-3454.

Formerly a bank, this funky and intimate drinkery is bedecked with contemporary, oversize paintings and attracts a mixed crowd of office workers, locals, and tourists with nightly live jazz. Small cabaret tables with black club chairs face a small stage; the old bank safe is used as a private room and a wine storage area. Over 150 different wines are served from the half-moon-shaped bar. Open daily from 4pm to 2am.

Admission: Free, except during occasional performances.

THE NEW ORLEANS ROOM, in the Fairmont Hotel, 950 Mason St., at California St. Tel. 772-5259.

Solo jazz pianists perform Monday and Tuesday. Local jazz vocalists perform Wednesday. International jazz stars from bebop to fusion play Thursday through Saturday. Open nightly from 3pm to 2am.

Admission: Cover charge varies with artists, so call for details.

RASSELAS, 2801 California St. Tel. 567-5010.

One of my favorite jazz rooms is this prominently windowed corner, near Fillmore Street. An amply sized, casual jazzery, Rasselas is packed with small tables and comfortable couches, and is backed by a Victorian bar. Hot local jazz and R&B combos play nightly from 9pm to 1am. The adjacent restaurant serves Ethiopian cuisine under an elegant Bedouin tent. Open Sunday through Thursday from 5pm to midnight, Friday and Saturday from 5pm to 2am.

Admission: Free–$5.

DANCE CLUBS

The up-and-coming area South of Market Street (SoMa) is the center of San Francisco's nightlife scene. A virtual ghost town during the day, once the sun sets SoMa comes alive with boisterous activity and entertainment of every variety.

The very nature of the club scene demands frequent fresh faces, outdating recommendations before the ink can dry on a page. Most of the venues below are promoted as different clubs on various nights of the week, each with its own look, sound, and style. The weekly-listings magazines *San Francisco Bay Guardian* and *San Francisco Weekly* contain the latest entertainment information. Discount passes and club announcements are often available at trendy clothing stores; shop along upper Haight Street.

Three Babes and a Bus (tel. 552-2582) runs regular nightclub trips on Friday and Saturday nights to the city's busiest clubs. See "Organized Tours" in Chapter 7 for complete information.

CITY NIGHTS, 715 Harrison St. Tel. 546-7938.

Open only on Friday and Saturday from 9:30pm to 3am, this popular club at Third Street sprawls over three levels and has one of the largest dance floors in the city. The weekend has been divided into two distinctly different programs, each with its own name, personality, and crowd. Wednesday and Friday is **The X** (tel. 561-1432), a modern music party with caged dancers and a multimedia show that rivals any in San Francisco. Saturday is **City Nights** (tel. 561-9782), playing contemporary, Top 40, house, and hip-hop music. Call for information on occasional live performances. Drinks run $3.50 to $4.

Admission: $10.

CLUB DV8, 540 Howard St. Tel. 777-1419, or 957-1730 for recorded information.

Kind of the South of Market (SoMa) club scene, DV8 has been attracting the black-clothes-and-pointy-shoes crowd longer than almost any other establishment. There are two DJs spinning music on separate dance floors, each perpetually packed with a lively 20-something crowd. The decor is an interesting mix of trompe l'oeil, pop art, candelabra, mirrors, and some extraordinary Daliesque props. Several quieter V.I.P. lounges provide necessary relief from the pounding. Open Thursday through Sunday from 9pm to 4am.

Admission: Thurs $5, Fri $10, Sat $10, Sun $5. Usually free before 10pm.

OASIS, 278 11th St. Tel. 621-8119.

Club O, on 11th at Folsom Street, is one of the trendiest danceterias in the city. Live bands alternate with in-crowd themes nights. In addition to the usual light show and videos, there's a Plexiglas dance floor on top of a swimming pool; its sometimes uncovered for parties. Open Tuesday through Sunday from 9pm to 2am.

Admission: Free–$10 (call for details).

OZ, in the St. Francis Hotel, 32nd Floor, Powell St. Tel. 774-0116.

Euro-chic DJs mix contemporary American dance music with the latest European sounds. Reached via glass elevator, Oz has a marble dance floor and good lighting, including mirrored columns with Tivoli lights bounce to the beat. The interior attempts to mimic a forest glade, complete with birch trees, ferns, and rockery. Look out the windows for superb views of the glittering city. Open Sunday through Thursday from 9pm to 1:30am and on Friday and Saturday from 9pm to 2:30am.

Admission: Sun–Thurs $8, Fri–Sat $15.

PARADISE LOUNGE, 1501 Folsom St. Tel. 861-6906.

Labyrinthine Paradise features three dance floors simultaneously vibrating to different beats. Smaller auxiliary spaces include a pool room with half a dozen tables. Open daily from 3pm to 2am.

Admission: $5–$15.

TEN 15 FOLSOM, 1015 Folsom St. Tel. 431-0700.

Three levels, and three dance floors, have long made 1015 Folsom, at Sixth Street, a stylish stop on the nightclub circuit. Weekends are best, when the club is a carnival of beautiful people. Currently, Friday is Club Martini (tel. 431-1200), one of the city's hottest tickets, and Saturday is gay night (tel. 431-BOYS). Open Saturday from 10pm to 6am, and on Sunday from

5pm to 2:30am, plus various other special days; call the club for information.
Admission: $5–$15.

---

3. THE BAR SCENE

There are so many bars in San Francisco it would be impossible to catalog them all. It would be pointless, too, since you don't want to visit every one. Below is a good cross section of the best the city has to offer.

ALBION, 3139 16th St. Tel. 552-8558.
This Mission District club is a gritty, leather, in-crowd place packed with artistic slummers and various SoMa hipsters. Open daily from 2pm to 2am.

CARIBBEAN ZONE, 55 Natoma St. Tel. 541-9465.
Not just another restaurant bar, Caribbean Zone is a visual Disneyland, jam-packed with a cluttered tropical decor that includes a full-size airplane fuselage. They don't have this in Iowa. Open Monday through Thursday from 11:30am to 10pm, Friday 11:30am to 11pm, Saturday and Sunday 5 to 11pm.

EDINBURGH CASTLE, 950 Geary St. Tel. 885-4074.
Opened in 1958, this legendary Scottish pub is still known for unusual British ales on tap and the best selection of single-malt scotches in the city. The huge pub, located near Polk Street, is decorated with Royal Air Force mementos, horse brasses, steel helmets, and an authentic Ballantine caber, used in the annual Scottish games. You might want to avoid Saturday nights, when live bagpipers supplement the jukebox. Fish and chips and other traditional foods are always available. Drinks cost $3 to $5. Open Monday through Thursday from 5pm to midnight; Friday from 5pm to 2am; Saturday from 2pm to 2am; and Sunday from noon to midnight.

HARRY DENTON'S, 161 Stuart St. Tel. 882-1333.
The dismantling of the Embarcadero Freeway after the 1989 earthquake has had the effect of revitalizing the Rincon Center neighborhood below. Harry Denton's, just a short walk away, in the shadow of the Ferry Building, is a popular restaurant, but is even better known as a great bar with lots of energy. Especially happening during early evenings with working "suits" and their tennis-shoed secretaries, the bar bustles until late. Harry Denton's is always a safe bet for a drink. The food, unfortunately, is not as memorable. Open Monday through Friday from 7am to 1:30am, Friday and Saturday from 8am to 1:30am.

JOHNNY LOVE'S, 1500 Broadway. Tel. 931-6053.
Attracting the same youngish power crowd as Harry Denton's (see above), Johnny Love's is a happy place, perpetually packed with corporate assistant–types and first-tier managers, who go directly here from work to buy rounds for their buddies. There's a small dance floor and live music several nights a week; when it's jumping, this joint is a real scene. Love's serves decent food, too, but your money is best spent here on drinks. Open nightly from 5pm to 1:30am.

LI PO COCKTAIL LOUNGE, 916 Grant Ave. Tel. 982-0072.

A divey Chinese bar, Li Po is made special by a clutter of dusty Asian furnishings and mementos that include an unbelievably huge ricepaper lantern hanging from the ceiling, and a glittery golden shrine to Buddha behind the bar. It would be the perfect place to hold a private party if it weren't for the video game machines and the bad sound system. Open daily from 2pm to 2am.

PERRY'S, 1944 Union St. Tel. 922-9022.

San Francisco's young, 30-something crowd has long patronized this attractive bar. Decorated with tiled floors, brass rails, a pressed-tin ceiling, and dark mahogany paneling, Perry's is pickuppy and attracts a successful urban clientele, most of whom are dressed as though they're ready to work. A separate, secluded dining room features breakfast, lunch, dinner, and brunch at candlelit tables. It's a good place for hamburgers, easy fish dishes, and pasta. Drinks run $3 to $5. Open daily from 9am to midnight.

PERSIAN AUB ZAM ZAM, 1633 Haight St. Tel. 861-2545.

Step through the forbidding metal doors and you'll feel as if you're in *Casablanca*. And although it's full of character, regulars come here for the acerbic owner/bartender, Bruno, who kicks almost everyone else out. Order a Finlandia vodka martini and you'll be allowed to stay. Sit at the bar; the tables are "closed." Usually open Monday through Friday from 4pm to midnight, and at the owner's whim.

THE SAVOY-TIVOLI, 1434 Grant Ave. Tel. 362-7023.

With your back to Chinatown, walk two blocks up Grant from Columbus Avenue to one of the area's most atmospheric neighborhood bars. The large room offers unobstructed sightlines, making it easy to see and be seen. It's popular with a wanna-be-artist, cigarette-smoking, Campari-and-soda crowd. Open Tuesday through Sunday from 3:15pm to 2am.

BREWPUBS

GORDON-BIERSCH BREWERY, in the Embarcadero, 2 Harrison St. Tel. 243-8723.

Gordon-Biersch Brewery is San Francisco's largest brew-restaurant, serving decent food and tasty homemade "barley-pop." There are always several brews to choose from, ranging from light to dark. Most of the brewery's well-dressed clientele look like the marketers from The Gap, whose headquarters are located across the street. Open Sunday through Wednesday 11am to 11pm, Thursday 11am to midnight, Friday and Saturday 11am to 1am.

SAN FRANCISCO BREWING COMPANY, 155 Columbus Ave. Tel. 434-3344.

Surprisingly low-key for an ale-house, this cozy brewpub serves its barley pop along with burgers, fries, and the like. It's located on North Beach's Columbus Avenue, at Pacific. Open Sunday from noon to 11:30pm, Monday through Thursday from noon to 12:30am, Friday and Saturday from noon to 1:30am.

20 TANK BREWERY, 316 11th St. Tel. 255-9455.

Right in the heart of SoMa's most "happening" strip, 11th Street at Folsom, this huge, upscale bar is known for enormous windows that look out onto the street, as well as a decent ale. Open daily from 11:30am to 2am.

CAFES/BARS

San Francisco in general, and North Beach in particular, is loaded with Italian-style cafes, many of which also have full bars. These character-laden places encourage patrons to linger, and are one of the city's greatest assets. See Chapter 6, "San Francisco Dining," for additional listings.

CAFE PICARO, 3120 16th St. Tel. 431-4089.

None of the tables match at this huge, informal literary cafe in the Mission. Picaro is part used-book store, part bohemian hangout, and part restaurant. Few cognoscenti, however, eat here. Wine and beer are served along with the cappuccinos. It's located on Columbus Avenue at Valencia Street. Open Sunday through Thursday from 9am to 10pm and on Friday and Saturday from 9am to midnight.

CAFFE TRIESTE, 601 Vallejo St. Tel. 392-6739.

Opera is always on the jukebox at this classic beatnik North Beach coffeehouse. It's somehow provincial European feel is augmented by live arias sung to the lucky few who get to squeeze in on Saturday afternoons. Open Sunday through Thursday from 6:30am to 11:30pm and on Friday and Saturday from 6:30am to 12:30am.

CAFFE GRECO, 423 Columbus Ave. Tel. 397-6261.

Relatively recent for North Beach, Caffè Greco opened about six years ago and has quickly become one of the best places to linger. Sophisticated and relaxed, it serves beer, wine, a good selection of coffee drinks, and delicious desserts. Open Monday through Thursday from 7am to 11pm and Friday through Sunday from 7am to midnight.

SPECS' ADLER MUSEUM CAFE, 12 Saroyan Place. Tel. 421-4112.

Specs' is located on Saroyan Place, a tiny alley at 250 Columbus Ave. that's named for William Saroyan, a local author and playwright who penned *The Time of Your Life*, which described a 1930s dive somewhat like this bar. Specs' is one of the liveliest—and most likable—pubs in North Beach. Inside this small wooden bar, near the intersection of Columbus Avenue and Broadway, you'll find one of the city's friendliest crowds. Maritime flags hang from the ceiling, while the exposed brick walls are lined with posters, photos, and various oddities. The "museum," protected beneath a few glass cases, contains memorabilia and items brought back by seamen who drop in between sailings. Beer and wine cost $2.50 to $3.50; mixed drinks, $3 to $5. Open Sunday through Thursday from 4:30pm to 2am and on Friday and Saturday from 5pm to 2am.

VESUVIO, 255 Columbus Ave. Tel. 362-3370.

Situated across Jack Kerouac Alley from the famed City Lights Book Store, this established cafe/bar at Broadway is one of North Beach's best beatnik-style hangouts. Popular with neighborhood writers, artists, songsters, and wanna-be's, Vesuvio also gets its share of longshoremen, cab drivers, and business types. Did I mention tourists? The walls are hung with a changing exhibition of locally produced art, complemented by an ongoing slide show. In addition to well-priced drinks, Vesuvio features an espresso machine, along with a staff that knows how to use it. No credit cards are accepted. Open daily from 6am to 2am.

COCKTAILS WITH A VIEW

THE CARNELIAN ROOM, in the Bank of America Building, 555 California St. Tel. 433-7500.

Between Kearny and Montgomery streets, on the 52nd floor of one of the city's tallest and most revered buildings, the Carnelian Room offers dramatic and spectacular uninterrupted views of the city. From a window-front table you feel as if you can reach out, pluck up the Transamerica Pyramid, and stir your martini with it. In addition to cocktails, sunset dinners are served nightly, for about $50 per person. Jackets and ties are required for men. Drinks are $5 to $7. Open nightly from 5pm to midnight.

CITYSCAPE, atop Hilton Tower I, 46th Floor. Tel. 776-0215.

Topped by a glass roof, Cityscape gives the illusion of drinking under the stars, with superlative views of the bay. There's dancing to a live orchestra Tuesday through Saturday from 8pm. The rich gold-and-blue carpeting, mirrored columns, and floor-to-ceiling draperies are both elegant and romantic. Drinks run $4 to $6. Open nightly from 6pm to 2am.

CROWN ROOM, in the Fairmont Hotel, 24th Floor. Tel. 772-5131.

Of all the bars listed below, the Crown Room is definitely the plushest. Reached by an external glass elevator, the magnificent panoramic view from the top will make you nurse your drink longer than usual. In addition to drinks, lunch and dinner buffets are served here (about $20 and $30, respectively). Drinks cost $4 to $6. Open Sunday through Thursday from 11am to 12:30am, Friday and Saturday from 11am to 2am.

EQUINOX, in the Hyatt Regency Hotel, 5 Embarcadero Center. Tel. 788-1234.

The "hook" of the Hyatt's rooftop Equinox is a revolving floor that gives each table a 360° panoramic view of the city every 45 minutes. In addition to cocktails, lunch and dinner are served daily. Drinks run $4 to $6. Open daily from 4pm to 1:30am.

SHERLOCK HOLMES, ESQ., LOUNGE, in the Union Square Holiday Inn, 30th Floor. Tel. 398-8900.

A theme bar, this 30th-floor lounge pays homage to the world's greatest fictional detective. Collections of related "memorabilia" are hung throughout this replica of Holme's study at 221B Baker Street, complete with recorded London street sounds. Hats and pipes aside, attractions include plush velvet chairs, two wood-burning fireplaces, a terrific 360° view, and live piano music Tuesday through Saturday. Drinks run $5 to $6. Open nightly from 4pm to 1:30am.

HARRY DENTON'S STARLITE ROOF, in the Sir Francis Drake Hotel, Powell and Sutter Sts. Tel. 392-7755.

One of the oldest high points in the city, this 21st-story bar is best known for nightly dancing to smooth combo music. Every table has a good view. Drinks go for about $7. Open Monday through Saturday from 4:30am to 1:30am.

TOP OF THE MARK, in the Mark Hopkins Hotel, atop Nob Hill, California and Mason Sts. Tel. 392-3434.

One of the most-famous cocktail lounges in the world, the Top of the Mark offers traditional drinks in a nostalgia-loaded atmosphere. During World War II it was considered de rigueur for Pacific-bound servicemen to toast their good-bye to the States here. The spectacular glass-walled room features an unparalleled view; nobody will mind if you wander around with your drink, sampling each direction. Sunday brunch is served from 10am to 2pm and costs about $28. Drinks cost $6 to $8. Open nightly from 4pm to 12:30am.

PIANO BARS

San Francisco is lucky to have several terrific piano bars. As in other cities, these specialized lounges are perfectly suited to the posh hotels in which they are usually located.

THE LOWER BAR, in the Mark Hopkins Hotel, 1 Nob Hill. Tel. 392-3434.

Drinks are served nightly in a delightfully intimate, skylighted room with hand-painted murals. It's located just off the lobby. Drinks run $5 to $8. Open Sunday through Thursday from 2 to 10pm, Friday and Saturday from 1pm to midnight.

THE PIAZZA LOUNGE, in the Parc Fifty Five Hotel, 55 Cyril Magnin St. Tel. 392-8000.

Sink into a handsome velvet chair, gaze out into the three-story atrium, and relax to a mix of old and new melodies played on a magnificent ebony grand piano. The hotel is located at Market and North Fifth streets. Drinks cost $5 to $6. Open daily from 1pm to 11pm.

THE REDWOOD ROOM, in the Four Seasons Clift Hotel, 495 Geary St. Tel. 775-4700.

A true art deco beauty, this ground-floor lounge is one of San Francisco's poshest piano bars. Its gorgeous redwood interior was completely built from a single 2,000-year-old tree. The piano player, Ricardo Scales, is easily one of the best in the city, while the staff is terrifically trained and particularly attentive. The Redwood Room is simultaneously intimate, luxurious, and fun. Drinks go for $6 to $7. Open Sunday through Thursday from 11am to midnight, Friday and Saturday from 11am to 2am.

GAY BARS & CLUBS

As with straight establishments, gay bars and clubs each attract a different clientele, from the leather crowd to three-piece–suite types. Because most of the area's lesbians live in Oakland, across the bay, clubs here are primarily male-oriented. The Castro, South of Market (SoMa), and Mission sections of town have especially good bar selections. Check the appropriate sections of the free weeklies, the *San Francisco Bay Guardian* and *San Francisco Weekly,* for listings of events and happenings. The dedicated gay papers the *San Francisco Sentinel* and the *Bay Area Reporter* have the most comprehensive listings, including a weekly calendar of events, social gatherings, art classes, sports events, meetings, and the like. All the above papers are free, and are distributed weekly on Thursday. They can be found stacked at the corner of 18th and Castro streets, and 9th and Harrison streets, as well as in bars, bookshops, and stores around town.

Listed below are some of the city's more established, mainstream gay hangouts.

KENNEL CLUB, 628 Divisadero St. Tel. 931-1914.

⭐ This warehouse bar features both DJ dancing and live bands in equal parts. On Thursday and Saturday nights it's called the Box, which is currently one of the best gay men and lesbian clubs around. For further details, call the club.

Admission: $5–$15.

RAWHIDE II, 280 Seventh St. Tel. 621-1197.

Gay or straight, this is one of the city's top country-and-western dance bars. Whether or not you brought your chaps, this is a jeans joint, patronized by both sexes. Free dance lessons are offered Monday through Thursday from 7:30 to 9:30pm. Rawhide II is located by Folsom Street. Drinks cost $2.50 to $5. Open daily from noon to 2am.

Admission: Free.

THE STUD, 399 Ninth St. Tel. 863-6623.

Despite its aggressive name, The Stud, on Ninth at Harrison Street, is a pretty mellow hangout. This classic South of Market (SoMa) place has been around forever, and is so tame that straights will feel comfortable here, too. The interior has an antique-shop look and a miniature train circling over the bar and dance floor. Music here is a balanced mix of old and new. Open nightly from 5pm to 2am.

Admission: Sun–Thurs free, Fri–Sat $3.

TWIN PEAKS TAVERN, 401 Castro St. Tel. 864-9470.

Right at the intersection of Castro, 17th, and Market streets is one of the Castro's most famous hangouts. This is a drinking bar catering to a 30-something crowd. Because of its relatively small size and great location, the place gets pretty full by 8pm or so. Drinks run $2 to $5. Open daily from noon to 2am.

Admission: Free.

---

4. MORE ENTERTAINMENT

The **San Francisco International Film Festival,** held in March of each year, is one of America's oldest film festivals. Tickets are relatively inexpensive, and screenings are very accessible to the general public. Entries include new films by beginning and established directors. For a schedule or information, call 931-FILM. Tickets can be charged by phone through BASS Ticketmaster (tel. 510/835-3849).

Even if you're not here in time for the festival, don't despair. The classic, independent, and mainstream cinemas in San Francisco are every bit as good as the city's other cultural offerings.

REPERTORY CINEMAS

CASTRO, 429 Castro St. Tel. 621-6120.

⭐ One of the largest and prettiest theaters in the city, the Castro is known for its screenings of classics and for its bold Wurlitzer organ, played before each show. There's a different feature here almost nightly, and more often than not it's a double feature. Bargain matinees are usually offered on Wednesday, Saturday, Sunday, and holidays. Phone for schedules, prices, and show times.

RED VIC, 1727 Haight St. Tel. 668-3994.

The worker-owned Red Vic movie collective recently moved from the Victorian building that gave it its name. The theater specializes in old Hollywood films, independent releases, and contemporary cultish hits. Phone for schedules, prices, and show times.

ROXIE, 3117 16th St. Tel. 863-1087.

Located on 16th at Valencia Street, the Roxie consistently screens the best new alternative films anywhere. The low-budget contemporary features shown here are largely devoid of Hollywood candy-coating; many are West Coast premieres. Films change weekly, sometimes sooner. Phone for schedules, prices, and show times.

CHAPTER 11

EASY EXCURSIONS FROM SAN FRANCISCO

Although you could spend a lifetime exploring San Francisco, save some time to take in the surrounding regions as well. The Bay City is a captivating Circe, but don't let it ensnare you to the point of ignoring its environs.

San Francisco is set amid the most fascinatingly diverse area in northern California—possibly in the United States. And the contrasts of the region are even more spellbinding than its beauties. There are silent forests of 1,200-year-old trees and smartly sophisticated seaside resorts. Humming industrial cities and serene, sun-drenched Spanish missions contrast with rolling wine country, wildly rugged mountain ranges, an island transformed into an oceanarium, and two of Am-erica's greatest universities.

With San Francisco as either your travel base or your springboard, you can reach any of these points in a few hours or less by car or public transport.

Tower Tours, 77 Jefferson St. (tel. 434-8687), operates regularly scheduled tours of San Francisco's neighboring towns and countryside. Half- and full-day trips visit Muir Woods, Sausalito, Napa, and Sonoma. Other excursions trek to Yosemite as well as to the Monterey Peninsula. Phone for price and departure information.

The purpose of this chapter is to give you a glimpse of some of the attractions beckoning beyond Coit Tower . . . how to get there and what to expect.

---

1. OAKLAND

10 miles E of San Francisco

GETTING THERE By BART Bay Area Rapid Transit (BART) makes the trip from San Francisco to Oakland through one of the longest underwater transit tubes in the world. Fares range from 80¢D to $3, depending on your station of origin; children 4 and under ride free. BART trains operate Monday through Saturday from 6am to midnight and on Sunday from 9am to midnight. Exit at the 12th Street station for downtown Oakland.

By Car   From San Francisco, Take I-80 across the San Francisco–Oakland Bay Bridge. Exit at Grand Avenue south for the Lake Merritt area.

ESSENTIALS   Downtown Oakland is bordered by Grand Avenue on the north, I-980 on the west, Inner Harbor on the south, and Lake Merritt on the east. Between these landmarks are three BART stations (12th Street, 19th Street, and Lake Merritt), City Hall, the Oakland Museum, Jack London Square, and several other sights.

For a recorded update on Oakland's arts and entertainment happenings, phone 510/835-2787.

Few San Francisco locals would suggest that any tourist leave the beautiful peninsula for Oakland, the East Bay's largest city. It's largely true; Oakland is chiefly a sprawling industrial city, and is almost entirely devoid of San Francisco's unique charm. It does, however, boast a number of outstanding attractions.

WHAT TO SEE & DO

Lake Merritt is the city's primary tourist attraction. Three miles in circumference, the tidal lagoon was bridged and dammed in the 1860s and has become the centerpiece of Oakland's most desirable neighborhood. Now a wildlife refuge, the lake is home to flocks of migrating ducks, herons, and geese. At the Sailboat House (tel. 510/444-3807), in Lakeside Park, along the north shore, you can rent sailboats, rowboats, pedal boats, and canoes for $5 to $20 per hour.

CHILDREN'S FAIRYLAND, Lakeside Park, Grand Ave. and Bellevue Dr. Tel. 510/452-2259.

Located on the north shore of Lake Merritt is one of the most imaginative and skillful children's parks in the United States. You can peer into old Geppetto's workshop, watch the Mad Hatter eternally pouring tea for Alice, see Noah's Ark overloaded with animal passengers, and view Beatrix Potter's village of storybook characters. Fairy tales also come alive during puppet-show performances at 11am, and 2 and 4pm.

Admission: $3 adults, $2.50 children 12 and under.

Open: Summer, Sat–Sun 10am–5:30pm, Mon–Fri 10am–4:30pm; spring and fall, Wed–Sun 10am–4:30pm; winter Fri–Sun and holidays 10am–4:30pm. **BART:** Exit at 19th Street and walk north along Broadway; turn right on Grand Avenue to the park. **Directions:** From I-580 south, exit at Grand Avenue; Children's Fairyland is at the far end of the park, on your left at Bellevue Avenue.

OAKLAND MUSEUM, 1000 Oak St. Tel. 510/238-3401, or 510/834-2413 for recorded information.

Located two blocks south of the lake, the Oakland Museum would be more appropriately called the Museum of California—it includes just about everything you'd want to know about the state, its people, history, culture, geology, art, environment, and ecology. Inside a graceful building, set down among sweeping gardens and terraces, it's actually three museums in one: works by California artists from Bierstadt to Diebenkorn; artifacts from California's history, from Pomo basketry to Country Joe McDonald's guitar; and re-creations of California habitats from the coast to the White Mountains. From time to time the museum has major shows of California artists, like an exhibit of 200 years of Californian folk painting and sculpture. A large show of California arts and crafts from 1890 to 1930 opened in 1993.

There are 45-minute guided tours leaving the gallery information desks on request. There is a fine cafe, inexpensive parking, and a gallery (tel. 510/834-2296) selling works by California artists. The book and gift shop is also an interesting place to browse. You'll find a wide variety of books, posters, and gift items, as well as attractive jewelry and wearable art by California artists. The cafe (tel. 510/834-2329) is open Wednesday through Saturday from 10am to 4pm and on Sunday from noon to 5pm.

Admission: $4 adults, $2 students and seniors, free for children under 12.

Open: Wed–Sat 10am–5pm, Sun noon–7pm. **Closed:** Thanksgiving Day, Christmas Day, New Year's Day, and July 4. **BART:** Lake Merritt station (one block south of the museum). **Directions:** From I-880 north, take the Oak Street exit; the museum is five blocks east at Oak and 10th streets. Alternatively, take I-580 to I-980 and exit at the Jackson Street ramp.

JACK LONDON SQUARE, Broadway and Embarcadero.

Jack London was an Oaklander who grew up here and spent most of his time along the waterfront. This square, at the foot of Broadway, is Oakland's only real tourist area. It fronts the harbor, and houses a complex of boutiques and eateries—about as far away from the call of the wild as you can get. In the center of the square is the small, reconstructed, rustic Yukon cabin in which Jack London lived while prospecting in the Klondike during the Gold Rush of 1897.

At 56 Jack London Square, at the foot of Webster Street, you'll find the oddly named First and Last Chance Saloon, where London did some of his writing and much of his drinking. The corner table he used has remained exactly as it was 75 or so years ago (except for his photos on the wall). Have a schooner in Jack's memory. Also in the square are the mast and nameplate from the U.S.S. *Oakland*, a ship that saw extensive action in the Pacific during World War II.

Open: Most restaurants and shops Mon–Sat 10am–9pm (some restaurants stay open later). **BART:** 12th Street station; then walk south along Broadway (about half a mile) or take bus no 51a to the foot of Broadway. **Directions:** Take I-880 to Broadway, turn south, and go to the end.

ALICE ARTS CENTER, 1428 Alice St. Tel. 510/238-7222.

The $14-million Alice Arts Center, a five-story mixed-use building four blocks from downtown Oakland opened to raves in 1993. Situated on a quiet residential street, the complex houses the Oakland Ballet, Oakland Ensemble Theater, and City Center Dance. The latter is primarily a school of jazz, Caribbean, and African dance. Dimensions Dance Theater, the Bay Area's oldest modern dance company, performs here as well as in downtown's spectacular Paramount Theater (tel. 510/465-6400).

Prices: $5–$20, depending on the program.

2. BERKELEY

10 miles NE of San Francisco

GETTING THERE   By BART   Berkeley station is two blocks from the university. The fare from San Francisco is $1.80.

By Car   From San Francisco, take I-80 east to the University exit. Drive straight to the university. Count on walking some distance because chances are you won't find a place to park near the university.

ESSENTIALS   Telegraph Avenue is the main drag for the student populace. It is most colorful around Bancroft Way and Ashby Avenue. Telegraph Avenue deadends at the university's Sproul Plaza and the Student Union.

Phone Visitor Hotline (510/549-8710) for general information on events and happenings in Berkeley.

Berkeley is actually an East Bay factory town that has achieved fame, glory, and notoriety through harboring an educational institution that has produced 15 Nobel Prize winners—more than any other university—and spawned some of the worst (best?) campus riots in the nation. More than any other city, Berkeley conjures up images of dissent and is closely identified with the radical activities of the 1960s. Politically, the student populace has moved somewhat to the right, but come Election Day this college town still becomes more boisterous than most.

Telegraph Avenue, the main shopping and strolling street, is seemingly lined in equal numbers by coffee bars and bookshops, both overflowing with students. It's also packed with people selling everything from T-shirts and jewelry to I Ching and tarot-card readings. On Telegraph Avenue the 1960s have never left.

Just before Telegraph Avenue runs into the university campus, it crosses **Bancroft Way.** This is the hub of student activities, a great many of which seem to take place right on the corner. Stand here for a few minutes, and you're bound to have leaflets thrust at you, hear an impromptu debate, or the jingling and rattling of a Hare Krishna chant. And you can likely purchase anything from a curried-beef pie to falafel from food stands here while you're being converted to the current cause. The university's **Sproul Plaza** is across the street and contains the Student Union, a lively building as spacious and hectic as the rest of the university. Go to the information desk on the second floor to pick up a free map of Berkeley, as well as the local student newspaper.

WHAT TO SEE & DO

UNIVERSITY OF CALIFORNIA—BERKELEY. Tel. 510/642-5215.

You might call Berkeley a city with a split personality, or at least two faces. The western part is flat, chock-a-block with factories and garages, and decidedly drab. The eastern portion undulates over a series of hills, with little houses clinging all over them and lush green patches smiling right into the main shopping streets. This is the university section, dominated by students and professors, and

- ① Oakland
- ② Berkeley
- ③ Tiburon & Angel Island
- ④ Sausalito
- ⑤ Muir Woods & Mount Tamalpais
- ⑥ Point Reyes National Seashore
- ⑦ Marine World Africa USA
- ⑧ The Wine Country— Napa Valley

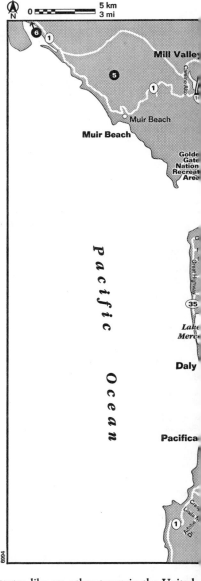

catering to their particular tastes like no other town in the United States.

You're not likely to see any rioting on campus in the now-tame 1990s, but you will see hordes of students. There are about 30,000 of them. Built in the wide-open California style, the campus is not exceptionally beautiful. Still, it's interesting to see.

The Visitor Information Center at UC—Berkeley offers free, regularly scheduled campus tours Monday, Wednesday, and Friday at 10am and 1pm. Phone ahead for information and reservations. No tours are offered from mid-December to mid-January.

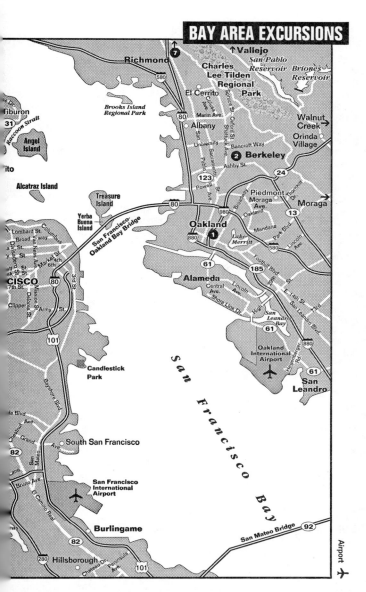

PEOPLE'S PARK, Berkeley.

In late 1967, the university demolished an entire block of buildings north of Telegraph Avenue. The destruction, which forced hippies and other "undesirables" from the slum housing that stood there, was done under the guise of university expansion and urban renewal—good liberal causes. But after the lot lay vacant for almost two years, a group of Berkeley radicals whose names read like a Who's Who of 1960s leftists—including Jerry Rubin, Bobby Seale, and Tom Hayden—decided to take the land for "the people." On April 29, 1969, hundreds of activists invaded the vacant lot with gardening tools and tamed the muddy ground into a park. One month later, Berkeley's Republican mayor sent 250 police officers into the park, and 4,000 demonstrators materialized to challenge them. A riot ensued, the police fired buckshot at the crowd, one rioter was killed and another blinded. Governor Ronald Reagan sent in the National Guard, and for the next seventeen days the Guardsmen repeatedly gassed innocent students, faculty, and passersby. Berkeley was a war zone, and People's Park became the 1960s' most important symbol of "people power."

People's Park once again sparked controversy in 1992 when university officials decided to build volleyball courts there. In August of that year, a park activitst broke into the campus home of the university's chancellor. When a police officer arrived, the activist lunged at him with a machete and was shot dead. On the victim's body was a note with the message: "We are willing to die for this land. Are you?" On news of the comtemporary radical's death, more than 150 of her supporters rioted. Today you can visit the park and watch the volleyballers self-consciuosly setting, bumping, and spiking.

TAKARA SAKE USA INC., 708 Addison St., Berkeley. Tel. 510/540-8250.
Sho Chiku Bai sake, one of this country's most popular brands, is not Japanese, it's made here in Berkeley by Takara Sake USA, America's largest sake maker. Unfortunately, there are no regularly scheduled tours of the plant, but you can learn about sake-making from a slide presentation, and taste three different types of rice wine. The tasting room is open daily from noon to 6pm.

WHERE TO STAY

Bed and Breakfast International, P.O. Box 282910, San Francisco, CA 94128 (tel. 415/696-1690, or toll free 800/872-4500, fax 415/696-1699), accommodates tourists and visitors in more than 80 private homes and apartments in the Berkeley area. The cost of these private B&Bs ranges from a reasonable $45 to $69 per night, and there's a two-night minimum. The Berkeley Convention and Visitor's Bureau, 1834 University Ave., 1st Floor, Berkeley, CA 94703 (tel. 510/549-7040 or 510/549-8710) can also find accommodations for you.

MODERATE

FRENCH HOTEL, 1538 Shatuck Ave., Berkeley, CA 94709. Tel. 510/548-9930. 18 rms. TV TEL **BART:** Berkeley. **Directions:** From I-80 north, take the University exit and turn left onto Shattuck Avenue; the hotel is six blocks down on your left.
$ Rates: $85–$125 single or double. Government employee, university, and group rates available. AE, CB, DC, MC, V. **Parking** Free.
If Gallic contemporary is your cup of tea, Berkeley has that too—at the French Hotel, directly across from Chez Panisse (see "Where to Dine," below). It's a small establishment with a charming cafe

IMPRESSIONS

*The only city I'd be sorry to leave in the United States is
San Francisco.*
—GRAHAM GREENE

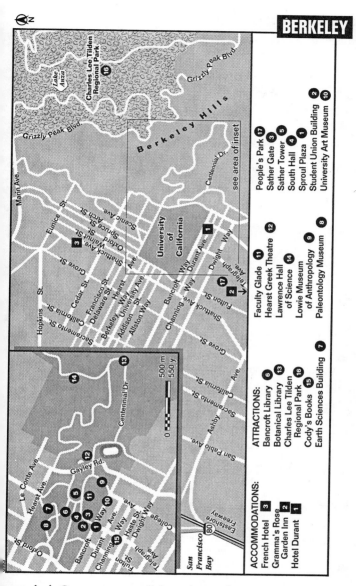

ACCOMMODATIONS:
French Hotel ⬛3
Gramma's Rose Garden Inn ⬛2
Hotel Durant ⬛1

ATTRACTIONS:
Bancroft Library ❻
Botanical Library ⓭
Charles Lee Tilden Regional Park ⓰
Cody's Books ⓯
Earth Sciences Building ❼
Faculty Glade ⓫
Hearst Greek Theatre ⓬
Lawrence Hall of Science ⓮
Lowie Museum of Anthropology ❾
Paleontology Museum ❽
People's Park ⓱
Sather Gate ❸
Sather Tower ❺
South Hall ❹
Sproul Plaza ❶
Student Union Building ❷
University Art Museum ⓾

attached. Guest rooms are light and airy, done in quiet grays and blues with warm maroon carpeting. The furnishings are attractive and practical, as the hotel's name would suggest. There are downy blue comforters and floral-pattern throw cushions in complementary colors. In lieu of a dresser, stacked sliding white baskets are provided for your personal things. No-smoking rooms are available.

The downstairs cafe is casual, with exposed brick walls, rust-colored concrete floor, and outdoor tables for enjoying espresso, croissants, and fresh orange juice. It's also a relaxed gathering spot for locals.

GRAMMA'S ROSE GARDEN INN, 2740 Telegraph Ave., Berkeley, CA 94705. Tel. 510/549-2145. Fax 510/549-1085. 40 rms, all non-smoking. TV TEL **BART:** Ashby. **Directions:** Take I-80 north to the Ashby exit and turn left onto Telegraph Avenue; the hotel is located four blocks up.

$ Rates (including breakfast): $85–$150 single or double. AE, DC, MC, V. **Parking** Free.

Gramma's charming, restored Tudor houses (a main house, carriage house, garden house, and the Fay house) offer guest rooms furnished in period style with antiques, floral-print wallpapers, and pretty patchwork quilts on the beds. Accommodations in the restored carriage house overlook a garden and have fireplaces and king-size beds.

Guests are served a complimentary breakfast in the downstairs dining room or on the deck overlooking the garden. Sunday brunch is served free to guests staying over Saturday night.

HOTEL DURANT, 2600 Durant Ave., Berkeley, CA 94704. Tel. 510/845-8981, or toll free 800/238-7268. Fax 510/486-8336. 140 rms, 10 suites. TV TEL **BART:** Berkeley. **Directions:** Take I-80 north to the University exit, turn right onto Shattuck Avenue and left onto Durant Avenue. The hotel is five blocks ahead on the right.

$ Rates (including breakfast): $85–$95 single; $95–$105 double, from $180 suite. AE, DC, DISC, MC, V. **Parking** $5.

Just one block from the university is the very pleasant Hotel Durant, at Bowditch Street. Built in 1928, it's the only full-service hotel this close to the university. New ownership restored it nicely to keep the best of its earlier days while providing conveniences now expected by vacationers and travelers. The rooms are straightforwardly furnished; and all have cable TV, movies, and radio. Some of the rooms can be connected for families, and no-smoking units are available.

The hotel's restaurant, Henry's Publick House and Grille, serves English-pub-style food.

BUDGET

HILLEGASS HOUSE, 2834 Hillegass Ave., Berkeley, CA 94705. Tel. 510/548-5517. 4 rms. TEL

$ Rates (including breakfast): $65–$75 single, $80–$90 double. Extra person $20. No credit cards. **Parking** Free.

Built in 1904, the house is filled with many antiques, most of which date from turn of the century. The tradeoff for being situated as much as ten minutes by car from the university is a nice, quiet neighborhood. Guest rooms are outfitted with either king- or queen-size beds, private baths, and voice-mail telephones. There is a sauna on the property, and large, inclusive breakfast is served either indoors or out.

WHERE TO DINE

You can **eat on campus** Monday through Friday in the building directly behind the Student Union. The least-expensive food is available downstairs in the Cafeteria, on Lower Sproul Plaza. Adjacent to it are the Bear's Lair Pub and Coffee House, the Deli, and the Ice Creamery. Upstairs, at the Terrace you can get braekfast, snacks, and lunch. Also on this level of the building is the handsome Golden Bear Restaurant. All the university eateries have both indoor and outdoor seating.

Telegraph Avenue has a wonderful array of small restaurants of many nationalities. Walk along, read the posted menus, and take your pick.

EXPENSIVE

CHEZ PANISSE, 1517 Shattuck Ave. Tel. 510/548-5525.
 Cuisine: CALIFORNIAN. **Reservations:** Restaurant, essential; cafe, accepted for lunch, not accepted for dinner. **BART:** Berkeley. **Directions:** From I-80 north, take the University exit and turn left onto Shattuck Avenue.
$ Prices: Appetizers $6–$8; main courses $13–$18; lunch $14–$18; fixed-price dinner $35–$65. AE, CB, DC, MC, V.
 Open: Restaurant, dinner seatings Mon–Sat at 6, 6:30, 8:30, and 9:15pm. Cafe, lunch Mon–Thurs 11:30am–3pm, Fri–Sat 11:30am–4pm; dinner Mon–Thurs 5–10:30pm, Fri–Sat 5–11:30pm.

Between Cedar and Vine streets is Alice Waters's extraordinary Chez Panisse. Californian cuisine is so much a product of Water's genius that all other restaurants following in her wake should be dated "A.A.W." (After Alice Waters). This delightful redwod-and-stucco cottage is entered via a brick terrace filled with flowering potted plants. There are two separate dining areas—the upstairs cafe and the downstairs restaurant, both offering a Mediterranean-inspired cuisine.

In the upstairs cafe there are displays of pastries and fruit, and large bouquets of fresh flowers adorning an oak bar. The menu is posted daily out front, and luncheon dishes are à la carte. Offerings might include a delicately smoked gravlax or a roasted eggplant soup with pesto, followed by lamb ragoût garnished with apricots, onions, and spices served with couscous. Your luncheon tab includes gratuity and tax. A glass of wine will usually add another $4. Brick-oven pizza; salads; a fabulous calzone, stuffed with mozzarella, goat cheese, and prosciutto; and homemade pastas are among the exceptional dinner offerings. Even the ice creams and sherbets are homemade. Since dinner reservations are not taken for the cafe, your wait may be lengthy, but it's worth it.

In the cozy downstairs restaurant, only one fixed-price five-course gourmet dinner is served each night. The menu, which has changed daily since the restaurant opened in 1971, is posted outside the restaurant on Saturday for each day of the week. The dining area is redwood-paneled and has a working fireplace, art deco lamps, and big bouquets of flowers everywhere. A typical meal might include pan-fried oysters with Chino Ranch curly endive, spinach-and-fennel soup, veal saltimbocca, straw potatoes, salad, and orange ice cream in almond cookie cups. Is this expensive? Of course. Is it worth it? Absolutely. The wine list ($20 to $200) is also excellent.

BUDGET

BISHOP'S SWEET POTATO PIE COMPANY, 1786 Shattuck Ave. Tel. 510/841-1277.
 Cuisine: MEAT AND FRUIT PIES
$ Prices: $1.65–$3 per mini-pie; $7–$13 per large pie. No credit cards.
 Open: Mon–Sat 7:30am–7pm.
This tiny take-out at Delaware Street bakes some of the best meat and fruit pies to be found anywhere. As the name says, sweet-potato pie is the house specialty, but pecan, apple, pumpkin, and

berry are also recommendable. Hearty entrée-type pies include chicken, beef, and vegetable. Most every flavor comes in single serving pies and full-pie sizes.

BLONDIE'S PIZZA, 2340 Telegraph Ave., Berkeley. Tel. 510/548-1129.
   Cuisine: PIZZA
$ Prices: $7–$14 pizza; $1.50 slice of cheese. No credit cards.
   Open: Mon–Thurs 5pm–1am, Fri–Sat 5pm–2am, Sun noon–midnight.
Always busy, loud, and somewhat messy, this pizza parlor with the decidedly un-Italian name is a Berkeley institution. Pizza is the only menu item—your choice of thick, thin, or whole-wheat crust.

CAFE INTERMEZZO, 2422 Telegraph Ave. Tel. 510/849-4592.
   Cuisine: SALADS/SANDWICHES
$ Prices: $3–$5. No credit cards.
   Open: Daily 10am–10pm.
Although Intermezzo's menu is strictly salads and sandwiches, it's easy to understand why this is one of the busiest restaurants in Berkeley: ingredients are of uniformly high standards, portions are huge, and prices are rock-bottom. Roast beef, ham, turkey, salami, tuna, chicken, egg, and vegetables are mounded between slices of homemade, thick-sliced bread. Huge natural salads contain lettuce, avocado, egg, beans, tomatoes, cabbage, and more. Order cafeteria-style, then take a seat at one of about 15 varnished wooden tables. At lunchtime, during the school year, there's a line out the door.

NOAH'S BAGELS, 2344 Telegraph Ave., Berkeley. Tel. 510/849-9951.
   Cuisine: JEWISH
$ Prices: $1–$7. Cash only.
   Open: Mon–Fri 7am–9pm, Sat–Sun 7:30am–6pm.
I've never had a good bagel in San Francisco. Until now. Noah's corner shop is permeated by a heavenly smell of fresh baking. A large appetizing section contains six different kinds of cream cheese, a dozen varieties of salads, and several smoked-fish sections. In deference to their native Berkeley customers, peanut butter and humus are also available. It's still not New York, but you can get the Sunday *Times* too, at a newsstand just a block away.

TRIPLE ROCK BREWERY COMPANY, INC. 1920 Shattuck Ave., Berkeley. Tel. 510/843-2739.
   Cuisine: AMERICAN. **Reservations:** Not accepted.
$ Prices: $6–$9. Cash only.
   Open: Sun–Thurs 11:30am–1am, Fri–Sat 11:30am–2am.
Although I don't particularly recommend eating here, this top-notch brewpub/restaurant is a must for any beer lover worthy of the title. It's not much to look at—very frat-like with wooden floors and a good juke box—but the beer is among the tastiest around.

---

3. TIBURON & ANGEL ISLAND

8 miles N of San Francisco

GETTING THERE By Ferry Ferries of the **Red and White Fleet** (tel. 415/546-2700, or toll free 800/229-2784 in California) leave from Pier 43½ (Fisherman's Wharf) and travel to both

Tiburon and Angel Island. Boats run on a seasonal schedule; phone for departure information. The round-trip fare is $9 to Tiburon, $8 to Angel Island; half price for kids 5 to 11.

Alternatively, you can drive to Tiburon (see below), then board the **Angel Island Ferry** (tel. 415/435-2131, or 415/388-6770) for the short, 15-minute hop to the island. The round-trip costs $5.

By Car Take U.S. 101 to the Tiburon/Belvedere exit and then follow Tiburon Boulevard all the way into downtown, a 40-minute drive from San Francisco. Catch the ferry from the dock located at Tiburon Boulevard and Main Street.

ESSENTIALS Orientation Tiburon is tiny. The aptly named Main Street is the town's primary thoroughfare. It fronts the water and is a popular bike path. Main intersects with Tiburon Boulevard (known as Paradise Drive). Opposite is a handsome and posh shopping and eating plaza with wood-shingled buildings and brick walkways overlooking its own small body of water. Just across the Beach Road Bridge is Belvedere Island, a pretty little place full of fancy houses.

Angel Island is only 730 acres. There are picnic sites with tables, benches, and barbecue pits, and rest rooms at Ayala Cove, where you land. Miles of hiking trails lead you around the island and to the peak of Mount Caroline Livermore, 776 feet above the bay.

INFORMATION The rangers at Angel Island State Park (tel. 415/435-1915) will be happy to answer any of your questions.

A federal and state wildlife refuge, Angel Island is the prettiest of the San Francisco Bay's three islets (the other are Alcatraz and Yerba Buena). Most of the people who visit here never leave the large green lawn that fronts the docking area; they bring picnics and enjoy the view of Tiburon across the way. Behind the lawn, inside the ranger station, are displays detailing the history of this largest bay island. Angel Island has been, at various times, a prison, a favorite site for duels, a quarantine station for immigrants, and a Nike missile base. Today, in addition to picnics, it is popular for hiking and biking. More than 12 miles of trails include the Perimeter Road, a partly paved path that circles the island and wends its way past disused troop barracks, former gun emplacements, and other military buildings. Sometimes referred to as the "Ellis Island of the West," Angel Island held Chinese immigrants from 1910 to 1940 while their citizenship papers were being processed. You can still see some faded Chinese scrawlings on the walls of the barracks where the immigrants were held. During the warmer months it's possible to camp on the island. There are a limited number of sites, and reservations are required. Call 415/323-2988 for information.

Tiburon, situated on a peninsula of the same name, looks like a cross between a fishing village and a Hollywood western set—imagine San Francisco reduced to toy dimensions, with just a dash of stagecoach atmosphere thrown in. This decidedly odd seacoast town rambles over a series of green hills and ends up at a spindly, multicolored pier on the waterfront, like a Fisherman's Wharf in miniature. But in reality it's an extremely plush patch of yacht-club suburbia, as you'll see by both the marine craft and the homes of their owners. This, ladies and gentlemen, is the "good life."

Main Street is lined with ramshackle, color-splashed old frame houses that hide chic little boutiques, expensive antiques shops, and art galleries. Other roads are narrow, winding, and hilly, and lead up to ultramodern villas that stand in glaring contrast to the old village atmosphere of the shopping center. But this contrast is the town's primary charm. The pace here is sleepy, the bay view bewitching, and the hill setting glorious. The view of San Francisco's skyline and the islands in the bay is almost worth the price of living here.

Whether you reach Tiburon by car or by boat, it'll give you a pang of envy for its lucky inhabitants, who enjoy city sophistication and village air in one breath. Several hundred upper-bracket businesspeople feel exactly the same way; that's why they live here and commute daily to their San Francisco offices.

WHAT TO SEE & DO

The main thing to do here is stroll along the waterfront, pop into the boutiques, and end up at a restaurant in time for lunch or dinner. While you're at it, enjoy a taste of the Wine Country at **Windsor Vineyards,** 72 Main St. (tel. 415/435-3113, or toll free 800/214-9463). Their Victorial tasting room dates from 1888. You may choose from more than 35 fine Windsor Vineyards wines, including many award winners, for complimentary sampling. Windsor has been awarded more than 200 medals at prestigious wine-tasting competitions. They also carry a good selection of wine accessories and gifts—glasses, cork pullers, gourmet sauces, posters, maps, and so on. Carry-packs are available (they hold six bottles). Ask about personalized labels for your own selections. The shop is open daily from 10am to 6pm.

WHERE TO DINE

MODERATE

GUYAMAS RESTAURANTE, 5 Main St. Tel. 415/425-6300.
   Cuisine: MEXICAN. **Reservations:** Accepted. **Ferry:** Walk about 10 paces from the landing. **Directions:** From U.S. 101, exit at Tiburon/Belvedere; follow Tiburon Boulevard 5 miles and turn right onto Main Street. The restaurant is situated directly behind the bakery.
$ Prices: Appetizers $3–$8; main courses $7–$15. AE, CB, DC, MC, V.
   Open: Mon–Fri 11am–9:30pm, Sat–Sun 11am–10:30pm.
Guyamas is quite possibly the only restaurant in the Bay Area offering both authentic Mexican regional dishes and a spectacular panoramic view of San Francisco and the bay. In good weather, dining on either one of the two outdoor patios is particularly pleasing. Bright pink walls are hung with colorful Mexican masks, illuminated by modern track lighting. To the rear of the dining room is a rounded fireplace reminiscent of those shaped by Native Americans of the Southwest.

Guayamas is named after a fishing village on Mexico's Sea of Cortez. Both the town and the restaurant are famous for their camarones (giant shrimp). In addition, the restaurant features ceviche, handmade tamales, and charcoal-grilled beef, seafood, and fowl. Save room for dessert—among the tempting choices is an outrageously delicious fritter with "drunken" bananas and ice cream, or you might opt for the white-chocolate mousse with fresh strawberry sauce. In addition to a good selection of California wines, the restaurant offers an exceptional variety of tequilas, Mexican beers, and mineral waters flavored with flowers, grains, and fruits.

SAM'S ANCHOR CAFE, 27 Main St. Tel. 415/435-4527.

Cuisine: SEAFOOD. **Reservations:** Accepted. **Ferry:** Walk from the landing. **Directions:** From U.S. 101, exit at Tiburon/Belvedere; follow Tiburon Boulevard four miles and turn right onto Main Street.

$ Prices: Appetizers $4–$9; main courses $8–$16. AE, MC, V.

Open: Mon–Thurs 11am–10pm, Fri 11am–10:30pm, Sat 10am–10:30pm, Sun 9:30am–10pm.

Summer Sundays are liveliest in Tiburon, when weekend boaters tie up to the docks of waterside restaurants. For over 70 years now, the traditional place to dock is Sam's, which boasts two 110-foot piers and a large wooden deck that's filled to overflowing with blithe Sunday spirits. Sam's is the kind of place where you can take off your shoes and shirt—everyone's home-away-from-home neighborhood bar. During Prohibition days, it was a rendezvous point for bootleggers, who used to pull in under the restaurant and bring liquor in through trapdoors.

At lunch you might order a bay shrimp, tomato, and Cheddar-cheese sandwich on a toasted English muffin, or the soup du jour and half a sandwich for $4.50 to $9.95. Dinner might be any one of the fresh seafood specials, or deep-fried oysters served with fresh vegetables. Delicious sourdough bread and butter comes with all main courses.

BUDGET

SWEDEN HOUSE BAKERY-CAFE, 35 Main St. Tel. 415/435-9767.

Cuisine: SWEDISH/AMERICAN. **Reservations:** Not accepted. **Ferry:** Walk from the landing. **Directions:** From U.S. 101, exit at Tiburon/Belvedere; follow Tiburon Boulevard five miles and turn right onto Main Street.

$ Prices: Omelets $5–$6; sandwiches $6–$8. MC, V.

Open: Mon–Fri 8am–5pm, Sat–Sun 8am–7pm.

This quaint little eatery with gingham-covered walls adorned with copperware and other kitchen things is one of my favorite places in Tiburon. I love sitting on the terrace, gazing out over the bay with an espresso in one hand and a home-baked Swedish pastry in the other. The raspberry-iced, cream-filled napoleon is especially good.

Full breakfasts are served daily—perhaps scrambled eggs with cheese, mushrooms, shrimp, or slices of smoked salmon? Everything comes with the restaurant's own toasted Swedish limpa bread. At lunch there are traditional open-face sandwiches like avocado and bacon, or delicious asparagus tips rolled in Danish ham; you can also order such American standards as chicken and garden salads. Beer and wine are available.

4. SAUSALITO

5 miles N of San Francisco

GETTING THERE By Ferry Ferries of the **Red and White Fleet** (tel. 415/546-2700, or toll free 800/229-2784 in California)

218 • EASY EXCURSIONS FROM SAN FRANCISCO

leave from Pier 43½ (Fisherman's Wharf) and cost $9 round-trip, half price for kids 5 to 11. Boats run on a seasonal schedule; phone for departure information.

By Car   From U.S. 101 north, take the first right after the Golden Gate Bridge (Alexander exit). Alexander becomes Bridgeway in Sausalito.

ESSENTIALS   Sausalito's main street is Bridgeway, which runs along the water. Just about everything notable is somewhere on or just off this roadway that plays the combined role of shopping center and promenade.

Sausalito makes no attempt to hide what it is—a slightly bohemian, nonchalant, and studiedly quaint adjunct to San Francisco, designed for folks who want to have their metropolitan cake and eat it outdoors too. With approximately 7,500 residents, Sausalito feels rather like St. Tropez on the French Riviera—minus the starlets and the social rat race. It has its quota of paper millionaires, but they rub their permanently suntanned shoulders with a good number of hard-up artists, struggling authors, shipyard workers, and fishermen. Next to the swank restaurants, plush bars, and expensive antiques shops, you'll see hamburger joints, beer parlors, and secondhand bookstores.

Above all, Sausalito has scenery and sunshine, for once you cross the Golden Gate Bridge you're out of the San Francisco fog patch and under blue Californian sky. The town's steep hills are covered with white houses that overlook a forest of masts on the water below. The gleaming spires of bustling San Francisco can be seen in the comfortably far-off distance.

WHAT TO SEE & DO

BAY MODEL VISITORS CENTER, 210 Bridgeway. Tel. 415/332-3871.

In this 1½-acre model of San Francisco's bay and delta, the U.S. Army Corps of Engineers can make water behave as it does in the bay and observe just what changes in water flow will mean. It's a scientific tool used by engineers, scientists, and planners to analyze problems that can't be resolved through textbooks, experience, or mathematical models alone. The model reproduces (in scale) the rise and fall of tides, the flows and currents of water, the mixing of fresh and salt water, and indicates trends in sediment movement.

An introductory film that lasts about ten minutes orients visitors to the purpose and operation of the bay model. Here you can see the impact of pollution, view the Sacramento and San Joaquin rivers flowing into the bay, and even see the swift flow of water around Alcatraz. In addition to rangers, who are usually available to answer questions, the center has a 30-minute tour on tape in English, Russian, Japanese, German, French, and Spanish. The model is most interesting when it's actually in operation, and that happens only when a test is being conducted. It pays to call and ask about testing before you go.

Admission: Free.

Open: Winter, Tues–Sat 9am–4pm; summer, Tues–Fri 9am–4pm, Sat–Sun 10am–6pm.

SHOPPING

A mecca for handmade, original, and offbeat clothes and footwear, Sausalito boasts many charming shops, featuring a wide variety of unusual arts and crafts, antiques, gifts, and souvenirs. The town's best offbeat shops can be discovered by prowling through the alleys, malls, and second-floor boutiques reached by steep, narrow staircases on an off **Bridgeway.** Shops here come and go fairly quickly, as the goods are fairly pricey. But the merchandise is original, and its always colorful and fun.

If you have energy enough to push on farther, new shops, pubs, and restaurants are mushrooming on **Caledonia Street,** which runs parallel to, and one block inland from, Bridgeway. This street may be as busy as the main drag by the time this book is in your hands, but, as yet, the strollers are mainly natives, and the baseball game in the schoolyard helps remind you that this tourist-thronged town on woody hillsides has real people in residence.

VILLAGE FAIR, 777 Bridgeway.

This is Sausalito's closest approximation to a mall. It's a fascinating complex of 30 shops, souvenir stores, coffee bars, and gardens. Leaning against the hillside and spilling over in all directions from what used to be an old warehouse, Village Fair is almost a community unto itself, and could occupy an afternoon's exploring, **Quest Gallery** (tel. 415/332-6832) features fine ceramics, whimsical chess sets, contemporary glass, hand-painted silks, woven clothing, art jewelry, and graphics. The shop specializes in celebrated Californian artists, many of whom sell exclusively through this store.

Most shops are open daily from 10am to 6pm; restaurants stay open later.

BURLWOOD GALLERY, 721 Bridgeway. Tel. 415/332-6550.

Visit this gallery for one-of-a-kind redwood furniture plus fine jewelry, metal sculptures, hand-blown glass, Oriental rugs, and other interesting gifts. It's well worth browsing. Open daily from 10am to 6pm.

PEGASUS LEATHER COMPANY, 30 Princess St. Tel. 415/332-5624.

Turn right off Bridgeway onto Princess Street and look into the Pegasus store, vendors of beautiful leather clothing and extensive accessories collections. Some of the leathers are so soft they seem to be made of flowing fabric and in colors sure to add excitement to a wardrobe. Clothing will be custom made, and altered for a perfect fit at no extra charge. Along with jackets, coats, skirts, and blouses, there are handsome leather belts, gloves, and purses. Open daily from 10am to 5:30pm.

PEGASUS MEN'S STORE, 28 Princess St. Tel. 415/332-1718.

Pegasus Men's Store offers ruggedly good-looking jackets in award-winning designs. The men's shop is where you'll find a fine selection of leather briefcases, belts, hats, and wallets. Open daily from 10am to 5:30pm.

THE SAUSALITO COUNTRY STORE, 789 Bridgeway. Tel. 415/332-7890.

This place sells oodles of wonderful handmade country-style goods. Many of these items—ceramic, stuffed, and painted-wood animals, aprons, baskets, embossed quilt prints, and lithographs—are made by local artists and artisans. Open daily from 10am to 6pm.

STONEFLOWER GALLERY, 795 Bridgeway. Tel. 415/332-2995.

The shop speciaizes in wood, ceramics, and unusual hand-crafted creations with a somewhat ethnic flair. The Stoneflower carries artwork from major American and international artists. Open daily from 10am to 6pm.

WHERE TO STAY

CASA MADRONA, 801 Bridgeway, Sausalito, CA 94965. Tel. 415/332-0502, or toll free 800/288-0502. Fax 415/332-2537. 34 rms, 1 suite. MINIBAR TEL **Ferry:** Walk across the street from the landing. **Directions:** From U.S. 101 north, take the first right after the Golden Gate Bridge (Alexander exit); Alexander becomes Bridgeway in Sausalito.

$ Rates: $105–$225 single or double; $370 Madrona Villa suite. Extra person $10. Two-night minimum stay on weekends. AE, MC, V. **Parking** $5.

Sooner or later most visitors to Sausalito look up and wonder at the ornate mansion on the hill. It's part of Casa Madrona, a hide-away-by-the-bay built in 1885 by a wealthy lumber baron. The epitome of luxury in its day, the mansion slipped, with the passage of time, into decay. It was saved by a Frenchman, Henri Deschamps, who converted it into a hotel and restaurant. Successive renovations and additions have included a rambling New England–style building that was added to the hillside below the main house. Now a certified historic landmark, the hotel offers rooms, suites, and cottages. The 16 newest units are each uniquely decorated by different local designers. The "1,000 Cranes" is Asian in theme, with lots of ash and lacquer. "Artist's Loft" is reminiscent of a rustic Parisian artist's studio, complete with easel, brushes, and paint. "Summer House" is decked out in white wicker, and "Château Charmant" evokes the genteel French countryside. Up in the mansion, the rooms are also decorated in a variety of styles; some even have Jacuzzis. Amenities include quilts and baskets of luxury shampoos, soaps, and bath gels in the bathroom. Other rooms have fireplaces and their newest rooms are located on the water with panoramic views of the San Francisco skyline and bay.

The Casa Madrona Restaurant (tel. 415/331-5888), offering breathtaking views of the bay, serves contemporary American cuisine. It's open for lunch Monday through Friday and for Sunday brunch from 10am to 2:30pm, and for dinner nightly. A meal will cost $30 to $40 without wine.

WHERE TO DINE

MODERATE

FENG NIAN CHINESE RESTAURANT, 2650 Bridgeway. Tel. 415/331-5300.
Cuisine: CHINESE. **Reservations:** Accepted. **Directions:** From U.S. 101 north, take the first right after the Golden Gate Bridge (Alexander exit); Alexander becomes Bridgeway in Sausalito. The restaurant is located near the intersection of Bridgeway and Harbor Dirve, before downtown Sausalito.

$ Prices: Appetizers $4–$6.50; lunch specials $4–$5.50; main courses $6–$13. AE, DISC, MC, V.
Open: Mon and Wed–Fri 11:30am–9:30pm, Sat 11:30am–10pm, Sun noon–9:30pm.

Some of the best and most interesting Chinese food outside of San Francisco proper is served in this pretty restaurant with an orange awning, at the south end of a small mall.

Feng Nian has such a wide selection of appetizers that a combination of several would make a delicious meal in itself. The crispy roast duck is a personal preference, but if you'd like an assortment, try the flaming combination (enough for two) that includes egg roll, fried prawn, paper-wrapped chicken, barbecued ribs, fried chicken, and teriyaki ($9.50). There are nine soups, including a sizzling rice soup with sliced chicken, prawns, mushrooms, and snow peas on a golden rice crust; or go for broke and order a truly exceptional, rich crabmeat/shark's-fin soup with shredded crab-leg meat.

Choosing one of the chef's suggestions isn't easy. The Peking duck requires about a half hour of patience before it arrives, but it's always superb. If you especially enjoy seafood, try the Twice Sizzling Seafood, with prawns, scallops, squid, and fresh vegetables in oyster sauce; it's prepared at your table. Beef dishes are prepared in almost every conceivable manner: Mongolian, Szechuan, Hunan, Mandarin; with ginger, curry, and broccoli—just to name a few of the choices. The restaurant offers over 90 main dishes, including a select number of main courses for vegetarians.

GUERNICA, 2009 Bridgeway. Tel. 415/332-1512.

Cuisine: FRENCH/BASQUE. **Reservations:** Recommended. **Directions:** From U.S. 101 north, take the first right after the Golden Gate Bridge (Alexander exit); Alexander becomes Bridgeway in Sausalito.
$ Prices: Appetizers $2.50–$6.50; main courses $10–$18. AE, MC, V.
Open: Dinner only, daily 5–10pm

French-Basque proprietor Roger Minhondo runs this terrific restaurant with a firm but friendly hand. The atmosphere is homey; Roger greets regulars by name and welcomes first-timers with a smile. In its decade of operation, Guernica has developed quite a large following, both in Sausalito and in San Francisco. The small dining room is tastefully decorated, with walls of stone, brick, wood, and white stucco, large wood-and-leatherette booths, and white-colored tables with flowers and candles. On one wall there's a large print of Picasso's *Guernica*. Classical music plays softly in the background.

Begin with an appetizer of artichoke hearts or escargots. Some of the main courses from which you can choose are grilled rabbit with a spicy red *diablo* sauce, the daily fresh-fish special, paella, and médaillons of veal with mustard sauce. Terrific desserts include such in-season specialties as strawberry tarte and peach Melba.

HORIZONS, 558 Brideway. Tel. 415/331-3232.

Cuisine: SEAFOOD/AMERICAN. **Reservations:** Accepted weekdays only.
$ Prices: Appetizers $3–$10, main courses $9–$14, salads and sandwiches $4–$10. AE, MC, V.
Open: Mon–Fri 11am–10pm, Sat–Sun 10am–10pm.

Everybody goes to Horizons for the view. On warm days you can sit out on the wooden waterside terrace and watch dreamy sailboats glide past San Francisco's toylike skyline. The heavily varnished, clunky built-in furnishings inside are hardly as inviting. The food here can't touch the view, but it's pretty good. Seafood dishes are the main bills of fare and include steamed clams and mussels, and freshly shucked oysters. Almond chicken, dungeness crab, and bay shrimp lead a long list of salads, and lunchtime sandwiches are filled with chicken or turkey breast. Dinners are heartier and include tiger prawns sautéed in basil-sherry cream sauce, chicken Dijon, and a variety of pastas.

In fine Marin tradition, Horizons has an herb tea bar, and is a totally no-smoking restaurant.

SCOMA'S, 588 Bridgeway. Tel. 415/332-9551.

Cuisine: ITALIAN/SEAFOOD. **Reservations:** Not accepted. **Ferry:** Walk five minutes south from the landing. **Directions:** From U.S. 101 north, take the first right after the Golden Gate Bridge (Alexander exit); Alexander becomes Bridgeway in Sausalito.

$ Prices: Appetizers $6–$8; main courses $10–$26. AE, CB, DC, MC, V.

Open: Thurs–Mon 11:30am–10pm, Tues–Wed, 5:30–10pm.

Scoma's is yet another one of Sausalito's attractive right-on-the-bay eateries. Boxes of geraniums line the entranceway, and the interior is beautifully furnished with gray wood-paneled walls and select antique furnishings. A scrumptious cioppino and linguine with clam sauce are among the Italian-style seafood dishes at this charming establishment. A la carte main courses usually come with a vegetable and pasta or rice.

INEXPENSIVE

THE SPINNAKER, 100 Spinnaker Dr. Tel. 415/332-1500.

Cuisine: AMERICAN. **Reservations:** Accepted. **Ferry:** Walk from the landing. **Directions:** From U.S. 101 north, take the first right after the Golden Gate Bridge (Alexander exit); Alexander becomes Bridgeway in Sausalito. The restaurant is located just off Bridgeway, near the ferry landing.

$ Prices: Appetizers $3–$6; main courses $7–$14; fixed-price dinner $12–$20. AE, CB, DC, MC, V.

Open: Daily 11am–11pm.

The food at the Spinnaker is not as great as the superb panoramic view of the bay. The restaurant itself actually projects out onto the bay, and diners sit on comfortable tufted banquettes facing 14-foot-high picture windows overlooking the water. Fir-trunk columns add a warm, natural, nautical air. Main courses include the likes of rex sole meunière, New York steak, and scallops sauté. A good selection of chicken, pasta, and veal dishes is also available.

PICNIC SUPPLIES & WHERE TO EAT THEM

There are picnic areas and benches all along **Bridgeway,** offering superb views of the bay. On a nice day, picnicking beats a restaurant meal hands-down.

THE STUFFED CROISSANT, ETC., 43 Caledonia St. Tel. 415/332-7103.

The most notable shop on Caledonia, in my hungry opinion, is the Stuffed Croissant, where you can get anything from a nosh to a meal. There are all sorts of gourmet croissants filled with almond-chicken salad or a scrumptious roast-beef barbecue with garlic and onions, bagels, plus soups and stews. Hot meals like chicken curry and Italian meatballs are also popular. For your sweet tooth there are croissants stuffed with fruits—strawberries and cream cheese, or apples, raisins, and cinnamon, as well as pain au chocolat—and a fantastic variety of delicious fresh muffins, like honey bran, pumpkin raisin, carrot pineapple, poppy seed, banana nut, and blueberry. All these goodies are freshly baked, and they cost a mere $1.50 to $4.50 each. There's always a variety of gourmet coffees brewing (including cappucino and espresso), and juices, tea, and mineral waters are available.

Open: Mon–Wed 6:45am–9pm, Thurs–Sat 6:45am–10pm, Sun 7:30am–8pm.

VENICE GOURMET DELICATESSEN, 625 Bridgeway. Tel. 415/332-3544.

This place has all the makings for a superb picnic—wines, cheese, fruits, stuffed vine leaves, mushroom-and-artichoke salad, quiche, delicious sandwiches made to order on sourdough bread, olives, and fresh-baked pastries.

Open: Daily 9am–6pm.

---

5. MUIR WOODS & MOUNT TAMALPAIS

20 miles N of San Francisco

GETTING THERE By Car To get to **Mount Tamalpais,** drive across the Golden Gate Bridge and take the exit for Calif. 1/Mount Tamalpais. Follow the shoreline highway about 2½ miles and turn onto the Panoramic Highway. After about 5½ miles, turn onto Pantoll Road and continue for about a mile to Ridgecrest Boulevard. Ridgecrest winds to a parking lot below East Peak. From there, it's a 15-minute hike up to the top.

To get to **Muir Woods,** follow the Mount Tamalpais directions to the Panoramic Highway. After about a mile, take the signed turnoff and follow successive signs.

Also in Marin County, but in silent, majestic contrast to the bustle of the seacoast towns, lies one of America's most enchanting nature preserves. Mount Tamalpais is the great landmark of the county, its outline towering over the entire scenery. At its foot nestle the Muir Woods.

WHAT TO SEE & DO

Amid the quiet grandeur of the forest are the world-famous **California redwoods**. Although these magnificent trees have been successfully transplanted to five continents, their homeland is a 500-mile strip along the mountainous coast of southwestern Oregon and northern California, where they grow inland "as far as the fog flows"—about 30 miles.

The coast redwood, or *Sequoia sempervirens,* is the tallest tree in that section of the earth—the largest-known specimen towers 367.8 feet. It has an even larger relative, the *Sequoiadendron giganteum* of the California Sierra Nevada, but the coastal variety is stunning enough. There is no other forest like it anywhere in the world—soaring like a wooden cathedral up to the sky while spreading over a lush green carpet of ferns underfoot.

You can drive the 2,600 feet to the top of Mount Tam, as the locals call it, or hike along one of two clearly marked trails (one gentle, the other fairly rough) to the summit. The mountain offers a special picnic camp and some wonderful forest trails undulating for miles beneath the spreading green canopy above. The redwoods range from months-old seedlings to 1,200-year-old elders that were fully grown when Charlemagne ruled France. And from the peak you get a 100-mile sweep in all directions, from the foothills of the Sierras to the western horizon.

What is known as Marin today, incidentally, was actually the first "New England." In June 1579, Sir Francis Drake sailed his sturdy *Golden Hinde* into the bay named after him. One of his first acts was to order a "plate of brasse, fast nailed to a great and firm post," claiming his discovery for his tough and level-headed sovereign, Queen Elizabeth I of England. He then named the land "Nova Albion."

However, this turned out to be one of the rare historical instances when the English were unable to follow through on their exploration by occupation—they were too busy elsewhere on the globe. Instead, the Spaniards arrived two centuries later and made Marin part of their empire.

6. POINT REYES NATIONAL SEASHORE

35 miles N of San Francisco

GETTING THERE By Car From San Francisco, cross the Golden Gate Bridge and stay on U.S. 101 north. Shortly before Corte Madera, turn left onto Sir Francis Drake Boulevard and drive 20 miles to Bear Valley Road. The information center is half a mile down Bear Valley Road. To get to the lighthouse, return to Sir Francis Drake Boulevard and continue to its end at a parking lot. The lighthouse is a half-mile walk down a paved road.

ESSENTIALS This 65,000-acre park encompasses several surf-pounded beaches, beautiful bird estuaries, and open swaths of land with roaming elk. Before you leave for the lighthouse, call the **visitor center** (tel. 415/669-1534) for a weather and whale-activity report.

This remarkable, beautiful stretch of shoreline is located about an hour's drive from San Francisco. Comprised primarily of sand beach and scrubland, it's home to birds, sea lions, and a variety of tidepool creatures.

WHAT TO SEE & DO

There are three distinct areas of interest that you can visit:

Point Reyes Beach faces the Pacific and withstands the full brunt of ocean tides and winds—so much so that the water is much too rough for swimming, surfing, or even wading. It's a wild, tormented, and moody place to walk in . . . and not one you'll soon forget.

Drake's Beach, along the south coast, evokes different feelings entirely. The waters here are as tranquil and serene as Point Reye's waters are turbulent. Drake's Beach was named for the English explorer who landed here. Locals come here to sun and picnic; occasionally a hearty soul ventures into the quiet but cold waters of Drake's Bay.

The main road of the park, Sir Francis Drake Boulevard, which passes by Point Reyes Beach and branches off to reach Drake's Beach, leads right out to Point Reyes itself. The **Point Reyes Lighthouse** juts out almost 15 miles from the mainland and is one of the best places on the West Coast to watch for whales. Gray whales pass by the point as they migrate between Alaska and the lagoons of Baja California. The annual round-trip encompasses 10,000 miles and represents one of the longest mammal migrations known. The whales head south in December and January, and return north in March. The last group of migraters are mothers swimming with their newborn calves.

If you plan to drive out to the lighthouse to whale-watch, be sure to arrive early since there's a limited amount of parking space. If possible, come on a weekday. On a weekend or holiday it's wise to park at the Drake's Beach Visitor Center and take the free shuttle bus to the lighthouse. Be sure to dress warmly—it's often quite cold and windy. Also, bring binoculars if you have any.

But whale-watching, as spectacular as it is, is not the only interesting activity the Point Reyes National Seashore offers. There are excellent ranger-conducted tours: You can walk along the **Bear Valley Trail,** where you'll see the wildlife and inhabitants of the ocean's edge; get a good look at the birds and some of the very secretive waterfowl of Fivebrooks Pond; explore tidepools; view some of North America's most beautiful ducks in the wetlands of Limantour; hike to the promontory overlooking Chimney Rock to see the sea lions, harbor seals, and sea birds; or take a guided walk along the San Andreas fault to look at the site of the epicenter of the famous 1906 earthquake and learn about the regional geology. And this is just a sampling. Since available tours and their lengths vary seasonally, you can either call the ranger station (tel. 415/663-1092), with pencil and paper handy, or ask to be sent a copy of *Park Paper,* which includes a schedule of activities and much other useful information. Many of the tours are suitable for the disabled. Two important no-no's: Pets are not permitted on any trails, and no swimming or wading is permitted at the outer Point Reyes beaches—surf and rip tides are extremely dangerous.

WHERE TO DINE

STATION HOUSE CAFE, Main St., Point Reyes Station. Tel. 415/663-1515.
   Cuisine: AMERICAN. **Reservations:** Recommended.
$ **Prices:** Breakfast $4–$6.50; appetizers $4.50–$7; main courses $8.50–$15. MC, V.
   Open: Sun–Thurs 8am–9pm, Fri–Sat 8am–10pm.
I don't know why sea air gives you an appetite, but when it does, treat yourself to the remarkable gastronomic glories of the Station

House located in the tiny town of Point Reyes Station. The cafe has a fireplace, an open kitchen, a full-service bar, live music on weekends, and a lovely garden for dining—in addition to superb food. For breakfast, you might be offered bread pudding with stewed-fruit compote, or fritatta with asparagus, goat cheese, and olives. Regular omelets and Belgian waffles are also on offer. The lunch special might be fettuccine with fresh local mussels steamed in white wine and butter sauce, or two-cheese polenta served with fresh spinach sauté and grilled garlic-buttered tomato. Organically grown beef is always on the menu; it's raised locally and is of an exceptionally superior quality. Rounding out the delicious choices are homemade chili, steamed clams, fresh soup made daily, and fish and chips. The cafe has an extensive list of fine California wines, plus local imported beers.

---

7. MARINE WORLD AFRICA USA

30 miles NE of San Francisco, 10 miles S of Napa

GETTING THERE By Ferry The **Red and White Fleet** (tel. 415/546-2700, or toll free 800/229-2784 in California) operates a high-speed catamaran service from Pier 41 at Fisherman's Wharf. The pretty cruise, passing Alcatraz and the Golden Gate Bridge, takes 55 minutes, including a brief bus ride. The round-trip, including park admission, is $36 for adults, $30 for seniors 62 and over and students 13 to 18, and $20.50 for kids 4 to 12. Service is limited; call for departure times.

By Car From San Francisco, take I-80 north to Calif. 37 and follow the signs to the park; it's less than an hour's drive.

Marine World Africa USA, Marine World Pkwy. in Vallejo (tel. 707/643-ORCA for a recording), is a kind of Disney-meets-Wild-Kingdom theme park, where humans and animals perform for visitors. The park is the interesting conjunction of Marine World, which specializes in aquatic attractions, and Africa USA, which features trained animals of land and air in daily shows.

A variety of events are scheduled continuously throughout the day. There's a **Killer Whale and Dolphin Show** where the front seven rows of seats are saved for guests who want a thorough drenching. In the **Sea Lion Show** you can pet some of the oldest and largest performers in the country. **Shark Experience,** a moving walkway through a clear acrylic tunnel, brings visitors through a 300,000-gallon tropical shark-filled tank.

When you cross the bridge over the waterfall, heading through the trees and past the flamingos, you enter "Africa USA." Here you'll find **Elephant Encounter,** where guests can interact with the park's 11 Asian an African elephants. In addition to shows, elephant rides costing $3 per person are offered. At **Tiger Island,** a habitat for the park's hand-raised Bengal tigers, you can see trainers and tigers playing and swimming together. An informative show about the park's exotic and endangered animals is performed in the **Wildlife Theater.**

The **Bird Show** is one of the park's best and proves that the bird's peanut-sized brains are capable of more than we think!

There's also an enclosed **Butterfly World,** and a **Small Animal Petting Kraal** (with llamas) that are particularly popular with kids. Even better is **Gentle Jungle,** a unique playground that combines education, fun, and adventure. It's one of the most innovative play areas of its type. Inside the **Prairie Crawl,** children can crawl through burrows in the prairie dog village and pop up into Plexiglas domes so they can see he world as these cute little animals view it.

And finally there's a 55-acre lake that is the stage for a **Waterski and Boat Show** April through October. Daredevil athletes jump, spin, and even create a human pyramid while wearing waterskis.

A wide variety of fast food is available at Lakeside Plaza—everything from burgers and sandwiches to nachos and chicken. Prices are moderate, averaging about $6 to $7 for a light bite. A sit-down restaurant completes the food choices. Or you can bring your own picnic—there are barbecue facilities on the grounds. The best way to cope with the full schedule of shows is to get there early, make up your own itinerary from the leaflet and map given to you at the entrance—and then stick to it. Otherwise, you'll find yourself missing parts of each presentation and feeling frustrated.

Admission is $24.95 for adults, $16.95 for kids 4 to 12, and $19.95 for seniors over 60, free for children under 4. Carte Blanche, Diners Club, MasterCard, and Visa are accepted. The park is open from Memorial Day through Labor Day, daily from 9:30am to 6pm; the rest of the year, Wednesday through Sunday from 9:30am to 5pm.

---

8. THE WINE COUNTRY— NAPA COUNTY

55 miles N of San Francisco

Just a short drive from the city are some of the world's greatest vineyards. Have fun in the country discovering new vintages on a wine-tasting tour of the Napa Valley.

GETTING THERE By Car From San Francisco, cross the Golden Gate Bridge and continue north on U.S. 101. Turn east on Calif. 37, then north on Calif. 29. This road is the main thoroughfare through the Wine Country.

ESSENTIALS Orientation California Highway 29 runs the length of Napa Valley, which is just 35 miles. You really can't get lost—there's just one north-south road, on which most of the wineries, hotels, shops, and restaurants are located. Towns are small and easy to negotiate. Any local can give you directions.

Information For a detailed description of the following and many other wineries, pick up free Wine Country maps and brochures from the Wine Institute at 425 Market St., Suite 1000, San Francisco, CA 94105 (tel. 415/512-0151). Once in the Napa Valley, make your first stop the **Napa Chamber of Commerce,** 1556 First St., in downtown Napa (tel. 707/226-7455). They have information on the local vineyards, as well as listings of antiques dealers and walking tours. All over Napa and Sonoma, you can pick up a very informative—and free—weekly publication called *Wine*

Country Review. It will give you the most up-to-date information on wineries and related area events.

Most of the delicious California wines you've been enjoying with your meals in San Francisco hail from a warm, narrow valley about 90 minutes' drive from San Francisco. Napa Valley's fame began with cabernet sauvignon and, except for white chardonnay, more acreage is devoted to the growth of this grape than any other. The valley is home to about 225 wineries, and an exceptional selection of fine restaurants and hostelries at all price levels. If you can, plan on spending more than a day here, if you'd like to tour even a small segment of the valley and its wineries. The valley is just 35 miles long, so whether you stay in Napa, Yountville, Rutherford, or St. Helena, you can dine, wine, shop, and sightsee without traveling very far.

WHEN TO GO

The beauty of the valley is striking any time of the year but is most memorable in September and October. This is when the grapes are being pressed and the very air in the valley seems intoxicating. It's the time of the year when the rain in Napa has its own quiet love affair with the hills, where the mists lie softly and lovingly. The colors are breathtaking as the vine leaves change to gold, rust brown, and deep maroon—all in preparation for the next season of grapes.

THE WINERIES

Most wineries offer tours daily from 10am to 5pm. And there's considerably more to them than merely open vineyards. Huge presses feed through an elaborate system of pipes into blending vats. From there, wines are mellowed gracefully in giant oak casks in the deep cellars. As you drive through the Napa Valley, you'll see nonstop welcoming signs put out by rows of wineries, most of which not only take visitors on conducted tours but also offer samples of their product, most of them free. Be careful—just a few visits can affect your driving in no uncertain manner.

Wineries and towns listed below are organized by geography, from south to north along Calif. 29, beginning in Napa village.

NEWLAN VINEYARDS, 5225 Solano Ave., Napa, CA 94558. Tel. 707/257-2399.

This small family-owned winery produces only about 10,000 cases a year. It all started in 1967 when Physicist Brunc Newlan planted 11 acres of cabernet sauvignon along Dry Creek. Three years later 16 more acres were planted, and in five years Bruce and his wife, Jonette, had a winery. Cabernet sauvignon, pinot noir, chardonnay, zinfandel, and late harvest Johannisberg riesling are estate bottled. Excellent tours are offered, by appointment only.

TREFETHEN VINEYARDS, 1160 Oak Knoll Ave. (P.O. Box 2460), Napa, CA 94558. Tel. 707/255-7700.

To reach Trefethen Vineyards from Calif. 29, take Oak Knoll Avenue east. The winery is ahead on your left. Tours are offered here by appointment only, and are well worth arranging. Listed on the National Register of Historical Places, the vineyard's main building was built in 1886, and remains Napa's only wooden, gravity-powered winery. The bucolic brick courtyard is surrounded with oak and cork trees. Unlike many of the region's wineries that try to outdo one another with modernity, Trefethen embraces its history, displaying old farming tools and machines along with plaques explaining their functions. Although it is one of the region's granddaddy's, Trefethen's first case of chardonnay wasn't vinified until 1973. Since that time the vineyard has succeeded in winning awards year after year. Tastings take place in their brick-floored, jazz-filled tasting room, under a wood-beamed ceiling.

Open: Daily 10am–4:30pm; tours by appointment year round.

STAG'S LEAP WINE CELLARS, 5766 Silverado Trail, Napa, CA 94558. Tel. 707/944-2020.

Our next stop in Napa is Stag's Leap Wine Cellars. For the most part, the Silverado Trail parallels Calif. 29, and you can get there by going east on Trances Street or Oak Knoll Avenue, then north to the cellars. The man who has guided the destiny of this now famous winery and attacted the attention of France's noted wine experts is Warren Winiarski. A hill hides the group of buildings at its foot that comprise the cellars. The first building, which once housed the entire operation, now houses a summary exhibit of wine making from start to finish. Undoubtedly one of the best-known wines is the Cabernet Sauvignon Cask 23. Winiarski also offers good-value wines under the Hawk Crest label. You can taste current releases during sales hours for $3 per person.

Open: Sales and tasting daily 10am–4pm; tours by appointment only.

DOMAINE CHANDON, California Dr., Yountville, CA 94599. Tel. 707/944-2280.

Back on Calif. 29 at its intersection with California Drive, you'll find Domaine Chandon. The firm produces about 450,000 cases annually of méthode champenoise sparkling wines, Chandon Brut Cuvée, Carneros Blanc de Noirs, Chandon Réserve, and Etoile. Founded in 1973, this is a California version of a champagne house. You can take a guided tour here to find out all about the making of sparkling wines. Wines are sold by the bottle or glass and are accompanied by complimentary hors d'oeuvres. There's also a gift shop and a small gallery housing artifacts from the vineyard's parent company, Moët et Chandon, depicting the history of champagnes. The Domaine Chandon restaurant is one of the best in the valley (see "Where to Dine" in "Yountville," below, for complete information).

Open: Nov–Apr, Wed–Sun 11am–6pm; May–Oct, daily 11am–6pm.

ROBERT MONDAVI WINERY, 7801 St. Helena Hwy. (Calif. 29), Oakville, CA 94562. Tel. 707/963-9611.

If you continue on Calif. 29 up to Oakville, you'll arrive at the Robert Mondavi Winery. This is the ultimate high-tech Napa Valley winery, housed in a magnificent mission-style facility. Almost every processing variable in their wine making is computer controlled—and absolutely fascinating to watch.

Reservations are recommended for the guided tour. It's wise to make them one to two weeks in advance, especially if you plan to go on a weekend. After the guided tour, you can taste the results of all this attention to detail with selected current wines. The Vineyard

Room usually features an art show, and you'll find some exceptional antiques in the reception hall. During the summer the winery has some great outdoor jazz concerts.

Open: May–Oct, daily 9:30am–5:30pm; Nov–Apr, daily 9:30am–4:30pm.

INGLENOOK–NAPA VALLEY WINERY, 1991 St. Helena Hwy. (Calif. 20), Rutherford, CA 94573. Tel. 707/967-3362.

Farther north on Calif. 29 (opposite Rutherford Cross Road), you will reach Rutherford and the Inglenook–Napa Valley Winery. Inglenook's history dates back to 1879, when the vineyards were bought by Gustave Niebaum. The original winery, designed and built by Captain McIntyre, the architect of several neighboring wineries, is now the tasting room and starting point for tours. You can taste current releases as well as older vintages during sales hours.

Open: Daily 10am–5pm.

BEAULIEU VINEYARD, 1960 St. Helena Hwy. (Calif. 29), Rutherford, CA 94573. Tel. 707/963-2411.

A bit farther on from Inglenook is the Beaulieu Vineyard, founded by a Frenchman named Georges de Latour. The original winery looks as French baronial as a turn-of-the century transplant can be. The winery is larger than when first built, but you can still see the complete tradition-oriented process of wine making from start to finish—beginning with the crusher, on to bottling, and then the tasting, the last step being yours.

Open: Daily 10am–5pm; tours, daily 11am–3:30pm.

FLORA SPRINGS WINE CO., 1978 W. Zinfandel Lane, St. Helena, CA 94574. Tel. 707/963-5711.

Flora Springs Wine Co. is at the end of West Zinfandel Lane, off Calif. 29. While this handsome stone winery dates back to Napa Valley's early days, the Flora Springs label first appeared in 1978. The current owners have vineyards throughout Napa Valley and select choice lots for their own label. They are especially known for their barrel-fermented chardonnay, a cabernet sauvignon, and Trilogy, a Bourdeaux-style blend.

Flora Springs offers an excellent two-hour "familiarization seminar," which almost everyone interested in wines would enjoy. And best of all, it's tailored to all levels of wine enthusiasts. Limited to groups of ten, the course is held Monday through Thursday and Saturday at 10am. The program begins in the vineyards, where you'll see a good-growing vine and taste the grapes. While the grapes are being crushed, you taste the must (just-pressed juice) and ultimately see how it becomes a beautiful, clear wine. Then you are taught how to evaluate wines: You'll blind-taste different ones and learn to distinguish between them, trying an older and a younger wine, for example, to see what happens with aging. You'll also learn to pair wines with different foods.

Your two hours here will prove to be among the most interesting and enjoyable you'll ever spend.

Open: By reservation only; call Fritz Draeger (tel. 707/963-5711) or write to him at the above address.

BERINGER VINEYARDS, 2000 Main St. (Calif. 29), St. Helena, CA 94574. Tel. 707/963-7115.

Be sure to stop just north of St. Helena's business district at Beringer Vineyards, if only to look at this remarkable Rhine House and view the hand-dug tunnels carved out of the mountainside, the site of the original winery.

Beringer Vineyards was founded in 1876 by brothers Jacob and Frederick. The family owned it until 1971, when it was purchased by the Swiss firm of Nestlé, Inc. In true Swiss fashion, the business has prospered. It is the oldest continuously operating winery in the Napa Valley. "What about Prohibition?" you might ask. Beringer made "sacramental" wines during the dry years.

The modern working winery on the opposite side of the road is not open to the public, but you can get a general look at it from the Rhine House. Tasting of current products is conducted during sales hours in the Rhine House. Tasting of Reserve Wines is available in the Founders' Room (upstairs in the Rhine House) during sales hours. A modest fee is charged per taste. Tours are conducted by very knowledgeable guides.

Open: Daily 9am–5pm.

STERLING VINEYARDS, 1111 Dunaweal Lane, Calistoga, CA 94515. Tel. 707/942-3344, or toll free 800/726-6136.

Sterling Vineyards is just south of the town of Calistoga and approximately half a mile east of Calif. 29. The winery is probably more startling in appearance than any of its neighbors. Perched on top of an island of rock, it looks more like a Greek or even an Italian mountaintop monastery than a Napa winery. Yet reaching this isolated facility is relatively easy—via aerial gondola (there's a $6-per-person visitor fee). Gravity moves the wine. You'll go downstairs to fermentors, then down to the aging cellar, and farther down still to the final aging cellar. A climb up to the top of the rocky perch will be rewarded by a tasting. The very informative tour is directed by signs, not by guides, so you can set your own pace. The winery has changed hands twice since its founding in 1969; its current owner is the Seagram Classics Wine Company, which produces over 200,000 cases per year.

Open: Sales and tasting, daily 10:30am–4:30pm.

NAPA

The town of Napa is the commercial center of the wine country. This gateway to the valley is situated at the juncture of two streams; it was served by ferries and steamboats as early as the mid-1800s and later by the Napa Valley Railroad.

WHAT TO SEE & DO

NAPA VALLEY WINE TRAIN, 1275 McKinstry St. Tel. 707/253-2111, or toll free 800/522-4142.

The Wine Train is a deliciously relaxing rolling restaurant that makes a three-hour, 36-mile journey through the vineyards of Napa, Yountville, Oakville, Rutherford, and St. Helena. The cars—finished with polished Honduran mahogany paneling, brass accents, etched-glass partitions, and fine fabrics, and colored burgundy, champagne, and grapeleaf green—re-create the opulence and sophistication of the 1920s and '30s. Gourmet meals are served by an attentive staff, complete with all the accoutrements of gracious living—damask linen, bone china, silver flatware, and etched crystal. Menus are fixed, consisting of three or four courses, which might include poached Norwegian salmon court bouillon or Black Angus filet mignon served with a cabernet and Roquefort sauce.

In addition to the luxuriously appointed dining rooms, the train pulls a Wine Tasting car, a Deli Car, and three 50-passenger lounges. Tours depart from, and return to, Napa's McKinstry Street depot, near First Street and Soscol Avenue.

Admission: Train fare only $29 brunch and lunch trains, $14.50 dinner train; for fixed-price meals, $22 for brunch, $25 for lunch, $40 for dinner.

Open: Departures for brunch trains, Sat–Sun and holidays at 8:30am; lunch trains, Mon–Fri at 11:30am, Sat–Sun and holidays at noon; dinner trains, Tues–Sun and holidays at 6pm. Reduced departure schedule during winter; call for information.

CHARDONNAY CLUB, Calif. 12. Tel. 707/257-8950.

South of downtown Napa, 1.3 miles east of Calif. 29, is a classy, stunning, mean, beautiful, and challenging 36-hole land-links golf complex with first-class service. You pay just one fee, which makes you a member for the day. Privileges include the use of a golf cart, the practice range (including a bucket of balls), and services usually found only at a private club. The day that I played, a snack cart came by on the course with a full complement of sandwiches and soft drinks. And at the end of the round, my clubs were cleaned. Chardonnay is not surrounded by condominiums, and there are no tennis courts or swimming pools; it's just beautiful championship golf—a test of strength, accuracy, and touch. The course ambles through and around 325 acres of vineyards, hills, creeks, canyons, and rock ridges. There are three nines of similar challenge, all leaving from the clubhouse so that you can play the 18 of your choice. Five sets of tees provide you with a course measuring from 5,300 yards to a healthy 7,100. Starting times can be reserved up to one week in advance.

Chardonnay Club services include the golf shop, locker rooms, and a restaurant and grill. The course is open year round.

Greens fees are $55 Monday through Thursday, $70 Friday through Sunday, including mandatory cart and practice balls.

WHERE TO STAY

Expensive

SILVERADO COUNTRY CLUB & RESORT, 1600 Atlas Peak Rd., Napa, CA 94558. Tel. 707/257-0200, or toll free 800/532-0500. Fax 707/257-2867. 281 rms, 28 suites. A/C MINIBAR TV TEL **Directions:** Drive north on Calif. 29 to Trancas Street; then turn east to Atlas Peak Road.

$ Rates: $175 studio; $235 one-bedroom suite; $340–$465 two- or three-bedroom suite. Seasonal packages available. AE, CB, DC, MC, V. **Parking** Free.

Silverado is a 1,200-acre resort, lavishly spread out in the Wine Country foothills. It features spacious accommodations, ranging from very large studios with a king-size bed, kitchenette, and a roomy, well-appointed bath, to one-, two-, or three-bedroom cottage suites, each with a wood-burning fireplace. Each room is individually decorated. The setting is superb: The cottage suites are in private, low-rise groupings, each sharing tucked-away courtyards and peaceful walkways. The arrangement allows for a feeling of privacy and comfort despite the size of the resort.

The main building looks more like an old southern mansion than a California country resort.

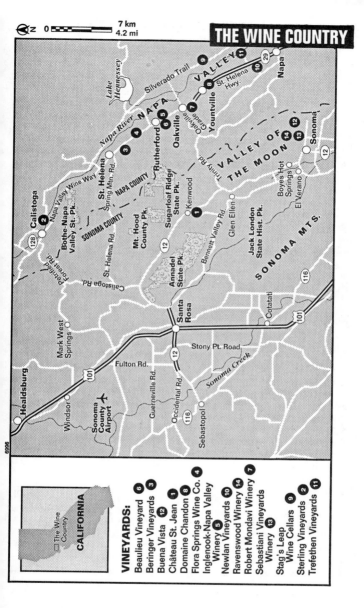

THE WINE COUNTRY

0 — 7 km / 4.2 mi

VINEYARDS:

Beaulieu Vineyard ⑥
Beringer Vineyards ③
Buena Vista ⑫
Château St. Jean ①
Domaine Chandon ⑧
Flora Springs Wine Co. ④
Inglenook-Napa Valley Winery ⑤
Newlan Vineyards ⑩
Ravenswood Winery ⑭
Robert Mondavi Winery ⑦
Sebastiani Vineyards Winery ⑬
Stag's Leap Wine Cellars ⑨
Sterling Vineyards ②
Trefethen Vineyards ⑪

Dining/Entertainment: The Royal Oak is the quintessential steak restaurant, with high-back chairs, carved-wood tables, and exposed beams and brickwork. Vintner's Court offers superb Californian cuisine in a chandeliered salon with a view of the surrounding eucalyptus and beautifully groomed flowerbeds. The Silverado Bar & Grill is a large indoor terrace/bar and outdoor deck that overlooks the North Course and serves breakfast, lunch, and cocktails.

Services: Room service, concierge, laundry.

Facilities: Occupying some 360 acres, the hotel's two golf courses are very cleverly designed by Robert Trent Jones, Jr. The South Course is 6,500 yards, with a dozen water crossings; the North Course is 6,700 yards, somewhat longer but a bit more forgiving. There is a staff of pros on hand. Greens fee is $95 for 18 holes on either course, including a mandatory cart. There are also a tournament's worth of tennis courts and several swimming pools, as well as a tour desk. No-smoking rooms are available.

Moderate

CEDAR GABLES INN, 486 Coombs St., Napa, CA 94559. Tel. 707/224-7969. Fax 707/224-4838. 6 rms. **Directions:** From Calif. 29 north, exit onto First Street and follow signs to "Downtown." The house is at the corner of Oak Street.

$ Rates (including breakfast): $79–$149 single or double. AE, MC, V.
Easily one of the best buys in tab-happy Napa, Cedar Gables is a darling Victorian mansion made cozy by the personal attention of Inkeepers Margaret and Craig Snasdell. The thoroughly romantic bed-and-breakfast, located in Old Town Napa, was built in 1892. Rooms are decorated with tapestries and antiques, and gilded in rich, old-world colors. Some include fireplaces and others have whirlpool tubs. The biggest room, called Churchill Chamber, was the mansion's original master bedroom. The inn's ground-floor sunken family room is cozy and contains a large-screen television.

CHATEAU HOTEL, 4195 Solano Ave., Napa, CA 94558. Tel. 707/253-9300, or toll free 800/253-6272 in California. Fax 707/253-0906. 115 rms, 6 suites. A/C TV TEL **Directions:** From Calif. 29 north, turn left just past Trower Avenue, at the entrance to the Napa Valley wine region.

$ Rates (including buffet breakfast): Nov–Mar, $70 single; $80 double. Apr–Oct, $85 single; $95 double. AE, CB, DC, MC, V. **Parking** Free.
The Château is a contemporary two-story hotel complex with the exterior charm of a country inn and the interior look of a Motel 6. Rooms are spacious and are furnished with individually controlled heating and air conditioning, direct-dial phones, cable TVs, and oversize beds. Most have refrigerators, and ten rooms are especially designed for disabled guests. No-smoking units are available as well. The bath is well sized and comes with a separate vanity-dressing area. Rates include breakfast and a daily newspaper.

If you're used to a daily swim, the Château has a heated pool and spa. If you prefer golf, tennis, bicycling, or even hot-air ballooning, the staff will be happy to arrange it.

TALL TIMBERS CHALETS, 1012 Darms Lane, Napa, CA 94558. Tel. 707/252-7810. 8 cottages. A/C MINIBAR TV **Directions:** From Calif. 29 north, turn left onto Darms Lane before you reach Yountville.

$ Rates: Dec–Feb Sun–Thurs $75 single or double, Fri–Sat and holidays $90–$105 single or double; Mar–Nov, Sun–Thurs $80–$95 single or double, Fri–Sat and holidays $95–$125 single or double. Extra person $10. Children under 11 stay free in parents' room. AE, MC, V. **Parking** Free.
Tall Timbers is a group of eight whitewashed, roomy cottages surrounded by pines and eucalyptus. It ranks as one of the best

bargains in the Napa Valley; the rates are exceptional, the location convenient. The cottages' close proximity to Yountville makes it ideal for sightseeing, shopping, and dining. It's also a good starting point for trips through the surrounding countryside and up to Calistoga. The Newlan Vineyards are located next door, and Domaine Chandon is within walking distance.

All the cottages are nicely decorated and well furnished. Amenities include a refrigerator, a toaster-oven, and a coffeemaker, all located in a stoveless breakfast nook. And it's really quite pleasant to find, on your arrival, a basket of fresh fruit in the breakfast area of your cottage, as well as breakfast treats in the refrigerator and a complimentary bottle of champagne. There are no phones in the cottages, but there is one in the main office. Each unit can sleep four (there's a bedroom plus a queen-size sofa bed in the living room). Several have decks—ideal for watching the colorful hot-air balloons as they float over in the morning. No smoking is allowed in the cottages.

While the Tall Timbers Chalets is not particularly difficult to find, be sure to ask for specific directions.

Budget

NAPA VALLEY BUDGET INN, 3380 Solano Ave., Napa, CA 94558. Tel. 707/257-6111. 58 rms. A/C TV TEL **Directions:** From Calif. 29 north, turn left onto the Redwood Road turnoff and go one block to Solano Avenue; then turn left and go half a block to the motel.

$ Rates: $40–$57 single; $46–$66 double. AE, DC, DISC, MC, V. **Parking** Free.

The location of this no-frills lodging is excellent—close to Calif. 29 and just across the street from a pleasant minimall. Rooms are simple, clean, and comfortable. Local calls are free, and there is a small heated pool on the premises.

WHERE TO DINE

THE RED HEN CANTINA, 5091 St. Helena Hwy., Napa. Tel. 707/255-8125.
Cuisine: MEXICAN. **Reservations:** For large parties only.
$ Prices: Appetizers $4–$10, main courses $8–$14; lunches $4–$9. AE, DC, MC, V.
Open: Sun–Thurs 11am–9pm, Fri–Sat 11am–10pm.

Looking very much like a Swiss chalet that got lost somewhere south of the border, the Red Hen is one of the most popular taquerias north of San Francisco. Both moderately priced and decorated, the cantina contains several good-sized dining rooms and a large outdoor dining deck.

Gastronomically speaking, Mexican traditionals are dotted with a healthy number of seafood dishes that include burritos, tacos, and pollo Mexicano (chicken strips sautéed in white wine, onion, mushrooms, and tomatoes).

YOUNTVILLE

Yountville is both casual and posh, and inarguably the most charming village along Calif. 29. Of less historical interest than St. Helena or Calistoga, it is nonetheless an excellent jumping-off point for a wineries tour or for the simple enjoyment of the beauty of the valley. What's more, it has several lovely places to stay, good shops, and excellent restaurants at various price levels. Best of all, intimate Yountville is walkable—you can easily take a very enjoyable stroll from one end of the town to the other.

WHAT TO SEE & DO

At the center of the village is **Vintage 1870** (tel. 707/944-2451), once a winery (from 1871 to 1955) and now a gallery with specialty shops selling antiques, wine accessories, country collectibles, and more. It is also home to three restaurants. One of the best shops in the complex is **Basket Bazaar,** where, in addition to wickery, you'll also find lamps, wine wreaths, chairs, chests, baskets, and rockers. And then there's **Gami's** for Scandinavian and European imports—Copenhagen figurines, jewelry, and a troll or two to take along.

Ballooning silently over the grape vines is a popular Napa pastime. **Adventures Aloft,** Vintage 1870 (P.O. Box 2500), Yountville, CA 94599 (tel. 707/252-7067), is Napa Valley's oldest hot-air balloon company, with full-time professional pilots. Groups are small and flights last about an hour. Like all ballooneries, Adventures Aloft flies in the early morning, when the winds are gentle and the air is cool. The cost includes a preflight continental breakfast, a postflight champagne brunch, and a framed First-Flight certificate. The cost is $165 per person.

WHERE TO STAY

Expensive

VINTAGE INN, 6541 Washington St., Yountville, CA 94599. Tel. 707/944-1112, or toll free 800/351-1133. Fax 707/944-1617. 72 rms, 8 suites. A/C MINIBAR TV TEL **Directions:** From Calif. 29 north, take the Yountville exit and turn left onto Washington Street.

$ Rates (including continental breakfast): $134–$174 single; $144–$184 double; $184–$204 minisuites and villas. Extra person $25. AE, CB, DC, MC, V. **Parking** Free.

The Vintage Inn, built on an old winery estate in the center of town, is a contemporary-styled, luxury country inn. The brick-and-board exterior fronts a warm and handsome reception lounge, furnished with a brick fireplace, lavender couches, and shuttered windows. Guest rooms mimic this cozy style. Each contains a fireplace, cable color TV with HBO, overside beds, a coffeemaker, and a refrigerator. Did I mention the private Jacuzzi and plush bathrobes? You will be welcomed into your room with a complimentary bottle of wine to share on your secluded patio or veranda. The inn also provides nightly turndown service and sports a 60-foot, year-round heated swimming pool, an outdoor heated whirlpool, and tennis courts reserved for the exclusive use of the guests. A California-continental champagne breakfast (cereals, yogurt, pastries, egg salad, and fruit) is included with your stay and served daily in the Vintage Club, as is afternoon tea. No-smoking rooms are available. Nice place.

Moderate

BURGUNDY HOUSE COUNTRY INN, 6711 Washington St. (P.O. Box 3156), Yountville, CA 94599. Tel. 707/944-0889. 5 rms (all with bath). A/C **Directions:** From Calif. 29 north, take the Yountville exit and turn left onto Washington Street.

$ Rates (including breakfast): $100 single; $115 double. MC, V. **Parking** Free.

Decidedly charming, this distinctly French country inn was built in the early 1870s of local fieldstone and river rock. Burgundy House is tiny yet impressive, with exposed hand-hewn beams and handsome antique country furniture. Each of the five cozy guest rooms has colorful quilted spreads and comfortable beds. All are no-smoking rooms. Delightful touches include fresh flowers in each of the rooms and a complimentary decanter of local white wine. The full breakfast can be taken inside, or outdoors in the inn's lovely garden.

WHERE TO DINE

Expensive

DOMAINE CHANDON, California Dr. Tel. 707/944-2892.
Cuisine: CALIFORNIAN/FRENCH. **Reservations:** Required.
Directions: From Calif. 29 north, take the California Drive exit; the restaurant is on the west side of the highway.

$ Prices: Appetizers $7–$11; main courses $13–$19 at lunch, $22–$28 at dinner. AE, DC, MC, V.

Open: Summer, lunch daily 11:30am–2:30pm; dinner Wed–Sun 6–9pm. Winter, lunch Wed–Sun 11:30am–2:30pm; dinner Wed–Sun 6–9pm. Closed: First three weeks of Jan.

Inside this French-owned champagne house is one of California's most-exquisite restaurants, and one of the most celebrated. The winery building is a low, ultramodern stone-and-concrete structure that seems like part of the hillside. A creek shaded by large trees contributes to this idyllic setting. Domaine Chandon forsakes the usual old-fashioned Wine Country quaintness for understated modern elegance. Its multilevel interior contains several dining rooms with arched fir-paneled ceilings. It is one of the most dramatic and beautiful settings in the Wine Country. Large picture windows open onto vineyard views, while candles illuminate tabletops by night.

On nice days you can eat lunch outdoors, a meal that might begin with a salad of arugula with prosciutto, Parmesan, truffle oil, and home-baked Calimyrna fig bread. Main courses change daily but might include lamb shank braised in chardonnay and herbs, with garden vegetables. There are superb desserts, including such mouthwatering choices as the hot chocolate soufflé served with a white-chocolate sauce or the espresso and mascarpone ice-cream terrine with a crunchy peanut-butter layer and bittersweet-chocolate sauce! Ready for dinner? The roast California quail is served with chanterelles, soft polenta, and acorn squash. Sweetbreads come in shallot-prosciutto butter and truffle juice. Need I say, the wine list is impeccable and includes some marvelous dessert wines and cognacs?

Moderate

CALIFORNIA CAFE BAR AND GRILL, 6795 Washington St., Yountville, Tel. 707/944-2330. Directions: The restaurant is located directly on Highway 29 at Madison Street.

Cuisine: INTERNATIONAL. **Reservations:** Accepted.

$ Prices: Appetizers $3–$8, main courses $10–$19; lunch $5–$11. AE, MC, V.

Open: Mon–Thurs 11:30am–9:30pm, Fri–Sat 11:30am–10pm, Sun 10am–9:30pm.

Both upscale and laid-back, California Café's big, bright, and airy dining room is as Californian as it gets. Smoky scents from the restaurant's wood-burning oven permeate the room; its products include smoked duck and hickory-roasted game hen. Spicy chili onion rings can be followed with pastas like black-pepper fettucini or rigatoni with mixed vegetables, or a respectable paella—mussels, shrimp, chicken, and spicy sausage mixed with saffron rice. A large selection of salads like warm cabbage with spicy beef and sandwiches like fried oysters on a baguette are available at lunch. Sunday brunch is popular. The regular menu features scrambled eggs with fried oysters, smoked bacon, spinach, and potatoes; and an omelete with artichokes, spinach, roasted peppers, and fontina cheese.

MUSTARDS GRILL, 7399 St. Helena Hwy. (Calif. 29). Tel. 707/944-2424.

Cuisine: CALIFORNIAN. **Reservations:** Recommended

$ Prices: Appetizers $3–$8; main courses $11–$18. CB, DC, MC, V.

Open: Apr–Oct, daily 11:30am–10pm; Nov–Mar, daily 11:30am–9pm.

Look for the humorous bronze sculpture of a bowler-topped gentleman on the west side of the road and you have found Mustards. As you enter this barnlike structure, you'll see beamed cathedral ceilings, a black-and-white tile floor, and a small bar. The main dining room is on two levels and includes an airy, glass-enclosed outer dining area for a simulated al fresco experience.

The atmosphere is light, festive, and relaxed. Mustards is a favorite with local wine makers and growers. The blue-jeaned, white-shirted servers are friendly and knowledgeable. Specials are listed on a blackboard, along with featured local wines ranging from $4 to $9 a glass. If you bring your own bottle, the restaurant charges a $10 corkage fee. From the looks of things, I'd guess that more wine per table is consumed here than in any San Francisco restaurant.

Tables are immediately topped with sliced, warm, crusty baguettes, served with sweet butter. Among the starters are such gems as home-smoked salmon with pasilla corncakes, warm goat cheese with roasted beets, and Chinese chicken salad. Sandwiches include chicken breast with guacamole and onion relish, and grilled ahi tuna with basil mayonnaise and ginger. Main courses are reasonably priced and range from wood-burning–oven specialties (barbecued baby back ribs, pork chops with Thai marinade, or smoked Long Island duck) to grilled items like Sonoma rabbit and "mallet" chicken with seasonal vegetables. The menu changes every three months to accommodate the season's offerings.

Budget

THE DINER, 6476 Washington St. Tel. 707/944-2626.
Cuisine: AMERICAN/MEXICAN. **Reservations:** Not accepted.
Directions: From Calif. 29 north, take the Yountville exit and turn left onto Washington Street.
$ Prices: Breakfast $4–$7; lunch $6–$10; dinner $8–$12. No credit cards.
Open: Tues–Sun 8am–3pm; dinner 5:30–9pm.

It's a diner, all right, decorated in shell pink, with track lighting, and boasting a friendly and unpretentious atmosphere. The restaurant features a functioning Irish Waterford wood stove, a collection of vintage diner water pitchers, and an art exhibit that changes monthly. Seating is at the counter or in wooden booths.

The menu is extensive, the portions are huge, and the food is good. Breakfast offerings include such California staples as *huevos Jalisco* (eggs scrambled with fresh red and yellow peppers). French toast and eggs are also available.

Lunch and dinner dishes include a host of toothsome Mexican and American dishes such as tamari-basted chicken breast salad on baby greens, grilled fresh fish, giant burritos, and thick sandwiches made with house-roasted meats and homemade bread. Homemade desserts usually include fresh fruit cobblers and sundae sauces. They have a cappuccino machine and stock fresh-squeezed orange juice along with natural-fruit sodas, beer, and wine by the glass.

OAKVILLE & RUTHERFORD

Driving north again on the St. Helena Highway (Calif. 29) you soon come to the Oakville Cross Road. There you will find the **Oakville Grocery Co.,** 7856 St. Helena Highway, Oakville, CA 94562 (tel. 707/944-8802). Stop! Its name, its location, and its exterior disguise one of the finest gourmet food stores this side of New York's Dean & Deluca. Here you can obtain provisions for a memorable picnic or for a very special custom gift basket. You'll find the best of breads, the choicest selection of cheeses in the Northern Bay Area, pâtés, fresh foie gras (domestic and French, seasonally), smoked Norwegian salmon, smoked sturgeon and smoked pheasant (by special order), fresh caviar (Beluga, Sevruga, Osetra), and an exceptional selection of Californian wines.

Hard-to-find wines and vintages are also available here. If you find the wine decision difficult, there are sampler sets to help you along. The Oakville Grocery Co. will prepare a picnic-basket lunch for you if you give them 24 hours' notice. Delivery service is available to some areas. It's open daily from 10am to 6pm.

WHERE TO STAY

RANCHO CAMUS, 1140 Rutherford Rd. (P.O. Box 78), Rutherford, CA 94573. Tel. 707/963-1777. Fax 707/963-5387. 26 suites. A/C TV TEL **Directions:** From Calif. 29 north, turn right onto Rutherford Rd; the hotel is ahead on your left.
$ Rates (including continental breakfast): $115–$135 single or double, from $225 Master Suite, $295 two-bedroom suite. AE, MC, V.

As restful as the quiet town of Rutherford itself, this Spanish-Mediterranean–style inn is one of our top Wine Country picks.

Every suite in this two-story, red-tile–roofed Rancho opens onto the hotel's plant-filled courtyard. It's a colorful place, outfitted with hand-carved black walnut furniture, stained-glass windows, and bright bedspreads and wall hangings woven by Ecuadorian Otavalon Indians. Most suites have split-level sleeping areas and wood-burning adobe fireplaces. The extra luxurious Master Suites also have kitchenettes and large Jacuzzi baths.

Breakfast, which includes fresh fruit and breads, coffee, and juice, is either delivered to your room or served in the inn's Garden Grill restaurant.

WHERE TO DINE

AUBERGE DU SOLEIL, 180 Rutherford Hill Rd., Rutherford. Tel. 707/963-1211.

Cuisine: CALIFORNIAN. **Reservations:** Recommended. **Directions:** From Oakville, take the Oakville Crossroad east to the Silverado Trail; turn left, heading north to Rutherford Hill Road, then turn right, up to Auberge du Soleil.

$ Prices: Main courses $14–$18 at lunch $25–$30 at dinner; desserts $7–$8; fixed-price dinner $52. AE, DISC, MC, V.

Open: Breakfast daily 7–11am; lunch daily 11:30am–2:30pm dinner daily 6–9:30pm.

This romantic country hideaway, nestled in an olive grove overlooking the lovely Napa Valley, is a stunning setting for Chef David Hale's classic Wine Country cuisine. Inside, a magnificent fireplace, huge wood pillars, pink tablecloths, and fresh flowers combine to create a warm rustic ambience. Light classical music plays in a room that opens out to a wisteria-decked, umbrella-topped terrace with a panoramic view of the valley below.

The food here is as good as the atmosphere is peaceful. Chef Hale employs the freshest local ingredients to create his delicacies. Lunch appetizers may include a dungeness crab quesadilla with local Sonoma Jack cheese, or grilled venison-cranberry sausage served with pear-apricot chutney. Among the lunch entrees are gourmet pizzas, seafood pastas, and a particularly endorsable grilled pork chop served with onion rings and a spicy tomato sauce. A la carte dinner dishes run the gamut from grilled Hawaiian ahi with rosemary polenta to rack of lamb accompanied by goat-cheese soufflé. Like everything else on the menu, desserts are very tasty. A good selection of country concoctions like bread pudding with brandy sauce and bittersweet chocolate and hazelnut rum cake are always on hand.

ST. HELENA

Reminiscent in some ways of the south of France, with its tall plane trees arching over the roads, St. Helena also suggests feudal England, with mansions overseeing the vineyards and valleys from high hillside perches. Many of the buildings in the main part of town date from the 1800s and are worth a look. The modern wares in a variety of shops are also worth browsing. This is a friendly place, with some excellent restaurants and inns.

Literary buffs and other romantics won't want to miss the **Silverado Museum,** 1490 Library Lane (tel. 707/963-3757), devoted to the life and works of Robert Louis Stevenson, author of *Treasure Island, Kidnapped,* and other classics. It was here that Stevenson honeymooned in 1880, at the abandoned Silverado Mine.

More than 8,000 museum items include original manuscripts, letters, photographs, portraits of the writer, and the desk he used in Samoa. It's open Tuesday through Sunday from noon to 4pm. Admission is free.

WHERE TO STAY

Expensive

BARTELS RANCH AND COUNTRY INN, 1200 Conn Valley Rd., St. Helena, CA 94574. Tel. 707/963-4001. 4 rms. A/C. **Directions:** From downtown St. Helena, turn east on Pope St., cross Silverado Trail and continue onto Howell Mountain Rd. After about 1 mile, bear right, onto Conn Valley Rd. The inn is 2 miles ahead.

$ Rates: $135–$275, single or double. AE, DISC, MC, V.

Encompassing more than one hundred acres of rolling meadows, Bartels is an alluring resort packed with beauty and charm. Innkeeper Jami Bartels, a hands-on proprietor, provides picnic baskets and blankets with each guest room and can lend you bicycles, arrange massages or personal wine-country tours, or just direct you to the lounge for the cookies, coffee, and tea that are served all day.

Although it's not particularly fancy, every room has a private bath and terry robes, and two rooms have fireplaces. There's a communal sundeck as well as a game room filled with books, a billiard table, and a stereo. Complimentary wine, fruit, and cheese are served each afternoon.

ZINFANDEL INN, 800 Zinfandel La., St. Helena, CA 94574. Tel. 707/963-3512. 3 rms. A/C TV TEL **Directions:** From Calif. 29 north, turn right onto Zinfandel Lane; the inn is 1 block ahead on your left.

$ Rates (including full breakfast): $150–$250 single or double. AE, MC, V.

Innkeepers Jerry and Diane Payton have turn their own smoke-free home into a charming bed-and-breakfast that's thoroughly recommendable. There are only three rooms here. The Chardonnay Room, which features bay windows and a large stone fireplace, contains a king-size bed, sofa, and its own private garden entrance. The huge Zinfandel Suite holds a king-size bed, a large sitting area, and old-fashioned blue-steel fireplace, a large private deck, and an enormous bathroom outfitted with a Jacuzzi tub positioned by an octagonal window with garden views; an adjacent shower has two heads. The Petite Sirah Room is the smallest, but charmingly decorated with antiques, a featherbed, and windows that overlook the Napa Valley.

The home's public areas are equally as well cared for as the rooms. The kitchen, with its well-stocked refrigerator, is open to all guests throughout their stay, and a casual family room is also available for guests' use. Outside, a wooden deck leads to the house's backyard, which contains a hot tub, lagoon pool, waterfall, and fish pond. A full breakfast is served in the formal dining room.

Moderate

WINE COUNTRY INN, 1152 Lodi Lane, St. Helena, CA 94574. Tel. 707/963-7077, Fax 707/963-9018. 21 rms, 3 suites (all with bath). A/C TEL **Directions:** From Calif. 29 north, turn right onto Lodi Lane, in the middle of St. Helena.

$ Rates (including continental breakfast: Jan 3–Apr 15, $91–$155 single or double, from $155 suite; the rest of the year, $97–$160 single or double, from $205 suite. Extra person $20. AE, MC, V. **Parking** Free.

The Wine Country Inn, set on a hillside overlooking the vineyards, is one of the most romantic hostelries I've ever seen. Its rooms are individually decorated in New England style. Many of them have fireplaces, balconies or patios, country antique furnishings, stitchery hangings on the walls, and patchwork quilts on the beds. And to add to the aura of quiet relaxation, the inn has an elegant pool and Jacuzzi. Don't stay here alone.

WHERE TO DINE

TRA VIGNE RESTAURANT AND CANTINETTA, 1050 Charter Oak Ave., St. Helena. Tel. 707/963-4444.
   Cuisine: ITALIAN. **Reservations:** Recommended.
$ Prices: Appetizers $5–$8, main courses $9–$17; cantinetta $4–$8. CB, DC, DISC, MC, V.
   Open: Daily noon–9:30pm; cantinetta daily 11:30am–6pm.

Looking like a small sandstone winery on the east side of Calif. 29, Tra Vigne has garnered raves throughout its half-dozen years of existence. Dramatically large green-marble columns on either side of the front door give way to a striking dining room designed with immense curved windows that open onto a large veranda.

The food here is terrific, with many of the best items coming from a wood-burning oven. Upon arrival, each table is presented with a demi-loaf of freshly baked bread that might be cracked wheat or rosemary raisin. Entrees include house-smoked duck, braised oxtail, grilled Sonoma rabbit, and a small selection of fresh fish. Gourmet pizzas and a variety of pastas and salads are also available. Lunch is also available at the bar, where a large assortment of wines, beers, ports, grappas, cocktails, and coffees are served. Desserts too are usually on the mark, and include *lasagna di cioccolata* (layers of whipped chocolate, sour cherries, and chocolate sponge cake with lemon sauce).

The restaurant's more casual side, called the Cantinetta, offers a small selection of sandwiches, pizzas, and lighter meals like chicken and vegetable stew. They also pack picnics, and sell about 20 flavored olive oils infused with roasted garlic, basil, chiles, hazelnuts, lavender, rosemary, or mint; sprinkle a little on a crouton and see which ones you like best.

CALISTOGA

San Brannan became California's first millionaire by building a hotel and spa to take advantage of this area's natural geothermal springs. His entrepreneurial instincts combined "California" with "Saratoga," a popular East Coast resort, and in 1859 Calistoga was born.

Located at the northern end of the lush Wine Country, the town remains popular. Today, Calistoga's main street is still only about six blocks long, and no building is higher than two stories. It's not fancy at all, but Calistoga is a delightfully simple place in which to relax and indulge in mineral waters, mud baths, Jacuzzis, massages—and, of course, wines.

WHAT TO SEE & DO
A Mud Bath

The main thing to do here is what people have been doing for the last 150 years: take a bath. The bath is composed of local volcanic ash, imported peat, and naturally boiling mineral–hot-springs water, all mulled together to produce a thick mud at a temperature of about 104°F. Once you overcome the hurdle of deciding how best to place your naked body into the mushy stone tub, the rest is pure relaxation—you soak with surprising buoyancy for about 10 to 12 minutes. A warm mineral-water shower, a mineral-water whirlpool bath, and a mineral-water steam-room visit follow; these are then followed by a relaxing blanketwrap to cool your delighted body down slowly. All of this takes about 1½ hours and costs about $45; with a massage, add another half hour and $20. The outcome is a rejuvenated, revitalized, squeaky-clean you. Mud baths are not recommended for people with high blood pressure or for pregnant women.

All spas also offer a variety of other treatments, such as hand and foot massages, herbal wraps, acupressure face-lifts, skin rubs, and herbal facials. Prices range from $29 to $100, and appointments are necessary for all services; call at least a week in advance. Calistoga spas include: **Dr Wilkinson's Hot Springs,** 1507 Lincoln Ave. (tel. 707/942-4102); **Lincoln Avenue Spa,** 1339 Lincoln Ave. (tel. 707/942-5296); **Golden Haven Hot Springs Spa,** 1713 Lake St. (tel. 707/942-6793); and **Calistoga Spa Hot Springs,** 1006 Washington St. (tel. 707/942-6269).

Other Attractions

CALISTOGA DEPOT, 1458 Lincoln Ave. Tel. 707/942-5556.
The tiny town's defunct railroad station now houses a variety of shops, a restaurant, and the Calistoga Chamber of Commerce. The Depot occupies the site of the original railroad station, built in 1868; alongside it sit six restored passenger cars dating from 1916 to the 1920s, each of which also houses some enticing shops.

OLD FAITHFUL GEYSER OF CALIFORNIA, 1299 Tubbs Ln. Tel. 707/942-6463.
One of three Old Faithful geysers in the world, this one has been blowing off steam at regular intervals for as long as anyone can remember. The 350°F water spews out every 40 minutes or so, day and night (varying with natural influences such as barometric pressure, the moon, tides, and earth tectonic stresses). The performance lasts about three minutes, and you'll learn a lot about the origins of geothermal steam. You can bring a picnic lunch with you and catch the show as many times as you wish. A gift and snack shop is open every day.
Admission: $5 adults, $4 seniors, $2 children 6–12, free for children under 6.
Open: Summer, daily 9am–6pm; winter, daily 9am–5pm. **Directions:** Follow the signs from downtown Calistoga; it's situated between Calif. 29 and Calif. 128.

PETRIFIED FOREST, 4100 Petrified Forest Rd. Tel. 707/942-6667.
Although you won't see thousands of trees turned into stone, you will find many interesting petrified specimens, including

redwoods that have turned to rock through the slow infiltration of silicas and other minerals. Volcanic ash blanketed this area after the eruption of Mount St. Helena three million years ago. Earlier specimens of petrified seashells, clams, and marine life indicate that the water covered this area even before the redwood forest.

Admission: $3 adults, $1 children 4–11, free for children under 4.

Open: Summer, daily 10am–5:30pm; winter, daily 10am–4:30pm. **Directions:** From Calif. 128, turn right onto Petrified Forest Road, just past Lincoln Avenue.

WHERE TO STAY

Expensive

MOUNT VIEW HOTEL, 1457 Lincoln Ave., (Calif. 29), Calistoga, CA 94515. Tel. 707/942-6877. Fax 707/942-6904. 22 rms, 3 cottages, 8 suites. A/C TV TEL

$ Rates: $85–$120 single or double; $140–$165 suite. Packages available. AE, MC, V. **Parking** Free.

Located on the main highway, near Fairway Street, in the middle of Calistoga, the Mount View Hotel offers art deco rooms, three self-contained cottages, and eight glamorous suites named for movie idols of the past. The Carole Lombard Suite has peach-colored walls and light-green carpeting, while the Tom Mix Suite has a western theme. Facilities also include a heated swimming pool, European spa, and Jacuzzi.

Valeriano's, a northern Italian restaurant, serves dinner nightly. A fairly standard menu of pastas and meats are accompanied by an extensive and reasonably priced selection of local wines. A separate cafe serves breakfast and lunch daily and has live entertainment on weekends.

Moderate

DR. WILKINSON'S HOT SPRINGS, 1507 Lincoln Ave., (Calif. 29), Calistoga, CA 94515. Tel. 707/942-4102. 42 rms. A/C TV TEL MINIBAR

$ Rates: Winter, $44–$79 single; $49–$99 double. Summer, $59–$84 single; $64–$94 double. Weekly discounts available. AE, MC, V. **Parking** Free.

Another good Calistoga choice is Dr. Wilkinson's Hot Springs. On the main highway in the middle of Calistoga, near Fairway Street, it's a typical motel, distinguished mostly by the mud baths on the premises. All rooms have drip coffeemakers, and some have kitchens. No-smoking rooms are available. Facilities include three swimming pools (two outdoor and one indoor). Packages are available; call for details.

WHERE TO DINE

ALL SEASONS CAFE, 1400 Lincoln Ave., Tel. 707/942-9111.
Cuisine: CALIFORNIAN. **Reservations:** Recommended on weekends.

$ Prices: Appetizers $4–$9; main courses $6–$17 at lunch, $9–$23 at dinner. MC, V.

Open: Continental breakfast Mon–Thurs 9–10:30am; brunch Fri–Sun 9–10:30am; lunch Thurs–Tues 11:30am–3pm; dinner Thurs–Mon 5–10pm (store, Thurs–Mon 9am–4pm and 5–9pm, Tues 9am–4pm).

For a delightful meal served in a treasurehouse of wines, wend your way to the All Seasons Café, on the main highway at the corner of Washington Street, in the middle of Calistoga. You can choose to eat in or prearrange a box lunch or picnic platter. Don't overlook the luncheon and dinner specials and the fresh desserts. Recent luncheon dishes included a baked eggplant, tomato, and mozzarella sandwich served with tomato sauce; and penne pasta with mushrooms, smoked chicken, garlic, sun-dried tomatoes, and romano cheese. The cafe also serves homemade soup and a wide selection of appetizers.

---

9. SONOMA

45 miles N of San Francisco, 20 miles W of Napa

GETTING THERE By Car From San Francisco, cross the Golden Gate Bridge and stay on U.S. 101 north. Exit at Calif. 37 and after ten miles turn north onto Calif. 121. After another ten miles, turn north again onto Calif. 12 (Broadway), which will take you into town.

From the town of Napa, take Calif. 121 south to Calif. 12. The road is well marked with directional signs.

ESSENTIALS Orientation The town's geographical and commerical center is called the Plaza and sits at the top of a T formed by Broadway (Calif. 12) and Napa Street. Most of the surrounding streets form a grid pattern around this axis, making Sonoma easy to negotiate.

Information Before you begin your explorations of the area, visit the **Sonoma Valley Visitors Bureau,** 453 First St. E., Sonoma, CA 95476 (tel. 707/996-1090; fax 707/996-9212). It's located right on the Plaza and offers free maps and brochures about local happenings. It's open daily from 9am to 5pm.

The **Sonoma County Convention and Visitors Bureau,** 5000 Roberts Lake Rd., Rohnert Park, CA 94928 (tel. 707/586-8100, or toll free 800/326-7666; fax 707/586-8111), offers a free "Visitors Guide" with information relating to the county as a whole. It also provides specialized information on historical attractions, wine tours, walking tours, carriage rides, hot-air ballooning, swimming, fishing, boating, bicycling, camping, golf, rock climbing . . . you name it. Write as far in advance as possible.

Sonoma is not far from Napa Valley, but it is special enough to warrant separate attention. The town of Sonoma is the seat of the county of the same name. Its pleasant mix of architectural styles looks like a cross between early California Mission and western Victorian. Sonoma is rich in history; much of the area is still preserved as it was in the mid-1800s, when a brilliant Mexican army officer, Gen. Mariano Guadalupe Vallejo, was in charge of the

Sonoma mission. In fact, so many of the town's historical monuments and landmarks are intact that it almost seems as though time has stood still.

The center of town is the Plaza—the largest town square in California and the site of City Hall. The Plaza's Bear Flag Monument marks the spot where the crude Bear Flag was raised in 1846, signaling the end of Mexican rule. The symbol was later adopted by the state of California. The eight-acre park surrounding the Plaza contains two ponds full with ducks and geese, and is a lovely place for picnicking. Provisions are available directly across the street (see "Where to Dine," below).

On your way to or from Sonoma, visit the **Old Sonoma Barn's World of Birds,** 23570 Arnold Dr. (Hwy. 121), Sonoma (tel. 707/996-1477). Rare parrots and $15,000 macaws are on display (and for sale) here, as are a small herd of llamas. Nearby, **Angelo's Wine Country Deli,** 23400 Arnold Dr., Sonoma (tel. 707/938-3688), sells all types of smoked meats, special salsas, and homemade mustards. Angelo's deli is especially known for half-dozen types of homemade beef jerky, meats that this closet enthusiast heartily endorses. It's open daily from 9am to 6pm.

WHAT TO SEE & DO

The best way to see the town of Sonoma is to pick up a free copy of **"Sonoma Walking Tour,"** available from the Sonoma Valley Visitors Bureau (see "Information," above). With the help of this pamphlet, you can learn about all the historic spots in and around Sonoma Plaza. Highlights include General Vallejo's 1852 Victorian-style home; Sonoma Barracks, erected in 1836 to house Mexican army troops; and the Blue Wing Inn, an 1840 hostelry built to accommodate tourists and new settlers while they built homes in Sonoma (John Frémont, Kit Carson, and Ulysses S. Grant were guests).

MISSION SAN FRANCISCO SOLANO DE SONOMA, Sonoma Plaza, at the corner of First St. E. and Spain St. Tel. 707/938-1519.

Founded in 1823, Sonoma's mission is the northernmost and last mission built in California. It was the only one established on the northern coast by the Mexican rulers, who were afraid of expansionist Russian fur traders.

Admission: $2 adults, $1 children 6–12, free for children under 6.

Open: Daily 10am–5pm.

ARTS GUILD OF SONOMA, 521 Broadway. 707/996-3115.

Step in and treat yourself to some truly exceptional works of art. Exhibits change frequently and include a wide variety of styles and media. Everything on display has been produced by local artists. The Arts Guild is a nonprofit organization run by its artist members. Since its organization in 1977, the guild has provided local professionals with an outstanding showcase. The guild also sponsors art shows by other county art groups, as well as international exhibitions.

Admission: Free.

Open: Spring–summer, daily 10am–6pm; fall–winter, daily 10am–5pm.

JACK LONDON STATE PARK, London Ranch Rd. Tel. 707/938-5216.

About eight miles north of Sonoma (a mile west of Glen Ellen), this 800-acre park includes a museum built by Jack's wife, Charmian, in 1919 for the purpose of housing the considerable collection of objects and memorabilia from the author's life. The cottage of the Londons is also here, along with the ruins of the mansion and their graves.

Admission: $5 per car, $4 per car for seniors over 62.

Open: Park, daily in winter 10am–5pm, summer 10am–7pm; museum, daily 10am–5pm.

SONOMA CATTLE COMPANY, in Jack London State Park, London Ranch Rd. Tel. 707/996-8566.

The Sonoma Cattle Company offers guided tours on horseback. You'll ride on the same trails that author Jack London once followed, and pass through London's eucalyptus grove and wood-frame cottage on your way to the top of Mount Sonoma for magnificent views of the countryside. The stables are in Jack London State Park, located in the northern part of Sonoma Valley. Rides cost $35 for a two-hour ride.

Open: By appointment daily, weather permitting.

WINERIES

Sonoma is the site of California's first winery, founded in 1857. Chardonnay is the single white variety for which Sonoma is noted and represents almost one-quarter of the acreage in vines. Like Napa, the Sonoma Valley produces some of the finest wines in the United States. Nearly all the operations are small or medium-size, and many are family owned. But you won't see the polished, city-bred look of the Napa Valley here. As you head north out of Sonoma on Calif. 12, the scenery evolves from an untidy backyard finish to the rough-hewn look of ranch country. The terrain varies by the mile, and with each change, small variations in climate–known as "microclimates"—create the differences in the wines.

SEBASTIANI VINYARDS WINERY, 389 Fourth St. E. Tel. 707/938-5532, or toll free 800/888-5532.

Sebastiani has the most interesting and informative guided tour, and its place in the development of the region is unique. It's the only winery in Sonoma Valley to offer both a guided tour and tastings from a full selection of wines that have won 95 awards. The tour, through aging stone cellars containing more than 300 carved casks, is fascinating and well worth the time. You can see the winery's original turn-of-the-century crusher and press, as well as the largest collection of oak-barrel carvings in the world. If you don't want to take the tour, go straight to the tasting room, where you can sample an extensive selections of wines. The lashing room also offers a large assortment of winery gifts. A picnic area is adjacent to the cellars. Tours are 25 minutes long.

Open: Daily 10am–5pm (last tour begins at 4pm).

RAVENSWOOD WINERY, 18701 Gehricke Rd. Tel. 707/938-1960.

Built right into the hillside to keep it cool inside, this traditional, small stone winery crushed their first grapes in 1976 for their inaugural zinfandel. Today the winery is best known for red wines, including zinfandel, merlot, and cabernet sauvignon. Visitors are also offered younger wines, often blends, that are less expensive than older vintages. Tours follow the wine-making process from grape to glass and include the oak-barrel aging rooms. Reservations are required.

This winery is located in the Sonoma hills; follow the signs.

Open: Daily 10am–4:30pm.

BUENA VISTA, 18000 Old Winery Rd. Tel. 707/938-1266.

Buena Vista, the patriarch of California wineries, is located slightly northeast of the town of Sonoma. It was founded in 1857 by Count Agoston Haraszthy, the Hungarian émigré who is called the father of the California wine industry. A close friend of General Vallejo, Haraszthy returned from Europe in 1861 with 100,000 of the finest vine cuttings, which he made available to all wine growers. Although Buena Vista's wine making now takes place in an ultramodern facility outside Sonoma, the winery still maintains a tasting room here, inside the restored 1862 Press House.

Open: Daily 10:30am–4:30pm.

CHATEAU ST. JEAN, 8555 Sonoma Hwy. (Calif. 12), Kenwood, CA 95452. Tel. 707/833-4134.

It's worth the 20-minute drive to visit Château St. Jean, founded in 1973 by a family of grape growers. The winery is situated at the foot of Sugarloaf Ridge, just north of Kenwood and east of Calif. 12 on a private drive, on what was once a private 250-acre country retreat built in 1920. Château St. Jean is notable for its exceptionally beautiful buildings, magnificent grounds, and elegant tasting room. A meticulously maintained lawn is now a picnic ground, complete with a fountain surrounded by grass and benches.

There is a self-guided tour with detailed and photographic descriptions of the wine-making process. At the end of the tour, be sure to walk up to the top of the tower for a magnificent view of the valley. Back in the tasting room, you are invited to sample a good range of St. Jean's wines at no charge. From each vintage, Château St. Jean offers several chardonnays, cabernet sauvignon, Fume blanc, merlot, Johannisberg riesling, and Gerwürtztraminer. Since 1984 the winery has been part of the Suntory family of premium wineries.

The toll-free, interactive Château St. Jean "wine line" (tel. 800/332-WINE) offers free recorded reports from the Sonoma Wine Country, including updated information on vineyard conditions, interviews with wine makers and growers, information on what's happening at the winery, and descriptions of currently available wines.

Open: Self-guided tour, daily 10:30am–4pm; tasting room, daily 10am–4:30pm. **Closed:** Major holidays.

SONOMA SHOPPING

Most of the town's multitude of shops are located around the Plaza. They offer everything from food and wines to clothing and books.

THE MERCATO, 452 First St. E.

Located around Sonoma's main plaza, the Mercato is a small shopping center with several good stores selling unusual wares. Interesting shops include **Papyrus** (tel. 707/935-6707), which has a vast collection of lovely paper products and is open Monday through Saturday from 10am to 5:30pm and on Sunday from 11am to 4pm.

WINE EXCHANGE, 452 First St. E., Sonoma, CA 95476. Tel. 707/938-1794.

One of the most intriguing shops of its kind, this handsomely decorated establishment bears a slight resemblance to a proper old pub. Up front there's an old grape press and to the rear is a stack of casks behind a full tasting bar for trying wine by the glass. The Wine Exchange carries more than 600 California wines, plus some French wines and champagnes. The beer connoisseur will be happy to find more than 250 beers from around the world, including a number of exceptional domestic beers that I guarantee you've never seen before. Draft choices include Anchor Old, Fog Horn, Hübsch Braü, and Cellis White Lager. The Wine Exchange has wine and beer tastings daily. It also has a number of useful books on wines, guides to the Wine Country, and copies of the *Wine Spectator* and *Wine Journal*. It's a great place to shop, and it ships everywhere in the United States via air freight. The shop is open daily from 10am to 6pm.

WHERE TO STAY

VERY EXPENSIVE

SONOMA MISSION INN & SPA, 18140 Calif. 12, Boyes Hot Springs, CA 94576. Tel. 707/938-9000, or toll free 800/358-9022, 800/862-4945 in California. Fax 707/938-4250. 170 rms, 3 suites. A/C MINIBAR TV TEL **Directions:** From central Sonoma, drive 3 miles north on Calif. 12.

$ Rates: Nov–Apr, $105–$225 Historic Inn room; $145–$310 Wine Country room. May–Oct, $145–$260 Historic Inn room; $175–$395 Wine Country rooms. Year-round, from $325 suite. AE, DC, MC, V. **Parking** Free.

This hostelry is off Calif. 12, set back on eight acres of lush landscaping and surrounded by a stucco wall. It's a sweeping three-story pink structure with mission towers, beautifully groomed lawns, bougainvillea, pines, eucalyptus trees, and a pink fountain near the entry. The Sonoma Mission Inn & Spa's guest facilities and services are every bit as impressive as the entryway. The huge lobby sports an exposed-beam ceiling that hints of an old Spanish mission. Tall palms break up the length of the room, along with a large fireplace. In 1993 the inn re-tapped underground hot springs which now fill their pools and whirlpools.

Guest rooms are spacious and designed with elegance and taste, from the attractively framed watercolors to the simple styling of the ceiling fans. There are few things I appreciate more than having a large bathroom replete with all the thoughtful touches that make for easy living. Each room has a scale, a hairdryer, oversize bath towels, and an ample supply of Mission Inn toiletries.

Wine Country rooms are in a newer building and are furnished with king-size beds, desks, and refrigerators. Some have fireplaces, and many have balconies. The older Historic Inn Rooms are located in a historic building and decorated in country style. They are slightly smaller, and most are furnished with queen-size beds. All rooms have VCRs and come with a complimentary bottle of wine.

Dining/Entertainment: Should you require superior sustenance, the Mission Inn offers excellent Wine Country cuisine in the Grille inside or on the outdoor Terrace Grille (weather permitting). Their casual bistro-style cafe serves Italian cuisine.

Services: Room service, concierge, laundry.

Facilities: There are body wraps, body scrubs, hair and scalp treatments, back treatments, and beauty-salon services beyond belief. After all that, if you're not too relaxed to care, strike out for the exercise class, an early-morning hike, a picnic hike, or the tennis courts. Private tennis lessons, fitness training, nutritional consultation, and slimming meals are all available. The tariff schedule of individual spa and salon services ranges from $14 to $155. The use of the spa's bathhouse, which includes a sauna, steam room, whirlpool, outdoor exercise pool, and gym with weight equipment, costs $10 weekdays, $20 weekends.

MODERATE

EL DORADO HOTEL, 405 First St. W., Sonoma, CA 95476. Tel. 707/996-3030, or toll free 800/289-3031. Fax 707/996-3148. 27 rms. A/C TV TEL

$ Rates (including continental breakfast): $90–$145 single or double. AE, MC, V. **Parking** Free.

The El Dorado Hotel is a true California beauty. The entrance to the hotel faces bucolic Sonoma Town Square and Park and has an inviting air that suggests comfort, warmth, and relaxed elegance.

Each guest room has expansive French windows and small terraces, some with lovely views of the Town Square, others overlooking the hotel's private courtyard and heated pool. The El Dorado's country-style rooms afford its guests continental luxury in a setting created for comfort. Light peach-tone walls surround terra-cotta floors, which are topped by wine-colored rugs and four-poster beds. Each guest room has a color TV with remote control and a private bath with plush towels. All rooms, with the exception of those with access for the disabled, are on the second floor. The two lovely rooms on the ground floor are off the private courtyard, and each has its own partially enclosed patio.

Breakfast is served either inside or outside and includes coffee, fruits, and freshly baked breads and pastries. The regional Italian cuisine in the hotel's Ristorante Piatti (tel. 707/996-2351) is prepared in an open, wood-burning oven. The restaurant is open daily for lunch and dinner; reservations are recommended.

SONOMA HOTEL, 110 W. Spain St., Sonoma, CA 94576. Tel. 707/996-2996. 17 rms (5 with bath).

$ Rates (including continental breakfast): Winter, Mon–Fri $65 single or double without bath, $95 single or double with bath; Sat–Sun $75 single or double without bath, $115–$120 single or double with bath. Summer, $75–$85 single or double without bath, $115–$120 single or double with bath. AE, MC, V. **Parking** Free.

Located on Sonoma Town Square, the Sonoma Hotel is a small, classic, historic beauty. Its accommodations evoke feelings of a different time—warm, romantic, and gracious. Each of its rooms is decorated in an early California style with magnificent antique furnishings, beautiful woods, and floral-print wallpapers—all with an emphasis on European elegance and comfort. Some of the rooms feature a handsome, American brass bed. You may even choose to stay in no. 21—the third-floor in which Maya Angelou wrote *Gather Together in My Name.* Five of the seven rooms on the third floor, in European tradition, share immaculate bathing quarters and toilet facilities off the hallway; all have private wash basins. Rooms with private baths have beautiful, deep, luxurious clawfoot tubs. The Sonoma Hotel has neither a TV nor a telephone in its rooms. However, for your convenience there is a hall phone on the second floor, or you can make a call at the downstairs desk.

When you arrive you're greeted as a friend, with an offering of wine. Each evening there's turndown service; each morning there's a complimentary continental breakfast with fresh-baked pastries. And what more could you ask of staying in Sonoma than being situated right at the corner of the Plaza, within walking distance of picnic spots, art galleries, and historical landmarks? During the summer season, reserve at least a month in advance.

The superb dining room and saloon are both open daily. The food is something to write a long letter home about (see "Where to Dine," below, for complete information).

BUDGET

EL PUEBLO MOTEL, 896 W. Napa St., Sonoma, CA 94576. Tel. 707/996-3651, or 707/996-3652. 38 rms. A/C TV TEL

$ Rates: Sun–Thurs $66 single or double, Fri–Sat $77 single or double; during the Thanksgiving and Christmas holidays, $80 single or double. AE, MC, V. **Parking** Free.

Low-cost lodgings in Sonoma are simply not that easy to come by. This place, on Sonoma's main east-west street, eight blocks from the center of town, offers just about the best-priced accommodations around. Rooms here are quite pleasant, having post-and-beam construction, exposed brick walls, and brown carpeting throughout. All have an Early American look with light wood headboards, and furnishings, geometric-print bedspreads, and desk and chairs. All rooms have king-size beds and individually controlled heat and air conditioning. A nice touch for early risers is a drip coffee machine supplied with packets of coffee. If possible, reservations should be made at least a month in advance during the spring and summer months.

WHERE TO DINE

MODERATE

DEPOT 1870 RESTAURANT, 241 First St. W. Tel. 707/ 938-2980.
Cuisine: NORTHERN ITALIAN. **Reservations:** Recommended.
$ Prices: Appetizers $5–$8; main courses $6–$12 at lunch, $7–$18 at dinner. AE, DC, DISC, MC, V.
Open: Lunch Wed–Fri 11:30am–2pm; dinner Wed–Sun 5–9pm.
This pleasant restaurant just one block north of Sonoma Plaza is in a handsome, historic stone building that has seen several lives. The original 1870 owners opened their living room as a bar. In 1900 eight hotel rooms were added to the second floor. During Prohibition all was closed and the building once again became a private residence. Restoration work was begun in 1962, and the Depot 1870 was reopened as a restaurant and wine bar. It now has a

comfortable country finish, polished to a fresh glow. To the rear you overlook a fenced-in terra-cotta patio with lots of greenery, plantings, and trees, and a small pool surrounded by dining tables. The main dining room is airy, with pink linen over burgundy cloths. A lovely antique chandelier with droplets of crystal hangs above the cozy room.

Chef Michael Ghilarducci, who has owned the restaurant since 1985, has received the honor of Grand Master Chef of America and is listed in the National Registry of Master Chefs, along with such well-known California names as Alice Waters, Wolfgang Puck, Jeremiah Towers, and Philippe Jeanty (of Napa's Domaine Chandon).

A number of dishes, although not all, are northern Italian cuisine designed by chef Ghilarducci to feature the locally produced meats, poultry, seafood, bread, cheeses, and vegetables. At lunch there's a delicious sandwich of prosciutto and Sonoma Jack cheese served on French bread. You might also begin with an appetizer of paper-thin slices of raw filet mignon and capers touched with parmesean cheese and olive oil. For those whose eyes gleam at the thought of a creamy pasta, the tortellini Ghilarducci is a path to sheery joy—stuffed with ricotta, veal, and chicken and touched with a delicate cream sauce and freshly grated Parmesean cheese.

As for main courses, you may find such dishes as veal scaloppine; chicken and Italian sausage with polenta; and prawns sautéed with white wine, shallots, and lemon. For desserts, the tiramisù is a best-seller. Here, it's a creation of sponge cake layered with freshly grated chocolate and mascarpone (an imported Italian cream cheese) and sprinkled with espresso and rum. For those almost lacking a sweet tooth, there is always fresh fruit and cheese.

OLD SWISS HOTEL, 18 W. Spain St. Tel. 707/938-2884.

Cuisine: CONTINENTAL. **Reservations:** Accepted.
$ Prices: Appetizers $5–$7; lunch $3–$11; main courses $8–$16. MC, V.
Open: Lunch Mon–Fri 11am–2:30pm dinner daily 5–9:30pm. Bar open daily 11am–2am.

The historic Old Swiss Hotel, located right in Sonoma's center, is one of the town's true landmarks. Now a restaurant, recently reopened after extensive restoration, the building retains its seasoned charm, complete with slanting floors and aged beamed ceilings. The turn-of-the-century long oak bar, located to the left of the entrance, is decorated with black-and-white photographs of pioneering Sonomians. Cold beers are kept in an antique wood-and-glass meat cooler.

The restaurant's bright white dining room and rear dining patio are both intimate and colorful. Lunch offerings include entrees like penne with chicken and mushrooms, as well as a variety of sandwiches and California-style pizzas fired in a wood-burning oven. Dinner might start with a warm winter salad of pears, walnuts, radicchio, and blue cheese; or minestrone soup. Entrees run the gamut from linguine with a spicy tomato sauce, to filet mignon wrapped in a cheese crust, to duck in a red wine sauce.

SONOMA HOTEL, 110 W. Spain St. Tel. 707/996-2996.

Cuisine: CALIFORNIAN. **Reservations:** Strongly recommended.
$ Prices: Appetizers $6–$11; main courses $6–$9 at lunch, $15–$17.50 at dinner; Sun brunch $10. AE, MC, V.

Open: Lunch daily 11:30am–3pm; dinner daily 5:45–8:30pm (in summer to 9pm).

Dining at the Sonoma Hotel, on Sonoma Town Square, is truly a visual and gastronomic treat that you don't want to pass up. The Sonoma is a respectful restoration of the original hotel, which dates back to the 1880s. There's a magnificent old bar of oak and mahogany, plucked right out of the turn of the century. The Saloon is a guileless charmer—an inviting, relaxed, comfortable spot out of another time—great for wine tasting, cocktails, conversation, waiting for your dinner partner, or a pleasant after-dinner drink.

The dining room has antique oak tables, decorative panels of stained glass, fresh flowers, comfortable oak chairs, and simply superb food. The menu changes every two weeks and specials are offered each evening. There are always great choices, whether your taste that evening happens to be for an exceptional beef, seafood, veal, chicken, or pasta dish. And the chef always includes seasonal vegetables, herbs from the hotel's garden, and homemade or locally produced ingredients.

The wine list is first-rate and there's a good selection of wines for $3 to $4.50 per glass. Should you decide to bring a bottle you may have selected at one of the vineyards, the corkage charge is $7.

INEXPENSIVE

LA CASA, 121 E. Spain St. Tel. 707/996-3406.

Cuisine: MEXICAN. **Reservations:** Recommended on weekends and summer evenings.

$ Prices: Appetizers $4–$6; main courses $4.95–$10; lunch or dinner specialties $5.95–$10.50. AE, CB, DC, MC, V.

Open: Daily 11:30am–9pm.

Located on Sonoma Town Square, across from the mission, this is a no-nonsense Mexican restaurant made to satisfy your urge for enchiladas, fajitas, and chimichangitas. Did I mention margaritas? La Casa opens onto a lounge and bar, a two-tiered softly lit dining area, and onto a new patio overlooking the El Paseo Courtyard.

When available, the ceviche is made of fresh snapper marinated in lime juice and served on two crispy tortillas. Tortilla soup is made from a base of homemade chicken soup. The real treats are to be found among the specialties *de la casa*. Tamales freshly made in La Casa's kitchen are prepared with corn husks spread with corn masa, stuffed with chicken filling, and topped with mild red chile sauce. Then there are the enchiladas Suiza—deep-dish enchiladas with corn tortillas filled with chicken. It's served with rice and a green salad. But if the fresh snapper Veracruz is available, that tops the menu. The filet is grilled and topped with a mild tomato sauce, onions, bell peppers, olives, capers, and melted cheese, and served with refried beans, rice, and a green salad. Wine is available by the bottle or glass, as is both Mexican and American beer.

FEED STORE CAFE AND BAKERY, 529 First St. W. Tel. 707/938-2122.

Cuisine: CALIFORNIAN. **Reservations:** Accepted; recommended Sun.

$ Prices: Appetizers $4–$9; main courses $4–$8 at lunch, $8–$14 at dinner; breakfast $3–$9. MC, V.

Open: Daily 7am–9pm.

You'll first notice that the Feed Store, on Sonoma Plaza at the corner of West Napa Street, is attractive, airy, and fresh. The staff is particularly nice and is always full of suggestions on what to see and do in the Bay Area. The dining room is large and features high ceilings typical of turn-of-the-century feed stores. An open kitchen adds to the spacious feel.

During warm weather you might enjoy al fresco dining on the lovely patio at the rear of the restaurant, beautifully done with lots of flowers and a genteel gurgling fountain. On warm summer nights the staff rolls back the multicolored awning so that you can dine under the stars.

Food here is first-rate, reasonably priced, and plentiful. For breakfast, the Feed Store Cafe has more varieties of eggs than you could eat in a month's stay. Choices also include such delectables as the Sonoma Mission Scrambler on tortilla strips, huevos rancheros, and a delicious special-recipe French toast. Lunch is designed to match any appetite from quesadillas to burgers or a grilled Mexican chicken-breast. Dinner specials change daily, although the mainstays of the menu are seafood, chicken, and enormous salads. Burgers and sandwiches are also available.

Under the same roof is the Bakery at the Feed Store, offering a marvelous selection of baked goods from mini coffee cakes, and a variety of muffins, to New York cheesecake. Their homemade breads are perfect for picnics.

BUDGET

HOME GROWN BAGELS, 122 W. Napa St. Tel. 707/996-0166.

Cuisine: DELI. **Reservations:** Not accepted.

$ Prices: Bagel sandwiches or salads $3–$6. No credit cards.

Open: Mon–Fri 6:30am–2:30pm, Sat–Sun 7am–2pm.

This small bakery/restaurant just half a block from Sonoma Plaza may not be visually impressive, but it offers a good selection of bagels and bialys filled with any number of tasty items. In addition to the traditional cream cheese and lox, you can have more substantial fillings like pastrami, turkey, salami, and cheese. If a somewhat more traditional breakfast is your style, there's ham and egg, bacon and egg, or Canadian bacon and egg on a bagel. Salads, veggies, and salad plates are always available.

As you might expect, the establishment serves the usual hot beverages, as well as cappuccino. Soft drinks are also to be had. The bagelry is on the breakfast circuit; it's a mob scene after 8:30am, so be prepared to wait or get there early.

PICNIC SUPPLIES

Although Sonoma has plenty of restaurants, the Plaza park is a lovely place for a picnic, complete with tables.

SONOMA CHEESE FACTORY, 2 Spain St., on the Plaza. Tel. 707/996-1000.

Offering an extraordinary variety of imported meats and cheeses, the factory also sells caviar, gourmet salads, pâté, and homemade Sonoma Jack cheese. Sandwiches are available, too. While you're there, you can watch a narrated slide show about cheese making.

Open: Mon–Fri 8:30am–5:30pm, Sat–Sun 8:30am–6pm.

SONOMA SAUSAGE CO., 453 First St. W. Tel. 707/938-8200.

Follow your nose to Sonoma Sausage; the fragrance of hand-made sausage wafts over Sonoma Plaza. In addition to making and selling smoked, cooked, and Louisiana-style sausages, the company purveys smoked meats, pâtés, and lunch meats. There are more than 85 delicious varieties of sausages and lunch meats in all. Smoked meats are fully cooked and ready for picnicking. While I admit that I haven't tried every sausage here, the ones that I have had are delicious. Sonoma sausages are made with 100% pure meat and contain no cereals, soy concentrates, or other fillers. They come with complete cooking instructions, along with excellent recipes. The company has won many awards over the past several years. Sonoma Sausage Company will ship orders to any state, although a few items are recommended to be hand-carried.

Open: Daily 10am–5pm.

VELLA CHEESE COMPANY, 315 Second St. E. Tel. 707/938-3232, or toll free 800/848-0505.

Located one block north of East Spain Street, this is where they make and sell the original Dry Jack cheese, a carefully aged, perfect accompaniment to wine. Vella Cheese also makes a ruch, buttery Montery Jack, a naturally seasoned Jack, and a superb sharp white Cheddar. Among other cheeses for which Vella has become famous is Oregon Blue, made at Vella's factory in

INDEX

RESTAURANTS

SAN FRANCISCO

EXCURSION AREAS

Key to abbreviations B = Budget; E = Expensive; I = Inexpensive; M = Moderately priced; VE = Very expensive.

Please Send Me the Books Checked Below:

FROMMER'S COMPREHENSIVE GUIDES
(Guides listing facilities from budget to deluxe, with emphasis on the medium-priced)

	Retail Price	Code		Retail Price	Code
☐ Acapulco/Ixtapa/Taxco 1993–94	$15.00	C120	☐ Morocco 1992–93	$18.00	C021
☐ Alaska 1994–95	$17.00	C131	☐ Nepal 1994–95	$18.00	C126
☐ Arizona 1993–94	$18.00	C101	☐ New England 1994 (Avail. 1/94)	$16.00	C137
☐ Australia 1992–93	$18.00	C002	☐ New Mexico 1993–94	$15.00	C117
☐ Austria 1993–94	$19.00	C119	☐ New York State 1994–95	$19.00	C133
☐ Bahamas 1994–95	$17.00	C121	☐ Northwest 1994–95 (Avail. 2/94)	$17.00	C140
☐ Belgium/Holland/ Luxembourg 1993–94	$18.00	C106	☐ Portugal 1994–95 (Avail. 2/94)	$17.00	C141
☐ Bermuda 1994–95	$15.00	C122	☐ Puerto Rico 1993–94	$15.00	C103
☐ Brazil 1993–94	$20.00	C111	☐ Puerto Vallarta/ Manzanillo/Guadalajara 1994–95 (Avail. 1/94)	$14.00	C028
☐ California 1994	$15.00	C134	☐ Scandinavia 1993–94	$19.00	C135
☐ Canada 1994–95 (Avail. 4/94)	$19.00	C145	☐ Scotland 1994–95 (Avail. 4/94)	$17.00	C146
☐ Caribbean 1994	$18.00	C123	☐ South Pacific 1994–95 (Avail. 1/94)	$20.00	C138
☐ Carolinas/Georgia 1994–95	$17.00	C128	☐ Spain 1993–94	$19.00	C115
☐ Colorado 1994–95 (Avail. 3/94)	$16.00	C143	☐ Switzerland/ Liechtenstein 1994–95 (Avail. 1/94)	$19.00	C139
☐ Cruises 1993–94	$19.00	C107	☐ Thailand 1992–93	$20.00	C033
☐ Delaware/Maryland 1994–95 (Avail. 1/94)	$15.00	C136	☐ U.S.A. 1993–94	$19.00	C116
☐ England 1994	$18.00	C129	☐ Virgin Islands 1994–95	$13.00	C127
☐ Florida 1994	$18.00	C124	☐ Virginia 1994–95 (Avail. 2/94)	$14.00	C142
☐ France 1994–95	$20.00	C132	☐ Yucatán 1993–94	$18.00	C110
☐ Germany 1994	$19.00	C125			
☐ Italy 1994	$19.00	C130			
☐ Jamaica/Barbados 1993–94	$15.00	C105			
☐ Japan 1994–95 (Avail. 3/94)	$19.00	C144			

FROMMER'S $-A-DAY GUIDES
(Guides to low-cost tourist accommodations and facilities)

	Retail Price	Code		Retail Price	Code
☐ Australia on $45 1993–94	$18.00	D102	☐ Israel on $45 1993–94	$18.00	D101
☐ Costa Rica/Guatemala/ Belize on $35 1993–94	$17.00	D108	☐ Mexico on $45 1994	$19.00	D116
☐ Eastern Europe on $30 1993–94	$18.00	D110	☐ New York on $70 1994–95	$16.00	D120
☐ England on $60 1994	$18.00	D112	☐ New Zealand on $45 1993–94	$18.00	D103
☐ Europe on $50 1994	$19.00	D115	☐ Scotland/Wales on $50 1992–93	$18.00	D019
☐ Greece on $45 1993–94	$19.00	D100	☐ South America on $40 1993–94	$19.00	D109
☐ Hawaii on $75 1994	$19.00	D113	☐ Turkey on $40 1992–93	$22.00	D023
☐ India on $40 1992–93	$20.00	D010	☐ Washington, D.C. on $40 1994–95 (Avail. 2/94)	$17.00	D119
☐ Ireland on $45 1994–95 (Avail. 1/94)	$17.00	D117			

FROMMER'S CITY $-A-DAY GUIDES
(Pocket-size guides to low-cost tourist accommodations and facilities)

	Retail Price	Code		Retail Price	Code
☐ Berlin on $40 1994–95	$12.00	D111	☐ Madrid on $50 1994–95 (Avail. 1/94)	$13.00	D118
☐ Copenhagen on $50 1992–93	$12.00	D003	☐ Paris on $50 1994–95	$12.00	D117
☐ London on $45 1994–95	$12.00	D114	☐ Stockholm on $50 1992–93	$13.00	D022

FROMMER'S WALKING TOURS
(With routes and detailed maps, these companion guides point out the places and pleasures that make a city unique)

	Retail Price	Code		Retail Price	Code
☐ Berlin	$12.00	W100	☐ Paris	$12.00	W103
☐ London	$12.00	W101	☐ San Francisco	$12.00	W104
☐ New York	$12.00	W102	☐ Washington, D.C.	$12.00	W105

FROMMER'S TOURING GUIDES
(Color-illustrated guides that include walking tours, cultural and historic sights, and practical information)

	Retail Price	Code		Retail Price	Code
☐ Amsterdam	$11.00	T001	☐ New York	$11.00	T008
☐ Barcelona	$14.00	T015	☐ Rome	$11.00	T010
☐ Brazil	$11.00	T003	☐ Scotland	$10.00	T011
☐ Florence	$ 9.00	T005	☐ Sicily	$15.00	T017
☐ Hong Kong/Singapore/ Macau	$11.00	T006	☐ Tokyo	$15.00	T016
☐ Kenya	$14.00	T018	☐ Turkey	$11.00	T013
☐ London	$13.00	T007	☐ Venice	$ 9.00	T014

FROMMER'S FAMILY GUIDES

	Retail Price	Code		Retail Price	Code
☐ California with Kids	$18.00	F100	☐ San Francisco with Kids (Avail. 4/94)	$17.00	F104
☐ Los Angeles with Kids (Avail. 4/94)	$17.00	F103	☐ Washington, D.C. with Kids (Avail. 2/94)	$17.00	F102
☐ New York City with Kids (Avail. 2/94)	$18.00	F101			

FROMMER'S CITY GUIDES
(Pocket-size guides to sightseeing and tourist accommodations and facilities in all price ranges)

	Retail Price	Code		Retail Price	Code
☐ Amsterdam 1993–94	$13.00	S110	☐ Montréal/Québec City 1993–94	$13.00	S125
☐ Athens 1993–94	$13.00	S114	☐ Nashville/Memphis 1994–95 (Avail. 4/94)	$13.00	S141
☐ Atlanta 1993–94	$13.00	S112	☐ New Orleans 1993–94	$13.00	S103
☐ Atlantic City/Cape May 1993–94	$13.00	S130	☐ New York 1994 (Avail. 1/94)	$13.00	S138
☐ Bangkok 1992–93	$13.00	S005	☐ Orlando 1994	$13.00	S135
☐ Barcelona/Majorca/ Minorca/Ibiza 1993–94	$13.00	S115	☐ Paris 1993–94	$13.00	S109
☐ Berlin 1993–94	$13.00	S116	☐ Philadelphia 1993–94	$13.00	S113
☐ Boston 1993–94	$13.00	S117	☐ San Diego 1993–94	$13.00	S107
☐ Budapest 1994–95 (Avail. 2/94)	$13.00	S139	☐ San Francisco 1994	$13.00	S133
☐ Chicago 1993–94	$13.00	S122	☐ Santa Fe/Taos/ Albuquerque 1993–94	$13.00	S108
☐ Denver/Boulder/ Colorado Springs 1993–94	$13.00	S131	☐ Seattle/Portland 1994–95	$13.00	S137
☐ Dublin 1993–94	$13.00	S128	☐ St. Louis/Kansas City 1993–94	$13.00	S127
☐ Hong Kong 1994–95 (Avail. 4/94)	$13.00	S140	☐ Sydney 1993–94	$13.00	S129
☐ Honolulu/Oahu 1994	$13.00	S134	☐ Tampa/St. Petersburg 1993–94	$13.00	S105
☐ Las Vegas 1993–94	$13.00	S121	☐ Tokyo 1992–93	$13.00	S039
☐ London 1994	$13.00	S132	☐ Toronto 1993–94	$13.00	S126
☐ Los Angeles 1993–94	$13.00	S123	☐ Vancouver/Victoria 1994–95 (Avail. 1/94)	$13.00	S142
☐ Madrid/Costa del Sol 1993–94	$13.00	S124	☐ Washington, D.C. 1994 (Avail. 1/94)	$13.00	S136
☐ Miami 1993–94	$13.00	S118			
☐ Minneapolis/St. Paul 1993–94	$13.00	S119			

SPECIAL EDITIONS

	Retail Price	Code		Retail Price	Code
☐ Bed & Breakfast Southwest	$16.00	P100	☐ Caribbean Hideaways	$16.00	P103
☐ Bed & Breakfast Great American Cities (Avail. 1/94)	$16.00	P104	☐ National Park Guide 1994 (Avail. 3/94)	$16.00	P105
			☐ Where to Stay U.S.A.	$15.00	P102

Please note: if the availability of a book is several months away, we may have back issues of guides to that particular destination. Call customer service at (815) 734-1104.